D1615157

WITHDRAWN

LIVERPOOL JMU LIBRARY

3 1111 01423 2761

The Making of Modern Tourism

The Making of Modern Tourism

The Cultural History of the British Experience, 1600–2000

Edited by

Hartmut Berghoff

Barbara Korte

Ralf Schneider

and

Christopher Harvie

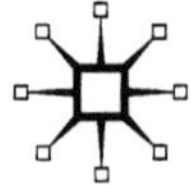

Editorial matter and selection © Hartmut Berghoff, Barbara Korte, Ralf Schneider and Christopher Harvie 2002
Chapters 1–2, 4–9 and 11–14 © Palgrave Publishers ltd 2002
Chapter 3 © Chloe Chard 2002
Chapter 10 © Christopher Harvie 2002

All rights reserved. No reproduction, copy or transmission of this publication may be made without written permission.

No paragraph of this publication may be reproduced, copied or transmitted save with written permission or in accordance with the provisions of the Copyright, Designs and Patents Act 1988, or under the terms of any licence permitting limited copying issued by the Copyright Licensing Agency, 90 Tottenham Court Road, London W1T 4LP.

Any person who does any unauthorised act in relation to this publication may be liable to criminal prosecution and civil claims for damages.

The authors have asserted their rights to be identified as the authors of this work in accordance with the Copyright, Designs and Patents Act 1988.

Published by
PALGRAVE MACMILLAN
Houndmills, Basingstoke, Hampshire RG21 6XS and
175 Fifth Avenue, New York, N. Y. 10010
Companies and representatives throughout the world

PALGRAVE MACMILLAN is the global academic imprint of the Palgrave Macmillan division of St. Martin's Press, LLC and of Palgrave Macmillan Ltd. Macmillan® is a registered trademark in the United States, United Kingdom and other countries. Palgrave is a registered trademark in the European Union and other countries.

ISBN-13: 978–0–333–97114–7
ISBN-10: 0–333–97114–0

This book is printed on paper suitable for recycling and made from fully managed and sustained forest sources.

A catalogue record for this book is available from the British Library.

Library of Congress Catalog Card Number: 2001036489

Printed and bound in Great Britain by
CPI Antony Rowe, Chippenham and Eastbourne

Contents

List of Figures vii

Acknowledgements ix

Notes on Contributors x

Hartmut Berghoff and *Barbara Korte* 1
Britain and the Making of Modern Tourism
An Interdisciplinary Approach

Helga Quadflieg 21
Approved Civilities and the Fruits of Peregrination
Elizabethan and Jacobean Travellers
and the Making of Englishness

Chloe Chard 47
From the Sublime to the Ridiculous: The Anxieties
of Sightseeing

Stephen Prickett 69
Circles and Straight Lines
Romantic Versions of Tourism

Gerhard Stilz 85
Heroic Travellers - Romantic Landscapes
The Colonial Sublime in Indian,
Australian and American Art and Literature

John K. Walton 109
British Tourism Between Industrialization
and Globalization - An Overview

John Beckerson 133
Marketing British Tourism
Government Approaches to the Stimulation
of a Service Sector, 1880-1950

Hartmut Berghoff 159
From Privilege to Commodity?
Modern Tourism and the Rise of the Consumer Society

Sue Wright 181
Sun, Sea, Sand and Self-Expression
Mass Tourism as an Individual Experience

Christopher Harvie 203
Engineer's Holiday: L.T.C. Rolt,
Industrial Heritage and Tourism

Alexander C.T. Geppert 223
True Copies - Time and Space Travels
at British Imperial Exhibitions, 1880-1930

Tobias Döring 249
Travelling in Transience
The Semiotics of Necro-Tourism

Eveline Kilian 267
Exploring London
Walking the City - (Re-)Writing the City

Barbara Korte 285
Julian Barnes, *England, England*
Tourism as a Critique of Postmodernism

Index 305

List of Figures

'The APOLLO BELVEDERE', engraved by L.P. Boitard, 32.1 x 18.6 cm; Plate XI of Joseph Spence, *Polymetis: or, An Enquiry Concerning the Agreement between the Works of the Roman Poets, and the Remains of the Antient Artists*, second edition (London: R. and J. Dodsley, 1755) 53

Emma Hamilton performing one of her attitudes, engraved by Thomas Piroli after a drawing by Friedrich Rehberg, 26.8 x 20.7 cm; Plate XII of Frederick Rehberg, *Drawings Faithfully Copied from Nature at Naples, and with Permission Dedicated to the Right Honourable Sir William Hamilton* (Rome, 1794) 54

'The FARNESE HERCULES', engraved by L.P. Boitard, 32.3 x 18.4 cm; Plate XVI of Joseph Spence, *Polymetis* 58

Nicolas Poussin, *The Massacre of the Innocents*, aquatint by Jean Claude Richard de Saint-Non, from a drawing by Jean-Baptiste Fragonard, 14.1 x 18.2 cm, in Saint-Non, *Fragments Choisis dans les peintures et les tableaux les plus intéressants des palais et des églises de l'Italie* ([Paris?] 1772-5) 63

Thomas and William Daniell, *The Waterfall at Papanasam, Tinnevelly*. Source: Maurice Shellim, *Oil Paintings of India and the East by Thomas Daniell, RA (1749-1840), and William Daniell, RA (1769-1837)* with a foreword by Mildred Archer (London: Inchcape, 1979), 11 90

Eugene von Guérard, *North-east view from the northern top of Mount Kosciusko*. Source: *Creating Australia: 200 Years of Art 1788-1988* (Adelaide: The Art Gallery of South Australia, 1988), 47 97

Thomas Moran, *Grand Canyon of the Yellowstone*. Source: The U.S. Department of the Interior Museum, Washington, D.C. 103

'An early Travel Association graphic, with a somewhat optimistic dual message.' (Source: courtesy of the British Tourist Authority Library) 145

'Historic landscape juxtaposed against a symbol of modernity and confidence, in a postwar cover for the TA magazine *Coming Events*.' (Source: courtesy of the Cambridge University Library) 151

The Empire Stadium, in: Larson Collection, Special Collections Library, California State University, Fresno 227

London's Underground Plan of the British Empire Exhibition, showing its Accessibility by Train, Omnibus and Tram. London 1925, in: British Empire Exhibition Collection, Gen. I., Cricklewood Community History Library and Archives, London Borough of Brent 228

The Old London Bridge between the Indian Pavilion and the Burmese Pagoda, in: Larson Collection, Special Collections Library, California State University, Fresno 239

PRO, RAIL 633/425, 411/655; from Laurent Tissot: "How did the British Conquer Switzerland? Guidebooks, Railways, Travel Agencies, 1850-1914", in: *Journal of Transport History* 116 (1995), 30 241

Acknowledgements

The editors would like to thank the British Council and the University of Tübingen for supporting the Tübingen Centre for Interdisciplinary British Studies, out of which this volume emerged.

The book could not have been completed without the editorial assistance of Dorothea Flothow and Stefanie Lethbridge, and above all, the efforts of Ursula Schröter, who produced the camera-ready copy.

Every effort has been made to trace copyright holders for all illustrations in this book. The editors regret if there has been any oversight and suggest the publisher is contacted in any such event.

Notes on Contributors

John Beckerson is a museum curator, oral historian and researcher for universities, heritage bodies and government. He is currently working in the field of British economic and social history at UEA Norwich. He has published on the history of tourism in *Business Archives* and in the *New History of the Isle of Man* (2000). A volume on Isle of Man boarding houses is at press (2001).

Hartmut Berghoff is director of the Institute of Economic and Social History at Göttingen University, Germany. Among his recent publications are, as editor, *Konsumpolitik: Die Regulierung des privaten Verbrauchs im 20. Jahrhundert* (1999) and, together with Cornelia Rauh-Kühne, *Fritz K. (1885-1980): Ein deutsches Leben im zwanzigsten Jahrhundert* (2000). He is working on various themes related to business history and the social and economic history of consumption.

Chloe Chard is a literary historian who has published widely on travel writing and art criticism. She is currently a Getty Scholar at the Getty Research Institute, Los Angeles, where she is working on a study of laughter, unease and the viewing of paintings and sculptures. Her most recent book is *Pleasure and Guilt on the Grand Tour: Travel Writing and Imaginative Geography, 1600-1830* (1999).

Tobias Döring teaches literature and cultural studies in the English Department of the Freie Universität Berlin, Germany, where his current project is concerned with performances of mourning in early modern theatre and culture. His book-length study *Caribbean-English Passages: Intertextuality in a Postcolonial Tradition* will be published in 2002.

Alexander C.T. Geppert is Research Associate and PhD candidate in the Department of History and Civilization at the European University Institute in Florence, Italy. He is currently completing his dissertation on imperial exhibitions and urban space in *fin-de-siècle* London, Paris and Berlin, and editing a collection of essays, *European Ego-Histoires: Historiography and the Self, 1970-2000*, together with Luisa Passerini. His previous publications are in the fields of oral history, history of sexuality, and urban history.

Christopher Harvie has been Professor of British and Irish Studies at Tübingen University, Germany, since 1980; he has honorary chairs at Aberystwyth and Strathclyde. His publications include *The Centre of Things: Political Fiction in Britain from Disraeli to the Present* (1991), *The Rise of Regional Europe* (1994), *Fool's Gold: The Story of North Sea Oil* (1994), *Travelling Scot: Essays on the History, Politics and Future of Scots* (1999) and *The Road to Home Rule: Images of Scotland's Cause* (with Peter Jones, 2000). He is currently writing a study of the society and culture of the Atlantic coast, 1860-1920, and his *Scotland: A Short History* will be published in 2002.

Eveline Kilian has been teaching English Literature at Tübingen University, Germany since 1991. Her publications include a study on Dorothy Richardson's *Pilgrimage*, which analyzes Richardson's various uses of the Moment and places them in the context of the history of ideas (*Momente innerweltlicher Transzendenz*, 1997), as well as articles on various aspects of gender and Modernism, on Jane Austen and the first women's colleges in Britain. She co-edited collections of essays on Feminist Literary Studies (*Bildersturm im Elfenbeinturm*, 1992) and on Generation and Gender (*GeNarrationen*, 1999). She is currently working on a book-length project on the construction of gender identity in contemporary English literature.

Barbara Korte is Professor of English Literature at Tübingen University, Germany. Her recent book publications include *Body Language in Literature* (1997), *English Travel Writing* (2000), and, as co-editor, *Many Voices – Many Cultures: Multicultural British Short Stories* (1997), *Unity in Diversity Revisited? British Literature and Culture in the 1990s*

(1998) and *Anthologies of British Poetry: Critical Perspectives from Literary and Cultural Studies* (2000).

Helga Quadflieg teaches English literature at the University of Würzburg, Germany. She has published books and articles on late nineteenth-century literature and contemporary English literature, as well as on architecture and film history. Presently she is working on a study of early modern travel writing. She is co-editor of the series *KritBrit: Die Bibliothek des kritischen Britannien.*

Stephen Prickett is Professor Emeritus of English Language and Literature at the University of Glasgow. He has published one novel and numerous monographs and articles on Romanticism, literature and theology, and related topics. Among his recent publications are *Reading the Text: Biblical Criticism and Literary Theory* (1991), *Origins of Narrative: The Romantic Appropriation of the Bible* (1996), and, as editor with Robert Carroll, the *World's Classics Bible* (1997). His latest book, co-authored with David Jasper, is *The Bible and Literature: A Reader* (1998). His new book, a major study of Western pluralism entitled *Narrative, Science and Religion: Fundamentalism versus Irony, 1700-1999*, will appear early in 2002.

Gerhard Stilz is Professor of English Literature at Tübingen University, Germany. Since 1970, he has substantially contributed to widening the canon of English Literature in German universities. His book publications and research papers include English, Irish, Indian, Australian, Canadian, New Zealand and comparative topics. He is the executive editor of the *ZAA* quarterly journal and two monograph series. Since 1999 he has been Chair of the European Association of Commonwealth Literature and Language Studies. Recent book publications include *Australienreisen: Von der Expedition zum Tourismus* (1995), *Gold, Geld, Geltung: Ressoucen und Ziele der australischen Gesellschaft* (1997) and *Colonies, Missions, Cultures in the English-speaking World* (2001).

John Walton is Professor of Social History and Director of Research in History at the University of Central Lancashire, Preston, UK. His main research interests involve seaside tourism, sport and urban and regional identities in England and Spain. His most recent books are *Blackpool* (1998), and *The British Seaside: Holidays and Resorts in the Twentieth Century* (2000).

Sue Wright is completing a doctoral thesis on mass tourism as an individual experience in the History Department at Sheffield Hallam University, UK. She is a graduate of St Martin's University College, Lancaster, and obtained a Distinction on the MA in Modern Social History at Lancaster University.

Britain and the Making of Modern Tourism
An Interdisciplinary Approach

Hartmut Berghoff and Barbara Korte

1. Tourism as an Economic and Cultural Force

At the turn of the twenty-first century, tourism is an impressive social as well as economic force. It has become the world's largest single industry. 'Over 125 nations consider tourism a major industry, and in nearly a third of those countries it is a leading industry, a top earner of foreign exchange and a critical source of employment [...].'[1] In 1992 some 130 million people world-wide worked in the tourism sector, and total expenditure on tourism in 1994 represented 12 per cent of the world's Gross National Product. International tourist receipts alone grew from US $ 2.1 billion in 1950 to 70 in 1984 and 373 in 1995. At the same time, world scheduled air traffic rose from 31 to 832 million passengers, which underlines the almost explosive growth of this service industry.[2]

However, tourism is not only an economic factor. It has also become, and been recognized, as a major cultural force in contemporary Western life and is sometimes even seen as an epitome of its displacement, restlessness and image orientation.[3] Tourism today is certainly an area of culture that intersects with many other areas of cultural existence in Britain and elsewhere in Western societies. It seems symptomatic in this light that the London Millennium Dome (itself conceived and marketed as a major new tourist attraction) devoted one of its themed areas to 'Journeys'. Appropriately sponsored by the Ford motor company, this section presented mobility and an urge to explore the world as an anthropological constant in the past, the present - and the future.

Tourism at the turn of the twenty-first century is a global phenomenon, but Britain, as the first industrial nation, played a pivotal role in creating and shaping modern tourism. The very term 'tourism' was coined in the British Isles, emerging in the English language early in the nineteenth century.[4] In the eighteenth and nineteenth centuries, Britain's economic lead enabled more of her wealthier citizens to indulge in travelling for sheer pleasure before any of their continental neighbours. The 'first modern nation' was not only richer but also more mobile, both socially and spatially. By the end of the eighteenth century, British travellers had become conspicuous all over Europe, noted with some suspicion by famous Germans abroad. In Goethe's *Faust Part II*, Mephistopheles is astonished *not* to find any British travellers amidst the griffins, sphinxes and other fantastical creatures of the Walpurgis-Night:

> Are there any Britons around?
> They have a mania for antiquity;
> Walking the ground
> Of old battle fields;
> Staring at scenically pleasing waterfalls,
> And dreary old ruins
> With crumbling walls;
> They'd love it here for their holidays.[5]

Heinrich Heine's account of his Italian travels is full of remarks on the English: 'they are now too numerous in Italy to be overlooked, they swarm across this country, [...] run around everywhere to see everything, and one can no longer imagine a lemon tree without an English woman sniffing at it.'[6]

This omnipresence of visitors from Britain is no surprise considering that tourism in our modern understanding is, in a way, a British invention. Long before the nineteenth century, the British were noted as ardent individual travellers, for instance the Grand Tourists since the Renaissance. In the nineteenth century, however, Britain's economic lead translated swiftly into the evolution of a tourist infrastructure which, for the first time in history, served a mass market. By 1911 in England and Wales a total of 145 seaside resorts existed with an out-of-season population of over 1.6 million or 4.5 per cent of the total population.[7] In other words, British seaside tourism had become a sizeable industry with a considerable share in the labour market and a model for resort development all over Europe.

Moreover, the most important economic innovation in the tourist industry, the package tour, had its origin in Britain thanks to Thomas

Cook, and the country remained at the industry's cutting edge. In 1936, two years before the Holidays-with-Pay Act, Billy Butlin created the British Holiday Camp – a completely new and tremendously successful product. Today's club holidays are a booming segment of the international tourist market whose pedigree reaches back to Butlinism. In the 1950s, British charter operators paved the way for cheap air travel and opened up Southern Europe for mass tourism. 'Britain led the way by pioneering a system of cheap packaged holidays that offered the chance of Mediterranean sunshine to a new class of people who had hitherto been content with Blackpool or Southend.'[8] British independent airlines made a considerable contribution to breaking up the high-price IATA cartel operated by the big national carriers. Entrepreneurs like Freddie Laker created a new type of highly price-conscious customer by offering flights without prior booking and without any frills at rock-bottom prices. Together with the deregulation of air transport in the United States in 1978 and similar landmark decisions in other parts of the world, these aggressive strategies exerted a continued downward pressure on air fares. In the 1980s and 1990s flying finally lost all characteristics of a privilege and shared the experience of so many former luxury products whose destiny turned out to be the mass market. Just as the railways had created a national market for tourism in the nineteenth century, deregulated air transport by the end of the twentieth century has opened up a global market for the average consumer, for whom the sky now literally is the limit.

The reasons for this astonishing success story are manifold. In terms of economics, the increase of disposable incomes and the amount of leisure on the demand side combined with the simplification and cheapening of travel on the supply side. This does not, however, explain why millions of people want to travel in the first place and what their expectations really are. Tourism is also a social and cultural phenomenon, centred – not exclusively but essentially – around dreams of alternatives to everyday life. Tour operators sell images and dreams to customers who often have primarily hedonistic anticipations, but who may also have an interest in encountering other cultures and expect an educational experience. These images, of which the pleasure-focussed dominate today's advertisements for tourist products, were constructed and sustained, invented and remoulded over a long process, which started well before the technological and economic foundations of modern mass tourism emerged. It seems that without this distinctive historical 'cultural baggage', represented and dispersed in many signifying practices, the modern tourist would not have checked in on the remarkable social practice called holidays. Even if tourism in terms of the numbers involved saw its most spectacular development in the nineteenth and twentieth centuries, it rests on a cultural foundation inaugurated in the early modern period. 'The making of modern tourism' was a long-term process, deeply rooted in the cultural and intellectual, economic and social history of Britain.

2. The Cultural Foundation of Modern Tourism

The cultural history of travel and tourism in Britain manifests itself in a broad variety of types that frequently overlap in their historical emergence.[9] A drive to widen one's knowledge of the world characterizes much travel activity from the early modern discoveries and mappings of new worlds to the scientifically 'enlightening' voyages of exploration in the eighteenth century, to the nineteenth-century venture into the interior of Africa. Domestic travel between the Renaissance and the eighteenth century also often had a primary purpose of collecting knowledge. Early modern antiquarians like John Leland and William Camden travelled to collect facts about their country's past and present, as did an early eighteenth-century traveller like Daniel Defoe. His *Tour of the Whole Island of Great Britain*, with its wealth of observations on national economy, was intended to demonstrate to a rising middle class that a politically united England and Scotland held an enormous economic potential that just waited to be exploited and thus make Britain even greater. Apart from the great European project of accumulating knowledge, many of these travels also had a clear ideological purpose: they were driven by patriotism and were often undertaken with the prospects of material gain and political hegemony. The desire to know other worlds than one's own led to colonialism and imperialism.

However, from the beginnings of European travel, other types of travel were associated with non-material subjective gain. The pilgrims of the late Middle Ages may have been curious about the foreign world (although they rarely admitted this), but their travel was certainly linked to gaining spiritual welfare. The Grand Tour of the eighteenth century was a form of cultural tourism with the aim of finishing the traveller's education – not only in the sense of accumulating useful and fashionable knowledge about the classical past and sociopolitical present of those parts of Europe perceived as civilized by the standards of the Enlightenment. Going on the Tour was also considered essential for developing the traveller's personality.

The romantic type of travel for the enjoyment of nature and landscape is often considered the epitome of travel for 'subjective' purposes. Engendered as a reaction against increasing utilitarianism and the beginnings of industrialization, romantic travel into a natural world that seemed to be still 'authentic' was seen (again) as a source of (re-)gaining spiritual welfare (in some cases also physical health), and as an opportunity of escape and alternative existence.

Romanticism essentially contributed to the redefinition of nature that was needed to set up and establish tourist destinations. This mechanism of cultural construction is best illustrated by the history of the Alps. Traditionally perceived as a dreadful, life-threatening barrier between Northern and Southern Europe, they were re-defined as a sublime experience under the impact of pre-romantic and romantic aesthetics *and* an accompanying critique of culture. As early as 1732, the Swiss scientist, statesman and poet Albrecht von Haller published his enormously successful poem 'Die Alpen', in which he claimed that in the Alps a deep unity between men and nature was preserved, which had elsewhere been destroyed by civilization. As 'nature's disciples', the inhabitants of the Alps would still know Vergil's 'Golden Age' and be close to paradise.[10]

Numerous Grand Tourists of the later eighteenth century included the Alps as a 'must' in their itinerary, like William Wordsworth, who depicted his crossing of the Simplon Pass in Book six of his autobiographical poem, *The Prelude*.[11] The new, virtually sublimated, image of the Alps permeated romantic painting and poetry and was passed on to the Victorians. Continuing the romantic discourse, John Ruskin, the Victorian 'high priest' of the Alps, described its mountains as the 'great cathedrals of the earth' and thought them comparable to the 'walls of lost Eden' in beauty and sublime effect.[12] Many Victorian tourists had read these rhapsodies and even took such books with them on their journeys. Some expressly followed the routes which the poets had taken or recited poems on reaching a summit.

In retrospection, it seems that our modern notion of tourism, with its element of temporary escape from the everyday, has its most immediate roots in romantic travel – even though this travel, with its emphasis on authentic and individual experience was still far removed from the mass experience which the modern notion of tourism normally entails. The package tour attracted criticism almost as soon as it emerged in the mid-nineteenth century. It was seen as the essence of a consumerist culture easily satisfied with superficial impressions.[13] 'Real', that is, individual travellers in the later nineteenth and throughout the twentieth century habitually tried to distinguish themselves from tourist herds - although, as tourism research has shown meanwhile, such distinctions between traveller and tourist seem spurious as deriding tourist travel has rather become an integral strategy of tourism itself:

> The touristic critique of tourism is based on a desire to go beyond the other 'mere' tourists to a more profound appreciation of society and culture, and it is by no means limited to intellectual statements. All tourists desire this deeper involvement with society and culture to some degree; it is a basic component of their motivation to travel.[14]

What all the above-mentioned types and phases in the history of travel have in common is that we would know nothing about them, and they would mean nothing to us, if they had not been translated into signs, if travel experiences had not been written about and represented in visual images. Indeed, for most tourists, travel experience crucially entails a mediation through texts and images. They produce texts (postcards) and their own photographs. They usually have a *Baedeker* and perhaps other travel literature in their luggage; above all, they have images in their minds with which they confront the countries travelled. These images are literal ones seen on other people's postcards and slides, in travel brochures, guidebooks, on video, television, etc. - but they are also images in the metaphorical sense: cultural preconceptions, stereotypes and mentalities.

The images linked with tourism have always been full of ambivalence, and the discourse centring around tourism is vastly contentious. Tourism has been much derided and denounced from its beginning; yet, none of its critics managed to prevent it from spreading and prospering. Tourism has remained a controversial phenomenon and is still seen as a double-edged sword, a blessing and a blight. It has a profound effect on its target areas, their labour markets, their social, economic and cultural structures. It is an environment-intensive industry selling natural assets, which are highly fragile and especially vulnerable to extensive use. Tourism lives off the beauty of the environment and at the same time plays a major role in obliterating it. A closely related dilemma is the quest for individual experience which easily translates itself into mass action. Both the ecological problem and the criticism of tourism's de-individualizing qualities still pose fundamental predicaments for the tourist industry.

As these introductory notes have shown, tourism is thus not only a social and economic fact but a semiotic and media-based phenomenon. Significantly, the tourist industry has never confined itself to selling transport and accommodation, but has always offered a more comprehensive set of culturally pre-constructed promises. The study of tourism thus calls for an interdisciplinary approach. This volume brings together essays from fields seemingly as far apart as literary studies and economic history but with a high potential for stimulating transdisciplinary communication under the umbrella of a cultural studies approach. Together, these contributions view the 'making of modern tourism' as a process going on since the beginnings of European travel, with a longish run-up phase and a significant acceleration in the late nineteenth and twentieth centuries, that is, with the culmination of bourgeois and industrial culture.

3. An Interdisciplinary Approach with Common Themes

This book does not offer a coverage of 400 years of travel and tourist history but rather focusses on emblematic developments and paradigmatic changes. The individual essays illuminate travel and tourism from very different angles to stress the highly multifarious character of these phenomena, which would be unduly simplified by a one-dimensional approach. Therefore this volume covers a wide field not only in terms of historical time but also in terms of subjects and methodology. There is, however, a strong focus on common core themes that connect the articles across temporal and disciplinary borders. All contributors are aware of the fact that cultural images and representations have shaped tourist practices. Each essay therefore scrutinizes for its particular subject the making or re-making of tourism's cultural foundations. Three specific topics serve as central points of reference giving the contributors directions on their protracted journey from Renaissance to Postmodernity.

Firstly, recent research has underlined the centrality of shifting modes of vision for the construction of the tourist experience. The making of tourist sites hinges on fixing, framing and positioning as well as signifying and interpreting specific views in order to endow them with cultural significance. Taking up John Urry's concept of the tourist gaze[15] as the essential mechanism operating in tourism, several essays deal with changing modes of vision and perception. In what way did new forms of visuality and new ways of reading landscapes interact with economic and technological transformations? What were the consequences for the emergence of distinctive travel and tourist practices?

This volume wants to identify historical continuities by tracing the invention and re-invention of key tourist images, preconceptions and stereotypes. As already mentioned, the aesthetic and emotional concepts of nature that emanated from romanticism are still operational today and belong to the standard tool-box of tourist marketing. Many landscapes and architectural sights of early modern and nineteenth-century travelling remain prime tourist attractions in the twenty-first century. And yet, they are supplemented by new tourist sights which were created later and for entirely different reasons. Whereas the romantic idealization of nature reacted to the emergence of the industrial world, the preservation and touristification of obsolete transport and production technologies from the mid-twentieth century onwards is a response to de-industrialization and the incomprehensibility of contemporary technologies. The heritage movement celebrates tangible and understandable machines. Their smell, noise and heat have been a menace for generations of workers who would only be too surprised to learn that their descendants have redefined steam locomotives and steel converters into tourist attractions. The industrial heritage also gained cultural and touristic significance because it had formed the basis of Britain's former industrial glory and therefore symbolizes the country itself and a heroic epoch of its history.[16]

This leads on to the second central theme of this book, the interrelation between national identity on the one hand and travelling and tourism on the other. Despite its transnational character tourism plays a prominent role in the formation of national identities and stereotypes. The encounter with the unfamiliar forces the traveller to reflect on his or her home country, to define his or her own place in the world and to erect borderlines between him or herself and the foreign. Tourists not only use geographical but also imaginative maps that depict cultural and political topographies and prefigure their perception.

Certain destinations are purposefully constructed to build up and reinforce national characters. This is true for great exhibitions and monuments, museums and heritage sites, battlefields and venues of other historic events as well as memorials and graves. Advertising tourist products has always strongly relied on the creation and exploitation of national stereotypes. Furthermore, this volume looks at touristic habits that were pioneered by the British and disseminated all over the world like the package tour. On the other hand, certain practices remained idiosyncratic - like the British holiday camp - and proved unable to be transplanted into different surroundings.

Thirdly, there is a dynamic historical relationship between tourism and the rise of modern consumer society. The construction of culturally significant images and places is closely linked with their commodification and marketing. Besides, tourism relies on new ways of allocating time and money, on the transgression of everyday patterns of spending and behaving and on licences for hedonistic experiences. Therefore it comes as no surprise that the intellectual debate on tourism has always been a centrepiece of the broader discourse on consumerism and the condition of mankind in general.

The deep-seated ambiguity of tourism is reflected in the writing associated with this cultural practice. On the one hand, literary texts and paintings helped to create tourist sights and prompt marketing strategies. On the other hand, their aesthetic depiction proved to be 'too successful' when growing numbers of people actually followed the literary signposts and made the sights 'commonplace'. Because many authors had an elitist concept of nature veneration, they resented this outcome of their writings. John Ruskin, for example, who had lavishly praised the beauty of the Alps, was disgusted when more and more people wanted to participate in his experiences. On Cook's entry into Switzerland, Ruskin burst out in a vehement reproach:

> you have made race-courses of the cathedrals of the earth. Your one conception of pleasure is to drive in railroad carriages round their aisles, and eat off their altars [...], the Alps themselves, which your own poets used to love so reverently, you look upon as soaped poles in a bear garden, which you set yourself to climb and slide down again with 'shrieks of delight'. All tourist destinations are covered by 'a consuming white leprosy of new hotels'.[17]

The essays of this volume are roughly arranged in chronological order and illuminate the cultural significance of British tourism and its predecessors from early modern to postmodern times. From Tudor and Stuart travel accounts, *Helga Quadflieg* reconstructs the importance which encountering otherness has had in the process of constructing the modern self and, at the same time, notions of 'Englishness'. In both processes of identity formation, subjective and national, travel was of great significance, not least since the phase in European cultural history investigated here was one in which the spatial (alongside the temporal and social) coordinates which define the individual were under radical reconstruction and could be experienced as a spatial correspondence to the dissolution of religious and political European (pseudo-)universalism, the beginning formation of the nation state, and so on. Visiting other countries, with their often radically different religious, social and political practices provided Elizabethan and Jacobean English travellers with a foil against which the de- and re-constructions in their own culture could be put in perspective. These travels at first sight seem to have little to do with today's understanding of tourism as a leisure activity. The sixteenth and seventeenth centuries were a period when hedonistic pleasure and the frisson of the exotic had not yet become accepted purposes for travel. At least in official discourse, travel had to be legitimized with practical, useful and serious pursuits, above all the 'collection' of knowledge, either in the service of colonial expansion or the great project of humanist learning.[18] Nevertheless, at least occasionally, travellers of the period like Fynes Moryson and Thomas Coryate convey in their accounts something of a proto-touristic attitude, admitting their sheer curiosity, taking pleasure in exotic food and customs and clearly enjoying the seeing of 'sights'.

The late eighteenth-century 'tourists' discussed by *Chloe Chard* come closer to now-contemporary notions of tourism – not only in name: when the Grand Tour ceased to be a purely aristocratic pursuit, this type of travel within Europe gradually encompassed travellers from the emerging bourgeois class and even included a certain amount of female travellers. These tourists also opened a new chapter in the negotiation of travel and pleasure. Even towards the end of the eighteenth century travel was still the subject of a lively debate about the usefulness or harm of this kind of activity.[19] Nevertheless, tourists now also spoke more openly and frequently about the *pleasure* of sightseeing – immediately facing a dilemma of this touristic discourse. After all, like tourists at the turn of the twenty-first century, the tourists discussed by Chard did not travel on untrodden paths. They went to see sights pre-defined for them, already semiotically 'marked' as sights (in the terminology used by Jonathan Culler[20]), including a pre-definition of the appropriate response to the sight. The tourist knew that he or she would have to encounter the sight with a proper sense of wonder, and that the proper way of communicating this reaction would be a rhetoric of hyperbole. Hyperbolic touristic discourse, however, had already become clichéd and thus developed into a problem for those who strove for a more original way of communicating their experience. As Chard demonstrates, travellers and especially travel *writers* thus developed an anxiety of influence which they tried to deflect through a counter-rhetoric of irony, bathetic intervention and humour. A similar anxiety of proper reaction and expression still marks the tourist experience today, as 'sights' have been even more heavily infrastructured and pre-signified. A 'cool', understated reaction is a strategy to deflect the dilemma that can still be overheard at many tourist sites. Despite mass tourism and the continual presence of 'wonders' on the television screen, those individuals who first see, say, the Niagara or Victoria Falls, may still be overwhelmed by what they see - but hesitate to express this response since they feel embarrassed in succumbing to a rhetoric which is now more strongly associated with the language of advertising than the discourse of the 'cultured' traveller.

Chard deals with a form of travel that originated in the Renaissance, when it was still primarily associated with education, but which, by the later eighteenth century, had been extended to accommodate a new, romantic sense of travel as an adventure of the self that expects to be titillated by wonders - whether those of artefacts (which still absorbed much of the time of a Grand Tourist) or those of nature and landscape, with which romantic travel is most intimately associated.

During the later phase of European romanticism, landscapes that could be perceived under the fashionable aesthetic categories of the 'sublime' and the 'picturesque', started to be developed for scenic tourism.[21] This process began with guidebooks - like those by the painter William Gilpin - for individual travellers who wanted to explore, for instance, the beauties of the Lake District by coach or on foot. As the nineteenth century progressed, however, the pleasures of landscape ceased to be the privilege of a happy few, leisured and economically privileged tourists in the traditional sense. Travel to spots of scenic beauty became an infrastructured and more democratic activity for increasing numbers of tourists in the emerging mass-tourist sense. *Stephen Prickett* points out to what extent the new railway lines, such as the Kendal-Windermere railway opened in the 1840s, helped to accelerate this process and how William Wordsworth, whose poetic work must be considered a major semiotic 'motor' in the development of the new tourism, reacted to the mass transport of travellers, many of them day-trippers, to formerly secluded landscapes. As far as Wordsworth was concerned, the railway with its straight and thus speedy lines of transport between fixed stations opened up travel for these masses, but at the same time it endangered a way of touring that had only fairly recently emerged with the romantic sensibility – and it threatened to destroy or at least spoil the very landscapes themselves. It seems an ironic afterthought that the Lake District was later saved by railway money, provided, for instance, by the fortune that Beatrix Potter made on railway shares.

Gerhard Stilz pursues another line of travel during the romantic period: not the touring of poets and artists within their home country or the sublime mountain ranges of Europe, but the travels of artists to various exotic or 'wild' regions of the British colonies overseas. As Stilz argues, the painters and poets who saw these foreign scenes through the optic of aesthetic concepts that had been constructed in Europe to turn terror into pleasure, above all the picturesque and the sublime, paved the way for the further mental and emotional, but also the very practical appropriation of these lands by other colonials. The Alpine sublimation model was transferred to the colonies, but it also reverberated back on Europe, which became accustomed to visualizing the colonial in sublime and picturesque terms – even long after colonialism: many of the natural wonders of Australia and the United States and, in the case of India, architectural sights aestheticized in the examples discussed by Stilz are still among the prime tourist sites of the respective countries today. Safe and comfortable travel has made the aesthetic sublimation of fear redundant, but the aesthetic patterns originally activated for that purpose still operate as frames of perception for the touristic sight – not least because they are repeated in innumerable brochures and posters for mass tourism.

John Walton, from the perspective of a social historian, offers a somewhat different narrative and challenges the interpretation of modern tourism as a result of the democratization of elitist practices. For him this variegated phenomenon has several, very different roots that cannot be bound together under linear concepts such as the trickle-down-theory which assumes an unbroken continuity between pre-industrial travel and modern tourism. According to Walton the rise of industrial society marked a watershed that fundamentally altered the conditions of supply and demand. Nevertheless, modern tourism incorporated various predecessors. Social emulation was definitely at work in the spas and on the Grand Tour, but seaside tourism as the most important contribution of industrial Great Britain to mass tourism all over the world cannot be interpreted along this line, namely as a cheap copy of the spas or a popularized version of the romantic approach to nature. The visitor to the seaside did not primarily search for beauty, sublimity, let alone solitude. On the contrary, he or she experienced his or her stay as a social activity with carnivalesque elements for which a multitude of other people were essential. Seaside resorts were 'able to surf the rising tide of industrialization' because they could build up on popular traditions of sea bathing and seasonal festivities. Moreover they benefitted from the mounting pressures of industrial discipline which called for a safety valve. After a comment on the historiography of tourism Walton unfolds a broad and colourful panorama by looking at the multifarious origins of modern tourism and its remarkable fanning out into even more diversity. He emphasizes that Britain has been well to the fore in every aspect of tourism's modern development, especially in its globalization but also in the development of literary tourism and the discovery of heritage tourism.

John Beckerson broadens this perspective even further by drawing attention to the generally forgotten fact that tourism – apart from being a cultural and socio-economic phenomenon – is also an object of political intervention and promotion. His analysis of the transition from private to state action in marketing British tourism provides a contribution to recent historical studies of both tourism and consumer culture that seek to 'bring the state back in'. He demonstrates that in Britain the development of tourism was left to greater extent to market forces than in most of the follower-on nations who relied more strongly on public money and initiatives. Beckerson thus maps out a long and twisted road that led from the pure market approach dominant in the mid-Victorian heyday of liberalism via the humble beginnings of collective action under the badge of voluntarianism to state-sponsored action culminating in the foundation of the Travel Association in 1921 and finally in the Tourist and Holidays Board in 1948. For a country so much ingrained in the dogma of laissez-faire it proved a difficult and protracted endeavour to switch over to collective, tax-financed marketing practices. Beckerson shows that change came from below. By the late 1880s seaside resorts increasingly discovered the need to advertise themselves as a whole. At first, voluntary organizations were created to co-ordinate this work and to raise money. Soon, however, demand for support from local government grew, as the weakness of the voluntary approach became obvious. The gradual advance of public spending into resort publicity reflected a general change of attitude towards the scope of local government during the late Victorian and Edwardian period, although central government's opposition remained formidable.

After World War I economic and political parameters had shifted fundamentally and tourism became to be viewed as a valuable national asset, especially a source of foreign exchange. Nevertheless, progress remained slow and the first national tourist organization under the Board of Trade suffered from chronic underfunding. After 1945 the dollar gap and the rising tide of interventionism convinced the new Labour government to set up the British Tourist and Holidays Board. From then on, state-funded tourist bodies became generally accepted and firmly established. From now on tourism was regarded as a commodity of vital importance for the balance of payments and regional development alike. There was no reason to treat it differently from any other commercial activity.

The commodification of tourism, however, was not of recent origin but rather the result of a long-drawn-out process, as the essay of *Hartmut Berghoff* demonstrates. He interprets the rise of modern tourism as an integral part of the emerging consumer society and tries to fathom the dialectical relationship between the multiply-intertwined phenomena of tourism and consumerism. While historical consumer studies have long been preoccupied with material consumption, tourism is centred around immaterial consumption, namely on images and experiences, and therefore requires a much broader approach.

Tourism has acted as a symbol as well as a motor of consumerism. It has always had a distinct demonstration effect which meant that forms of conspicuous consumption practised on holiday spilled over to everyday life. Holidaymaking in fact widened consumers' horizons. The widespread denunciation of tourism as a malign force of de-individualization and a paradigmatic expression of harmful consumerism can be traced back mainly to 'propaganda from a war for contested social territory' in which holders of travel privileges fought against those challenging their exclusivity. Although social emulation was a powerful force in the process of disseminating tourism and consumerism, the trickle-down mechanism is only one part of the story as certain habits entered the mass market via trickle-up processes. Besides, there are plenty of examples of behaviour that people adopted for their own, intrinsic motives rather than imitating social groups above, below or beside them. Finally this article challenges the view that modern tourism was a child of the industrial revolution dependent on mass production techniques and a high degree of uniformity that deprived the individual of chances for personal choice. Although standardization is indeed a key phenomenon of modern tourism, a multitude of options are available within and outside the package sector.

This result is confirmed and underscored by *Sue Wright*. In her in-depth analysis of post-war package tourism she disputes the contention that 'mass tourism' and package holidays are interchangeable concepts. Both, the elitist as well as the left-wing critique deny agency to package holidaymakers, who are looked down upon, either because their experiences are allegedly limited to the tour operator's 'bubble', or because they seem to be 'capitalist pawns'. By drawing attention to the enormous range of packages that have been available since the 1950s, Wright refutes the idea of a monolithic as well as passive mass experience. Instead holidaymakers played an active role in the composition of their experiences. Interviews with package holidaymakers enable Wright to see beyond the stereotypes and give voice to the tourists themselves. With the help of this fascinating, innovative material this essay demonstrates that 'mass tourists', rather than passively consuming uniform, standardized products, accepted certain parts of the package and rejected others. Selective behaviour and the construction of individual meaning led to a multiplicity of experiences that belies the clichés of mass tourism.

The relation between tourists and host cultures, which is often described in terms of cultural and economic exploitation, must also be more correctly described as a mutual and negotiated process. By taking a close look at the history of Benidorm, Wright outlines how local people and international investors co-operated in putting a new destination on the map and how travel guides redefined and signposted the location without depriving tourists of chances to develop individualistic ways of discovering and appropriating the place. The package tour allowed for a multiplicity of experience and for many served even as a springboard for independent holidays in the same region.

The following group of essays points out how the economic side of tourism is really inseparable from the issue of tourism's wider cultural impact. *Christopher Harvie* provides a biographical introduction to the beginnings of industrial heritage tourism, initiated by amateur enthusiasts, who strove to preserve historic technology in the first place and found out later in the process that they had created popular tourist destinations. One of the most influential of them was the engineer-historian L.T.C. Rolt, a pioneer of canal and railway restoration. His projects, which were to have a considerable impact on tourist development within Britain, were embedded in Rolt's wider politico-social value system and especially his literary-cultural criticism, which came from the same sources as Ruskin, Yeats and T.S. Eliot.

Heritage tourism provides opportunities for time travels by creating the illusion of stepping back into history. Popular exhibitions also appeal to the masses because they permit similar experiences of seemingly moving backward and forward in time and space. The Great Exhibition of 1851 systematically exploited what we today would call virtual travel but which was of course intimately linked to 'real' travel when the first organizer of mass tourism, Thomas Cook, cashed in on the exhibition's attraction and used the train system to take millions of visitors to the Crystal Palace. As a result, the history of travel was both continued and also significantly altered. As Cook's organization of foreign travel has already been well documented and analyzed,[22] this volume includes an essay on early and hitherto neglected versions of virtual travel, in which Cook also participated. Despite its Victorian origins this form of travel is still of particular significance today, when phenomena such as the Millennium Dome or the Expo are designed as mega tourist attractions. *Alexander Geppert* investigates the 'time and space travel' opportunities provided by the British Imperial Exhibitions between 1880 and 1930. Through their 'true copies' of sights remote in space and time, these exhibitions provided opportunities to see the world - or at least the Empire - without leaving the urban setting of London. Visitors were thus in two spaces at the same time: the 'real' setting of London (where they might have come as tourists in the first place), and the space which, with Jean Baudrillard, has to be termed as the simulacrum.[23] As Geppert shows, the simulacra of the British Imperial Exhibitions served to uphold a British sense of imperialism until the outbreak of World War II, which must be seen as a caesura for (British) tourism in more than one respect. The exhibitions' topography that centred around the British government's pavilion symbolically replicated the relation between London and the colonies. The exhibitions not only visualized, but at the same time also commodified the imperial project by turning it into a spectacle for millions of visitors.

One of the culturally most remarkable aspects of tourism development after 1945 is the way in which new kinds of market segments and new approaches of winning customers have been continually developed. Among these, specialized forms of 'cultural tourism' (including heritage tourism) have aroused the attention not only of researchers, but also of creative writers who read tourism as indicative of the state of contemporary culture.

Tobias Döring's essay on the semiotics of necro-tourism reminds us that currently popular forms of cultural tourism often have a venerable tradition. A taste for 'tombstone-travelling' is found even in early modern travellers like Thomas Coryate. Döring shows which personal needs and cultural functions graveyard tourism has fulfilled in British culture from then until the present, for which Chris Rojek has observed that 'necro-fever' has acquired a particular popularity.[24]

Another currently booming branch of urban tourism is the city walk, a culturally prestigious alternative to the standard bus-conducted sightseeing tour. The city-walk business is used in a novel of late twentieth-century London life, Geoff Nicholson's *Bleeding London* (1997), to make a general statement on the *condition humaine postmoderne* and to point out the fundamentally constructive nature of all world-making. *Eveline Kilian* discusses this novel and other examples of recent London writing. Exploring the city as a tourist is read as emblematic of how everyone develops a mental image or map of a city, that is, constructs the city in signs in order to make sense of it. The city thus is always a text that can be read but that is at the same time also always written and re-written, with repercussions on the self that is writing it.

Barbara Korte's essay links up with Kilian's as far as a connection between the tourist industry and postmodern life is made. It also links up with the concept of the copy or simulacrum discussed in connection with the British Imperial Exhibitions. In a way, these exhibitions can be considered predecessors of the late twentieth-century phenomenon of the theme park which, together with heritage tourism, is the core idea for Julian Barnes's novel, *England, England* (1998). Only superficially is this novel about the transformation of the Isle of Wight into a condensed copy of England a satire about where the (heritage) tourist industry may take us. Rather, Barnes makes a much more serious statement when one takes the novel's depiction of tourism as a metaphor for the postmodern condition and the postmodern dilemma of England and English identity – that is, the very same issue investigated in the volume's essay on early modern travel.

Notes

1 L. Richter, *The Politics of Tourism in Asia* (Honolulu: University of Hawaii Press, 1989), 3.

2 OECD, *Tourism Policy and International Tourism in OECD Countries, 1984* (Paris: OECD, 1985), 62; see also P. Lyth and M.L.J. Dierikx, 'From Privilege to Popularity: The Growth of Leisure Air Travel since 1945', *Journal of Transport History* 15 (1994), 97-116, here 97; H. Dettmer (ed.), *Tourismus I. Tourismuswirtschaft: Arbeitsbuch für Studium und Praxis* (Cologne: Bachem, 1998), 14; A. Poon, *Technology and Competitive Strategies* (Wallingford: C.A.B. International, 1993), 7; F. Vellas and L. Bécherel, *International Tourism* (Basingstoke: Macmillan, 1995), 15-23.

3 See, for instance, C. Kaplan, *Questions of Travel: Postmodern Discourses of Displacement* (Durham: Duke University Press, 1996).

4 The *OED* (second edition) gives the following definition of 'tourism': 'The theory and practice of touring; travelling for pleasure. [...] Also, the business of attracting tourists and providing for their accommodation and entertainment; the business of operating tours.' The first quotation given for this use is dated 1811.

5 Goethe, *Faust Parts I and II*, in a new version by Howard Brenton (London: Nick Hern Books, 1995), Act II, Scene iv.

6 Heine, *Reisebilder [Pictures of Travel]*, in *Sämtliche Schriften in 12 Bänden*, ed. Klaus Briegleb (Munich: Hanser, 1969), III, 371 [our translation].

7 J.K. Walton, *The English Seaside Resort: A Social History, 1750-1914* (Leicester: Leicester University Press, 1983), 65-7.

8 Lyth and Dierikx, 'Privilege', 97; see also P.J. Lyth, 'The History of Commercial Air Transport: A Progress Report, 1953-93', *Journal of Transport History* 14 (1993), 166-80.

9 For more detailed outlines of the history of British travel and tourism see: B. Penrose, *Travel and Discovery in the Renaissance 1420-1620* (Cambridge/MA: Harvard University Press, 1952); E.S. Bates, *Touring in 1600: A Study in the Development of Travel as a Means of Education* (London: Century 1987 [1911]); G.B. Parks, *The English Traveler to Italy* (Rome: Edizioni di Storia e Letteratura, 1954); J. Parkes, *Travel in England in the Seventeenth Century* (Oxford: Clarendon Press 1968 [1925]); W. Stoye, *English Travellers Abroad 1604-1667: Their Influence in English Society and Politics* (London: Cape, 1952); J. Black, *The British and the Grand Tour* (London: Croom Helm, 1985); E. Moir, *The Discovery of Britain: The English Tourists 1540 to 1840* (London: Routledge and Kegan Paul, 1964); C. Hibbert, *The Grand Tour* (London: Methuen, 1987); J. Buzard, *The Beaten Track: European Tourism, Literature, and the Ways to 'Culture' 1800-1918*

(Oxford: Clarendon Press, 1993); A. Gregory, *The Golden Age of Travel, 1880-1939* (London: Cassell, 1991 [*L'Age d'or du voyage*, 1990]); J.A.R. Pimlott, *The Englishman's Holiday: A Social History* (London: Faber, 1947); J. Walvin, *Beside the Seaside: A Social History of the Popular Seaside Holiday* (London: Allen Lane, 1978); Walton, *The English Seaside Resort*; B. Cormack, *A History of Holidays 1812-1990* (London: Routledge, 1998); J. Towner, *An Historical Geography of Recreation and Tourism in the Western World 1540-1940* (Chichester: John Wiley, 1996); P. Brendon, *Thomas Cook: 150 Years of Popular Tourism* (London: Secker and Warburg, 1991); W. Schivelbusch, *The Railroad Journey: The Industrialization of Time and Space in the Nineteenth Century* (Leamington Spa: Berg, 1986).

10 See P. Faessler, 'Reiseziel Schweiz: Freiheit zwischen Idylle und "großer" Natur', in H. Bausinger et al. (eds), *Reisekultur: Von der Pilgerfahrt zum modernen Tourismus* (Munich: Beck, 1991), 243-8.

11 Lord Byron referred to the Alps as 'palaces of nature' in 'Childe Harold's Pilgrimage', Canto III, stanza lxii.

12 Ruskin, *Modern Painters*, in *Works of John Ruskin*, ed. E.T. Cook and A. Wedderburn (London: George Allen, 1904), VI, 425 and *Praeterita*, in *Works*, XXXV, 115.

13 See Brendon, *Thomas Cook*, 81-96.

14 D. MacCannell, *The Tourist: A New Theory of the Leisure Class* (New York: Schocken Books, 1976), 10. On the condemnation of tourism (versus 'real' travel) in twentieth-century travel writing see also B. Korte, *English Travel Writing: From Pilgrimages to Postcolonial Explorations* (Basingstoke: Macmillan, 2000), 130f.

15 J. Urry, *The Tourist Gaze: Leisure and Travel in Contemporary Societies* (London: Sage, 1990).

16 See R. Hewison, *The Heritage Industry* (London: Methuen, 1987) and Urry, *Tourist Gaze*, 104-12.

17 Quoted in Brendon, *Thomas Cook*, 81.

18 See, for instance, Francis Bacon's essay 'Of Travel' (1625), in *The Essays of Francis Bacon*, ed. Mary A. Scott (New York: Scribner's, 1908), 79-82.

19 See, for instance, Richard Hurd's 'Dialogues VII and VIII on the Uses of Foreign Travel: Between Lord Shaftesbury and Mr. Locke' (1763), in id., *The Works* (Hildesheim: Olms, 1969), IV, 85-229.

20 J. Culler, 'The Semiotics of Tourism', in id., *Framing the Sign: Criticism and Its Institutions* (Oxford: Blackwell, 1988), 153-67, who bases his observations on MacCannell, *The Tourist*.

21 For extensive coverage of this kind of tourism, see M. Andrews, *The Search for the Picturesque: Landscape Aesthetics and Tourism in Britain, 1760-1800* (Aldershot: Scolar Press, 1989).

22 See J. Pudney, *The Thomas Cook Story* (London: Michael Joseph, 1953); E. Swinglehurst, *The Romantic Journey: The Story of Thomas Cook and Victorian Travel* (London: Pica Editions, 1974) and Brendon, *Thomas Cook*.

23 J. Baudrillard, *Simulacra and Simulation* (Ann Arbor: University of Michigan Press, 1994).
24 C. Rojek, *Decentring Leisure: Rethinking Leisure Theory* (London: Sage, 1995), 160.

Approved Civilities and the Fruits of Peregrination

Elizabethan and Jacobean Travellers and the Making of Englishness

Helga Quadflieg

A last evening out in Jerusalem at the end of a fortnight of sightseeing in the Holy Land and on the eve of departure for an exciting trip to Egypt - could you imagine a more obvious way of passing time than go and make a reluctant old friar tattoo the name of your Sovereign, encircled by the crowns of England and Scotland, on your right arm? William Lithgow, a Scotsman who travelled across Europe, Asia Minor and parts of Africa in the years between 1609 and 1614, at least could not.[1] Ending up virtually inscribing his patriotism on his body after viewing the monuments and inscriptions of foreign cultures, Lithgow is probably unique among British travellers of the late sixteenth and early seventeenth century. In processing the experience of the foreign and the other into a manifestation of the familiar and the (national) self, however, he is fairly typical of travellers in general and of early modern travellers in particular.

1. New Maps

Since the days of the early Tudors travelling had become an issue on England's political, economic and cultural agenda. Long before the establishment of a tourism industry as a substantial branch of national and international economies and ecologies, travelling in a general sense became one of the more important factors in the development of basic features of early modern society in England. Henry VIII's ambition to establish Tudor England as a new force on the changing map of Europe's political powers led to an increase of travel activities between England and the Continent with a special focus on Italy.[2] Apart from travellers who moved along the established tracks of traditional pilgrimages, most of these journeys were motivated by a particular diplomatic or ecclesiastical mission. In the second half of the sixteenth century new modes of travelling and new types of travellers came to hold a more prominent place in public consciousness. On the one hand, public discourse was dominated by the promotional orchestration of the increasing number of voyages and travels overland which were embarked on with a decidedly economic target in mind: the discovery or opening of new trading routes, the discovery of new markets or first attempts at colonialization. Men like Anthony Jenkinson, Martin Frobisher or Francis Drake embodied the willingness of the new economic forces and powers in England to compete with Spain and Portugal for their share in the economy of a world whose boundaries had been extended so dramatically over the last five or six decades.[3]

On the other hand, the second half of the sixteenth century also witnessed an increase in journeys to the European continent, with a special preference for Italy, followed by France and Germany – journeys which were undertaken either for reasons of political diplomacy or, increasingly, journeys of young men who embarked on a circuit through Middle Europe as part of their educational curriculum. Humanism and the rediscovery of the classics had brought Italy (and Greece) into focus as the admired sites of the ancient texts. Moreover, the flourishing universities of Italy and France promised intellectual stimulation and a more profound and advanced education in 'modern' subjects like medicine or science than the conservative curriculae of the few English universities could offer. Apart from such concessions to a silently acknowledged cultural and educational superiority of the Continent, a more political *raison d'être* prompted the promotion of these forerunners of what was to become the Grand Tour: in the absence of formalized education programmes in geography, social or political science these early *Bildungsreisen* were supposed to acquaint members of socially dominating classes with the political and social organisation of the most important countries in Europe.[4]

2. 'Civill wisedome' and the 'good ancient Brittaine fashion'

This increase in travelling also led to an increasing debate on the appropriate aims and the potential dangers of travelling. The general consensus was that travelling expressly for pleasure, travelling explicitly and solely dedicated to enjoying oneself and the 'sights and wonders' of the world, was not an accepted activity for a serious member of Tudor and early Stuart society. This debate on the functions of travelling was part of a larger debate which unfolded around a general change of codes for social behaviour, both on a private and on a public level. This change found its linguistic expression in the gradual disappearance of the notions of 'nurture' and 'courtesy' in favour of the concept of 'civility'.[5] Travelling came to be considered a possible means of acquiring the 'civility' of mind and manner appropriate for a gentleman in a civil society. Therefore, reflections on travelling often appeared as parts of letters of advice to young gentlemen, as chapters in early conduct books such as James Cleland's *Hero-Paideia, or The Institution of a Young Nobleman* (1607), or as one amongst various other essays reflecting on diverse aspects of human behaviour and the development of the mind, such as Robert Johnson's *Essaies, or Rather Imperfect Offers* (1601) or Francis Bacon's *Essays* (1625). In a letter of advice to the Earl of Rutland, Robert Devereux, Earl of Essex, in 1596 recommended travelling in order 'to see the beauty of many Cities, knowe the manners of the people of many countries, and learne the language of many nations' and thereby gain that 'beauty of the mind' which he sees as the 'greatest ornament' of a gentleman. Travellers would come across 'infinite variety and manners of men' and, by learning to evaluate and choose among them, arrive at that 'fortitude, which is not given unto man by nature, but must grow out of discourse of reason'.[6]

Like Devereux, Robert Johnson in his *Essaies* advocated travelling as an important step in the development of the gentlemanly mind:

> They know best whose minds soare higher, and become greater by beholding the memorials of other mens glory and magnificence. [...] For this varietie of companie bettereth behaviour, subtelizeth artes, awaketh and exerciseth wit, ripeneth judgement, confirmeth wisedome, and enricheth the mind with many worthy and profitable observation.[7]

Completing their education by embarking on a journey rather than by immersing in the learned books of venerable authors made these travellers the vanguard of a new epistemological paradigm – empiricism and its privileging of direct experience over book-learning. In his 'Epistle to the Reader', B.F., the editor of Devereux's and Sidney's 'Letters of Advice', vehemently spoke out against critics of travelling who, like for example Joseph Hall, argued that all necessary knowledge was already available in books in adequately systematic and complete form.[8] In contrast to such forms of arm-chair travelling, B.F. emphasizes the interrelatedness of book-learning and immediate experience:

> Our sedentary Traveller may passe for a wise man, as long as hee converseth with dead men by reading. [...]
> He, that never travelled but in his Books, can hardly shew his learning without manifestation of his want of experience.[9]

In contrasting pure book knowledge and empirical knowledge, B.F. elaborates on an opposition which Francis Bacon theorized as the opposition of 'words' and 'matter': 'Here therefore is the first distemper of learning, when men study words and not matter.'[10] Travelling for Bacon was one of the means of furthering learning and empirical knowledge, for '[t]ravel in the younger sort is a part of education; in the elder, a part of experience'.[11]

For Bacon, learning and knowledge were not ends in themselves but part of the development of the mind and man's 'gift of reason' which was to be put 'to the benefit and use of men'.[12] Travelling therefore could be considered not only a necessary but a most 'natural' human activity, both in the interest of an individual and of his social community, as Haly Heron had already reasoned in his *Kayes of Counsaile* in 1579:

> Amongst all trades of life practised in sundrye sorte, since the beginning of the world, there is none more auntient and agreeable unto the Nature of man than Travel. For as the foule is bred to flye, fish to swimme [...], as naturally enclyned to that kind of motion: So is man likewise addicted unto labour, and paines taking [...]. And as birdes flye not all one waye, but some to the hilles, other into the fieldes [...]: Even so of diverse men diverse dispositions, and not all inclyned to one conversation, and trade of living. For what common wealth (I pray ye) can consist of one only Art and Societie? or what realme so ryche, what nation so fertile, that needeth no forraine help & suggestion? [...] Then if the good estate of every common wealth dependeth much upon travell, no doubte the frequent use thereof is no lesse worthy to bee allowed [...].[13]

In praising travelling as a most venerable necessity which ensures a community's well-being both on a material and on an intellectual level, Haly Heron is talking about all kinds of travels, from the voyage of discovery to the merchant's and the scholar's journey. Travelling is not merely a phase in education, let alone a pleasurable leisure activity; it is an aspect or expression of an innate human enthusiasm for work, and as such should and could hardly be open to criticism. Travelling for Heron, moreover, is more than a pre-ordained task for 'merchaunts, Legates, and adventurers' or 'wyse Philosophers' who travel as the 'Citizens of the whole worlde to whome all countreys are in common'. In accordance with authors like Sir Philip Sidney, Robert Johnson or James Cleland, Heron emphasizes the usefulness of the traveller returning 'armed with experience', whom he trusts to be 'more able to persever in the sundry service of our most noble Prince and famous Country'.[14]

The function of preparing young men[15] of the gentry for their future tasks as leading members of society was to remain one of the most important arguments in favour of travellers. Sidney explicitly disapproves of the kind of travelling which in modern terminology might be called 'touristy': 'If you should travell but to travell, or to say you had travelled, certainely you should prove a pilgrim, no more.' He insisted that the aim of travelling was 'to furnish your selfe with the knowledge of such things as may be serviceable for your Country and calling'.[16] James Cleland praises travelling as 'the true Science of Pollicie, and the good Schoole of al government',[17] and Robert Johnson commends travelling for providing opportunity to observe those 'particularities' which 'inspire us with civill wisedome, and inable our judgement for any active employment'.[18]

To ensure that none of these 'particularities' of a foreign country escaped the attention of the traveller, most of these books and letters of advice contained lists of variable lengths of the things to which the travellers should pay particular attention: the general description of the geography of the country visited, her commodities, infrastructure and climatic conditions, the social structure and the role and economic condition of particular social groups, the political system, the organization of jurisdiction and legislation, religion, universities, military defence systems, general habits of eating, drinking and dressing. What the travellers were expected to bring back was more or less encyclopedic knowledge about foreign countries which would be useful in organizing and consolidating the emerging English nation state. Some such imports, however, were less welcome than others. There is hardly any essay or letter which does not include advice or exhortation against bringing 'foreign' forms of social intercourse, specific ways of talking, of dressing or of entertainment, back to England. The imitation of foreign manners was warned against even by authors who took a sympathetic stance on travelling as an 'affectation [...] which is both displeasing and ridiculous'.[19] Like Roger Ascham decades earlier, Sidney warned the traveller to Italy against going 'Italian' and admonished his brother that 'English behaviour is best in England, and the Italians in Italie'.[20] The customs, habits and manners of a particular country were conceived of as pre-given, a-historical constants accepted as long as there was no transfer from one country to another. For Cleland, therefore, adopting foreign manners and fashions came close to betraying

> the good ancient Brittaine fashion for some fresh toies. These are not the fruits, which are expected of you by your peregrination. [...] Here the approved civilitie & Countreie language are more esteemed then ether the *Italian huffe* with a shoulder, or the *Duch puffe* with the pot, or the *French apishnesse* in ceremonies.[21]

Bacon in his essay 'Of Travel' at least seems to tolerate the occasional adoption of a foreign speciality, but overall he joins in with the general chorus of exhortation: 'let it appear that he doth not change his country manners for those of foreign parts, but only prick in some flowers of that he hath learned abroad into the customs of his own country.'[22]

3. Flowers from Abroad

The imitation of foreign manners and habits is seen as a threat to the integrity of the traveller and his identity. In their appreciation of the advantages of travelling and their awareness of the seductive potential of this kind of experience of the other, these early modern philosophers of travel describe one of the most important aspects of travelling: the role that the contact with various kinds of 'othernesses' plays for the definition or construction of the self both on an individual and social or national level.

Early modern travellers moved in a world in which the borders and limitations of the individual's perception of the world had changed in a radical way. The spatial, temporal and social coordinates which serve to position the individual had to be re-defined and adjusted to the new concepts of perceiving the world: to the de-centering of the earth within the universe, the de-centering of Europe in the geography of the world, the new notions of providence and the new conception of history as a potentially open linear series of events with a decisively new role of the individual in shaping this line of development. Travelling and travel writing constitute an important facet in this process of re-construction of the early modern self, which among other aspects, defines itself explicitly as 'English' (and occasionally European). What seem to be early forms of ethnography therefore, can also be described as early forms of an anthropology of the self, the writing, the construction of the individual and of the national self.

Of course, the definition of identity, of an 'I' with its subjectivity and individuality is always integrated in the permanent interplay of the 'self' and the 'other', which permanently reflects and modifies the momentary order the self has created for itself.[23] The interplay between 'self' and 'other' is, however, even more marked in situations where the 'other' tends to become the 'foreign' or the 'alien', and this applies particularly to the situation of the traveller. The change of location which is constitutive for travelling always implies the departure from the 'Regionen der Vertrautheit',[24] the regions where things appear familiar and as a matter of course. Travelling, therefore, always implies the meeting of different horizons of experience and of different cultures. This meeting of cultures and the discourse about it, is always pre-structured by the concepts and experiences of one's own culture, which influence not only what we see but also how we structure our image of the 'other'. Travelling and the experience of 'alterity' which goes hand in hand with it, can imply a modification of the 'own' in the face of an 'other' experience and can turn into the experience of 'alternativity'. On the other hand, travelling can imply the definition and affirmation of the 'own'. By describing the contours of the 'other' and excluding it as the 'alien', the character of the 'own' can become more clearly visible and is affirmed.

Exclusion of 'othernesses' also implies inclusion of 'samenesses', the formation of larger entities by appropriation or identification with what is perceived to be similar or equivalent. Such unifying concepts are particularly important in times of wide-ranging restructuring and redefinition processes which are often perceived as processes of disintegration and the loss of community:

> National unity, nation as unity, is an effect. It is an effect, first of all, of the process of collective identification with a common ob-

> ject which is accompanied by identification of individuals with each other.[25]

The concept of 'nation' as an entity unified by sharing a certain limited amount of characteristics by which it can be clearly distinguished from other entities,[26] therefore promised to provide coherence and stability in early modern times, which contemporaries like John Donne experienced as times when 'Tis all in pieces, all coherence gone'.[27]

The travellers' accumulation of 'othernesses' provided the foils for the construction and definition of new common grounds. Travelling in Elizabethan and Jacobean times, therefore, was one of the strategies which were to provide the grounds on which a national identity could be constructed. In accordance with this agenda, all instructions for travellers as well as those for voyagers always included the exhortation to write down their observations - the early modern increase of travelling both on the Continent and across the oceans therefore is closely connected to the emergence of the travelogue as a distinct genre of prose writing. The reports and narratives brought back by the travellers are, of course, much more than the simple, more or less structured, more or less personalized, record of this accumulation of knowledge. They are, on the one hand, documents for processes of restructuring and redefining identities; on the other hand, these travelogues themselves are part and parcel of these very processes.

4. Rarities, Antiquities and Luther's Bed

The collection of knowledge about non-English countries was to lead up to knowledge about England, or as Sidney put it in his letter to his brother: 'hard sure it is to know England without you know it by comparison with some other country'.[28] Like Tudor historiography,[29] travel writing can be said to have emerged as part of the agenda of constructing and defining the emergent nation state 'England' in providing various 'othernesses' in relation to which the English self gained contours. This applies also to those huge collections of reports about maritime enterprises and travels overland which Richard Hakluyt and Samuel Purchas published in 1598-1600 and 1625 respectively. Hakluyt's *Voyages and Discoveries* was explicitly devoted to the promotion of the maritime endeavours of what Hakluyt in his editorial calls the 'English nation'. In his 'Epistle to the Reader' he emphasizes the national didactics of his collection: 'So, though not in wax, yet in record of writing have I presented to the noble courages of this English Monarchie, the like images of their predecessors, with hope of like effect in their posteritie.'[30] Similarly, Purchas defined his *Pilgrimes*[31] as the documentation of an important 'English inheritance' although he – just as Hakluyt before – also included texts from non-English sources. Both Hakluyt and Purchas present the reports of contemporary English travellers as the highlight in an integrated grand narrative of England's role in a world which had to be radically re-organized after the disintegrative eruptions of the early sixteenth century.

The narrative variety and the polyphony of the vast number of reports assembled in Hakluyt's and Purchas's collections, which is discernible in spite of their editors' 'unifying' efforts, has its counterpart in the narratives of the English travellers to the Continent. Within the unifying framework described by the advice books appeared travelogues as diverse as Robert Dallington's *The View of France* and *A Survey of the Great Dukes States of Tuscany*[32] and Thomas Coryate's *Crudities*[33] or Lithgow's *Discourse of a Peregrination*. Dallington's reports about his journeys to France and to Italy concentrate on the comprehensive description of France and Tuscany respectively and would certainly have lived up to the expectations of those for whom the legitimate aim of travelling lay primarily in its politico-didactic pragmatics. In spite of the presence of a recognizable personal speaker, who comments and passes judgements on what he describes, the course and events of the journey, the hazards or pleasures of travelling remain subordinated to the systematic representation of the foreign countries. The description of France and of Tuscany dutifully records all (or most) of the 'regular' aspect of the country and allows hardly any space for the singular or spectacular.

Even travellers like Fynes Moryson, Thomas Coryate or William Lithgow, whose reports about their journeys allow the presence of speakers who seem to come fairly close to the 'touristy' aspect of travelling as an end in itself, cannot really do without some kind of didactic pragmatism. Thomas Coryate who travelled through Europe (France, Italy, Switzerland, Germany, Holland) in 1608 is exceptional among early seventeenth-century travellers.[34] His *Crudities*, published in 1611, present a speaker who takes a vivid interest in 'sights', especially in famous buildings, monuments and their inscriptions, the birthplaces of 'celebrities', their graves and tombstones. Coryate frequently gets carried away with his enthusiasm for sights, curiosities, festivities and spectacles and 'neglects' the systematic and comprehensive documentation of his host countries. Repeatedly he touches only cursorily on the political organization at the end of his descriptions of cities and countries, allowing the impression that he is only paying lip service to one of the traveller's supposed duties. Even for Venice he dedicates merely seven out of 180 pages to the description of government, although the constitution of the Republic of Venice enjoyed particular prominence in early modern political theory and travel writing. The particular fascination that Venice and her form of government held for Elizabethans and Jacobeans was due, on the one hand, to the unbroken continuity of her history and, on the other hand, to her continuing power and independence.[35] Coryate duly registers the 'Monarchicall, the Oligarchicall, and Democraticall' elements of Venetian politics;[36] his real interest, curiosity and enthusiasm, however, lies with the buildings and the monuments of the city and he is particularly fascinated by Venetian music. It is the 'variety of curious objects' as well as the variety of people of all classes and professions and their habits of everyday life, which makes Coryate's Venice. He even ventures into the world of Venice's (in)famous courtesans and mountebanks and into the Ghetto for a 'discourse with the Jewes about their religion'.[37] Like many English travellers before and after him,[38] Coryate falls for the splendour and beauty of Venice which he praises as 'this incomparable city'.[39]

It is not only in Venice, however, that Coryate succumbs to the pleasures of travelling and neglects his 'duties' as a chronicler. In Paris, Padua and Heidelberg, for example, he becomes so engrossed with viewing splendid architecture and curiosities, with the 'rarities and antiquities',[40] that he finally finds no time to visit the famous universities, all renowned among humanists and usually an indispensable feature of any early modern travel route.

Coryate accepts being criticized for this kind of travelling as a 'tombstone traveller' who neglects the traveller's task of describing politics. In response to this kind of criticism he explicitly tries to distance himself from the political and public dimensions of travelling:

> For which cause he branded me with the note of a tome-stone traveller. Wheras it had been much more laudable (said he) to have observed the government of common-weales, and affaires of

> state. I answer him, that because I am a private man and no statist, matters of policie are impertinent unto me.

Insisting on his role as a 'private' traveller, Coryate can even admit to 'pleasure' as a dominant motive for his travelling: 'Of all the pleasures in the world travell is (in my opinion) the sweetest and most delightful'. In spite of his insistence on the private, however, Coryate also emphasizes the educational function of travelling as part of a gentleman's preparation for his role in politics:

> it may perhaps yeeld some little encouragement to many noble and generose yong Gallants that follow your Highnesse Court [...]: seeing thereby they will be made fit to doe your Highness and their Countrey the better service when opportunity shall require.[41]

Fynes Moryson went on two prolonged tours through Europe in 1591/95 and 1595/97. In spite of his seemingly post-modern declaration that 'the fruit of travel is travel itself', his *Itinerary* (1617)[42] lives up to all the expectations which a title like that may have raised for Elizabethans. He meticulously describes touristic infrastructure, the political structure of countries and towns, the manners and everyday life of the inhabitants and he is a true 'statist' in giving detailed lists of mileages, prices and currencies. Moryson is the prototypical humanist 'collector' and 'schematizer' of that kind of factual knowledge the accumulation of which justified travelling even in the eyes of critics. Nonetheless, Moryson also registers objects which arouse his curiosity or his admiration for artistic craftsmanship, as for example when he comes across a portrait in a church in Lübeck: 'a picture, wherof both the eares of the head are seene, which painters esteeme a great master worke'.[43]

Although travellers like Lithgow, Coryate or Moryson are not 'tourists' in the modern sense of travelling for pleasure and moving along the meanwhile proverbial 'beaten tracks', some aspects of their travelling bear resemblance to modern tourism. Coryate admits to his 'pleasure' and Moryson once explicitly speaks of interrupting his stay in Heidelberg in order to go on 'a journey of pleasure to see the Cities lying upon the West Side of the Rheine'.[44] More importantly, the tracks on which these travellers move are, if not beaten, at least prepared. Even though the Grand Tour with its more or less prescribed itinerary was not yet established, the humanistic and the politico-didactic theories of travelling provided a list of places, buildings and monuments which a conscientious and successful traveller was supposed to have seen. They thus provided what Jonathan Culler has defined as one of the characteristics of modern tourism: 'a shared sense of what is significant, and a set of moral imperative: they all know what one 'ought to see' in Paris, that you 'really must' visit Rome [...].'[45]

These travellers are not adventurers who try to discover unknown countries or towns, although all of them occasionally elaborate on the dangerousness of a particular undertaking. What some of them, however, try to discover is the singular and spectacular or the particularly moving item within the range of traditional sights. Lithgow and Coryate in particular have an eye and an ear as well as a palate for the unusual within the usual. Lithgow, for example, foregoes describing the beauty of Venetian palaces explicitly because they have been described too often.[46] Instead, he revels in the description of a 'monster' – a pair of siamese twins – in Dalmatia or of a greedy crocodile killed on the Nile.[47] Occasionally, we even get a glimpse at a nascent tourism industry. Moryson, for example, indignantly comments on a kind of 'Luther industry' in Wittenberg, which tries to attract travellers to Luther's house. His empirical mind is particularly irritated by an inscription in Luther's study pointing out Luther's bed of death: 'So much they attribute to *Luther*, for this is not the place where hee died, neither was there any bed, yet suffer they not the least memory of him to be blotted out.'[48]

When Coryate describes his visit to Cologne Cathedral, he plays a typical tourist's game.[49] Like many other tourists before him, he is fascinated by the famous monument to the three Kings:

> Amongst many other worthy monuments that are contained in this Church, one is that which is the most famous of all Europe, whose fame has resounded to the farthest confines of all Christendome. For what is he of any meane learning or understanding that hath not at some time or other heard of the three Kings of Colen; Therefore because it is so remarkable a monument, and so much visited by all strangers [...], I visited it as well as the rest, and observed it after a more strict and curious manner then every stranger doth.[50]

Coryate is drawn between two antagonistic responses: on the one hand, he has to insist on the uniqueness of the sight, which accounts for its world-wide fame and which makes it a 'must' for every tourist. On the other hand, he insists on the uniqueness of the traveller himself who takes pride in having found something that no one else has ever seen before or at least in having taken a more thorough look than anybody else before him.

5. The Orkneys in Greece

In spite of occasional inclinations towards touristic travelling, none of these travelogues forgets about the overall frame of early modern travelling. In travelling through Greece, Asia Minor and Egypt, Lithgow for example seems to do what tourists frequently do: he travels with varying guides whom he either despises or patronizes, he buys souvenirs, he looks at all the established sights and he is quite willing to admire and marvel at what he sees, provided the monument is impressive and 'monumental' enough. The pyramids of Cairo, for example, leave Lithgow (almost) at a loss for adequate words to express his admiration.[51] Lithgow is, however, no longer the awe-stricken early humanist English traveller who writes from a feeling of cultural inferiority in the face of the superiority of the classics. His is the confident stance of the critical empiricist who believes only in what he has experienced himself. When he is shown the tombs of classic heroes in Troy, he is more than sceptical about the information the guide gives him; when he sees Arcadia or Athens, he can only register decay rather than the grandeur his book-learning would suggest.[52] His sceptical refrain from tribute based on the mere fact of antiquity also applies to the Holy Land. Although Lithgow repeatedly describes himself as a pilgrim,[53] his way of experiencing the sites of the Bible is worlds apart from medieval pilgrims and their awe in the face of 'holy' places. Lithgow takes pride in his own achievements and he rationally calculates the heuristic value of what he has seen:

> I have plainly described the monuments I saw within, and about *Jerusalem* [...]: the like heretofore was never by any *Pilgrime*, so truely manifested. But as I said in the beginning of my description, so I say now also at the conclusion, some of these things are ridiculous, some of manifest untruths, some also doubtfull and others somewhat more credible, and of apparent truth.[54]

Lithgow's confidence in the superior value of his personal experience is the self-confidence of an educated and worldly-wise 'modern' Scotsman who takes pride in his own cultural achievements. He is never really far from home, no matter how large the distance between himself and Scotland may be. When he wants to praise the kindness of a 'Dalmatian Maister', he compares him to a Scottish countryman, taking this comparison as a starting point for paying reverence to his native country, for whose glory he professes to have undertaken his pilgrimage:

> so I, for many weighty considerations (& especially for that high respect) indeavored my self, to the utmost of my power, to attempt this fastidious wandering, whereby I might manifest to my natives, that zeale I bore, in undertaking such dangers (as it were) for that never-conquered Kingdomes sake; leaving him to be the last witnesse, of that innated duty, which I did owe unto my dearest nation.[55]

Likewise, the vista of the Isles of Sporades triggered off a long eulogy to the Orkney and the Shetland islands, their inhabitants,[56] and even their climate which contrasts favourably with that of the Greek islands. His visit to Jerusalem found its climax in the patriotic tattoo mentioned at the beginning of this essay in which he expresses his double identity as English and Scottish, united in the tribute to King James.

Lithgow's omnipresent patriotism is by no means a sign of the individual eccentricity of a bizarre Scotsman. For all English early modern travellers England was always present as a reference point for descriptions, no matter what they described, and the comparison more often than not was in favour of England. It was, however, a patriotism which claimed to be based on empiricism and careful evaluation of differences. Coryate and Moryson occasionally are quite willing to concede that some particular things in England could be improved by adopting Continental customs. Both agree, for example, in their praise of the habit of Venetian gentlemen to go to the market themselves instead of sending their servants, and they exhort their countrymen to adopt this custom;[57] Coryate recommends the introduction of the Italian way of using a fork and he praises German drinking habits as more restrained than the English ones.[58] Moryson, who at the very beginning of his journey was struck by the hostility the citizens of Hamburg felt against the English, repeatedly stresses the importance of variety and calls for the acceptance of difference.[59] As one instance of the variety of manners and morals, he points out that what passes for lack of chastity in a woman in one country, may be perfectly acceptable in another:

> Thus the Italian erre, who comming into *England*, and seeing the familiar conversation of our Weomen, doe repute them for Harlots, who are much chaster then their Weomen would be, having like liberty as ours. Thus strangers may easily judge amisse, of the weomen in *Freesland* giving kisses to each man to whom they drink.[60]

Moryson seems to be acutely aware of the relativity of cultural values, but his very plea for acknowledgement of variety also implies an assertion of English superiority - should they be put to the test of 'liberty', Italian women actually would prove to lack the moral steadfastness of English women.

For Moryson and Coryate, England is just as superior to other European nations as it is for Dallington and other travellers. Coryate's patriotism is kindled whenever he encounters traces of the English: he feels proud when an orthodox bishop in Venice speaks favourably of the English and when he sees a portrait of King James hanging next to portraits of the Spanish and the French King in the Duke's Palace in Venice.[61] He can even go as far as praising the portrait of a Jesuit, as long as it depicts 'our famous English Jesuit, *Henry Garnet*'.[62] Moryson's systematic and 'objective' comparison of different countries with respect to a broad range of criteria, which makes up the third part of his *Itinerary*, attributes superiority to England in things as various as sepulchres, goldsmiths, architecture of churches and universities, fruit and mariners.[63] One aspect all English travellers take pride in is the new exchange in London.[64]

Dallington is the most overtly political writer among these travellers[65] in presenting the political situation in France as a warning against possible future developments in England. In contrast to Moryson and Coryate, he ends his discourse on France with a generalizing depiction of French national character - rash and impatient, inconstant and childish.[66] Italians find hardly more grace before Dallington's eyes. Englishness, in contrast to these, emerges as the ideal middle way between the extremes of the French and Italian characters:

For yee must observe of the French, that he entreth a Countrie like thunder, and vanisheth out againe like smoke. [...] A childish humour, to bee wonne with as little as an Apple, and lost with lesse then a Nut: Quite contrarie to the nature of the *Italian*, of whome yee shall in your travell shortly observe, that he is of so sullen and retired a fashion [...], wherein I would have you observe the vertue of the Englishman (for vertue is the mediocrity between two extremes) who is neyther so childishly and Apishly familiar, as the French; nor so scornefully and Cynically solitary as the other.[67]

Moryson and Coryate are more restrained about derogatory generalizations about individual nations' characters. Moryson describes the differences between European countries within the framework of a principal cultural difference and conflict between Northern and Southern Europe.[68] His identity as an Englishman integrates easily into that of a representative of Northern Europe. In his praise of the North one can still detect an element of the defensive and apologetic attitude towards the South as the abode of classical learning and the supposedly superior achievements in areas as diverse as wit, wisdom, cleanliness, prodigality, humour, luxury or length of life. This defensiveness is particularly pointed when he talks about religion. He apparently feels at an argumentative impasse when trying to fit his firm conviction of the sole 'truthfulness' of Protestantism to the undeniable fact of its comparative novelty, a lack of antiquity which contrasts strongly with religious continuity in the South. Justifying the fall from Rome as the result of early insight into 'the papall fraudes', he quotes 'our Northern Luther' as a model for truly religious constancy. Northern truthfulness thus contrasts favourably with Southern insincerity: 'Northern men are soone drawn with the love of Religion, the outside whereof the Southerne men can skilfully paint over.'[69] But this insistence on Protestantism's moral superiority over Catholicism obviously is not quite enough and he supports his claims by going back to pre-Reformation times, pointing to the longstanding superiority of the North as far as the material symbols and effects of religious zeal go:

If we behold the Temples, Monasteries, Bels, and other older ornaments or religious vestures of our Northern Iland England, no doubt they farre passe those of the South. I will only add in generall, that the English were allwayes Religiously affected, and while they were obedient to the Pope, yealded him in proportion more profitt then any other Kingdome.[70]

6. Papist Pagans and Pagan Papists

Moryson's uneasiness is typical of English travellers to the Continent who looked admiringly at the architecture and artistry of monuments and churches which belonged to the hated Papist tradition. They kept coming across a variety of religious practices which contrasted strongly with the claim of the English reformed Church to be sole agent of religious truth.

Religion and its social institutions were the one area in which the coordinates for the location of the self can be said to have been destabilized in a particularly marked way. The medieval world picture with its notion of a union of *oikumene* and *christianitas* had been shaken ever since the first voyages of discovery, during which the Spanish and Portuguese had discovered for themselves beings who were definitely human and part of the *oikumene*, but who quite as definitely were not part of Christianity. Within Europe the seemingly stable community of all Christians had been destabilized by the reformation; and renewed activities of strong counter-reformatory movements continued to cause anxieties as to where the individual 'rightly' was supposed to position itself. The seemingly universal absoluteness of the Christian faith had given way to a process of 'relativization' and 'territorialization'.[71] The confrontation with other countries and their religious rites and rituals therefore becomes the confrontation of the traveller with his own self, and the travelogue as the textualization of this experience becomes a means of implicit 'hidden theology'. The background against which these 'other' religions are described and evaluated is the catalogue of 'deviations' which mark the differences between Catholicism and Protestantism. This is particularly true for the early voyages into Russia and Asia, which focus on the different kinds of religious practice: again and again we have descriptions of monasteries and of the life of orthodox monks, descriptions of the role of priests and their influence on politics, of the role of the spoken or written Bible word, of the ornamentation or bareness of churches, of the number of ecclesiastical feasts, the number and character of sacraments, etc.[72]

This pattern of describing religious differences mainly in terms of 'Protestant' vs 'Papist' is not only applied to members of reformed or non-reformed churches. The same pair of binary opposition underlies Thomas Harriot's description of Algonquin rituals:

> This Uppowoc is of so precious estimation amongst them, that they thinke their gods are marvellously delighted therewith: whereupon sometime they make hallowed fires, and cast some of the pouder therin for a sacrifice: being a storme upon the waters, to pacifie their gods, they cast some up into the aire and into the water: so a weare for fish being newly set up, they cast some therin and into the aire [...].[73]

Harriot's description of the importance of tobacco (uppowoc) and the scenes of sacrifice he describes, very strongly call to mind Catholic rites of sacrifice and consecration. By rhetorically bridging Roman Catholic religious practices with those of the native Americans (which are absolutely unacceptable to him), Harriot's English Protestantism emerges as the only possible alternative. The same mechanism of rhetorical exclusion works, the other round, in the reports of travellers to the Continent. In describing the habits of Catholics in Rome's St Peter's Church, Lithgow derogates the rites of the Catholics by comparing them to those of 'ethnicke pagans':

> I espied the portrayed image of Saint *Peter*. [...] The fashion of the people is this, entring the Church, they goe strait to this Idoll, and saluting with many crosses his senselesse bodie, kisse his feete [...]: thus adoring that breathlesse masse of mettall, more then though it were a living creature. O wonderfull, and strange spectacle that these onlie titular Christians, should become worse of knowledge, then Ethnicke Pagans [...].[74]

Later on in Venice, Lithgow equates Jesuits and Jews: 'The *Jews* and the *Jesuits* are brethren in blasphemies; for the *Jewes* are naturally subtill, hatefull, avaritious [...]: And the ambitious *Jesuites* are flatterers, blody-gospellers, treasonable tale-tellers [...].'[75]

By rhetorically coupling Catholics with the socially and morally despised groups of Pagans and Jews, Catholicism *per se* appears unacceptable to English adherents of the 'true' religion. Coryate, Moryson and Dallington are generally less polemical than Lithgow in their descriptions of 'other' religions. In Venice, Coryate famously entered on a theological debate with some Jews in the Ghetto. Although he seriously criticizes their religious habits, he refutes some of the long-standing stereotypes about Jews.[76] Coryate, who always appreciates a good show when he sees one, is also frequently fascinated by the ceremonies and festivities of Catholicism and has to try to distance himself at least rhetorically from the spectacles described:

> There are two Churches in this towne, to the greatest whereof I went on Whitsun-day where I saw their Masse (but not with that superstitious geniculation, and elevation of hands at the lifting up of their consecrated wafer-cake, that the rest used) and many ceremonies that I never saw before. [...] Also I saw their mutilated sacrament, whereof I much heard before. For I saw the Priest minister the Sacrament to the lay people under one kind only, namely that of bread, defrauding them of the wine, contrary to the holy institution of Christ and his Apostles. [...] The high Priest [...] went abroad in Procession round about the Church-yard [...] having a rich silver crosse carried before him, and accompanied with many that carried silke banners and flags after a very ethnical and prophane pompe.[77]

Coryate sensually enjoys the rites of others as a spectacle, but he harbours no doubt about the righteousness of his own religion's habits. Moryson, who admits to occasional 'counterfeiting' as a Catholic in order to avoid falling prey to the inquisition refuses to acknowledge Catholic rites as an imaginable alternative to his own religion.

Both Dallington and Coryate mention examples of religious pluralism and tolerance; both, however, seem to have reservations about this kind of acceptance of variety. When Coryate talks about religious tolerance in Speyer, he describes it in terms of a lack or absence: 'This city doth not embrace that unity of religion [...] but is distracted into a double religion, Protestant and Papisticall.'[78] Although he cannot really cite examples of conflicts, he insinuates them by detecting 'a kind of murmuring between both parts'. Similar unease in the face of religious pluralism marks Dallington's report about French tolerance towards Huguenots, a tolerance which in his view leaves the Protestants with less freedom than '*Xantippus* allowed his Dogge'.[79] All these travellers thus clearly emerge as representatives of that kind of Protestantism which increasingly came to be seen as the only possible religion for an Englishman (or a Scotsman).

In times of a strong counter-reformatory movement the travelogue thus becomes the site of the assertation of an English self which emerges to be indissolubly linked to Protestantism.

On a broader social or 'national' level we can observe similar mechanisms of identity construction at work. Among the most frequently applied criteria for evaluating the inhabitants or natives the travellers and voyagers come across is the existence of a structured socio-political community – which is, of course, to say that the travellers find something on which they can project their own notions of political organisation. This always and exclusively implies hierarchical and monarchical structures. In his description of France, Dallington, for example, is drawn between his obvious admiration for the 'absolute authoritie' of Henri IV and his criticism of the relative freedom the French king allows, which for Dallington threatens to undermine authority and thereby stability. He is particularly irritated by the 'liberty of speech' and the freedom French people of all classes take in publicly criticizing their monarch.[80] Special attention is always paid to the splendour and spectacle of the (supposed) staging of power. Another aspect which is important in this context is the existence of laws which regulate life within the social community. The marked insistence on the well-orderedness of communities points to the potential instability of the Tudor state; the self, private and public, which seems to emerge here is the well-mannered, well-organized Protestant trade-oriented individual who is well aware of his national identity which contrasts favourably with other national identities which in themselves are taken for granted as a-historical constants.

Being 'English' is constructed as being unequivocally Protestant, experienced and worldly-wise, reasonable and rational, well-educated, well-mannered, well-balanced and well provided-for. Travelling to foreign countries provided the contrasts against which this English self was constructed; a construction which was to dominate English self-perception over the following centuries. Travellers came home with their Englishness under their skin; Lithgow even had it cut into his skin. The Scotsman Lithgow, however, also shows that this English identity was not yet a stable one. The gradual equation of 'English' with 'British' which was to subsume Scotland and Wales under the label of Englishness in the ensuing decades and centuries had not yet set in. In public and political discourse Scotland and England still formed separate and clearly distinguishable entities, as Moryson's description of Scotland as one among other European countries clearly indicates. Yet Lithgow already insists on having both his Scottishness and his Englishness documented. Apart from nationality, religion still provided the most important unifying force. For Moryson and his North European community, being Protestant still is a stronger identity marker than being English. Lithgow's staunch Protestant identity is dissolved into the community of Christians as soon as he moves outside Christian Europe, and on coming back from Egypt he thanks God for his 'safe return to Christendom'[81] although he has just arrived in Papist Ostia – different 'othernesses' make for different selves. Travellers in early modern times, just like modern and postmodern tourists, may go out in search of the foreign, but what they come back with is always themselves; travellers may search for their 'real' selves, but what they come back with is always an image or construction informed by the discourses and social formations of their starting point.

Notes

1 Lithgow, *Discourse of a Peregrination in Europe, Asia and Affricke* (London, 1614; repr. Amsterdam: Theatrum Orbis Terrarum, 1971), R3- R3v.

2 See C. Howard, *English Travellers of the Renaissance* (New York: John Lane, 1913); R.S. Lambert, *The Fortunate Traveller: A Short History of Touring and Travel for Pleasure* (London: Andrew Melrose, 1950).

3 See for the general context G.R. Elton, *England under the Tudors*, third ed. (London: Routledge, 1991); D.M. Palliser, *The Age of Elizabeth: England under the later Tudors 1547-1603*, second ed. (Harlow: Longman, 1992); J.A. Sharpe, *Early Modern England: A Social History 1550-1760* (London: Edward Arnold, 1987). For the more specific context see K.R. Andrews, *Trade, Plunder and Settlement: Maritime Enterprise and the Genesis of the British Empire, 1480-1630* (Cambridge: Cambridge University Press, 1984); John C. Appleby, 'War, Politics, and Colonization', in N. Canny (ed.), *The Origins of Empire, The Oxford History of the British Empire*, I (Oxford: Oxford University Press, 1998), 55-78; R. Brenner, *Merchants and Revolution: Commercial Change, Political Conflict, and London's Overseas Traders, 1550-1653* (Princeton: Princeton University Press, 1993); H. Blumenberg, *Säkularisierung und Selbstbehauptung* (Frankfurt/M.: Suhrkamp, 1974).

4 See E.S. Bates, *Touring in 1600: A Study in the Development of Travel as a Means of Education* (London: Century Hutchinson, 1987 [1911]); B. Korte, *English Travel Writing: From Pilgrimages to Postcolonial Explorations* (Basingstoke: Macmillan, 2000); J. Stoye, *English Travellers Abroad: 1604-1667*, rev. ed. (New Haven: Yale University Press, 1989).

5 See A. Bryson, *From Courtesy to Civility: Changing Modes of Conduct in Early Modern England* (Oxford: Clarendon Press, 1998); N. Elias, *The Civilizing Process*, 2 vols (Oxford: Blackwell, 1978-1982).

6 Devereux, 'The Late E. of E. his advice to the E. of R. in his travels' (1596), quoted from the edition printed in *Profitable Instructions* (London: Benjamin Fisher, 1633), here 31, 32, 46 and 47f. respectively.

7 Johnson, *Essaies or Rather Imperfect Offers* (London: J. Barnes, 1601), E2-E2v.

8 J. Hall, *Quo Vadis? A Just Censure of Travell* (1617; repr. Amsterdam: Theatrum Orbis Terrarum, 1975), 23 and 34.

9 *Profitable Instructions*, A2-A2v and A6v-A7.

10 Bacon, *The Advancement of Learning; and, New Atlantis*, ed. Arthur Johnston (Oxford: Clarendon Press, 1974), 26. For a discussion of the semiotic dimensions of Bacon's word/matter opposition see A. Easthope, *Englishness and National Culture* (London: Routledge, 1999), esp. 63-6.

11 Bacon, 'Of Travel', in *Essays* (1625), ed. John Pitcher (Harmondsworth: Penguin Books, 1985), 113f.

12 Bacon, *Advancement*, 36.

13 Heron, *A New Discourse of Morall Philosophie, Entitled The Kayes of Counsaile* (1579), ed. V.B. Heltzel (Liverpool: University of Liverpool Press, 1954), 63.

14 Ibid., 63, 71 and 79 respectively.

15 'Men' in this context actually means 'male persons'. Most theoretical reflections on travelling up to the later seventeenth century either do not mention women travellers at all or, for varying reasons, explicitly exclude women from the range of possible travellers.

16 Sidney, 'Advice to His Brother' (c. 1578); quoted from the edition printed in *Profitable Instructions*, 74-103, here 77f. and 79.

17 Cleland, *Hero-Paideia, or The Institution of a Young Noble Man* (Oxford: Barnes, 1607), 251.

18 Johnson, *Essaies*, E3.

19 Devereux, 'The Late E. of E. his advice', 49.

20 Sidney, 'Advice'. See also Roger Ascham, *The Scholemaster* (1570), ed. L. Ryan (Ithaca/NY: Cornell University Press, 1967).

21 Cleland, *The Institution*, 270.

22 Bacon, 'Of Travel', 114.

23 P. Burke, 'Representations of the Self From Petrarch to Descartes', in R. Porter (ed.), *Rewriting the Self: Histories from the Renaissance to the Present* (London: Routledge, 1997), 17-28; M. de Certeau, *Heterologies: Discourse on the Other* (Minneapolis: University of Minnesota Press, 1988); J. Sawday, 'Self and Selfhood in the Seventeenth Century', in Porter (ed.), *Rewriting the Self*, 29-48; R. Smith, 'Self-Reflection and the Self', in Porter (ed.), *Rewriting the Self*, 49-60; B. Waldenfels, *Der Stachel des Fremden* (Frankfurt/M.: Suhrkamp, 1990).

24 H. Plessner, 'Über das Welt-Umweltverhältnis des Menschen', in id., *Gesammelte Schriften*, VIII (Frankfurt/M.: Suhrkamp, 1983), 77-87, here 85.

25 Easthope, *Englishness*, 22.

26 See B. Anderson, *Imagined Communities: Reflections on the Origin and Spread of Nationalism* (London: Verso, 1983).

27 Donne, 'An Anatomy of the World: The First Anniversary', in *John Donne: The Complete English Poems*, ed. A.J. Smith (Harmondsworth: Penguin, 1971), line 213.

28 Sidney, 'Advice', 81f.

29 See E. Jones, *The English Nation: The Great Myth* (Stroud: Sutton, 1998); see also, on the role of discourses like the common law or chorography in the construction of Englishness: R. Helgerson, *Forms of Nationhood* (Chicago: University of Chicago Press, 1992).

30 Hakluyt, *The Principal Navigations, Voyages, Traffiques & Discoveries of the English Nation*, 8 vols (London: J.M. Dent, 1907), here I, 39.

31 Purchas, *Hakluytus Posthumus or Purchas His Pilgrimes*, 20 vols (Glasgow: MacLehose, 1905).

32 Dallington, *The View of Fraunce* (1604), ed. W.P. Barrett, Shakespeare Association Facsimile No. 13 (Oxford: Oxford University Press, 1936); *A Survey of the Great Dukes State of Tuscany* (1605; repr. Amsterdam: Theatrum Orbis Terrarum, 1974).

33 Coryate, *Coryat's Crudities, Hastily gobled up in five Monethes travells in France, Savoy, Italy, Rhetia ... Newly digested in the hungry aire of Somerset, and now dispersed to the nourishment of the travelling Members of this Kingdome* (1611; repr. Glasgow: MacLehose, 1905), 2 vols; all subsequent references are to the following reprint: *Coryat's Crudities; reprinted from the Edition of 1611, to which are now added His Letters From India* (London: W. Cater et al., 1776), 3 vols.

34 See C. Nicholl, 'Field of Bones', *The London Review of Books*, 2 September 1999, 3-7; M. Strachan, *The Life and Adventures of Thomas Coryate* (Oxford: Oxford University Press, 1962).

35 See A. Hadfield, *Literature, Travel, and Colonial Writing in the English Renaissance 1545-1625* (Oxford: Clarendon Press, 1998), esp. 22-68. I cannot agree with Hadfield's equation of Coryate's representation of Venetian politics with that of authors like Starkey or Lewkenor as it seems to overlook the predominance of the interest Coryate takes in the spectacular or curious in comparison to the role politics seem to have for him.

36 Coryate, *Crudities*, II, 63.

37 Ibid., I, 216 and 301.

38 For a general look at the particular fascination of Venice and Italy for English travellers and writers see: E. Chaney, *The Evolution of the Grand Tour: Anglo-Italian Cultural Relations Since the Renaissance* (London: Cassell, 1999); M. Pfister and B. Schaff (eds), *Venetian Views, Venetian*

Blinds: English Fantasies of Venice (Amsterdam: Rodopi, 1999).
39 Coryate, *Crudities,* II, 75.
40 Ibid., I, 189f.
41 Ibid., 'Epistle to the Reader', I, n.p.
42 Moryson, *An Itinerary Containing His Ten Years Travell through the Twelve Dominions of Germany, Bohmerland, Sweitzerland, Netherland, Denmarke, Poland, Italy, Turky, France, England, Scotland & Ireland. Divided into III Parts* (1617; repr. Amsterdam: Theatrum Orbis Terrarum, 1917), here Part III, Book I, chapter 1, 8. The unpublished fourth part of the *Itinerary* was published in extracts as *Shakespeare's Europe: Unpublished Chapter of Fynes Moryson's Itinerary,* ed. Charles Hughes (London: Sherratt and Hughes, 1903).
43 Ibid., Part I, 4.
44 Ibid., Part I, 33.
45 J. Culler, 'The Semiotics of Tourism' , in id., *Framing the Sign: Criticism and Its Institutions* (Norman: University of Oklahoma Press, 1988), 153-167, here 158.
46 Lithgow, *Discourse of a Peregrination,* C3v.
47 Ibid., D2v and S2 respectively.
48 Moryson, *Itinerary,* Part I, 8.
49 Culler, 'Semiotics of Tourism', 158.
50 Coryate, *Crudities,* III, 6.
51 Lithgow, *Discourse of a Peregrination,* S1-S1v.
52 Ibid., G4v, E3, E4 respectively.
53 Ibid., A2v, E1.
54 Ibid., R3.
55 Ibid., D1. The fact of never having been conquered is also one of the assets of Venice which keeps turning up in various travelogues. The most famous example for connecting 'maidenhood', 'nonconqueredness' and (market) value is probably Raleigh's appraisal of Guyana.
56 Ibid., G2v, G3.
57 Coryate, *Crudities,* II, 31f.; Moryson, *Itinerary,* Part III, 149.
58 Coryate, *Crudities,* I, 106f. and II, 330.
59 Moryson, *Itinerary,* Part III, 10f.
60 Ibid., Part III, 34.
61 Coryate, *Crudities,* I, 295 and II, 73.
62 Ibid., III, 52.
63 Moryson, *Itinerary,* Part III, 63, 68, 69, 147, 149.
64 Coryate, *Crudities,* I, 30 and 212; Moryson, *Itinerary,* Part III, 68; Dallington, *A View of Fraunce,* C4.
65 For a discussion of the direct political implications of Dallington's reports on France and Tuscany see Hadfield, *Literature, Travel and Colonial Writing,* 34-44.
66 Dallington, *View of France,* T1v, x1, x1v-x3.
67 Ibid., x1-x1v.

68 Moryson, *Itinerary*, Part III, 37-43.
69 Ibid., Part III, 42.
70 Ibid., Part III, 43 and Moryson, in *Shakespeare's Europe*, 285.
71 Anderson, *Imagined Communities*, 24.
72 See, for example, Hakluyt, *Voyages* I, 291; I, 434; II, 81; VI, 251.
73 Harriot in Hakluyt, *Voyages*, VI, 177.
74 Lithgow, *Discourse of a Peregrination*, B3.
75 Ibid., C3v.
76 Coryate, *Crudities*, I, 296-301.
77 Ibid., I, 3f.
78 Coryate, *Crudities*, II, 398.
79 Dallington, *View of Fraunce*, R4v.
80 Ibid., E2v and T1v.
81 Lithgow, *Discourse of a Peregrination*, T1v.

From the Sublime to the Ridiculous: The Anxieties of Sightseeing

Chloe Chard

1. Sights and Wonders

There are various ways of defining the concept of the Grand Tour – a concept formed with reference to a specific practice of travel in Europe, over the period – roughly – 1600 to 1830. The Tour can be defined, for example, as a journey down from the cold North to the warm South, with its own specific narrative of movement across the Alps towards Rome, as a mode of travelling that necessarily entails combining pleasure seamlessly with benefit, and as an encounter with a not-so-distant topography of the foreign, heavily mediated by familiar works of art and literature.[1] The Grand Tour also embodies an assumption that travel is structured as a progression through an itinerary of sights and wonders. Travellers register a desire to visit places or objects that others before them have deemed worth seeing. Hester Lynch Piozzi, describing her journey to Naples in her *Observations and Reflections Made in the Course of a Journey through France, Germany and Italy* (1789), anxiously checks that she is indeed witnessing Mount Vesuvius itself, and not some lesser volcano in the vicinity that just happens to be erupting in an overwhelmingly dramatic and striking manner:

> Vesuvius, vomiting fire, and pouring torrents of red hot lava down its sides, was the only object visible; and *that* we saw plainly in the afternoon thirty miles off, where I asked a Franciscan friar, If it was the famous volcano? 'Yes', replied he, 'that's our mountain, which throws up money for us, by calling foreigners to see the extraordinary effects of so surprising a phænomenon'.[2]

Sights and wonders, as objects to be translated into forms of language, supply travellers with an opportunity to demonstrate that they are capable of one of the main pleasures that they are expected to proclaim in their writings, in affirming their ability to appropriate the topography of alterity: the pleasure of experiencing the topography of the foreign as a domain that is dramatically different from the familiar. Sights exhibit a form of dramatic otherness that supplements the alterity of the topography in which they are located: the alterity supplied by singularity. In the case of the special category of sights known as wonders, such singularity is classified as especially extreme. Stephen Greenblatt, in his essay 'Resonance and Wonder', notes the power of the wonder 'to stop the viewer in his tracks, to convey an arresting sense of uniqueness, to evoke an exalted attention'.[3] Piozzi, in her anxious question to the friar, expresses her eagerness to experience such a sense of uniqueness.

The rhetorical figure that travellers see as most compellingly prompted and invited by points of extreme singularity is that of hyperbole. This figure, however - in which the speaker employs forms of language that move beyond the bounds of everyday, mundane utterances, or, in more audacious instances, beyond the bounds of verisimilitude - is one of the dominant tropes of travel writing in general, and is constantly employed to describe all sorts of objects of commentary encountered by travellers. Travel writings of the period with which this essay is concerned - roughly, 1750 to 1830 - make especially conspicuous use of a rhetoric of hyperbolic emotional responsiveness.

Sights and wonders, then, present the traveller with the problem of finding hyperboles sufficiently specific in their focus - or sufficiently extreme - to register not only a generalized alterity but also a localized singularity. Piozzi, returning to the task of describing Vesuvius and its surroundings a few pages later, initially explains that Naples is singular because sights and wonders there seem almost to press themselves upon the traveller, rather than requiring that travellers should go out of their way to visit *them*:

> Our eagerness to see sights has been repressed at Naples only by finding every thing a sight; one need not stir out to look for wonders sure, while this amazing mountain continues to exhibit such various scenes of sublimity and beauty.

Soon after, she turns instead to an extravagantly extreme hyperbole, of a kind in constant use during the late eighteenth and early nineteenth centuries – the claim that the sight in question is so astonishing that the traveller cannot in fact hope to find words in which to describe it:

> Nor shall I ever forget the scene it presented one day to my astonished eyes, while a thick cloud, charged heavily with electric matter, passing over, met the fiery explosion by mere chance, and went off in such a manner as effectually baffles all verbal description.[4]

2. The Problems of Hyperbolizing

The rhetoric of hyperbole, however, is fraught with anxieties. Embarking on her ascent of Vesuvius, Piozzi visits the Hermitage on its slopes. When the Hermit describes his unusual dwelling-place, she registers her unease with his disinclination to employ the language of sublimity, despite his undoubted commitment to affirming the singularity of the spot: 'This Hermit is a Frenchman. *J'ai dansé dans mon lit tans de fois,* said he: the expression was not sublime when speaking of an earthquake to be sure.'[5] Wonders, she implies here, when they fail to prompt hyperboles of the right variety, may all too readily push the sightseer into an awareness of the ridiculous. Travel writings repeatedly suggest that the rhetoric of rapture, astonishment and sublimity that wonders excite in those who visit them is of so exalted a kind that it must necessarily tremble on the verge of bathos. Lady Sydney Morgan, describing her own ascent of Vesuvius in her travel book *Italy* (1821), relates how her party reach a spot 'which a few days before had been liquid fire, and from which smoke and a sulphureous vapour were emitted at frequent air-holes', and are startled when, 'by the sudden turn of an angle, we came unexpectedly upon a group of English dandies, of both sexes, of our acquaintance – the ladies with their light garments something the worse for the adventure, and all laughing, flirting, and chattering over a chasm, which exhibited the lava boiling and bubbling up within a few feet below where they stood'. Lady Morgan ironically maintains the language of aesthetic theory in her observation that 'this was a terrible sacrifice of the sublime to the agreeable!'[6]

Hyperbole leaves the traveller open not only to this risk of bathos, but also to accusations of affectation, pretentiousness, a naïve proclivity to be much too easily impressed, an undiscriminating effusiveness, or a reliance on the conventionalized formulations of others. Traveller-narrators of the late eighteenth and early nineteenth centuries are often defensive about their own hyperboles, and mercilessly contemptuous of the hyperboles of others.[7] Sydney Morgan, confronting the Tarpeian Rock, in Rome, from which prisoners were flung to their death, disparages female travellers, in particular, for affecting delight at such a sight:

> Away from every true woman's heart be the throb of pleasure excited by such an object. Let such affected raptures be left to those in whom exhibiting pretension takes place of all the finer and nobler feelings instilled by nature.[8]

The critical thrust of the term *affected raptures* is directed here, in part, towards the rhetoric of intense responsiveness that is widely adopted in writings of the late eighteenth and early nineteenth centuries, whether the author is proclaimed as male or female, or not specified as one or the other, through the names or other designations on the title pages of the works concerned. Women, Lady Morgan suggests, should, like men, demonstrate a responsiveness of a kind that is compatible with manly sincerity, and should restrain themselves from lapsing instead into effeminate affectation.[9] This gendering of 'affected raptures' – the insincere and pretentious responsiveness that brings in its wake a loss of authority – is explicitly charted by the Marquis of Normanby in his collection of sketches *The English in Italy* (1825): he proclaims that travel itself 'is the hot-bed of affectation', and continues:

> If there be a seed, a germ of it in the disposition, travel will force it to the light, and it is for this reason that womankind are so rarely improved by seeing foreign countries, and return in general so much more affected and ridiculous.[10]

Unsurprisingly, travel writings of this period often employ a self-protective irony, which acknowledges the risk of bathos and turns it to the traveller-narrator's advantage, reminding the reader that even when travellers allow themselves to be tempted by the rhetorical force of hyperbole, they may nonetheless retain some of their powers of critical detachment. Sydney Morgan, on Vesuvius, cheerfully quashes any expectation that she might herself be tempted to launch into unrelieved 'raptures' when confronting such a sight. Patrick Brydone, descending Mount Etna in his *Tour through Sicily and Malta* (1773), observes:

> It would appear, that in proportion as we are raised above the habitations of men, all low and vulgar sentiments are left behind; and that the soul, in approaching the ætherial regions, shakes off its earthly affections, and already acquires something of their celestial purity.

Running over the ice, however, he slips, and receives 'so violent a sprain, that in a few minutes it swelled to a great degree'. Unfortunately, 'in these exalted regions, it was impossible to have a horse, or a carriage of any kind; and your poor philosopher was obliged to hop on one leg, with two men supporting him, for several miles over the snow': This unfortunate accident prompts him to comment wryly on his previous language of sublime transcendence: 'our wags here allege, that he left the greatest part of his philosophy behind him, for the use of Empedocles's heirs and successors.'[11]

Travellers, it would seem, register a certain relief when they suspend their hyperbolic affirmations of sublimity and astonishment, and, allowing themselves to be distracted by bathetic interventions in their visits to wonders, turn instead to the other main trope of travel writing: the more disorderly trope of digression. The eighteenth-century text that affirms most strongly the liberatory irreverence of digressiveness on the Grand Tour is, of course, Laurence Sterne's *Sentimental Journey through France and Italy* (1768), in which the traveller-narrator, Yorick, self-consciously replaces the established sights of the Grand Tour with a series of episodes of trivial social exchange - for the most part, flirtatious encounters with women - and declares that this strategy of sightseeing is prompted by his interest in the female heart:

> It is for this reason, Monsieur le Compte, continued I, that I have not seen the Palais royal - nor the Luxembourg - nor the Façade of the Louvre - nor have attempted to swell the catalogues we have of pictures, statues, and churches - I conceive every fair being as a temple, and would rather enter in, and see the original drawings and loose sketches hung up in it, than the transfiguration of Raphael itself.[12]

The displacement of hyperbole by such digressiveness is marked, as Yorick continues, by his pointed reference to his journey as 'a quiet journey of the heart in pursuit of NATURE, and those affections that rise out of her'.[13] Through his digressiveness, in other words, Yorick is able to lay claim to manly simplicity and sincerity, as opposed – implicitly – to the effeminate affectation of the purveyor of hyperboles. Hester Piozzi, in her exchange with the hermit on Vesuvius, deploys a similar digression into trivia in order to claim these same qualities: after she has upbraided him mildly for his lapse from sublimity, he replies in a way that displaces the sublime entirely, and almost diverts the traveller from her progression onwards towards the crater:

> 'Did I never see you before, Madam?' said he; 'yes, sure I have, and dressed you too, when I was a hair-dresser in London, and lived with Mons. Martinant, and I dressed pretty Miss Wynne too in the same street. *Vit'elle encore? Vit'elle encore?* Ah I am old now,' continued he; 'I remember when black pins first came up.' This was charming, and in such an unexpected way, I could hardly prevail upon myself ever to leave the spot.[14]

In accounts of paintings and sculptures, abandoning hyperbole for trivia allows travellers to maintain a certain ease, while appealing to a discourse of art criticism which, they repeatedly suggest, all too easily attracts suspicions of affectation and awkwardness.[15] In many commentaries, the traveller-narrator accomplishes the shift into a bathetic domain of trivial social exchange or trivial gossip in a pointedly casual manner, so as to suggest that he or she is used to moving easily between the two areas of experience, and is no more daunted by the one than by the other. Byron, having described the great sights of Rome as 'quite inconceivable', moves sharply into the domain of trivial gossip: 'The Apollo Belvidere is the image of Lady Adelaide Forbes – I think I never saw such a likeness' (Fig. 1).[16] The famous classical sculpture invites, in other words, the humorous response that Coleridge defines as an awareness of the finite – in this case, the amusingly epicene good looks of a London society woman – in relation to the infinite: the beauty of a god who represents the life-giving force of the sun.[17]

Emma Hamilton, a woman who, through her 'attitudes' (Fig. 2), and later her scandalous behaviour, becomes one of the sights of Naples in the 1780s and 1790s, supplies travellers with a convenient

Fig. 1: 'The APOLLO BELVEDERE', engraved by L.P. Boitard.

Fig. 2: Emma Hamilton performing one of her attitudes, engraved by Thomas Piroli after a drawing by Friedrich Rehberg.

point at which to move nonchalantly between art, on the one hand, and, on the other, the same domain of trivial social exchange that Byron invokes in naming Lady Adelaide Forbes; Emma is seen as striking in the one domain for her extraordinary taste and talent, and, in the other, for her astonishing vulgarity. The Earl of Minto concludes his praise of her attitudes in a half-sentence that lapses abruptly into bathetic malice, as he mockingly attempts to transcribe her provincial accent:

> Nothing about her, neither her conversation, her manners, nor figure announce the very refined taste which she discovers in this performance, besides the extraordinary talent that is necessary for the execution [...] and besides all this, says Sir *Willum*, 'she makes my apple-pies'.[18]

3. Laughter and Sightseeing

An element of unease about the need to encounter sights and wonders and respond hyperbolically is registered not only through such self-protective plunges into bathos and deflections to trivia, but also through accounts of situations in which sightseeing goes comically awry. John Galt, in *The Life and Studies of Benjamin West, Esq.* (1816), tells a story about West's visit to Rome in which the possibilities of comic cross-cultural misunderstanding are affirmed first through a social encounter and then through a visit to one of the great sights of the city. The young American painter is taken to see 'the celebrated Cardinal Albani', who is blind, and who, 'fancying that the American must be an Indian, exclaimed, "Is he black or white?" and on being told that he was very fair, "What as fair as I am?" said the Cardinal still more surprised'. Galt comments: 'This latter expression excited a good deal of mirth at the Cardinal's expense, for his complexion was of the darkest Italian olive, and West's was even of more than the usual degree of English fairness.' Afterwards, the Cardinal's interest 'occasioned inquiries respecting the youth: and the Italians concluding that, as he was an American, he must, of course, have received the education of a savage, became curious to witness the effect which the works of art in the Belvidere and Vatican would produce on him'. When West sees the *Apollo Belvedere*, 'the Artist felt himself surprised with a sudden recollection altogether different from the gratification which he had expected; and without being aware of the force of what he said, exclaimed, "My God, how like it

LIVERPOOL JOHN MOORES UNIVERSITY
LEARNING SERVICES

is to a young Mohawk warrior!"' Unfortunately, the Italians present, when the remark is translated, are 'excessively mortified to find that the god of their idolatry was compared to a savage'. After West has explained the precise character of the beauty of the Mohawk Indians, however, 'the Italians were delighted, and allowed that a better criticism had rarely been pronounced on the merits of the statue'.[19]

Laughter, in such commentaries, can be seen as a way of confronting the unease and anxiety entailed in translating sights and wonders into forms of language.[20] William Hazlitt, in his essay 'On Wit and Humour', describes laughter as arising in situations in which oddity and absurdity distract us from some disagreeable or distressing circumstance, so that 'the ludicrous prevails over the pathetic, and we receive pleasure instead of pain from the farce of life which is played before us'.[21] Freud puts forward a similar analysis of the liberatory effect of humour, which, like Hazlitt's observation, provides a useful model for examining the rhetorical purposes of humorous anecdotes: 'The ego [...] insists that it cannot be affected by the traumas of the external world; it shows, in fact, that such traumas are no more than occasions for it to gain pleasure.'[22] Laughing at the story of West's visit to the *Apollo Belvedere* deflects a sense of the difficulties of providing fresh and new hyperboles, in response to such a famous sight, by presenting such difficulties as specific to the experience of an American visitor.

The laughter through which the unease of sightseeing is deflected is occasionally directed towards foreigners who utter ill-informed commentaries on their own wonders, and who, in doing so, display an airy irresponsibility, of a kind that the traveller is unable to emulate without loss of authority, but that supplies a welcome excuse for veering away from the rhetoric of reverence or enthralment. Thomas Gray, in Rome in 1740, comments, in an addition to one of Walpole's letters:

> *À-propos du Colisée*, if you don't know what it is, the Prince Borghese will be very capable of giving you some account of it, who told an Englishman that asked what it was build for: 'They say 'twas for Christians to fight with tigers in'.[23]

More often, the traveller-narrator's mirth is directed towards other travellers. Paintings and sculptures, as sights that demand not only a rhetoric of hyperbole but also a language of specialized expertise, are seen as posing particular difficulties for the traveller. In accounts of those who have failed in this task, the difficulties of responding to sights and wonders in a composed, fluent and authoritative manner can be classified as mere products of individual vanity or pretension, of some other individual 'oddity or absurdity' (to use Hazlitt's terminology) or of the oddity of some particular category of traveller-spectator. One such category is the connoisseur, a figure who, in Bergson's terms, abandons the flexibility of 'natural', untutored responsiveness. John Moore, in his *View of Society and Manners in Italy* (1781), remembers the downfall of 'a gentleman who affected an enthusiastic passion for the fine arts' on a visit to the Palais Royal with a party of fellow-sightseers. At one point, the gentleman cries: 'The Virgin, you'll observe, gentlemen, is only fainting, but the Christ is quite dead. Look at the arm, did you ever see any thing so dead?' As this admirer of the arts violently upbraids another of the party for failing to appreciate Raphael's *St John the Baptist*, it is revealed that the painting in question is a mere copy, 'a very wretched daubing'. 'How the connoisseur looked', Moore remarks, 'I cannot say. It would have been barbarous to have turned an eye upon him'.[24] Such stories are common in travel writings: 'In the Church of St. Sepulchre at Parma', William Parsons claims in his *Poetical Tour* (1787), 'there is a very fine Picture of Correggio, generally visited by Travellers, and the affected Connoisseur is often discover'd by his admiration of another which is only a cover for it'.[25]

A second category of traveller-spectator onto whom the unease of commenting on art is deflected is that of the female spectator. John Moore, putting forward his own view of the *Farnese Hercules* (Fig. 3), at the Palazzo Farnese, in Rome, mockingly introduces a woman who, in unselfconsciously adopting the language of everyday, casual assessment of masculine 'charms' (a term that Moore himself uses ironically here), nonetheless assumes a crucial role in allowing the spectator to acknowledge, obliquely, the problems of assimilating this sculpture within a classical ideal that endorses the smooth-limbed male body, in which muscles and inner organs are carefully kept in their place, behind the uninterrupted surface of the skin.[26] Moore notes that this woman, on seeing the work in the Palazzo Farnese, in Rome, 'turned away from it in disgust'. With a fausse naïveté that refuses to acknowledge how easily 'large brawny limbs' and protruding muscles can threaten the aloofness of this ideal, he then comments: 'I could not imagine what had shocked her.' Her explanation touches on the power of the sculpture to evoke a robust, troubling sexuality:

Fig. 3: 'The FARNESE HERCULES', engraved by L.P. Boitard.

> She told me, *after recollection*, that she could not bear the stern severity of his countenance, his large brawny limbs, and the club with which he was armed; which gave him more the appearance of one of those giants that, according to the old romances, carried away virgins and shut them up in gloomy castles, than the gallant Hercules, the lover of Omphale. Finally, the lady declared, she was convinced this statue could not be a just representation of Hercules; for it was not in the nature of things, that a man so formed could ever have been a reliever of distressed damsels.[27]

The rhetorical difficulties of three travellers in a third category - spectators who adhere to their respective national stereotypes - are described by Martin Sherlock, as he recounts a visit to St Peter's in his *Lettres d'un Voyageur Anglois* (1779), translated by the author himself *as Letters from an English Traveller* (1780). Adopting a formula disconcertingly familiar to the twenty-first century reader, Sherlock begins:

> I went thither with a Pole, a Frenchman, and an Englishman: the Englishman looked for beauties; the Frenchman for faults; the Pole looked for nothing. When we were at the end of the church, 'Behold,' says the Frenchman, 'that *Charity* of Bernini, how bad it is! the air of her head is affected, her flesh is without bone, and she makes frightful faces.' 'These remarks appear to me just enough,' replies the Englishman, 'but, look on the other side of the altar, you will see one of the finest pieces of modern sculpture, the *Justice* of Guglielmo della Porta.' 'You are in the right,' says the Frenchman (without looking at it), 'but that child at the foot of *Charity* disgusts me more than its mother.' While the Englishman continued to praise *Justice*, and the Frenchman to criticize *Charity*, the Pole was observing the door at which he entered, and said to me, that the church was much longer than he imagined.[28]

The comic failure of the Pole to rise to the occasion, in this last remark, distracts the reader from an uneasy realization that all sorts of aspects of the foreign may prove to have dimensions beyond those that the traveller has anticipated.

4. Tourism

The way in which travellers manage the rhetorical dangers of commenting on sights and wonders is determined, too, by the demands of a new approach to travel that is formulated around the end of the eighteenth century: an approach that can usefully be termed *tourism*. This approach – in common with another new attitude that might loosely be called *romantic travel* – is dependent upon a new option of defining travelling not only as an opportunity for gathering and ordering knowledge of the world, of the kind that it is seen as supplying in the eighteenth century, but, rather, as an adventure of the self. The romantic approach defines this adventure as one that entails crossing symbolic as well as geographical boundaries, experiencing travel as a means of self-exploration and self-realization, and encountering various forms of destabilization and danger. The approach of the tourist, formulated in opposition to this romantic outlook, recognizes the possibility that the traveller may be drawn into plots of transgression and destabilization, but insists that it is still feasible to keep any major threat to the self and to identity at bay. In individual writings, and even in brief individual utterances, from the end of the eighteenth century onwards, the subject of commentary constantly oscillates between these two positions. While both approaches are still adopted in twenty-first-century commentary on the foreign, neither new approach, in its initial form, marks an end to the set of assumptions and arguments about travel that can be seen as crucial to the Grand Tour. The touristic attitude, for example, does not preclude the view that pleasure should merge seamlessly with benefit, and it positively exploits the uses of defining travel as a progression through an itinerary of sights and wonders – a definition that allows danger to be kept at bay by providing a means of carefully delimiting the experience with foreign places.[29]

While seeking to exclude or distance any potentially destabilizing elements within the topography, the touristic approach, as just noted, nonetheless entails an acknowledgement of such elements as an alarming possibility. Charlotte Eaton, describing the *Apollo Belvedere* in *Rome in the Nineteenth Century* (1820), launches into an elaborate hyperbole of indescribability ('Description would be the excess of absurdity; even the best copies are vain', she begins). She then considers the extreme reactions that might be prompted by such a work:

> You will think me mad - and it were vain to deny it - but I am not the first person who has gone mad about the Apollo. Another, and a far more unfortunate damsel, a native of France, it is related, at the sight of this matchless statue, lost at once her heart and her reason. Day after day, and hour after hour, the fair enthusiast gazed and wept, and sighed her soul away, till she became, like the marble, pale, but not like the marble, cold. Nor, like the lost Eloisa, nor the idol of her love, could she 'forget herself to stone,' till death at last closed the ill-fated passion, and the life, of the maid of France.[30]

In concluding her account of this unfortunate art lover, however, Eaton reassures the reader by declaring robustly: 'But I have not the least intention of dying.'[31] She counters the possibility of destabilization, in other words, by a resolute jocularity: an insistence that extreme responsiveness is always in danger of tipping over into absurdity. Anna Jameson, in her *Diary of an Ennuyée* (1826), introduces a similar note of jocularity into an account of extreme - if less unhappy - responses to one of the wonders of Rome. She observes a young artist 'transported out of his senses' in the Coliseum, and describes the man's embarrassment when he realizes that she is watching his 'extraordinary antics and gestures':

> Sometimes he clasped his hands, then extended his arms, then stood with them folded as in deep thought; now he snatched up his portfolio as if to draw what so much enchanted him, then threw it down and kicked it from him as if in despair [...].

The story ends in a shared sense of the absurd: 'I met the same man afterwards walking along the Via Felice, and could not help smiling as he passed: he smiled too, but pulled his hat over his face and turned away.'[32]

Jocularity, then, in early nineteenth-century travel writing, supplies one of the rhetorical devices through which the touristic traveller keeps destabilization at bay. Gastronomic and culinary metaphors, in writing of this period, are often deployed to suggest that the elevated pleasures of sightseeing may not be so far removed from the more down-to-earth gratification of eating and drinking as we might expect. Sydney Morgan, coming upon the unexpected social gathering beside the crater of Vesuvius, remarks how provoking it is to climb so far, in search of 'Nature, all solitary and sublime', and then 'to be put off with a *rechauffée* of the St. Carlos party of the preceding evening'.[33] William Hazlitt, describing the cascade at Terni in his *Notes of a Journey through France and Italy* (1826), deploys an unexpected metaphor of this kind in order to indicate that Byron's strategy of hyperbolic rapture, in a famous passage of Canto IV of *Childe Harold's Pilgrimage* (1818), is not the only possible approach to this celebrated feature of the Italian countryside:

> To say the truth, if Lord Byron had put it into *Don Juan* instead of *Childe Harold*, he might have compared the part which her ladyship has chosen to perform on this occasion to an experienced waiter pouring a bottle of ale into a tumbler at a tavern. It has something of the same continued, plump, right-lined descent.[34]

In Hazlitt's description of Raphael's *La Fornarina*, the title of the painting supplies him with his pretext for sliding into bathetic gastronomy, and so making it clear that he has no intention of allowing his admiration of the sights of Italy to become too overwhelming:

> Assuredly no charge can be brought against it of *mimini-piminee* affectation or shrinking delicacy. It is robust, full to bursting, coarse, luxurious, hardened, but wrought up to an infinite degree of exactness and beauty in the details. It is the perfection of vulgarity and refinement together. The Fornarina is a bouncing, buxom, sullen, saucy baker's daughter - but painted, idolized, immortalized by Raphael! Nothing can be more homely and repulsive than the original; *you see her bosom swelling like the dough rising in the oven*; the tightness of her skin puts you in mind of Trim's story of the sausage-maker's wife - nothing can be more enchanting than the picture [...].[35]

Joseph Forsyth, in *his Remarks on Antiquities, Arts, and Letters, during an Excursion in Italy* (1813), repeatedly describes works of art as assailed by the threat of the ridiculous, even in those cases where they do in fact, he decides, succeed in resisting comic absurdity. Commenting on Guido Reni's *St Michael*, in the church of Santa Maria della Concezione, in Rome, he declares that 'the very devil derives importance from his august adversary, and escapes the laugh which his figure usually produces'. In Poussin's *Massacre of the Innocents*, at the Palazzo Giustiniani, Forsyth concludes: 'Agony carried one point farther would fall into the ludicrous' (Fig. 4). Michelange-

Fig. 4: Nicolas Poussin, *The Massacre of the Innocents*, aquatint by Jean Claude Richard de Saint-Non, from a drawing by Jean-Baptiste Fragonard.

lo's *Moses*, in this travel book, is at grips with a proliferation of mirth: 'One critic compares his head to a goat's; another, his dress to a galley-slave's; but the true sublime resists all ridicule.'[36]

Moments of humour and comedy, then, in literature of the Grand Tour, over the late eighteenth and early nineteenth centuries, supply ways of deflecting the diverse forms of unease entailed in viewing and commenting on sights and wonders - often by making use of a movement from the sublime to the bathetic. Many of these humorous commentaries manage, at the same time, to retain the same sense of wonder and drama that hyperboles of indescribability establish. When Sherlock describes his three travellers in St Peter's, their attempts to comment on the church and its monuments affirm that the task of uttering appropriate words, when visiting this architectural wonder and encountering its famous works of art, is no easy one; the Pole's final comment, in fact, can be read as an utterance that, when quoted by Sherlock, supplies him with an ironic understatement with which to affirm the sublime grandeur of the building. The comic misunderstandings described by Galt, when he recounts the story of West's visit to the *Apollo Belvedere*, conclude with a general acceptance that the sculpture has been acclaimed as a wonder in a satisfactory manner.

Touristic jocularity, on the other hand, in not only deflecting an awareness of the anxieties of encountering the foreign but, more specifically, precluding or neutralizing any incipient intensity of responsiveness, risks a loss of the drama that plays a crucial role in affirming that the traveller-narrator has managed to experience the topography as a domain strikingly different from the familiar. Such jocularity has nonetheless proved useful to the rhetoric of touristic caution, and has survived long after the initial formulation of a touristic attitude towards the foreign. Gastronomy, moreover, continues to supply the traveller with metaphors for a reassuring absence of intensity: Evelyn Waugh, in his travel book *Labels: A Mediterranean Journal* (1930), follows the same strategy as Hazlitt at Terni, selecting a gastronomic product decidedly lacking in exotic associations to provide his metaphor, in describing the Acropolis as 'a singularly beautiful tone of very pale pinkish brown; the nearest parallel to it in Nature that I can think of is that of the milder parts of a Stilton cheese into which port has been poured'.[37]

Notes

1 For a more detailed discussion of ways of defining the Tour, see my *Pleasure and Guilt on the Grand Tour: Travel Writing and Imaginative Geography, 1600-1830* (Manchester: Manchester University Press, 1999), 9-26.

2 Piozzi, *Observations and Reflections Made in the Course of a Journey through France, Italy, and Germany*, 2 vols (London: A. Strahan and T. Cadell, 1789), II, 1f.

3 S. Greenblatt, 'Resonance and Wonder', in *Learning to Curse: Essays in Early Modern Culture* (London: Routledge, 1990), 161-83; here 170.

4 Piozzi, *Observations*, II, 4, 5.

5 Ibid., II, 63; Piozzi, in a footnote, translates the hermit's words as: 'I have danced in my bed so often this year.'

6 Morgan, *Italy*, 2 vols (London: H. Colburn, 1821), II, 343, 344.

7 Anna Jameson, in her *Diary of an Ennuyée*, presents her own susceptibility to 'illusions of romance', as she travels through Italy, as under attack from those travellers who spurn the strategy of hyperbolic responsiveness: travellers 'to whom enthusiasm is only another name for affectation - who, where the cultivated and the contemplative mind finds ample matter to excite feeling and reflection, give themselves airs of fashionable *nonchalance*, or flippant scorn'. Such travellers, she explains, are resolute in their avoidance of hyperboles when they encounter the great sights of Rome: to them 'the tomb of the Horatii and Curiatii is a *stack of chimneys*, the Pantheon *an old oven*, and the Fountain of Egeria *a pig stye*' (second ed., London: H. Colburn, 1826; 207f.).

8 Morgan, *Italy*, II, 180. The convention of mocking the hyperboles of precursors in travel continues long after the period under discussion here. Evelyn Waugh, in *Labels: A Mediterranean Journal* (Harmondsworth: Penguin, 1985), first published in 1930, satirizes the convention of declaring 'I shall never forget ...' - a convention deployed by Piozzi in her description of Vesuvius quoted above - when he observes: 'I do not think I shall ever forget the sight of Etna at sunset [...]. Nothing I have ever seen in Art or Nature was quite so revolting.' (139)

9 For a more detailed exploration of the ways in which concepts of gender become entangled in the rhetoric of responsiveness in travel writings of this period, see my *Pleasure and Guilt on the Grand Tour*, 103-8. Sydney Morgan is, of course, not the only writer of the time to suggest that women are especially inclined or encouraged to fall into the rhetorical trap of displaying their responsiveness in a manner completely incompatible with the qualities of sincerity and simplicity, viewed as marks of manliness, and so laying themselves open to the suspicion of effeminate affectation. In her *Vindication of the Rights of Woman* (1792), Mary Wollstonecraft, in a more general context, satirizes the 'lovely trembler' who turns to men for support 'in the most trifling danger' - exhibiting her tendency 'to feel rather than reason' at such perils as 'the frown of an old cow, or the jump of a mouse' (London: Penguin, 1985, 153).

10 Marquis of Normanby [Constantine Henry Phipps], *The English in Italy*, 3 vols (London: Saunders and Otley, 1825), II, 72f.

11 Brydone, *A Tour through Sicily and Malta: In a Series of Letters to William Beckford, Esq. of Somerly in Suffolk* (London: W. Strachan and T. Cadell, 1773), I, 217, 218, 219.

12 Sterne, *'A Sentimental Journey' with 'The Journal to Eliza' and 'A Political Romance'*, ed. I. Jack (Oxford: Oxford University Press, 1984), 84.

13 Ibid.

14 *Observations and Reflections*, II, 63; in a footnote, Piozzi translates the hermit's words: 'Is she yet alive? Is she yet alive?'

15 Travellers' mockery of stilted and awkward commentaries on art suggests that their writings incorporate, as an unspoken assumption, the argument later mapped out explicitly by Henri Bergson: that we laugh at language and gestures that conspicuously abandon the flexibility that we expect of the human mind and body, and appear mechanistic. See H. Bergson, *Le Rire: Essai sur la signification du comique* (Paris: Félix Alcan, 1906), passim.

16 George Gordon, Lord Byron, *Letters and Journals*, ed. L.A. Marchand, 13 vols (London: John Murray, 1973-94), V, 227.

17 See Samuel Taylor Coleridge's lecture 'Wit and Humour', as summarized by contemporaries in *Coleridge's Miscellaneous Criticism*, ed. Thomas Middleton Raysor (London: Constable, 1936), 111-30, here 113: 'Humour is also displayed in the comparison of finite things with those which our imaginations cannot bound; such as make our great appear little and our little great; or, rather, which reduces to a common littleness both the great and the little, when compared with infinity.' (The editor, in a footnote, points out that this sentence is a paraphrase of a passage in Jean Paul Richter's *Vorschule der Ästhetik*, section 32.)

18 *Life and Letters of Sir Gilbert Elliot, First Earl of Minto, from 1751 to 1806*, ed. the Countess of Minto, 3 vols (London: Longmans, Green, 1874), 366.

19 Galt, *The Life and Studies of Benjamin West, Esq., President of the Royal Academy of London, Prior to his Arrival in England; Compiled from Material Furnished by Himself* (London: T. Cadell and W. Davies, 1816), 103-6.

20 The stories of West's visit to Rome also register another source of unease: an awareness that travellers are themselves objects as well as subjects of vision, and may well be under scrutiny by critical foreigners. Such an awareness is registered in other anecdotes in travel writings of the time: Hester Piozzi, for example, in *Observations and Reflections*, tells a story about a Milanese woman who exclaims in astonishment at the 'slavery' endured by noblemen in England, the supposed land of liberty, in observing the custom of putting on a clean shirt every day (I, 105).

21 Hazlitt, 'On Wit and Humour', in *Lectures on the English Comic Writers* [1818] (Oxford: Oxford University Press, 1943), 5-30, here 2.

22 S. Freud, 'Humour' [1927], in *Art and Literature: 'Jensen's "Gradiva"', 'Leonardo da Vinci' and Other Works*, ed. Albert Dickson, *The Pelican Freud Library*, XIV (Harmondsworth: Penguin, 1985), 425-33, here 429.

23 *The Letters of Horace Walpole, Earl of Orford*, ed. P. Cunningham, 9 vols (London: Bickers and Son, 1880), I, 44.

24 Moore, *View of Society and Manners in Italy: With Anecdotes relating to some Eminent Characters*, second ed., 2 vols (London: W. Strahan and T. Cadell, 1781), I, 63-8. The painting was one of the three versions of Raphael's famous *St John the Baptist*, of which another was (and still is) in the Uffizi, Florence; the third was in Bologna. For Bergson's account of the effect of comedy generated by a lack of flexibility, see, for example, *Le Rire*, 9-11.

25 W. Parsons, *A Poetical Tour, in the Years 1784, 1785, and 1786: By a Member of the Arcadian Society at Rome* (London: J. Robson and W. Clarke, 1787), 33, in a footnote to 'The Man of Taste, An Epigram'; in the poem itself, Parsons describes the copy springing upwards to reveal the actual work as 'The Ciceronè pulls the string'.

26 For an analysis of commentaries on this sculpture that explores such problems, see my 'Effeminacy, Pleasure and the Classical Body', in *Femininity and Masculinity in Eighteenth-Century Art and Culture*, ed. G. Perry and M. Rossington (Manchester: Manchester University Press, 1994), 142-61; in particular, 142-5.

27 Moore, *View of Society and Manners*, II, 10f.

28 M. Sherlock, *Letters from an English Traveller, translated from the French original printed at Geneva: With Notes* (London: J. Nichols, 1780), 61. In the French original, the passage reads as follows: 'J'y suis allé avec un Polonais, un François et un Anglois: l'Anglois cherchoit des beautés; le François, des défauts; le Polonais ne cherchoit rien. Arrivés au bout de l'église; voyez, dit le François, cette Charité de Bernin, qu'elle est mauvaise! l'air de sa tête est affecté, sa chair est sans os, et elle fait des mines épouvantables: ces remarques me paroissent assez justes, répond l'Anglois, mais regardez de l'autre côté de l'Autel, vous verrez une des plus belles choses de la sculpture moderne, la Justice de Guglielmo della Porta; vous avez raison, dit le François (sans la regarder); mais cet enfant, au pied de la Charité, me dégoûte plus que sa mère. Pendant que l'Anglois continuoit à louer la Justice, et le François à critiquer la Charité, le Polonais regardoit la porte par laquelle il étoit entré, et me disoit, que l'Eglise étoit bien plus longue qu'il ne l'avoit cru.' *Lettres d'un voyageur anglois* (Geneva: privately printed, 1779), 127f.

29 For more detailed explorations of these two attitudes to the foreign, see my *Pleasure and Guilt on the Grand Tour*, 173-248.

30 Eaton, *Rome in the Nineteenth Century*, 3 vols (London: A. Constable, 1820), I, 169f. (In the text, the inverted commas begin just before the words *nor the idol of her love* [...].)

31 Ibid., I, 170.

32 Jameson, *Diary of an Ennuyée*, 185f.
33 Morgan, *Italy*, II, 343f.
34 Hazlitt, *Notes of a Journey through France and Italy* (London: Hunt and Clark, 1826), 329; for Byron's description of the cascade, see *Childe Harold's Pilgrimage*, Canto IV, stanzas 69-72.
35 Hazlitt, *Notes of a Journey*, 262f.; emphasis added.
36 Forsyth, *Remarks*, fourth ed. (London: T. Cadell and W. Davies, 1835), 190, 198, 188. Michelangelo's *Last Judgement* in the Sistine Chapel, in Forsyth's account, fails to escape the danger of mirth; in the 'dingy field' of this work, the traveller remarks dismissively, 'you stop only to smile at singularities' (207).
37 Waugh, *Labels*, 124.

Circles and Straight Lines
Romantic Versions of Tourism

Stephen Prickett

In 1844, the *Morning Post* – a London newspaper later absorbed by the *Daily Telegraph* – published a sonnet by the 74 year-old poet laureate, William Wordsworth, on the subject of the proposed Kendal to Windermere railway.

Is then no nook of English ground secure
From rash assault? Schemes of retirement sown
In youth, and mid the busy world kept pure
As when their earliest flowers of hope were blown,
Must perish; – how can they this blight endure?
And must he too the ruthless change bemoan
Who scorns a false utilitarian lure
Mid his paternal fields at random thrown?
Baffle the threat, bright Scene, from Orrest-head
Given to the pausing traveller's rapturous glance:
Plead for thy peace, thou beautiful romance
Of nature; and, if human hearts be dead,
Speak, passing winds; ye torrents, with your strong
And constant voice, protest against the wrong.[1]

As a poem, it has not proved to be one of Wordsworth's most famous works – and it is easy enough to see why. One does not have to be an avidly Freudian critic to suspect that the convoluted syntax may reflect convolutions and problems in the argument. It is hard to believe that Wordsworth was not at some level aware of the irony that he, who had probably done more than any other single person to popularize the natural beauties of his native Lake District, is now trying to stop people coming to admire them.

If the sonnet's clumsiness betrays something of Wordsworth's problems in being caught by the new tourism that he himself has done so much to create, it is not because he has not struggled with answers. The sonnet was accompanied by a letter which spelt out in greater detail his sense of outrage at the intrusion of the railway:

> the perception of what has acquired the name of picturesque and romantic scenery is so far from being intuitive, that it can be produced only by a slow and gradual process of culture; and [...] as a consequence [...] the humbler ranks of society are not, and cannot be, in a state to gain material benefit from a more speedy access than they now have to this beautiful region.[2]

Who, one wonders, *are* these people who want to come to the Lakes without having a proper appreciation of them? And what is Wordsworth, of all people, co-author of the *Lyrical Ballads*, whose name had become synonymous with poems about the poor, the downtrodden, and the destitute, doing trying to exclude 'the humbler ranks of society' from day-trips by train to Windermere?

To begin with, Wordsworth explains, he has no objection to tourists. This was just as well, since not merely had he and his sister, Dorothy, made a number of tours, both to Scotland, and to continental Europe, but he had helped to make such tours fashionable among the middle classes by publishing sequences of sonnets and other poems about his travels. Indeed, one might say that with the Wordsworths, travel had grown from being a leisure activity into a literary form. But these people are not legitimate 'tourists' because, he explains, 'the very word precludes the notion of a railway'.[3]

This is a point so semantically literal-minded as almost to baffle the modern reader. The word 'tourist' was in fact a very recent addition to the English language. One of the first recorded uses in the *OED* is in 1800, where Samuel Pegge, in his *Anecdotes of the English Language* notes that 'A traveller nowadays is called a tour-*ist*'. The model for this, of course, was the so-called 'Grand Tour' of Europe, which was almost an obligatory rite of passage for the young eighteenth-century English aristocrat. Wordsworth himself, when he came down from Cambridge, had gone to France in 1791 to learn French with the intention of becoming travelling tutor to some such wealthy youth.[4] What Wordsworth means in the quote above is that 'tourists' go on 'tours', that is they are independent travellers, free to plan a circular route: departing by one road, and returning by another. Railways, by contrast, only shuttle backwards and forwards by precisely the same path. This is a point worth unpicking with some care: not merely is this a thinly-veiled economic and class distinction between those who can afford to travel in their own or (in the case of the Wordsworths) hired carriages, and those who are forced to ride on public transport, but it reflects what seems to have been with hindsight a unique moment in the history of travel. Whether by wheeled vehicle or by horse, the rich and important had always travelled separately from ordinary people. Like its modern successor, the motor car, the horse-drawn coach was limited in where it went only by the state of the roads. The coming of the railway era in the 1830s and 40s in Britain not merely transformed the speed of travel, it totally transformed its *structure* as well.

When, in June 1837, the old king William IV died, the Earl Marshall, the Duke of Wellington, whose task it was to organize and oversee the coronation of the young Queen Victoria, was in Rome. When news of the king's death reached him, he had to return to London by the quickest means available to him - namely, a coach with frequent changes of horses. The journey from Rome to London took him rather longer than it would have taken a Roman Centurion rejoining his legion in, say, the second century A.D. - because the roads were in a considerably worse condition. There had been no basic change in means of transport for sixteen hundred years. 23 years later, in 1860, George Eliot and G.H. Lewes left London for Rome. They travelled by train, with dining and sleeping cars, only disembarking for the short voyage from Nice to Genoa, because the alpine tunnels, though already under construction, were still unfinished.[5] Despite some degree of fame, Eliot and Lewes were commoners, mere private tourists, without the financial and political clout of Wellington, yet they travelled with a degree of luxury, and with a cheapness unknown in the 1830s. No less significantly, had Wellington been doing the same journey in 1860, he too would undoubtedly have travelled by public transport. Though there were notable exceptions, such as the wealthy and eccentric Duke of Sutherland, who not merely had his own private train, but even had his own private locomotive, named 'Dunrobin', to pull it, by and large the nineteenth century is the only period in human history when the richest and most powerful travelled by the same transport system as the common people.

So much has often been noticed. From a cost of nearly a shilling a mile on a stage-coach, for many years in nineteenth-century Britain the price of the cheapest train ticket was a penny a mile. Nevertheless, so far from liberating the traveller there was another sense in which the railway also *restricted* travel in quite a new way. However bizarre Wordsworth's distinction between circles and straight lines, he has a point: that unlike the coach passenger (or the driver of a private car today) a traveller by train necessarily follows a fixed track. It follows that a railway implies a hitherto unimaginable density of traffic, irrevocably changing the scenery it passes through - and which its travellers have come to admire. Forty years later Wordsworth's disciple, John Ruskin, was to give this idea of loss of innocence with a railway a slightly different mythological twist. Protesting against the construction of another railway line - this time through Monsal Dale in Derbyshire - he wrote:

> There was a rocky valley between Buxton and Bakewell, once upon a time, divine as the vale of Tempe; you might have seen Gods there morning and evening - Apollo and all the sweet Muses of light - walking in fair procession on the lawns of it [...]. You cared neither for Gods nor grass, but for cash [...]. You Enterprised a Railroad through the valley - you blasted its rocks away [...]. The valley is gone, and the Gods with it; and now, every fool in Buxton can be at Bakewell in half-an-hour, and every fool in Bakewell at Buxton.[6]

Wordsworth's attitude towards his landscape, however, is less concerned with the antics of every fool in Buxton (or, as it might be, in Kendal) than with the attitudes symbolized by such shuttling as against the traditional 'tour'. If, as a young radical, he once believed that 'One impulse from a vernal wood' could teach more 'than all the sages can' he has now decided to join the sages. Feeling for nature matures through a slow process of growth and education. It is not something instinctive to the masses. Though the 74 year-old poet was worried that in publicizing such a view he might look as if he was going back on his youthful commitment to the cause of the poor, he stuck to his position, despite a storm of abuse. What he does not say in so many words, but was always evident, is that his admiration had always been for the rural independent poor, and in particular for the Cumberland 'statesmen' or smallholders, and not for the urban proletariat - for whom he had expressed some contempt in *The Excursion*.

But there is another element in that Ruskin quotation that strikes a familiar chord. The destruction of the beautiful Manifold valley by the railway is more than merely the destruction of natural beauty; it is in some sense a *violation* of it in an almost sexual sense. Again, this is an element already present in Wordsworth's 1844 poem. The logical problem on which the sestet of that sonnet founders is, of course, the clumsy personification of nature which is being invoked to keep the tourists at bay. This is presented in two stages. In the first, it is apparently the *view* itself, the 'bright Scene' (with capital 'S'), from 'Orrest-head', that is being invoked to somehow 'baffle' the threat posed by the new railway. The language is deliberately feminized: like the contemporary 'fair maid of Buttermere', of Schubert's maid of the mill, 'she' is the 'romance of nature' and the object of 'the pausing traveller's rapturous glance'. The implication of overwhelming physical beauty, coupled with the suggestion that she is 'pleading' is obviously meant to suggest rape – and, like Edmund Burke's famous response to the threatened Marie Antoinette, to rally the chivalrous reader to her defence.[7] If, however, as the poet plainly fears, no such chivalrous response will be forthcoming from his readers, then the protection of a more violently masculine nature of 'winds' and 'torrents' is invoked where human agency has failed.

That Wordsworth actually has rape in mind here is suggested by the curious diction of the opening line. 'Nook' is a special word in Wordsworth's vocabulary. It occurs twice, for instance, at key points in his poem 'Nutting', first published 44 years earlier, in the second volume of the 1800 *Lyrical Ballads*. On both occasions the context has a peculiar sexual charge:

> Among the woods,
> And o'er the pathless rocks, I forc'd my way
> Until, at length, I came to one dear nook
> Unvisited, where not a broken bough
> Droop'd with its wither'd leaves, ungracious sign
> Of devastation, but the hazels rose
> Tall and erect, with milk-white clusters hung,
> A virgin scene!

The violation of this 'virgin scene' by Wordsworth himself is even more explicit:

Then up I rose,
And dragg'd to earth both branch and bough, with crash
And merciless ravage, and the shady nook
Of hazels, and the green and mossy bower
Deform'd and sullied, patiently gave up
Their quiet being [...][8]

Intrusion and despoilation of this nook is an act of rape. The 'rash assault' of the railway is, it seems, more than a mere military metaphor. The conquest and possession of the land by the forces of industrial progress is not fruitful and productive, but a barren assertion of will: a sexual assault. The interweaving of garden and vaginal imagery is centuries old in English poetry: a 'nook' is for Wordsworth what a garden signified in an earlier vocabulary. The *hortus conclusus* is a place of stimulation and refinement of the senses. Comparisons between 'Nutting' and Andrew Marvell's 'Garden', for instance, make the point clearly.

Fair quiet, have I found thee
And Innocence, thy Sister dear?
Mistaken long, I sought you then
In busie Companies of Men.
Your sacred Plants, if here below,
Only among the Plants will grow.
Society is all but rude
To this delicious Solitude.

No white nor red was ever seen
So am'rous as this lovely green
[...][9]

Similarly, the nook is for Wordsworth a place of retirement and seclusion where he could sit 'voluptuous [...] among the flowers', and where 'with the flowers [he ...] played' – a place at once of lush sensuousness yet total innocence until the brutal arrival of man.

Only after a moment's reflection does the alert reader begin to puzzle over further the implications of what has to be called this 'train' of imagery. In feminizing and victimizing the Lake District landscape, Wordsworth is, it seems, deliberately making reference to another Burkian antithesis: that between the sublime and the beautiful. The 'sublime' is rugged, massive, mysterious and powerful – in short, masculine; by contrast, the 'beautiful' is distinctly feminine: gentle, curvacious, soft and passive. In terms of landscape, mountains are sublime; valleys, meadows and groves beautiful. So why is the jutting peak of Orrest-head, a famous local viewpoint which dominates the northern side of Windermere town, being invoked as 'beautiful' rather than 'sublime'? A logical case might, of course, be constructed to the effect that Orrest-head, at just under 300m, its not exactly on the same scale as the 1000m Helvellyn further up the valley, let alone that classical locus of sublimity, the Alps, but this, I think, is to miss the point. Orrest-head is being feminized because she needs our protection – protection from rape. But, of course, it is *not* actually Orrest-head which is being feminized at all: it is the 'Scene, *from* Orrest-head': not the mountain (which can presumably look after itself) but the *view*, which is in danger of being raped by the insertion of a railway terminus in the foreground.

Here, we notice, what is at stake is manifestly a human aesthetic construct: neither the raw power of nature, nor a lost pristine innocence, but a visual perspective, a way of looking at landscape. And, of course, Wordsworth's second line of defence, the masculine sublimity of the 'strong and constant' voices of wind and water, is no less an aesthetic and anthropomorphized human construct. Indeed, for all its apparent metaphorical power, it is by far the weaker line of defence. If people are not going to rise up and defend the landscape of Windermere from rape by the railway, then it is unlikely the voices of passing winds and local torrents are going to be very effective either.

Now, however, in this sonnet he strikes a new note. The 'schemes of retirement' (l.2) sound at first as if they belong in the same world as the 'garden' imagery of innocence and loss, but the word 'retirement' had acquired its modern meaning well before Wordsworth's time, and the contrast of youth and age underlines its main sense. This is not so much the contemplative aesthetic withdrawal of an Andrew Marvell or Shakespeare's William Iden, but a home for old age: perhaps not for too many of the Manchester bourgeoisie, but certainly for his new neighbours at Rydal Mount, the Arnolds, and other members of the educated classes capable of appreciating the landscape. Wordsworth's letter to the *Morning Post* is in many ways an astonishingly academic piece, stressing what a new aesthetic phenomenon the appreciation of mountain scenery was. He cites passages from Evelyn, Ray, Bishop Burnet, the 'other Burnet' and Gray, all of whom reacted with horror to the sublimity and loneliness of the high peaks. There is, he believes, a revolution in sensibility under way, and the new railway, with its promise of cheap and easy access to the wilderness, will destroy the very thing the more discerning travellers are in search of.

But Wordsworth is also playing politics – as the fact that he had chosen to make his attack via a London and national newspaper rather than a local one, indicates. Horror at rape is cunningly set alongside a solider economic interest. A railway, he believes, will lower land values and house-prices. Alongside the Lakeland 'statesman', whose rural patrimony is threatened by the 'false utilitarian lure' must stand another class of persons altogether: those whose future plans for retirement will (he believes) be blighted by the projected railway. This is a point he clarifies in his letter:

> Among the ancient inheritances of the yeomen, surely worthy of high respect, are interspersed through the entire district villas, most of them with small domains attached that the occupants would be hardly less annoyed by a railway passing through their neighbour's ground than through their own.[10]

What Wordsworth is trying to do, in effect, is put together a political coalition of local interests and visitors with an equal stake in preserving the landscape as it is – in short, shepherds like his own 'Michael' must finally put aside their suspicion of the wicked city and make common cause with the in-comers: the Arnolds, the Ruskins, Rawnsleys, and, of course, in the twentieth century, Beatrix Potter.

But Wordsworth has more formidable enemies ranged against him than cheap day-trippers. The 'false utilitarian lure' of the sonnet was more than simply the temptation to the statesman to sell his ancestral patrimony. Utilitarianism was an economic theory with direct implications for conservation and tourism. One example, in particular, had brought the matter close to home only a few years before.

In 1833 Thomas Babington Macaulay, the historian and liberal theoretician, had reviewed Southey's *Colloquies on Society* for the *Edinburgh Review*. By means of a series of conversations with the ghost of Sir Thomas More – now a time traveller visiting the early nineteenth century – Southey had highlighted a series of urgent social and economic problems, soon to be known by Carlyle's umbrella term as 'the condition-of-England question'. They included poverty, industrialization, Catholic emancipation, national education, emigration, the position of women, the decay of religion and the spread of revolutionary ideas by printing. In reply, Macaulay had vigorously defended the economic condition of Britain. Prompted, perhaps, by the ghostly presence of Henry VIII's one-time Lord Chancellor, he embarks on a brief economic history of England since Tudor times in order to show that despite 'all the misgovernment of her rulers' England

> has been almost constantly becoming richer and richer. Now and then there has been a stoppage, now and then a short regression; but as to the general tendency there can be no doubt. A single breaker may recede; but the tide is evidently coming in.[11]

He concludes by projecting the progress of the past into an England of a hundred years hence:

> If we were to prophesy that in the year 1930 a population of fifty millions, fed, better clad, and lodged than the English of our time, will cover these islands, that Sussex and Huntingdonshire will be wealthier than the wealthiest parts of the West Riding of Yorkshire now are, that cultivation, rich as that of a flower-garden, will be carried to the very tops of Ben Nevis and Helvellyn, that machines constructed on principles yet undiscovered will be in every house, that there will be no highways but railroads, no travelling but by steam, that our debt, vast as it seems to us, will appear to our great-grandchildren a trifling encumbrance, which might be paid off in a year or two, many people would think us insane.[12]

Though Macaulay, frightened perhaps that his readers might take him at his word, is quick to add 'we prophesy nothing', the passage is none the less a remarkable exercise in what Herman Khan calls 'futurology'. The National Debt has climbed to astronomical figures – and we have stopped worrying about it. From a population of 13.9 million (1831 census) Macaulay 'prophesies' a figure of 50 million: the actual figure in the 1931 census was 46 million. We can forgive him 'no travelling but by steam', for the internal combustion engine is still sixty years away and he has grasped the essential transformation of travel that the railway implies in the very year of the opening of the Liverpool and Manchester Railway. Prophetic also is the reference to Sussex and Huntingdonshire – both notoriously poverty-stricken areas of the period. By 1930 both had become prosperous railway commuter-belt country, while the textile industry of the West Riding of Yorkshire was already beginning to suffer from cheaper foreign competition. The 'machines constructed on principles yet undiscovered', despite its studied vagueness, was also a shot well ahead of its time. Such forecasts of technical progress were common enough by the 1880s, when the young H.G. Wells was attending the Normal School of Science in South Kensington, but a leap of imagination *beyond* steam (which we can now happily interpret as electricity) was rare, if not unique in 1830. Which brings us, of course, to the one notable failure in Macaulay's list - the notion that 'cultivation, rich as a flower-garden, will be carried to the very tops of Ben Nevis and Helvellyn' - a prophecy as notable for its *inaccuracy* as the others were accurate.

Macaulay's ideas of landscape, and the consummation of its 'improvement' in terms of flower gardens (or their equivalents) on the peaks of the Scottish Highlands and the Lake District declares its utilitarian ancestry as unmistakably as his views on economic progress. Indeed, it is part of his economic beliefs, and, like them, in some ways it is a deeply conservative vision - or rather, combination of visions, for we can detect in his throwaway prophecy two quite distinct attitudes to landscape. The first is the eighteenth-century equation of beauty with usefulness. An aesthetically pleasing landscape is a well-cultivated one. Where man is not clearly in evidence, nature is barren. Though it is by no means their only attitude towards landscape, it is one frequently found in Arthur Young and in William Cobbett.[13] Indeed, in view of our interest in the connotations of the word, it is worth noticing that Young's appointment as secretary to the newly-formed Board of Agriculture in 1793 was based partly on the prestige of his significantly-named *Tours in England and Wales* (1768-70) and later Ireland (1780). A similar journey around France on the eve of the Revolution in 1787, however, was published as *Travels in France*, which, despite its appearance in two weighty volumes in 1792, was clearly less comprehensive than the earlier 'tours'. One begins to see why, for Wordsworth, a 'tourist' is an altogether more substantial figure than a mere train passenger.

The second attitude to landscape directly relates to the cultivation of a hill or mountain right to its summit as an expression or symbol of human conquest and domination of nature. The obligatory tower or ruin in a Claude or early Turner painting implies either man's domination of the wilderness, or, as in John Dyer's poem, 'Grongar Hill' (1727), the reverse - human vanity and pride. Though Dyer's idyllic peak is triumphally 'crowned' by a ruined castle, it is now the unsavoury haunt of ravens, foxes and toads.[14] W.T. Pomeroy, author of *A General View of the Agriculture of Worcestershire* (1794) writes of 'the Aberly and Whitley hills [...] rising with a bold front, and most of them cultivated to their summits' with sheep 'hanging from their brows'.[15] Mountains are to be conquered, tamed and humanized. Thus Macaulay's vision is not merely one of utility, but horticultural lushness. Yet, as those who have climbed them will recall, Ben Nevis and Helvellyn are, on their upper slopes, as fine a pair of natural slag-heaps as one may find anywhere.

Robert Southey himself, on his tour to Scotland in 1819, had described Ben Nevis as 'a precipitous, rugged, stony, uninviting mountain, looking as if it had been riven from the summit to the base, and half of it torn away'.[16] In his *Colloquies*, moreover, among other forms of public works to alleviate unemployment, he had suggested the reclamation of waste and unprofitable land.[17] Macaulay, therefore, though he had not read Southey's opinion of Ben Nevis, is actually responding to what he *had* read of Southey's suggestions for land improvement. Laissez-faire will make Ben Nevis bloom. Certainly the idea of cultivation 'rich as a flower garden' is outrageous hyperbole, but that is, after all, the tone of the whole passage. To assert a future population of 50 million, or as wealthy a future for Sussex or Huntingdonshire as for Yorkshire would have seemed no less hyperbolic to many sceptical contemporaries. The idea of landscape as garden has a long and well-documented history. The biblical story of Eden, its return in the Earthly Paradise of Dante, medieval and renaissance allegories have all contributed to the rich deposit of association that Macaulay is able to invoke by that simple adjectival clause. Though the ostensible purpose is still one of 'utility', the rhetoric is of sanctuary, moral order, harmony - in short, of Wordsworthian 'nooks'.

And here, of course, is where Macaulay's rhetorical synthesis runs into trouble. The point he wishes to make against Southey's argument is essentially an economic one. Laissez-faire is, for Macaulay, the most efficient and productive way of encouraging agriculture, as it is of any other economic enterprise. 'We firmly believe that five hundred thousand pounds subscribed by individuals for rail-roads and canals would produce more advantage to the public than five millions voted by Parliament for the same purpose.'[18] But the argument cannot be allowed to develop into one of 'utility' versus 'beauty' as it had already done in town planning and architecture:

Pugin's *Contrasts*[19] is only three years away. For Macaulay, utility *is* beauty. A landscape conquered to the very highest peaks by organized agriculture is thus a visible aesthetic expression of progress. The agricultural improvements begun in the previous century will, Macauly believes, continue to a point we cannot yet imagine. The same spirit that greened the sandy wastes of the Norfolk brecklands in the eighteenth century will make a cottage garden out of Helvellyn in the nineteenth. Yet ironically, this faith in the future of scientific farming misses the conclusion of its own economic logic. If there really were to be such dramatic improvements in agricultural methods, then it would not be necessary to try and farm Helvellyn anyway. The rich soils of the Midlands and East Anglia would suffice to feed the swelling population of 50 million, and, so far from prospering, agriculture on the hill-farms would become increasingly marginal. And so it has proved, as the European Union taxpayers have learned to their increasing cost. The only conceivable reason for farming Helvellyn would be as a defiant demonstration that it *was* possible: as an assertion of human mastery over the most inhospitable and bleak places of the earth. But the purpose then would be unequivocally aesthetic: an attempt to obliterate the Wordsworthian distinction between garden and wilderness. A nook that covers the whole of England is, by definition, no longer a nook. Moreover any attempt to beautify a place of no inherent agricultural value would be precisely the kind of misuse of resources Macaulay has attributed to public funding. Macaulay's argument deconstructs itself.

But even rhetorical hyperboles have meaning. Why, for instance, pick on Helvellyn in the first place? Unlike Ben Nevis, the highest mountain in Scotland, Helvellyn is far from being the highest mountain in England. The Scawfells in the Lake District are both higher, and even Skidaw, towering directly over Keswick, where Southey lived, is almost as high. Could it be that Helvellyn had other, important, associations for Macaulay? Could it be its closeness to the home of the man who, more than any other, was to ensure that nobody, on either aesthetic or economic pretext, was ever to try any Macaulayan agricultural experiments on Helvellyn's summit, William Wordsworth?

By the mid-years of the nineteenth century Wordsworth's own crusade to defend his beloved landscape against 'utility' had gained two powerful groups of allies. One was centred on Ruskin and his circle at Brantwood, on Lake Conniston; the other on the Arnolds just across the valley from Rydal Mount at Fox How. The youthful

Matthew Arnold was taken to visit the Great Man at Rydal Mount. His niece, though born in Tasmania, made up for it by returning at the age of two, and (somewhat later) making the Lake District a vital part of the setting of two of her best-selling novels. Both Mrs Humphry Ward's novels *Robert Elsmere* and *Helbeck of Banisdale* rely on local topography for much of their atmosphere. At this same period the Vicar of Wray, on the far side of the lake from Orrest-head, was Canon Rawnsley, also an avid Wordsworthian.

It was he, together with Ruskin's friend, Octavia Hill, and Sir Robert Hunter, a lawyer, who founded the National Trust in 1895 for the express purpose of preventing the desecration of areas of outstanding natural beauty by property developers, inappropriate farming methods or tourist facilities.[20] They were soon to be aided by the almost inexhaustible funds of another Wordsworthian, a shy young Londoner whom Rawnsley had befriended as a child and later helped in the publication of her first book - *Peter Rabbit*. Beatrix Potter's family wealth had come from railway shares, but the phenomenal sales of her books had allowed her to buy first of all Hill Top Farm, at Sawrey in the Furness Fells, and then over 4,000 acres (1,600 hectares) of threatened Lake District territory - all of which were bequeathed to the Trust at her death in 1943. She had also been the means of rescuing an extraordinary little notebook which, inexplicably, had turned up in her ice-house at Hill Top Farm: Ann Tyson's Prompt Book. Ann Tyson was Wordsworth's landlady when he attended Hawkshead Grammar School in the 1780s. From it we know in detail much of his day-to-day life: his diet, his debts, who else was lodging in the house (as it happens, two other future poets) and much else besides. Hill Top Farm is now the biggest single tourist attraction in the Lake District.

What Macaulay had failed to prophesy was the growth of conservation movements like the National Trust - and that such movements are part of a tourist economy. The population of 50 millions, better clad, fed and housed than in the 1830s, travelling by railway (or even by such undiscovered principles as the petrol and diesel engine) would fight to *preserve* the very distinction between the garden and the wilderness that Macaulay had confidently assumed would be obliterated by the inevitable march of progress. As Wordsworth saw, the preservation of wilderness is a direct consequence of population pressure and increased prosperity. If we needed an example, we need look no further than Beatrix Potter herself, whose family money came from railway shares, and whose passionate interest in natural history and rural existence was driven by a city upbringing and an emotionally undernourished home-life. Of such stuff are Wordsworthians made.

Yet Wordsworth himself, for all his perspicacity, had also failed to see some of the consequences of his own argument. As we have seen, Macaulay, in the name of progress, had in fact conceived landscape in essentially conservative and outmoded terms that eventually contradicted themselves. Wordsworth, apparently the conservative, was surely correct in seeing himself as the spearhead of a radical shift in aesthetic sensibility that would, in the end, create a quite new attitude to wilderness. What he could not see was the fact that the present was no different from the past in that even the wilderness was in a process of evolution. In his second sonnet on the Kendal and Windermere Railway Wordsworth focussed his protest on human changes to the landscape.

> Proud were ye, Mountains, when, in times of old,
> Your patriot sons, to stem invasive war,
> Intrenched your brows; ye gloried in each scar:
> Now, for your shame, a Power, the Thirst of Gold,
> That rules o'er Britain like a baneful star,
> Wills that your peace, your beauty, shall be sold,
> And clear way made for her triumphal car
> Through the beloved retreats your arms enfold!
> Heard YE that Whistle? As her long-linked Train
> Swept onwards, did the vision cross your view?
> Yes, ye were startled; - and, in balance true,
> Weighing the mischief with the promised gain,
> Mountains, and Vales, and Floods, I call on you
> To share the passion of a just disdain.[21]

Macaulay's imagery of domination is now taken up by Wordsworth. This is an anthropomorphized landscape of war. The proud mountains, like old warriors, bear scars upon their brows. This time, however, the war is not metaphorical but real and human: the scars are iron-age hill forts. These scars of the past, however, have healed, and like the ruins in a classical landscape enhance rather than disfigure the view. The difference between ancient earthworks and modern railway embankments and cuttings, Wordsworth argues, is primarily one of *motive* rather than aesthetics. The former is a symbol of honourable patriotism, the latter of naked greed. The argument, like the quality of the verse, is distinctly doubtful. Wordsworth's invocation of ancient Britons, like Macaulay's trope of Saxon liberties, though a matter of intense and real emotion for many at this period, is historically weak.[22] Moreover, landscape is a matter of earthworks, not motives. Like Macaulay, Wordsworth is weakest on the economics of conservation, failing to see that prosperity would do more than poverty to preserve his wilderness of mountains, vales and floods. Nor could he recognize that the earthworks of the railway would, in their turn, become green furrows in the hillside, assimilated into the ever-changing synthesis of the rural landscape. When the railway line from Kendal to Windermere was closed in the 1970s there was a public outcry – not least from conservationist groups. It was then re-opened, with links to the highspeed passenger trains from London to Scotland, to offer day-return trips from London to Windermere. Two other steam railways, one on the far side of Windermere, the other a narrow-gauge in Eskdale, operate in summer purely for the tourist trade and are considered an enhancement to the environment. The National Trust approves.

Notes

1 Wordsworth, *Last Poems, 1821-1850*, ed. J. Curtis (Ithaca: Cornell University Press, 1999), 389-90.
2 Wordsworth, 'Kendal and Windermere Railway', in W.J.B. Owen and J.W. Smyser (eds), *The Prose Works of William Wordsworth* (Oxford: Oxford University Press, 1974), III, 349.
3 Wordsworth, 'Kendal and Windermere Railway', 341.
4 M. Moorman, *William Wordsworth*, vol I: *The Early Years, 1770-1803* (Oxford: Oxford University Press, 1957), 170.
5 See G.S. Haight, *George Eliot: A Biography* (Oxford: Clarendon Press, 1968), 322.
6 Ruskin, 'Fors Clavigera', in E.T. Cook and A. Wedderburn (eds), *The Works of John Ruskin* (London: George Allen, 1907), XXVII, letter 5, 86 (quoted again in the final chapter of *Praeterita* III, iv).
7 See Burke, 'Reflections on the Revolution in France', in *The Works of Edmund Burke* (London: Rivington, 1808), 149.
8 Wordsworth, 'Nutting', in J. Butler and K. Green (eds), *'Lyrical Ballads' and Other Poems, 1797-1800* (Ithaca: Cornell University Press, 1992), 219f., lines 13-20 and 41-6 respectively.
9 Marvell, 'The Garden', in H.M. Margoliouth (ed.), *Poems and Letters* (Oxford: Clarendon Press, 1971), I, 51, lines 9-18.
10 Wordsworth, 'Kendal and Windermere Railway', 352.

11 Macaulay, 'Southey's Colloquies on Society', in *Critical and Historical Essays Contributed to the 'Edinburgh Review'* (London: Longmans, Green, 1883), 120.
12 Ibid., 120f.
13 Young, *Tours in England and Wales,* Series of Reprints of Scarce Tracts in Economic and Political Science, no. 14 (London: London School of Economics, 1932), 6f. and Cobbett, *Rural Rides* (London: Cobbett, 1830).
14 Dyer, 'Grongar Hill', in R. Lonsdale (ed.), *The New Oxford Book of Eighteenth-Century Verse* (Oxford: Oxford University Press, 1984), 168, line 71.
15 Quoted in J. Barrell, *The Idea of Landscape and the Sense of Place 1730-1840* (Cambridge: Cambridge University Press, 1972), 76.
16 Southey, *Journal of a Tour in Scotland 1819* (Edinburgh: Thin, 1972), 202.
17 Southey, *Colloquies on Society* (London: Cassell, 1887).
18 Macaulay, 'Southey's Colloquies', 109.
19 A.W.N. Pugin, *Contrasts* (London: Pugin, 1836).
20 W.T. Hill, *Octavia Hill: Pioneer of the National Trust and Housing Reformer* (London: Hutchinson, 1956).
21 Wordsworth, *Last Poems*, 390.
22 For the emotive significance of these, and similar images, see J. Burrow, *A Liberal Descent: Victorian Historians and the English Past* (Cambridge: Cambridge University Press, 1982).

Heroic Travellers - Romantic Landscapes

The Colonial Sublime in Indian, Australian and American Art and Literature

Gerhard Stilz

1. Romantic 'Maps' for Colonial Travel

Consciously or not, the tourist industry of our day tends to follow the sentimental ways of travelling through the past. It does so for various good reasons. Even where historic nostalgia is not made as explicit as it is in heritage tourism, the beaten tracks are felt to provide safety, they largely offer a reliable and therefore economical infrastructure, and they are, above all, lined with the familiar sights, cultural memories and shibboleths of cosmopolitan education which make them attractive to the provincial mind ever suffering from territorial fixations.

Thus, the modes, attitudes, concepts and aims of travelling in past centuries, as reflected in art and literature, do not only create the charms of nostalgia, but they must be seen as the groundwork and basic conditions of tourism as a generally accepted individual and social activity. They need to be reflected upon in order to reveal why we travel, and where to.

This essay concentrates on the romantic impulse of travelling. Romantic travellers, moved by Edmund Burke's password of the 'sublime', not only revaluated solitary, remote and forbidding areas in Britain and Europe (such as the Lake District, the Scottish Highlands or the Alps), turning them into the glorious sites for experiencing a new relation between the individual self and its overpowering environment. They also informed colonial travellers overseas with the perceptions and discursive strategies of coping with alien realities. And they can be seen to play a formative role for the touristic appreciation and appropriation of the 'new worlds', both in a figurative and in a very material sense. Their images and descriptions of stormy seas and safe harbours, of mountainous deserts and grand canyons, still constitute a good number of those spectacular route maps and indispensable sights which are offered by modern tourism.

Colonial travellers of the eighteenth century were (or stylized themselves into being) a hardy lot. They set out into 'uncharted' realms, and they conquered 'unknown' areas which had previously been covered by metaphors of darkness and desolation. Their mission was to search these areas and possibly convert them into useful fields of cultivation. The prescribed metaphorical routes of colonial progress led from discovery through enlightenment to cultural gardening. Wavering between self-discipline and self-commiseration, colonial explorers felt the heroic choice between victoriously contributing to the colonial ideal or tragically sacrificing their lives against the overwhelming odds ominously characterized by ruins, wilderness and void infinities.

This concept of colonial exploration was informed and could be made aesthetically palatable by Edmund Burke's *Philosophical Enquiry into the Origin of our Ideas of the Sublime and the Beautiful* (1757). The emotions of danger or pain which, on immediate experience, produced terror, were found to be a source of delight when overcome or perceived from a safe distance. Romantic writers and artists, under Burke's magic keyword of the 'sublime', had been able to revalue that prime European landscape of terrors, the Alps. British travellers made major contributions to this process, above all William Wordsworth in his reflections on Mont Blanc or Simplon Pass included in his *Prelude* (1806/1850) and Percy Bysshe Shelley in his imaginative poetic praise of 'Mont Blanc' (1816/17). Certainly this revaluation presupposed a number of very palpable improvements in the technology and logistics of travelling itself. Without the increased safety, reliability and comfort of roads and vehicles, without the solid infrastructures supplied by stagecoaches, hotels and guest houses during the eighteenth century, neither travellers in Britain nor on the European continent would have thought of interpreting their immediate experiences as sublime and therefore delightful versions of terror.

On a larger canvas, this also applies to travels overseas, where enemies had to be subdued, pirates eliminated and peaceful networks established before travelling could be regarded as safe and the old terrors could be seen in the fascinating glow of Burke's aesthetics. Undoubtedly, from the late eighteenth century on, the strategy of aesthetic sublimation can be seen at work at the borders of the British Empire and - no less, though a little later - in the American West. Spectacular, wild landscapes and sombre ruins are evoked in order to make the colonial traveller's exploits appear heroic and to adorn the colonial settler's everyday work in all its weariness and boredom with the flavour of sublime emotions. This strategy can be traced in landscape descriptions as found in literature and painting. The occasional transfer of the Alpine sublimation model to the imperial fringe is hardly surprising though it sometimes verges on the grotesque. This essay will discuss and compare exemplary texts and views from India, Australia and America.

2. Views from India

In India, the impressions of British *litterateurs* and painters usually followed, but frequently also preceded, the British flag, especially in areas which were regarded as peaceful and friendly. Travelling by boat, on horseback or in a palanquin were old and well-organized activities in the Muslim and Hindu cultures where pilgrims, traders and family relations for time immemorial had regularly travelled over vast distances and society had been multicultural for at least three thousand years. British explorers of any kind - once they had been approved of by the East India Company - were therefore, as a rule, not exposed to insurmountable difficulties when applying for passports to Indian princely states adjoining British territory. Accounts of painters being arrested under suspicion of espionage are rare when compared with accounts of Indian princes entertaining such visitors and even commissioning artworks for their palaces.

Thomas and William Daniell (1749-1840 and 1769-1837), uncle and nephew, produced hundreds of sketches, aquatints and oil paintings. They spent nine years travelling as 'intrepid adventurers',[1] sketching and painting in India (1784-93), North and South, East and West. For many years after, they published and marketed their work in London, where there was a 'growing market [...] for views of distant lands, peoples, flora and fauna'.[2] The idea that foreign countries might supply valuable material for art collectors whose exotic fantasies could be satisfied for good money had been triggered off by the Grand Tour to mediterranean countries. This idea was charged with notions of the sublime, i.e. Edmund Burke's observation that dangers overcome or terrors remote and artistically reflected might be even more attractive and accompanied by stronger emotions than those positive pleasures which could be regarded as familiar, homely and beautiful.

In a classicist manner, the Daniells used a camera obscura (as Canaletto had done before), thus obtaining an architectural and topographical precision which was, even later, hardly matched by photography. At the same time, however, under the impression of the new picturesque fashion, they also added, removed or shifted elements, changed the light, reduced the size of human figures and heightened the effects of dramatic perspectives in order to appeal to the increasingly romantic taste which spread among both the colonial nouveau-riche in India and the retired Indian civil servants in England who could afford to decorate their buildings and impress their friends with these trophies of Indian scenery.

The Daniells travelled India at a time when the British paramountcy had only taken control of Bengal and a few coastal patches in Bombay and around Madras. In northern India, they first revisited and revised the sights sketched by William Hodges (Captain Cook's painter on his second voyage), who had been supported in Calcutta by Governor General Warren Hastings. But the Daniells soon pioneered into areas which no other European painter had ever seen. They were the first Europeans known to enter the Himalayas, and they bravely traversed South India only one year after the dreaded Tipu Sultan had been forced to retreat from the Carnatic in the Third Mysore war. More than once, their retinue had to be accompanied and protected by sepoys.

Srinagar, Fort and Bridge (1788), an oil painting,[3] takes us to Garhwal (a place not to be confused with Kashmir). The Himalayan foothills appear mainly dramatic for the daring construction of the rope bridge over the Alaknanda River (a Ganges tributary) and its composition with the rocky fort. Here, the effects of the picturesque are still rather derived from human structures than from a natural landscape. In fact, the Daniells have not left us a sublime picture of the high mountains. Their artistic impressions remained weak and distanced. Yet William Daniell was affected by the snow-clad Himalayas very much along Burke's new aesthetic when he confided to his journal:

> the appearance of a prodigious range of still more distant mountains, proudly rising above all that we have hitherto considered as most grand and magnificent, and which, clothed in a robe of everlasting snow, seem by their etherial hue to belong to a region

> elevated in the clouds, and partaking of their nature; having nothing in common with terrestrial forms. It would be in vain to attempt, by any description, to convey an idea of those sublime effects, which perhaps even the finest art can but faintly imitate.[4]

In *Madras, Fort St. George, 'a squall passing off'* (1833, sketches dating back to 1792),[5] another oil painting, we witness a sublime seascape with the British colonial fort triumphantly presented as the heroic survivor placidly enjoying its integrity above and behind the turmoil and rubble which expands in the foreground. Two aquatints from the Daniells' *Oriental Scenery* (under which title they fabricated six highly successful collections of 24 scenes each) show the *Trichinopoly Rock Fort* (Tamil Nadu) from different perspectives:[6] first a classicist vista, distanced and matter-of-fact, with a casual Cauvery river scene; but second a closer, awe-inspiring, sublime, wide-angled impression of inaccessibility, heightening the walls of the temple fort, which towers over crumbling, dark and gloomy rocks. The painting of the *Waterfall at Papanasam, Tinnevelly* (1792)[7] (Fig. 1) had originally belonged to Warren Hastings, Governor of Bengal. The sublime power of this cataract is enhanced by the praying and prostrate Indians. The objects of their devotion, which in reality are not visible from the chosen angle, were shifted into sight by the painters so that they could underline the terror of this awe-inspiring spectacle.[8]

More or less direct and lasting influences of the Daniells in British culture have been discerned by Mildred Archer: for Charles Cockerell's 'Indian' villa in Sezincote (Cotswolds), both the architect Samuel Pepys Cockerell and Humphry Repton, who was in charge of planning the garden including various monuments, consulted Thomas Daniell's works. Of the Brighton Pavilion, Daniell inspired at least Porden's Royal Stables and Riding School and John Nash's Pavilion, and between 1800 and 1830, 'most experiments in Indo-British architecture were based on his work'.[9] For Lord Curzon, British Indian Viceroy from 1899 to 1905, as well as for the Archaeological Survey of India, the Daniells' oil paintings offered 'important clues' for the conservation and restoration of Indian monuments. After 1947, the 'nostalgia for the Raj' ushered in a new enjoyment of the Daniells' work which, in turn, fostered the fascination of the exotic and still supports the desire to travel and see the places many of which have become well-known 'sights' made accessible by the infrastructure of modern tourism.[10]

Fig. 1: Thomas and William Daniell, *The Waterfall at Papanasam, Tinnevelly.*

In early Anglo-Indian colonial literature we find significant parallels to the concept of landscape painting and Burke's new aesthetics. In D.L. Richardson's poem 'Evening on the Banks of the Ganges' (c. 1830) we have a charming intertextual experiment in which the sublime and the beautiful are evidently contrasted as two complementary views and emotions characterizing East and West, the sombre province of the colony and the promising capital of the motherland. We are clearly urged to read this poem as an Eastern companion piece to Wordsworth's famous sonnet, 'Upon Westminster Bridge Sept 3, 1802':

> I wandered thoughtfully by Gunga's shore,
> While the broad sun upon the slumbering wave
> Its last faint flush of golden radiance gave,
> And tinged with tenderest hues some ruins hoar.
> Methinks this earth had never known before
> A calm so deep – 'twas silent as the grave.
> The smallest bird its light wing could not lave
> In the smooth flood, nor from the green-wood soar
> (If but the tiniest branch its pinions stirred,
> Or shook the dew-drops from the leaves) unheard.
> Like pictured shadows 'gainst the western beam
> The dark boats slept, while each lone helmsman stood
> Still as a statue! – the strange quietude
> Enthralled my soul like some mysterious dream![11]

The most obvious intertextual link between the two poems is the central formula of quietness ('a calm so deep'). Next to that, all significant topographical, temporal, perspectival and symbolic issues are mirrored and contrasted. Wordsworth focusses on a still, but promising, London morning, viewed Eastward across the Thames. Richardson replies with its Indian antithesis – a sunset scene viewed among the ruins near the Ganges, with the thoughtful spectator looking West. Yet the elegiac note in the latter poem does not permit an easy dismissal of the darkening colony waiting for nightfall vis-à-vis the brightening metropolis waiting for its thronging, majestic day. Quite apart from the valorizing companion character of the poem itself, the sublime elements seen and felt in the Indian landscape redeem it from contempt and keep the colonizer's gaze and mind open for its mysteries.

However, a darker note prevails in the Anglo-Indian colonial creed: the colonizer, during the nineteenth century, is usually shown to be attracted to or obliged to participate in the colonial cult, i.e. the task of colonization and cultivation. At the same time the colonizer and his or her culture are existentially (i.e. both physically and mentally) threatened by the colonized and their 'dark' nature. Landscape, climate, flora and fauna play a dominant role in the *im*personal variants of this conflict. British Indian colonial literature is full of tales where heat, drought, humidity, floods, thunderstorms, earthquakes, landslides or any of the other shake-ups that Indian nature might have in store, thwart the colonizer's purpose and drive him either back into safer and more familiar places or alternatively into madness or death.

Augustus Prinsep's tale 'A Man of Sentiment in the Mofussil' (1834)[12] is an early case where comparatively mild consequences of the Indian civil servant's life in a provincial place are described. The young first-person narrator, an assistant judge who has been educated by his books into becoming a romantic sentimentalist and who therefore 'desired banishment and solitude', is first disenchanted with the all but picturesque Indian landscape through which he is carried in a palanquin. The land is made up of 'interminable plains'. The narrator goes into some detail describing his disappointment:

> The dust even was welcome to shut out the painful prospect. The sun sunk behind the dreary and fatiguing landscape, falling like a huge ball of fire across a desert of sand, without a cloud in the firmament to reflect its glory, and without a tree or a hill to divide its rays.[13]

On the second day, he passes through

> a close and low jungul, thick enough to screen from me the refreshing breeze before the sun rose; yet not high enough to shelter me from its rays, when it took its highest station in the heavens. We proceeded for hours without encountering a native village, miserable as may be the variety which that affords.[14]

India's aesthetic shortcomings are intensified on the third day with 'a new and wilder scenery'.[15] There is, at last, a single hill standing 'erect in the middle of a wild plain', but its picturesque deficiency is immediately apparent: 'the sun was shining vertically above it, there were no shadows, no tints, and the sight was any thing but beautiful.' Later that day, the landscape is said to be 'more pleasing, but it impressed me with a more complete idea of the seclusion into which I was going'. After supper, the narrator notes 'the distant howl of beasts, rising upon the stillness of night, and all the terrific descriptions of Asiatic wildernesses recurred to my imagination'; on the fifth day, 'the dry bed of an immense river' is passed over 'where all was soft sand without a track to guide us, or a trace to mark the way'.[16] All these descriptions are heavily marked not only with emotional values but also with a highly significant symbolism revealing colonial fears and phobias. We have here, in fact, a full catalogue of tropical phobic landscapes. No wonder that the presumed romantic overland journey finally turns into a self-commiserative and very unromantic flight:

> Away! away! no rest! no rest! – Another day did I journey in the deprivation of every comfort, and with every misery aggravated. No prison could have been more wretched than my palankeen; no chains more painful than my unchanged posture.[17]

But even the arrival at the destination in the province, the Judge's bungalow, brings no relief. To his great chagrin, no one welcomes the Man of Sentiment at his new home: 'No one was at the door, but a single bearer asleep across the passage.'[18] In spite of all this, he succeeds in being served dinner, and he is almost able to appreciate a most romantic night scene from outside the bungalow (which happens to perch right on the banks of the Ganges).

In Prinsep's tale, the Indian natural and cultural landscapes are introduced as early indicators of the protagonist's ultimate fate of being marooned. The destructive impact of the colonized land on the colonial protagonist can be called comparatively mild because its effect is not fully dramatized. Indian nature does not immediately become instrumental in the hero's fate, but neither can it be domesticated with the delights of the sublime.

3. Views from Australia

Australian natural landscapes, in poetry and in painting, have not lost their notions of terror, even today. It is the vast deserts and scrublands of the outback and the 'never-never' that have earned, among Europeans, the mythical attributes of hostility and the horror of emptiness. Our tourist catalogues still offer safe coach tours to Alice Springs or to Ayers Rock as a courageous expedition if not a trip through hell. Until the middle of the nineteenth century, no explorer had traversed the continent anywhere close to its red heart. For almost 25 years of Australian settlement, no European had crossed the barrier of the Blue Mountains which limited the British settlement of New South Wales to a narrow strip along the Eastern coastline. After 50 years, only the most daring explorers had seen areas more than 200 kilometres inland. Most Australian artists therefore preferred to concentrate on the strange flora and fauna found in the coastal areas and they spent some energy on describing the efforts and achievements of creating homely settlements in the 'New Britannia under a Southern sky'.[19] Still, quite a few Australian authors and painters of the nineteenth century were also fascinated with their 'new' continent's rugged nature, particularly with the mountains – much less with the outback plains.

William Charles Wentworth (1793-1872) had been a member of the Blaxland and Lawson expedition which first crossed the Blue Mountains in 1813. He then stayed in England from 1817 to 1834, where he studied law at Cambridge (1817-20), published his widely influential *Statistical, Historical and Political Description of the Colony of New South Wales* (1819) and wrote his poem 'Australasia' (1823). This long poem in heroic couplets poses as a pastoral in the tradition of Pope's 'Windsor Forest' (1713). Its focus travels from the city of Sydney across the fields and rural villages of the coastal area to the mountains. The following excerpt expresses the sublime qualities which are attributed to the forbidding escarpment which, like the Alps in Europe, or the Sinai in the Old Testament, had blocked the promised land and stood in the way of salvation until its terrors were overcome:

Hail mighty ridge! that from thy azure brow
Survey'st these fertile plains, that stretch below,
And look'st with careless, unobservant eye,
As round thy waist the forked lightnings ply,
And the loud thunders spring with hoarse rebound
From peak to peak, and fill the welkin round
With deaf'ning voice, till with their boist'rous play
Fatigued in mutt'ring peals they stalk away; –
Parent of this deep stream, this awful flood,
That at thy feet its tributary mud,
Like the fam'd Indian, or Egyptian tide,

Doth pay, but direful scatters woe beside; –
Vast Austral Giant of these rugged steeps,
Within whose secret cells rich glitt'ring heaps
Thick pil'd are doomed to sleep, till some one spy
The hidden key that opes thy treasury;
How mute, how desolate thy stunted woods,
How dread thy chasms, where many an eagle broods,
How dark thy caves, how lone thy torrents' roar,
As down thy cliffs precipitous they pour,
Broke on our hearts, when first with vent'rous tread
We dared to rouse thee from thy mountain bed!
Till gain'd with toilsome step thy topmost heath,
We spied the cheering smoke ascend beneath,
And, as a meteor shoots athwart the night,
The boundless champain burst upon our sight,
Till nearer seen the beauteous landscape grew,
Op'ning like Canaan on rapt Israel's view.

The sense of the sublime is equally evident and outspoken in mid-century poems whenever Australian mountains are addressed. Charles Harpur's 'Dawn and Sunrise in the Snowy Mountains' (c.1850) exults in describing the intensity of light and colour in the swiftly changing atmosphere of a sunrise.[20] Imaginative overtones in comparisons and metaphors bring about the speaker's final mystical correlation of the alpine scenery with the ritual setting of a primeval sacrifice. The topography of the 'Australian Alps', greatly heightened and dramatized, also provides for the enthusiastic character of Henry Kendall's 'Dedication – To a Mountain' with its egotistic reflection of 'the awful Volume' of the 'majestic' and 'lordly' peak.[21] Evidently, the sublime effects of Wordsworth's and Shelley's devotional landscape poetry proliferated even in those colonies where the mountains did not reach the altitudes encountered in Europe.

In Australian painting, the grandeur of the local scenery is often reflected in coastal landscapes. Burke's notion of the sublime seems particularly appropriate here, since the delightful emotions arising from terrors overcome would of course be most intensively felt after having weathered the storms of the sea and reached a safe harbour. Conrad Martens's *View from the Crags above Neutral Bay* (1857/58),[22] showing Sydney Harbour from the North (70 years before the famous Harbour Bridge was built), can be taken as an instance; there are elements that suggest comparison to Thomas Daniell's *Madras,*

Fort St George. A storm breaks over Sydney Cove, leaving dark shadows in the foreground and dark clouds over the eastern suburbs and the Pacific, while a splendour of light illuminates the Government House in the centre and the city around – from St Andrew's Cathedral to the Windmill in King's Cross. Two tall ships anchor safely in the harbour and an ultra-modern steamer courageously sets out heading for the dark Pacific. Martens is said to have read and studied Ruskin, Constable and Turner for his presentation of atmosphere in rocks and clouds. But it is equally known that he was an astute observer of meteorological processes when journeying from Montevideo to Valparaiso as an artist-topographer on HMS Beagle. In any case, the effect of this picture is that the romantic sublime finds a new place in Australia, visibly reassuring the bright centre of this new world in the midst of the receding dangers which had surrounded it.

Heroic perseverance in a sublime seascape is also celebrated in Eugene von Guérard's *Castle Rock, Cape Schank* (1865).[23] A lighthouse stoically watches over the tremendous crags washed by heavy breakers during the hour of sunset. Dwarfed by this vast spectacle of nature we see a lonely boat and a fisherman who calmly walks ashore after his day's work. Eugene von Guérard (1812-1901), who was born in Vienna, came to Australia during the Gold Rush in 1852 and became curator of the National Gallery of Victoria in Melbourne and head of its art school, is also notable for his impressive panorama of the Snowy Mountains.[24] On 18 November 1862, he accompanied the German scientist Georg von Neumaier on his magnetic survey to Mount Kosciusko (where, however, Neumaier did not give him sufficient time to do any sketch). A second climb was made up Mount Townsend, where von Guérard made sketches until the party was surprised by bad weather. He (incorrectly) believed that they 'were the first men who had ever trodden' this peak.[25] In order to heighten the effect of the painting *North-East View from the Northern Top of Mount Kosciusko,* which von Guérard executed in 1863 (Fig. 2), he invented a forbidding tumble of dark rocks in the foreground which pile up into the sky on the left margin. They indicate the smallness of men vis-à-vis the magnificence of nature. Furthermore, he added the oncoming rainshowers which had forced the party to leave. The painting was meant to be 'a complete rebuttal of the theory, if such a theory now be held by anyone, that Australian scenery possesses no element of the sublime'.[26]

Fig. 2: Eugene von Guérard, *North-east view from the northern top of Mount Kosciusko.*

But, surprisingly, von Guérard's demonstration was not appreciated by Australian art connoisseurs. The painting appeared to hold too much of the sublime – or, to put it differently, the terror of the Australian landscape was still felt to be all too real and troublesome to Australian settlers so that it could not yet be enjoyed, not even in art. One of the critics observed:

> Here we are high up among the clouds; rocks, rocks, rocks, on every side, huge shattered basaltic fragments; a deep crater-formed abyss at our feet, riven by subterranean fires; the whole under a cold mantle of snows lying in the wildest confusion, flung deep and thick in parts, with the black traprock showing through. Terribly true to nature, but most uncomfortable to look at.[27]

The painting could not be sold in Australia; a European patron graciously bought it after more than ten years. No sooner than a century later it found its way to the Australian National Gallery in Canberra. Nevertheless, Australian mountains, though few and largely accessible (when compared to Europe, Northern India or America), did remain a source of the sublime in Australian art. Nicholas Chevalier's *Mount Arapiles and the Mitre Rock* (1863)[28] presents us with a rare view of Australian topography, which, on first sight, one would rather have located in the American West – had the sights of the Rocky Mountains existed when Chevalier first took his sketches. But Albert Bierstadt's and Thomas Moran's time was still to come.

4. Views from America

Although the United States of America, at the beginning of the nineteenth century, enjoyed their independence from Britain, the European colonial impulses and emotions remained strong when American explorers and settlers faced the interminable landscapes of the West. As far as the Prairies, the Rocky Mountains and the Pacific Coast (i.e. Oregon and California) are concerned, the colonizing Anglo-Americans came rather late. They had been preceded, in Texas and in the South West, by the Spanish conquistadores and the Franciscan missionaries, and in the North by the trappers and *couriers de bois* of French and Métis extraction. The weakening resources of these predecessors brought about by the Louisiana Purchase (1803) and by the Mexican revolution (1810-24) opened up the option of 'going west' for the citizens of New England. They did so rather reluctantly, and the 'Glory of the West' seems to have needed a good amount of governmental encouragement, active immigration policy and ideological pushing, in which art and literature were involved. James Fenimore Cooper's early Leatherstocking tales, following Walter Scott in romanticizing wild and exotic landscapes, recall, some 20 years after the event, the opening up of the prairie in 1804 (*The Pioneers*, 1823; *The Last of the Mohicans*, 1826; *The Prairie*, 1827). William Cullen Bryant's poem 'The Prairies' (1832/34), written on a visit to what is today Illinois, reflects the emotions generated by the vastness of 'the gardens of the Desert [...] for which the speech of England has no name'.[29] There is an element of the sublime in this poem, but the notion of terror is clearly subordinated to the unlimited promise of fruitful areas to be reached further West ('the palms of Mexico [...] the vines of Texas [...] the fountains of Sonora [...] the calm Pacific'). The promised lands are decorated with the elements of the biblical myth of paradise where the church returns to nature ('this magnificent temple of the sky') and God's heaven is closer to man than in the Eastern hills.

After the opening up of the Oregon trail in 1837, the annexation of Texas in 1846 and the acquisition of New Mexico and California (including today's Colorado, Utah, Arizona and Nevada) in 1848, the Rocky Mountains and the Great American Desert appeared on the Anglo-Americans' mental and emotional maps. These new and troublesome landscapes, which obstructed the routes to the Western paradise and cost the lives of many a hopeful migrant and settler, could not easily be accommodated in God's benevolent plan to settle the West. In Henry Wadsworth Longfellow's 'The Song of Hiawatha' (1855), the ambiguous role of the Rocky Mountains is approached.[30] Significantly, this is done in the neutralizing distance of an Indian myth mediated to Anglo-American readers. In part IV of this poem ('Hiawatha and Mudjekeewis') Hiawatha, the fearless youth living in the East, decides to travel to the Rocky Mountains, the kingdom of his father Mudjekeewis. His route is beset with ill omens, threats, dangers and hardship. But he courageously makes his way journeying 'westward, westward', and he now finds the 'awe'-struck Mudjekeewis full of joy. The king of the Mountains praises Hiawatha's heroic deed which brings him back 'his youth of passion'. Longfellow's poem was extremely popular for its mythical native lore. In a most romantic fashion it endorsed the colonial desire to be familiarized with the land – a desire that had found its first vivid and mythopoetic expression in the Pocahontas story located in Jamestown, Virginia (1609).

The first famous American painters of the West could tap 'an increasingly nostalgic view of American Indian life fanned by the relentless popularity of works like Hiawatha', but at the same time they catered for 'spectacular New World landscapes, which [in America] would surpass that for views of Europe'.[31] Thomas Moran's sublime presentations of the Yellowstone and the Grand Canyon of the Colorado were anticipated by Albert Bierstadt (1830-1902), a painter of German stock. In 1834, as a boy of four years, Bierstadt had come to New Bedford (Massachusetts) with his family. He studied in Düsseldorf and practised landscape painting (between 1855 and 1857) around Salzburg, Lucerne and, on a kind of Grand Tour, in Italy (Livorno, Rome and Naples).[32] In 1859 he set out on his first journey west with Colonel Frederick West Lander, the surveyor of a new route for the overland trail (after the Utah trail had been blocked by the Mormons of Salt Lake City – in league with Indians). He came back for a 'first great success'[33] in New York with romantic panoramas of the Rocky Mountains, particularly of the Wind River Country (Wyoming). On his second trip west (1863) he reached San Francisco via Salt Lake City and sketched his path-breaking paintings in the 'Yo Semite' before he returned to New York and Boston, in order to become America's most celebrated landscape artist. Several Government projects earned him between 25,000 and 40,000 dollars each. Bierstadt travelled fast and with professional aplomb: he was the first painter who enjoyed free tickets on railways – the companies had contracted him for his paintings, which they used for advertising their western services. The missing link between the Union Pacific and the Central Pacific (which was only closed in 1869) was covered by an overland stagecoach making a little over 100 miles in 24 hours. On his return via Panama (which was still faster than the overland trip), Bierstadt relied on boat services, while the isthmus itself had to be crossed by coach. His later tours were divided between Europe (Paris, Rome, Munich, Dresden, Berlin and Vienna) and the American West.

In October 1859, the London *Art Journal* suggested that Albert Bierstadt was William Turner's successor.[34] This comparison is best borne out by Bierstadt's *Storm in the Mountains* (undated),[35] one of his European paintings which, in the cloudy whirlpool reminiscent of Turner's *Aosta Valley* (1836/37),[36] is supposed to show a sublime glimpse of the Watzmann near Berchtesgaden – a subject which

Caspar David Friedrich (1824/25) had given a less turbulent if equally famous atmosphere of the sublime.[37] Bierstadt's *American* sceneries seem to be less indebted to Turner's sublime turbulences than to the idea of the picturesque cultivated by Andreas Achenbach or Max Joseph Wagenbauer, or even Caspar David Friedrich. In any case, the romantic notion of awe-inspiring wild nature domesticated and made delightful by the artist is predominant.

A contemporary critic, James Jackson Jarves (*The Art Idea*, 1864) praised the naturalism of Bierstadt's *The Rocky Mountains* (1863),[38] which shows a lively group of homely natives in the foreground and an awe-inspiring chain of snow-clad mountains rising behind them. At the same time, Jarves raised the objection that here we have 'two pictures in one, from different points of view'.[39] Both Indians and the majestic alpine scenery seemed to be worth presenting, yet this should have been done separately. The two kinds of terror whose sublime pacification was evoked here, appeared too different for being convincingly matched in one painting.[40]

Thomas Moran (1837-1926), the son of an immigrant from Bolton (Lancashire) who had settled in a suburb of Philadelphia, became Albert Bierstadt's most able competitor. He was a voracious reader admiring above all the Pre-Raphaelites and particularly Ruskin's *Modern Painters*, *The Elements of Drawing* and *Three Letters to Beginners* (1857). In quite a few of his early (imitative) works, he explicitly strove 'after Claude [Lorrain]' or 'after Turner'. Some of his imaginative journeys took him to the literary landscapes created by Shelley, Coleridge and Byron.[41]

In 1862 Thomas Moran and his elder brother Edward travelled to England to study Turner's paintings in the National Gallery in London. Thomas made direct copies after Turner, discovering for himself Turner's artistic licence of 'inaccuracy' within the bounds of 'naturalness'. He returned in 1862, painting a considerable number of romantic forest idylls which frequently focussed on solitary figures evoking reminiscences of the wandering poet-hero, very much along the lines of Shelley's *Alastor* (1816) or Byron's *Childe Harold* (1812-18).[42] In 1866 he left for his second trip to Europe (then married, with a child). There he did an artist's Grand Tour comprising Paris, the Alps, northern Italy and Rome, learning and exhibiting some of his American romantic paintings on the way (*Children of the Mountain*, 1867 and for example *The Woods Were God's First Temples*, 1867).

In 1870 Thomas Moran was commissioned by his friend Richard Watson Gilder, managing editor of *Scribner's Magazine*, to rework some field sketches from a strange land in the American West called the Yellowstone. In 1871 Ferdinand Vandeveer Hayden, geologist and surveyor, included Moran in his expedition. Moran gained some private funding, but the Northern Pacific Railroad supported him on the competitive expectation 'that he will surpass Bierstadt's Yosemite'.[43] At Green River crossing he sketched nostalgic views of American Indian life, while the railway had actually taken over that area, transforming the country with dams, bridges and settlements.

On the expedition to the Yellowstone, Moran was accompanied by William Henry Jackson, a young photographer. Their joint production of drawings, photographs and watercolour sketches were instrumental in moving the Congress in 1872, under the presidentship of Ulysses Grant, to proclaim the Yellowstone the first American National Park (the Yosemite followed in 1890). While Bierstadt had virtually laid claim to the Yosemite as his object of art, Moran was credited with having revealed if not 'made' the Yellowstone to be the place of wonder it still is to millions of tourists from America and all over the world.

His painting *Grand Canyon of the Yellowstone* (1872), (Fig. 3)[44] was put on private exhibit in New York in May 1872. It was praised by Clarence Cook in the *New York Tribune* (4 May 1872) for 'its own intrinsic truth, sublimity and beauty' as the 'finest historical landscape yet painted in this country'.[45] For the reviewer of the *New York Mail*, it was 'more an object of grandeur than of beauty'.[46] Soon after its private first show, the *Grand Canyon of the Yellowstone* – for 'the mine of scientific illustration to be found in it'[47] – was exhibited at the Smithsonian Institute. Obviously, Moran was able to serve both purposes at once: the romantic celebration of the American West as the sublime and heroic space for the 'ultimate secular pilgrim'[48] and the need for scientific knowledge about the newly acquired lands in the West. Significantly, he had positioned both Hayden and himself, the scientist and the painter, in the centre of the grand panorama. Two weeks later, Moran had succeeded in placing his grand tableau of the Yellowstone in the old Hall of Representatives where every member of Congress could see it.[49]

Soon after, Thomas Moran was invited to join Major Powell on his Colorado expedition at no cost. Instead he was promised 500 dollars for his picture of the Grand Canyon of the Colorado. The party reached the South Rim in August 1873. Moran was overwhelmed with 'by far the most awfully grand and impressive scene that I have

Fig. 3: Thomas Moran, *Grand Canyon of the Yellowstone*, 1872, oil on canvas. The U.S. Department of the Interior Museum, Washington, D.C.

ever seen' (as he wrote back to his wife). He decided to develop this in a companion piece to the *Yellowstone.*

When the *Chasm of the Colorado* (1873-74)[50] was finished, the 'brave picture' was credited with having all the appurtenances of the romantic sublime. *Appleton's Magazine* shuddered:

> The scene is a tumultuous and even appalling chaos of cliffs and chasms, a wildly-broken plain of cyclopean rocks without a tree or shrub to vary its savage grandeur. Midway in the picture, through a deep rift in the rocks, one traced far below the narrow thread of the Colorado; while in the near foreground are frightful chasms reaching to unknown depths. These dark abysms seem fairly infernal; it is as if hell itself were gaping [...] Altogether it is the wildest, and, we may say, fairly diabolical scene man ever looked upon.[51]

Other magazines joined in with this echo, and the texts of tourist advertisements have not disclaimed the impression to this very day. Within weeks, the Congress purchased the companion piece to the *Yellowstone* for 10,000 dollars. This picture was clearly instrumental, on the one hand, in constructing a special railway line for tourists to travel right up to the South Rim and stay in the new El Tovar Hotel (which Moran often visited during his lifetime for doing many more pictures of the Grand Canyon and securing the Santa Fe Railroad as his best patron). On the other hand, Moran's Grand Canyon panoramas also contributed to making the Grand Canyon (six years after Moran's death, in 1932) one of the largest, most famous and best-preserved National Parks in the United States.

Both commerce and conservation, it appears, can owe their impulses to the perceptions and emotions shaped and kept alive by *litterateurs* and artists. This at least becomes obvious from our examples of the colonial sublime gathered in three continents. Indeed, many of the landscapes and architectural sights highlighted and aestheticized in this fashion have become prime tourist attractions in the twentieth century. Up to the present day, the sights discerned as 'heroic' by the romantic notion of the sublime are still able to activate and rehearse the tourist's desire for terror and its sublimation in the judicial comfort of safe and civilized travel arrangements.

Notes

1 M. Shellim, *Oil Paintings of India and the East by Thomas Daniell, RA (1749-1840), and William Daniell, RA (1769-1837)* with a foreword by M. Archer (London: Inchcape, 1979), 18.

2 *India Yesterday and Today: Two Hundred Years of Architectural and Topographical Heritage in India.* Aquatints by T. and W. Daniell, modern photographs by A. Martinelli, text by G. Michell (Shrewsbury: Swan Hill Press, 1998), 11.

3 Ibid., 132.

4 Quoted in M. Archer, *Early Views of India: The Picturesque Journeys of Thomas and William Daniell 1786-1794* (London: Thames and Hudson, 1980), 91.

5 Shellim, *Oil Paintings of India*, 29.

6 *India Yesterday and Today*, 150.

7 Ibid., 168.

8 *Kalakkadu* (Kalkad near Cape Comorin), another aquatint from *Oriental Scenery* (*India Yesterday and Today*, 170f.), shows a partly shrouded mountain rising above the clouds in a truly transcendent fashion. Although this scenery is easily identifiable, there is some mystery about the solitary South Indian gopuram on the other side of the river pointing like a finger at the sublime spectacle. Mildred Archer, in her 'Foreword' to Shellim's *Oil Paintings of India*, flatly states that 'no such temple had ever existed' in this place (6). Antonio Martinelli, who revisited the sites between 1995 and 1997 in order to compare the art of the Daniells with the technical (im)perfections of contemporary photography, admits that 'it was impossible to precisely match the vantage point of the Daniells' and in this case fails to attach his photograph (*India Yesterday and Today*, 171).

9 Archer, 'Foreword' to Shellim, *Oil Paintings of India*, 4.

10 Ibid., 8f.

11 Reprinted in H.K. Kaul (ed.), *Poetry of the Raj: A Collection of British Poems on India* (New Delhi: Arnold-Heinemann, 1984), 61.

12 *The Baboo; and Other Tales Descriptive of Society in India* (London: Smith, Elder, 1834), 327-65.

13 Ibid., 328f.

14 Ibid., 329.

15 Ibid., 330.

16 Ibid., 331.

17 Ibid., 332.

18 Ibid., 333.

19 Wentworth, "Australasia" (1823), quoted in *My Country: Australian Poetry and Short Stories*, selected by L. Kramer (Willoughby: Ure Smith, 1991), I, 15f.

20 Reprinted in *The Oxford Anthology of Australian Literature*, ed. L. Kramer and A. Mitchell (Melbourne: Oxford University Press, 1985), 55. This anthology also contains Harpur's more extended treatment of a sublime southern mountain atmosphere (though not in the Australian 'Alps'), 'A Storm in the Mountains' (49-54).
21 *Oxford Anthology of Australian Literature*, 67-9.
22 *Creating Australia: 200 Years of Art 1788-1988* (Adelaide: The Art Gallery of South Australia, 1988), 82f.
23 Ibid., 40.
24 Ibid., 46f.
25 Ibid., 46.
26 Ibid.
27 Ibid.
28 Ibid., 41.
29 Bryant, 'The Prairies', in id., *Poems* (New York: Worthington, n.d.), 49-53.
30 *The Poetical Works of Henry Wadsworth Longfellow* (London: Frederick Warne, 1889), 254-308; 'Hiawatha and Mudjekeewis', 262-5.
31 N.K. Anderson, *Thomas Moran* (New Haven: Yale University Press, 1997), 50.
32 G. Hendricks, *Albert Bierstadt* (New York: Harrison House, 1988), 11-45.
33 Ibid., 91-110.
34 Ibid., 140.
35 Ibid., 186f.
36 J. Selz, *Turner* (Munich: Südwest Verlag, 1975), 57.
37 W. Geismeier, *Caspar David Friedrich* (Leipzig: Weltbild Verlag, 1994), 76.
38 Hendricks, *Bierstadt*, 150f.
39 Ibid., 144.
40 The self-reflexive inclusion of the painter's and explorer's party which we have in Bierstadt's *Yosemite Valley* (undated, presumably 1863ff., reproduced in Hendricks, *Bierstadt*, 143), seems to have been free from such criticism. It obviously adds to the peace of this grand nature and rather underscores than deflects from its artistic domestication.
41 Anderson, *Thomas Moran*, 24 and 26.
42 Ibid., 27-32.
43 Ibid., 48.
44 Ibid., 12f. and 88.
45 Quoted in Anderson, *Thomas Moran*, 53f. It is rather as a footnote that one might hint at Moran's artistic liberties which he took with western landscapes, especially in his later work. In *Hopi Village, Arizona* (1916, reproduced in Anderson, *Thomas Moran*, 178), apparently taken on the Second Mesa, he introduces a sombre mountain in the background which does not exist in that area. But it certainly adds to the sublime effect of this painting.
46 Ibid., 89.
47 Ibid., 54.

48 Ibid., 55.
49 Ibid., 54.
50 Ibid., 98.
51 Ibid., 56.

British Tourism Between Industrialization and Globalization
An Overview

John K. Walton

The British may not have invented tourism (as so often, the Romans have a prior claim, on most definitions of this variegated phenomenon), but British innovation, participation, investment and development have been well to the fore in most of its modern incarnations. This is a theme of the greatest importance in British cultural studies, especially when we look at the wider influence of tourism as exemplar and export beyond the bounds of the islands themselves. This chapter introduces and evaluates ideas about tourism in Britain and the British as tourists, beginning in the eighteenth century with the Grand Tour, the spa resort and the origins of the vogues for seaside, mountain and broader forms of 'cultural' tourism, and moving on to look at the democratization and transformation (in widely varying degrees) of these activities in the nineteenth and twentieth centuries. The historiography of twentieth-century British tourism (as opposed to its treatment by other disciplines) is still in its infancy, and this applies especially to the period of domestic crisis and accelerating change during the second half of the century, and especially its last quarter, the treatment of which will necessarily be speculative, exploratory and tentatively agenda-suggesting.[1]

1. Historians and Tourism

The underdevelopment of tourism as a mainstream theme in modern British historical writing is an interesting indicator of the cultural conservatism of the historical profession. Before looking at this further it will be helpful to chart the dimensions of the field as it currently exists. There are developing historiographies on (especially) early tourism as part of the extensive literature on eighteenth-century consumption and consumerism,[2] and on the nature and development of the seaside holiday and seaside resorts, especially in the nineteenth century.[3] There is also work on Thomas Cook and the (limited) democratization of travel, although the firm itself has an unhealthy grip on this output and much of it is recycled from one sponsored historian to the next. Here again a great deal more weight is given to the nineteenth century than to what followed.[4] More generally there has been interesting work, not always by professional historians and not necessarily the worse for that, on the British 'abroad', whether as travellers, tourists (a distinction to which I shall return) or expatriates, in western and southern France and the Mediterranean as well as across the formal and informal Empire.[5] Some of this work has reached out to cultural and what might be called anthropological tourism, conjuring up versions of Edward Said's much-debated concept of orientalism through the exploitation and classification of 'native' cultures.[6] In less exciting but also important ways the relationships between transport innovation, living standards and the popularization of tourism have also attracted attention, although railways, and to a lesser extent steamboats, have been a much stronger focus than the twentieth-century developments surrounding the internal combustion engine.[7] The rise of 'picturesque' travel and mountain tourism within Britain has generated a distinctive literature on perceptions, representations and experiences of landscape, especially as traversed and gazed upon by the pedestrian, which dissolves notional disciplinary frontiers between history, literary criticism and cultural studies.[8] Relatedly, questions surrounding the values attached to landscape, 'countryside' and rural societies, and the preservation and 'conservation' of them, have attracted increasing attention from historians of 'Englishness' and environmental historians as well as cultural geographers.[9] Liveliest of all, perhaps, is the debate on the presentation of 'history' in the 'heritage tourism' of museums, theme-parks and restored and sanitized industrial sites which Robert Hewison identified as a key and disturbing development of the 1980s, sparking fierce arguments over whether this constituted the prostitution and distortion of history for commercial and politically-disreputable ends, or whether it empowered visitors by making the past accessible and enjoyable, slotting in alongside other popular appropriations and re-creations of archaic artefacts, from railway preservation (which, as with other aspects of 'industrial archaeology', has a much longer pedigree) to do-it-yourself.[10] One clear outcome of this trend, whose implications historians have yet to explore, has been the rise of new kinds of tourist economy within the decaying fabric of old industrial towns, which emphasizes the apparent paradox that many of the places which were created as tourist destinations in the nineteenth century have languished and themselves decayed, like the Victorian industrial towns that they are, towards the end of the twentieth, although some are now striving to remake themselves by invoking a 'heritage' of their own.[11] This has also been an interdisciplinary debate, and tourism history is particularly notable for borrowing ideas and approaches from sociology, anthropology and the new cultural geography as well as from the textual analyses associated with literary criticism. This in turn makes aspects of the field particularly open to postmodernist influences, especially when we begin to query and dissect the value-judgements and cultural assumptions which underlie so many discourses of tourism in primary and (often) secondary sources.[12]

A lot of interesting things are happening in British tourism history, then, and it is disappointing to see its continuing marginal status in the eyes of the historical establishment, especially as the importance of tourism in economic, cultural and environmental terms is at last coming to be recognized more generally, and a whole new discipline of Tourism Studies is gathering momentum, fuelled by economics, cultural geography, anthropology and especially management studies, and in its turn so present-minded as to give history a very low profile in its activities. The textual and semiotic analysis of tourism-related literature and visual culture does reach eagerly into the past, but the ideas generated by this work are left to blossom within their own disciplines.[13] Meanwhile tourism gets short shrift in history textbooks and syllabi, apart from relatively specialized courses in the social history of leisure and popular culture at university level. The dominant agenda of political and diplomatic history pushes tourism to the margins as trivial and irrelevant to a top-down, centre-outwards, agenda based on jockeying for power in parliaments and chancelleries. Notions of triviality are reinforced by the embedded associations which the British seaside has acquired with vulgar aspects of popular culture: the carnivalesque of the comic postcard and fairground, the music-hall rudery of the pier comedian, the down-market connotations of fish and chips, the sexual associations of undressing and unscheduled bodily display on the liminal zone of the beach, and the assumption that the holiday is dead or suspended time, of no serious historical interest.[14] The lack of high-class international resorts in Britain (despite the pretensions of, especially, Torquay) reinforces these perceptions. Even the resort as site for international diplomatic initiatives, congresses or treaties, such as the Ems Telegram or the Yalta Conference, or as summer capital, transferring the intrigue and diplomacy of courts and governments to Biarritz, or San Sebastian, or Ostend, or Balchik, has never been a strong British theme: not that historians have developed it very far in other settings, despite the potential impact of distinctive resort surroundings and societies on the nature and outcomes of such gatherings and roles.[15] The cultural influence on international politics of the Grand Tour and, later, of the itineraries of statesmen from watering-place to watering-place, has likewise received short shrift from historians.[16] In Britain itself, little or nothing has been made of the significance of Brighton as George IV's summer capital (especially when he was Prince Regent, and before Queen Victoria shook its pebbles off her feet); or the international elite yachting gatherings at Cowes; or indeed the political culture associated with grouse-shooting or deer-stalking, which certainly come within most definitions of the tourism canon. Queen Victoria's seaside, rural and Highland retreats have attracted more attention, especially the time spent at Balmoral and with John Brown during the more difficult phases of her widowhood, when republicanism began to stir; but the political dimension to tourism history, on this slightly extended definition, is still almost completely undeveloped.[17] Economic history, for its part, has tended to concentrate on agriculture and manufacturing rather than services (except financial ones), and especially on the kinds of industry which are associated with heavy work for men, preferably accompanied by clouds of smoke and steam; while labour and working-class history retains a similar focus, concentrating on compact bodies of unionized workpeople and their organized struggles. Tourism is different: its product (although not its plant) is invisible, taking the form of satisfactions drawn from health and enjoyment, sociability and status; its consumers are taken to the raw materials and their consumption is enjoyed (repeatedly, although consumption changes the nature of what is consumed) at 'places on the margin', at the geographical periphery rather than the obvious political core; its workforce is predominantly female, casually and seasonally employed, lacking in the power to organize and locked into complex family economies whose survival strategies defy easy categorization; and, worst of all, its statistics are both 'soft' and scattered, making them resistant to tabulation and to econometric analysis, especially at national level.[18]

It is much easier to plough the established furrows of the discipline, contribute to the established controversies, gather up your citations, and stay within the 'respectable' mainstream. It is refreshing to contemplate the indications that this is beginning to change, although the only general survey around which a course (for example) might be organized, John Towner's *Historical Geography of Recreation and Tourism in the Western World, 1540-1940*, is a rather descriptive and derivative survey without a distinctively articulated point of view, useful though its distillations of existing research are as points of departure.[19]

2. Distinctions: Travellers, Tourists, Trippers

Each of the main themes in tourism history now has a literature which can be picked up and fed into wider analyses, however, and some really stimulating work can be found within the *genre*. Before we pursue this, however, we need to acknowledge that tourism is itself a contested category: indeed, much of the literature of Tourism Studies chases its tail in an unprofitable quest for precise (and therefore reassuringly quantifiable) definitions, in spite of awareness in other parts of the same forest of Foucauldian strictures against the innocent pursuit of such loaded objectives, products of the Enlightenment urge to control through classification and counting.[20] The idea of tourism itself soon acquired pejorative connotations, as tourists became detached from travellers as an inferior category in status and indeed class terms, following guidebooks to experience prescribed sensations in shallow ways which were inferior to the deeper insights of the independent and better-educated traveller, who also had access to the appropriate cultural capital for more satisfying, contextualized appreciation of architecture or evocative landscapes or artistic endeavours.[21] By the 1860s Cook's lower middle-class tourists were being stigmatized according to these criteria, as they scuttled through cathedrals or slid across glaciers against the clock, catching fleeting impressions of the significance of what they were seeing from babbling guide or simplified tourist manual.[22] To the Rev. Francis Kilvert, on holiday and seeing the prescribed sights with friends in Cornwall in the early 1870s, the 'tourist' was an alien being, rowdy and destructive, ruining what he came to visit and failing to respect his destination and those who were trying to enjoy it. No doubt these stigmatized creatures could have made their own commentary on Kilvert as snob and hypocrite; and the Victorian literature is riddled with these distinctions.[23] In part, of course, such distinctions were based on class, and the differential access to time, money and 'high' culture which followed the great divide between rent, profit, salary and wage as basis for income, social standing and attainable leisure preferences. But some aspects of the traveller/tourist divide ran across this grain, because part of the distinction to which 'travellers' laid claim was a kind of moral superiority, founded in a search for authenticity and cultural understanding, taking in the hidden and esoteric as well as what was commercially and conventionally presented to the 'tourist', and entailing a willingness to endure discomforts and take risks in pursuit of a special kind of experience. On such a scale of values the rambler, hiker or cyclist, escaping from a routine white-collar or factory job in an industrial town at the turn of the nineteenth and twentieth centuries, and exploring the hills, bridle-paths and byways of rural Britain, could feel superior not only to neighbours who made the annual pilgrimage to the commercial fleshpots of Blackpool, but also to the followers of fashionable convention at the great international watering-places of Europe.[24] A century later Alex Garland's novel *The Beach* could also make a distinction between authentic, morally-superior travellers and mere tourists, even within the ranks of backpackers passing through Thailand. This distinction is most clearly expressed by the narrator's friend Etienne, initiating a search for a legendary perfect beach and extrapolating from a guidebook's perception of the moving frontier between the 'spoiled' and the 'unspoilt' islands off the Thai coast:[25]

> 'This says travellers try new islands beyond Ko Pha-Ngan because Ko Pha-Ngan is now the same as Ko Samui.'
> 'The same?'
> 'Spoiled. Too many tourists. But look, this book is three years old. Now maybe some travellers feel these islands past Ko Pha-Ngan are also spoiled. So they find a completely new island, in the national park.'

Even within the footloose community of backpackers, whose travel experiences form a more democratic late twentieth-century Grand Tour rite of passage, these gradations of perceived authenticity can be recognized, and those 'remote' places which might seem to embody the ultimate authentic experience are the subject of something approaching a 'Golden Fleece' or 'Holy Grail' mythology, as the enormous success of book and film suggests.

Below the traveller and the tourist, in Victorian and subsequent parlance, lay the tripper, whose time was even more limited, and whose cultural pretensions (according to stereotype) stopped short at the immediate gratifications of food, drink, a splash in the sea (not necessarily observing the respectable conventions of the beach, which involved paying for suitable costume and disrobing space) and a burst of accessible entertainment. Where 'tourists' were middle-class, while the label had lower-middle-class connotations, 'trippers' were working-class, although here again the label lowered their status by equating them with 'roughs'.[26] 'Trippers', in this sense, were products of the railway age, taking advantage of cheap fares to spend anything between half a day and a week at accessible destinations; and this draws attention to the difference between the sedentary holidaymaker, staying in a single resort (the standard pattern at the British seaside, for example, until the motor age), and those who toured around enjoying the journeys for their own sake and trying out a variety of resort experiences.[27] In the twentieth century, anyway, 'tourist' has gradually become a more universal and less pejorative term in itself, supplemented by the neutral 'holidaymaker'; but the pejorative connotations attached to imagined holiday styles and cultures have been perpetuated by the loose but prevalent use of 'mass tourism' as a label connoting controlled, directed, lowest-common-denominator holidays pre-packaged for the undiscriminating: a perception whose value is not enhanced by its indiscriminate application to everything from early Cook's tourists to Club 18-30.[28]

3. The Legacy of the Eighteenth Century

The value-laden terminologies of tourism deserve detailed investigation in themselves; and John Urry's initial division of the 'tourist gaze', directed at sights worth seeing and in some sense appropriating, into the 'romantic' and the 'collective' has tended to perpetuate this binary distinction into (from some perspectives) sheep and goats, although this metaphor suffers from the sheep-like qualities which are attributed to the goats. The snobberies and status-consciousness which are expressed through these labels constitute a central and recurring theme in British tourism history, whether we are dealing with spas, seaside resorts, mountain tourism, or indeed heritage issues, and Urry's categories, debatable though they may be, have performed an important function in focussing the gaze of historians themselves.[29]

The Grand Tour certainly illustrates this theme, with its emphasis on the acquisition of social skills and cultural capital, offering an entry into a lexicon of shared experiences which could only be enjoyed and exchanged by men of privileged educational background for whom time and money were not constraints. Journeys and the narratives which represented them changed with the flux of fashion, as the sovereignty of Italy grew stronger and passing through the Alps became a desirably sublime experience, especially if glaciers and precipices were involved, rather than a grim and dangerous chore to be by-passed if at all possible.[30] But as the volume of travellers increased, and the way was eased by the provision of guidebooks, post-horses and accommodation to meet demand, exclusivity was undermined; and the sensitivity of those who felt themselves to be in the true 'Grand Tour' tradition, when forced to rub shoulders (however fleetingly) with aspiring and adventurous clerks, shopkeepers, and even frugal women who felt safe in organized groups, helps to explain the savage satire which was directed against the Cook's and other tourists who were invading the Continent from the 1860s. Travellers and the self-consciously superior increasingly had to seek out the exotic, distant or bucolic, or to take refuge in expensive specialized resorts or grand hotels, as an ever-expanding tourist market fragmented into niches in the later nineteenth century and the flight to ever more distant or protected destinations began in earnest.[31]

The other dominant tourism outlet for the British elite in the eighteenth century, the spa, was much more vulnerable to loss of exclusivity. This was not a British invention, even in its modern form, as the origins of the name in a small Ardennes resort should indicate; but its popularity grew in step with increasing mobility and fashion-consciousness among the expanding middle ranks of (especially) commercial and early industrial England. At its core was the pump-room and bath: a small space in which health was pursued expensively, under medical governance, but in combination with personal display and controlled sociability. But around it developed an array of entertainments which made up the spa's real *raison d'être* in the eyes of most of its visitors: assembly rooms, ballrooms, promenades and (for a time) gaming tables, at which the relative anonymity of a gathering drawn from a wide geographical area enabled people to bid for acquired status through fashion and accomplishments, rather than laying claim to ascribed status through lineage, known wealth and office, and property ownership. These places could not be kept exclusive: they were accessible to anyone who could afford a subscription and sustain the dress code, and by the later eighteenth century Bath, the most fashionable spa resort of the time, was already drawing in middle-ranking visitors and adventurers to mix with the titled, landed and otherwise affluent. Hence the need for a Master of Ceremonies; and social mixing was even more pronounced closer to London, and in the lesser provincial spas. The new spa resorts of the nineteenth century coped with the problem for a time, but most of the larger spas were becoming predominantly residential and retirement centres rather than tourism venues by the early railway age.[32]

4. Seaside Tourism

The votaries of fashion in health and pleasure were already transferring their affections to the seaside from the mid-eighteenth century onwards. Where the Grand Tour and the spa had been European phenomena with British incarnations, the seaside resort was a British, indeed an English invention, which proved to be almost infinitely adaptable and exportable. It was also, initially, an example of behaviour 'trickling up', giving the lie to simplistic assumptions about emulation as the prime mover in expanding tourism markets, which have also been challenged from more subtle perspectives which emphasize consumers' capacity to make choices according to their own values and preferences, even when those preferences are expressed 'on the ground' in ways which look similar to scaled-down or diluted versions of those of their 'betters'. Sea-bathing (and sea-water drinking) were popular therapeutic, prophylactic and pleasurable activities, often associated with calendar customs, which medical entrepreneurs adopted, theorized, wrote up, prescribed and made fashionable. Their success was reinforced by the emergence of new, positive ways of seeing and experiencing shorelines and seascapes, rendering them attractive in their sublimity, fecundity and associations with the Biblical past, and redefining their flora and fauna as interesting and worthy of collection and classification. Corbin's *The Lure of the Sea* is the classic presentation of this sea-change, and although it is much stronger on texts than on contexts and diffusion of ideas (and the author's claims to use English sources are nullified by the mistakes he makes about England), it is a mind-expanding contribution.[33]

Building on these trends, while benefiting from the relative accessibility and legal openness of the English shoreline and the scope for satisfying a variety of markets through a multiplicity of resorts and parts of resorts (and through 'different seasons for different classes'), the English seaside was able to surf the rising tide of industrialization and respond to the preferences of each social stratum and bundle of cultural preferences in turn, as they chose to adopt their versions of the seaside holiday. In this respect the seaside was like the cotton industry: a versatile product which was eventually able to cater for all but the poorest through the sheer variety and adaptability of its product. It also had the attractions of 'liminality', as gateway between land and sea where some of the inhibitions of everyday life could be cast aside, and where a carnivalesque spirit of reversing and upending the conventions of 'civilization' could be conjured up. But British seaside tourists brought their own internal constraints with them, and expected to encounter the inhibiting presence of neighbours and authority figures at their own resorts, so that the extent to which these ideas can be applied 'on the ground' is a source of developing debate. But the entertainments and architecture of the British seaside became distinctive, in ways which did relax conventions, and its place in popular culture became assured, summed up by star billing in children's books.[34] Not that this evolution was conflict-free: the politics of space and 'social tone' (a Victorian concept of lasting value and importance) are central to resort development, and the role of local government, in this sphere as in others (including entertainment provision and advertising), becomes a key theme from the mid-nineteenth century: the role of local authorities in mediating between conflicting interest-groups and cultural preferences, negotiating the balance between hedonism and convention, freedom and security, was crucial to the forging of resort identities and their adaptation or resistance to changing times and markets.[35] It was not until the late twentieth century that the British seaside began to falter, partly through competition from sunnier alternatives with newer plant in (especially) Mediterranean locations, partly through a novel failure to match the changing tastes of a new generation of visitors (which was also associated with the declining distinctiveness and status of its own place-identities), and partly through a broadening perception of pollution problems which had been around for many years but surfaced in the 1970s, threatening two hundred years of positive evaluations of maritime environments; but (unlike the cotton industry) reports of its death have been greatly exaggerated.[36]

5. Upland Tourism

The emergence of mountain regions as tourist destinations, like that of the seaside, was impelled by an eighteenth-century revaluation of what had previously been seen as barren, inhospitable, threatening and ugly environments. The new aesthetics of the picturesque and the sublime, in tandem with romanticism and the cult of the 'natural' and the 'wilderness', provided new fashionable grammars and vocabularies for gazing upon and evaluating upland landscapes: in effect, for inventing or constructing them as suitable objects of appraisal, informed by conventions of seeing and reporting.[37] The English Lake District was at the core of these new perceptions, developing infrastructures of access, accommodation and (before long) entertainment to cope with growing numbers of 'Lakers', and becoming a literary landscape under the aegis of William Wordsworth and the other 'Lake Poets' at the turn of the eighteenth and nineteenth centuries. Wordsworth's legendary walking feats helped to encourage a fashion for experiencing as well as gazing upon the mountains, even though he himself tended to stick to the roads; and the search for a recuperative closeness to 'Nature and Nature's God' through healthy outdoor exercise provided employment for guides and map-makers.[38] Appreciation of the Lakes, which for some also extended to an 'anthropological gaze' directed at an idealized, virtuous, hard-working peasantry (a perception not universally shared), thus required a measure of appropriate cultural capital, and visitors from outside this charmed circle were viewed with suspicion. Thus, when railways reached the fringes of the Lake District and promised (or threatened) to make its inner reaches accessible to working-class excursionists from the industrial towns, the resistance to sharing this privileged space was much stronger than at the seaside (where, however, it was far from negligible). More space was available to be enjoyed, but its enjoyment was predicated on a particularly demanding and exclusive version of the 'romantic gaze', so that tolerance of 'other' presences and alien ways was much reduced. This was a sacralized landscape, and its identification with a special, archaic, quintessential, prelapsarian Englishness helped to fuel opposition to development of any kind, beyond (of course) what was necessary to sustain the comforts of the existing tourists. The autonomous working-class tradition of walking, landscape appreciation and natural history was marginalized, and 'trippers' were assumed to be influences for depravity and despoliation. Out of the campaigns of the 1870s onwards against railways, reservoirs and quarries emerged the Lake District Defence Society (1883) and its successors, and the National Trust (1895).[39]

The English Lake District has been a particularly evocative crucible of conflict and contradiction, in which tensions simmered and sometimes boiled between advocates of preservation and protection against development of any kind, advocates of modest expansion on existing lines, and those who favoured job-creating popularization, industrial growth, and the practical conveniences arising from improved transport and communications (including, by the early decades of the twentieth century, low-cost telephone lines and electricity supplies, without the expensive concealment measures to protect landscape which the preservationists advocated). In this climate internal access for (what was assumed to be) the few by footpath was staunchly defended, while external access for the many by train was resisted. Where Britain lagged, however, was in introducing National Parks on the late-nineteenth century American or Australian model; and when legislation introduced them in 1949 they merely entailed stricter planning regimes, reflecting the lack of true British wilderness and the need to conciliate the interests of the working inhabitants. By this time the democratization of car ownership was already disturbing the solitudes which had been defended so fiercely by a Wordsworth-invoking elite; and, in another characteristic paradox, the emergence of Wordsworth as staple of the schools helped to encourage the popular crowds and direct their gaze. The analysis of Lake District tourism is particularly fruitful in raising complex issues involving conservation, development, literary landscapes, landscape and identity, the rights of private property and the role of the state, generating ideas which are transferable elsewhere but without quite the same resonance.[40]

Conflicts on similar lines have been widespread as British upland tourism has developed, especially since the later nineteenth century as the pressures of popular demand have increased. Attempts by deer forest owners to exclude walkers and mountaineers from their fastnesses have generated conflict in the Scottish Highlands, while grouse moors and water catchment areas have been similarly controversial in the Derbyshire Peak District (producing an iconic confrontation between hikers and gamekeepers, the Kinder 'mass trespass' of 1932), and the extension of slate quarrying and mountain railways in late Victorian North Wales did not go unopposed, although things were done here that would have been unthinkable in the Lake District, and the conflicts were inflected through an emergent Welsh Nationalism.[41] All these aspects of upland tourism deserve further attention, as does the role of the British as seekers after mountain landscape, as mountaineers and as pioneers of winter sports in the Alps and elsewhere.[42]

6. British Tourism Abroad

The British 'conquest of Switzerland', which was well under way by the mid-Victorian years (when Thomas Cook was joining in and the railway network began to spread in earnest), was one manifestation among many of the export of British tourist demand to a widening range of destinations across the Channel and far beyond. The search for relatively comfortable Grand Tour routes to Italy led to the 'discovery' of the French Riviera, a process which began in the later eighteenth century (there were already 110 English families in Nice in 1787) and was given added impetus, long before the arrival of the railway from Paris in 1864, by the laying out of the significantly-named *Promenade des Anglais* in the early 1820s and the arrival of Lord Brougham at Cannes in 1834. Consumptives staying for the winter in search of cure and alleviation eventually gave way to pleasure-seekers as amenities and numbers multiplied in the late nineteenth and early twentieth century, and enterprising hoteliers and shopkeepers made an early start in catering for English tastes in food and accommodation, while doctors and clergymen, English clubs and libraries soon followed, in a pattern that was to be repeated endlessly elsewhere.[43] Seasonal visitors became residents, laying claim in some cases to insider knowledge of local culture, but also establishing and sustaining their own shops and institutions, alongside the services provided by enterprising locals. The *Majorca Sun*, the 'first English newspaper in Spain', provided a guide to the English bars, tea-shops, clubs, makers of English-style biscuits, flower shops, night-clubs and teachers of bullfighting which catered for a mixed community of spinster annuitants, frisky divorcees, remittance men and hard-drinking retired army officers in Palma's Terreno district in the mid-1930s. By this time, the British expatriates were enjoying the low cost of living (especially of wines and spirits) in company with Americans, Germans, French and 'a babel of nationalities', and short-term visitor numbers ebbed and flowed with the seasons. Similar communities could be found across western Europe, from northern France to Portugal, welcoming suitable tourists and educating them in their versions of what constituted appropriate behaviour towards their hosts.[44] Within their adopted environments, expatriate communities based on commerce or administration rather than sunlit retirement might make a distinctive contribution to the development of tourist infrastructures, as in the case of Indian hill stations or the 'months of the English and the swallows' (December and March) at Argentina's fashionable Mar del Plata, where in 1913 the Buenos Aires expatriate business community took advantage of cheaper prices on the 'shoulder' of high season and colonized one of the less-fashionable beaches.[45] The cultural negotiations between British expatriate residents, short-stay tourists, other nationalities and the locals offer attractive opportunities for comparative research; and they were complicated in interesting ways by the development of democratized variants of the overseas package tour from the 1950s and especially the 1970s, bringing in a 'lower' class of visitor whose activities and demeanour were readily stigmatized by advocates of exclusivity and decriers of 'mass tourism' within Britain and among the established expatriates. Matters were further complicated, in turn, however, by awareness of the diversity of holiday experiences even within what could be made to seem a standard package tour and package resort format, and by the emergence of expatriate defenders of the British holidaymaker against the lazy exaggerations and over-simplifications of the British media in places like Benidorm.[46] The ways in which tourist experience of 'foreign' environments fed back into British society, a theme which immediately challenges notions of 'mass tourism' as something insulated from all but the most rendered-down of commercialized host cultures, constitute another potentially fascinating research agenda.

7. The Globalization of Tourism

We also need to consider the spectrum of issues involving the relationships between tourism and globalization, in which British initiatives played a formative role in the eighteenth and nineteenth centuries, only for the British contribution to be diluted and by-passed by wider traffic flows and new patterns of development (especially in the Pacific) as globalization developed in earnest under (especially) American auspices in the late twentieth century. British participation in the Grand Tour, followed by the spread (and adaptation) of seaside tourism and the development (pioneered by the Thomas Cook firm) of tourism across the British Empire and beyond from the second half of the nineteenth century, can be seen as part of the extended articulation of Wallerstein's 'European world-system' as it developed from beginnings in the fifteenth and sixteenth century.[47] The British were prominent among those who exported tourist infrastructures, and stimulated local responses to their demands and expectations, across the Mediterranean and throughout the Empire. We have already looked at the ambiguous role played by expatriates in this process. British perceptions of 'other' cultures, mediated through relationships of economic, military and administrative dominance and perceptions of superiority, have promoted an 'orientalist' frame of mind, seeking a sense of control through labelling, classifying and laying claim to superior external understanding, which has been incorporated into tourist itineraries, advertising, guidebooks and the 'tourist gaze'.[48] The objects of this gaze have agency of their own, of course, and are capable of manipulating and making capital out of such perceptions, engaging in a dialogue of desire which results in tourist provision that reflects the visitors' desire for some kind of authenticity or distinctive place-identity, however negotiated and refracted through a commercial prism this might be. Thus developed an economy of tourism-related signs and symbols, spreading across the European world-system, in which a shared grammar of desire and expectation was mediated through representations of the perceived and actual place-identities of particular destinations, to enable tourists to consume sights and experiences in accessible, secure form, through the staging of authenticity and the repackaging of traditions. Globalization has built on this and extended it to (so far) ever-expanding pleasure peripheries, as tourism extends its tentacles and deepens its penetration into Asian, Pacific and Latin American societies in an age of swift and widely-available long-haul transport.[49] In the process it feeds on local differences, puts the experience on sale, and through commodification converts it into artifice, transmuting the objects of the gaze by making them aware of the monetary value of an authenticity which, as a result, becomes illusory. 'Post-tourism' entails a knowing, nudging enjoyment of the artifice at work. Such a loss of innocence is inherent in all tourism, of course, and eighteenth-century writers lamented its first symptoms in (for example) the calculative behaviour of 'peasants' and fisherfolk in the English Lake District, the Swiss Alps and French fishing villages.[50] The search for the perfect, pristine, 'unspoilt' beach in Alex Garland's novel has, significantly, an unpopulated goal, and it is the people and their necessary organization and conflict that provoke the novel's tragic climax. This is an obvious variant on the older theme of the desert island and the search for an unmediated encounter with untrammelled nature (unfamiliar culture in a raw state being an even more threatening objective for the self-conscious consumer of experiences). Globalization, by bringing more and more of the world into the market-place (including the market for risk-free simulations of the castaway experience, as well as that for dangerous explorations in 'wilderness' situations), intensifies and generalizes these older processes.[51] What is novel is the sheer scale and pervasiveness of the new world of tourism; and as part of this process of generalization the British role has been diluted into something of very limited importance on the world stage.

8. Heritage Tourism

The issues raised by 'heritage tourism' for the conscientious professional historian are also very contentious, especially for those who do not find postmodernist irony and relativism particularly enticing, cleave to the notion that the pursuit of an approximation to 'truth' (and clarity of expression) is still a valid goal, and yet accept that history is about popular accessibility, agency and entertainment as well as about scholarly accuracy and earnest debate, and that 'heritage' tourism is capable of generating such enjoyment. Here, perhaps, the 'traveller' in time meets the 'tourist' and indeed the 'tripper', and the sparks of argument are bound to fly. The use of representations of a tourist destination's past as part of a portrayal of attractive cultural distinctiveness is almost as old as tourism itself, but in the British context it became controversial in the late 1980s, as Robert Hewison's polemic on the 'heritage industry' focussed on attempts to convert old industrial sites into vehicles for a tourism based on nostalgia for a sanitized, gift-wrapped recent past, and on commercial representations of history which massaged the past to make it seem attractive and uncontroversial, without troubling too much about notions of historical accuracy, debate or periodization. Defenders of the appropriation of history by tourist interests have argued that historians' own truth-claims are open to challenge, that the ownership of history should be popular rather than academic, and that it is better to arouse interest in the past, which might be taken further, through populist commercial outlets than to leave it to wither in academic aridity. The rise of 'heritage tourism' has extended even to the English seaside resort, as ailing coastal towns have sought to reinvent themselves by recycling aspects of their own pasts to make them attractive as visitor destinations in the age of the shopping mall and of virtual reality. This is an aspect of the history of tourism which links it to wider arguments about the nature of history and the ways in which it should respond or react to the challenges of postmodernism.[52]

Where Britain is distinctive, perhaps, is in the increasingly determined marketing of versions of its history to the rest of the world. In this respect it is fulfilling D.H. Robertson's prescient prophecy of 1926:

> It is even possible that the part ultimately reserved for the British Isles in the scheme of the international division of labour will be that of a playground and park and museum to exercise youth and soothe the declining years of the strenuous industrial leaders congregated on either side of the Pacific Ocean.[53]

This suggestion anticipated the worst fears of Robert Hewison in the late 1980s, and finds an echo in Julian Barnes's *England, England,* with its satirical vision of the Isle of Wight as theme park distilling and representing focus-group visions of quintessential Englishness; although youth is likely to find exercise in more strenuous settings, and the soothing of declining years is a more obvious role for British heritage tourism.[54] But, as Hewison was well aware, the British heritage market is regional and national as well as international, especially when we look at the proliferation of museums and makeovers in the decaying post-industrial provinces. The market for seaside and mountain tourism is mainly domestic, and where such sites attract across the world it is usually for other reasons: the Japanese who come to the Lake District to see Beatrix Potter's house, for example, or the international gay tourists who enjoy the nightlife and the ambience at Blackpool or Brighton.[55] Britain's place in global tourist markets and imagery is still dominated by a small number of sites and icons, mainly metropolitan; and here as elsewhere, the distinctiveness it lays claim to is increasingly protected and marketed as an asset, on a highly-competitive world stage. But what the British experience also makes clear is the continuing importance of local tourist markets, especially for day-trips and short breaks, which have the power to sustain the remaking and revival of 'traditional' holiday activities, the seaside included. The familiar paradox whereby globalization coexists with, and sometimes reinforces, the locally distinctive and even the reassuringly familiar, is very much at work in Britain.[56]

9. Conclusion

The current state of tourism history in Britain, broadly defined, is lively and expansive. It is nourished by questions and theories generated by a wide range of overlapping disciplines, and what it still lacks is full integration into what are perceived as the mainstream concerns of historians themselves. There is plenty of scope for such integration. The new cultural history, with its interest in consumption and identities, is the likeliest vector, alongside the interdisciplinary urban history which prioritizes the analysis of urban spatial and social systems and the meanings allocated to (and contested around) urban recreational spaces.[57] It will probably take longer for tourism's multiple relevances to a new, culturally-informed political history to become more widely appreciated within the empires of the profession. But there is an ample and exciting array of potential research themes, over and above the developing ones outlined above. The role of London as tourist metropolis is an obvious one, especially as it has constituted such an important gateway and generator of images of Britain for tourists from other cultures.[58] This leads into questions of tourism and national and regional identities, which are now beginning to be broached, and of the ways in which resorts act as vectors of cultural change and exchange, promoting them as well as responding to them.[59] Questions of identity are interesting historians at the individual as well as the collective level, and the reconstruction of tourist experiences and expectations at a personal level will help us to deconstruct the more dangerously heroic of the generalizations now current about such problematic phenomena as 'mass tourism'.[60] The recent, belated development of interest in twentieth-century British history, especially the second half of the century, offers particularly exciting opportunities, as the economic and cultural importance of tourism becomes obvious even to the most myopic or blinkered gaze. Here, most obviously, are theories to borrow and test from cognate disciplines (Urry, Shields, Said, even the crudely provocative notion of the resort product cycle which is so dear to Tourism Studies), bringing them into critical dialogue with evidence according to the classic *modus operandi* of the historian.[61] Historians of tourism also need to pay attention to gender, a theme which has been surprisingly neglected as a central focus, apart from work on Victorian female travellers from a literary perspective.[62] The full range of sources and approaches is available, from textual analyses of the construction and representation of the self through accounts of individual holidays, through grounded local studies in how resorts work using a cross-section of material, to surveys at national level through the archives and specialist journals of organizations, investigations undertaken by national and local government, and quantitative studies of resort population structures, visitor surveys or investment patterns. Taking the history of British tourism seriously opens out enticing vistas for future research which will shed light not only on resorts and their associated services, but also, and more importantly, on the lives, spending priorities and cultural values of that overwhelming majority of the population whose time spent as tourists enables us to access other aspects of their lives.

Notes

1 See, for an overview of British tourism in wider context, J. Towner, *An Historical Geography of Recreation and Tourism in the Western World, 1540-1940* (Chichester: Wiley, 1996).

2 P. Borsay, *The English Urban Renaissance: Culture and Society in the Provincial Town, 1660-1770* (Oxford: Clarendon Press, 1989).

3 J.K. Walton, *The English Seaside Resort: A Social History 1750-1914* (Leicester: Leicester University Press, 1983); J. Travis, *The Rise of the Devon Seaside Resorts 1750-1900* (Exeter: University of Exeter Press, 1993); A. Durie, 'The Development of the Scottish Coastal Resorts in the Central Lowlands, c. 1770-1880', *Local Historian* 24 (1994), 206-16; N. Morgan and A. Pritchard, *Power and Politics at the Seaside* (Exeter: University of Exeter Press, 1999); J.K. Walton, *The British Seaside: Holidays and Resorts in the Twentieth Century* (Manchester: Manchester University Press, 2000).

4 P. Brendon, *Thomas Cook* (London: Secker and Warburg, 1991); L. Withey, *Grand Tours and Cook's Tours* (London: Aurum Press, 1997), chapter 5.

5 See especially J. Pemble, *The Mediterranean Passion* (Oxford: Clarendon Press, 1987); Simona Pakenham, *60 Miles from England: The English at Dieppe, 1814-1914* (London: Macmillan, 1967).

6 Edward Said, *Orientalism* (London: Routledge and Kegan Paul, 1978).

7 J. Whyman, 'A Hanoverian Watering-Place: Margate before the Railway', in A. Everitt (ed.), *Perspectives in English Urban History* (London: Macmillan, 1973), 149-55; J. Simmons, *The Railway in Town and Country*

1830-1914 (Newton Abbot: David and Charles, 1986), chapter 8; D.N. Smith, *The Railway and Its Passengers: A Social History* (Newton Abbot: David and Charles, 1988); S. O'Connell, *The Car in British Society: Class, Gender and Motoring 1896-1939* (Manchester: Manchester University Press, 1998), chapter 5.

8 M. Andrews, *The Search for the Picturesque* (Stanford: Stanford University Press, 1989); A. Bermingham, *Landscape and Ideology: The English Rustic Tradition, 1740-1860* (Berkeley: University of California Press, 1986); I. Ousby, *The Englishman's England: Travel, Taste and the Rise of Tourism* (Cambridge: Cambridge University Press, 1990).

9 M. Wiener, *English Culture and the Decline of the Industrial Spirit* (Harmondsworth: Penguin, 1992); J. Lowerson, 'Battles for the Countryside', in F. Gloversmith (ed.), *Class, Culture and Social Change* (Brighton: Harvester Press, 1980); A. Howkins, 'The Discovery of Rural England', in R. Colls and P. Dodd (eds), *Englishness: Politics and Culture, 1880-1920* (London: Croom Helm, 1986), 62-88.

10 Key texts include R. Hewison, *The Heritage Industry* (London: Methuen, 1987); R. Samuel, *Theatres of Memory: 1, Past and Present in Contemporary Culture* (London: Verso, 1994); J.D. Marshall, *The Tyranny of the Discrete* (Aldershot: Scolar Press, 1997), 128-37; G. Shaw and A. Williams (eds), *The Rise and Fall of British Coastal Resorts* (London: Pinter, 1997), chapters 5 and 7.

11 Walton, *British Seaside*, 139f.

12 C. Rojek and J. Urry (eds), *Touring Cultures* (London: Routledge, 1997), 1-5.

13 J. Craik, 'The Culture of Tourism', in Rojek and Urry, *Touring Cultures*, 113-36, is one example among many.

14 The 'Introduction' of Walton, *British Seaside*, tries to turn these assumptions on their head.

15 M. Chadefaud, *Aux origines du tourisme dans les pays de l'Adour* (Pau: Université de Pau, 1987); J.K. Walton and J. Smith, 'The First Century of Beach Tourism in Spain: San Sebastian and the *Playas del Norte* from the 1830s to the 1930s', in M. Barke, J. Towner and M.T. Newton (eds), *Tourism in Spain: Critical Perspectives* (Wallingford: C.A.B. International, 1996), 35-61; Galerie CGER, *Villes d'eaux: Stations thermales et balnéaires en Belgique, XVIe-XXe siècles* (Brussels, 1987), 175-93; D. Mihailov and D. Marinov, *Bulgaria: A Guide* (Sofia: Sofia-Press, 1970), 159.

16 For the Grand Tour itself see especially J. Black, *The British Abroad: The Grand Tour in the Eighteenth Century* (London: Sutton, 1992).

17 D. Thompson, *Queen Victoria: Gender and Power* (London: Virago, 1990).

18 J.K. Walton, 'Seaside Resorts and Maritime History', *International Journal of Maritime History* 9 (1997), 125-47.

19 See above, note 1.

20 Rojek and Urry, *Touring Cultures*, 2.

21 J. Buzard, *The Beaten Track: European Tourism, Literature and the Ways to 'Culture', 1800-1918* (Oxford: Clarendon Press, 1993).

22 Withey, *Grand Tours*, 162-6.

23 W. Plomer (ed.), *Kilvert's Diary* (Harmondsworth: Penguin, 1977), 64f.

24 H. Taylor, *A Claim on the Countryside: A History of the British Outdoor Movement* (Edinburgh: Keele University Press, 1997).

25 A. Garland, *The Beach* (London: Penguin, 1997), 24f.

26 Walton, *English Seaside Resort*, especially chapter 8.

27 The advent of the motor car was expected to tip the balance towards touring in the 1920s, but the change took much longer to become widespread; see Walton, *British Seaside*, chapter 3.

28 For example A.M. Williams, 'Mass Tourism and International Tour Companies', in Barke et al. (eds), *Tourism in Spain: Critical Perspectives*, 119-23 (note qualification on page 123).

29 J. Urry, *The Tourist Gaze* (London: Sage, 1990), and id., *Consuming Places* (London: Routledge, 1995).

30 Black, *The British and the Grand Tour*; see also Towner, *Recreation and Tourism*, chapter 5.

31 See above, note 4.

32 Towner, *Recreation and Tourism*, chapter 5; Borsay, *English Urban Renaissance*; R.S. Neale, *Bath 1680-1850* (London: Routledge and Kegan Paul, 1981); P. Hembry, *The English Spa 1560-1815: A Social History* (London: Athlone Press, 1990).

33 A. Corbin, *The Lure of the Sea* (Cambridge: Polity, 1994).

34 Walton, *British Seaside*.

35 Morgan and Pritchard, *Power and Politics at the Seaside*; see also John Beckerson's essay in the present volume.

36 J. Demetriadi, 'The Golden Years: English Seaside Resorts 1950-1974', and J. Urry, 'Cultural Change and the Seaside Resort', in Shaw and Williams (eds), *British Coastal Resorts*, 49-75, 102-13; Walton, *British Seaside*, chapter 7 and 'Conclusion'.

37 See above, note 8.

38 N. Nicholson, *The Lakers* (London: Hale, 1955); K. Welberry, '"The Playground of England": A Genealogy of the English Lakes from Nursery to National Park, 1793-1951', unpublished Ph.D. thesis, La Trobe University, 2000.

39 J.D. Marshall and J.K. Walton, *The Lake Counties from 1830 to the Mid-Twentieth Century* (Manchester: Manchester University Press, 1981), chapters 8-9; O.M. Westall (ed.), *Windermere in the Nineteenth Century* (Lancaster: University of Lancaster, Centre for North West Regional Studies, 1991); J.K. Walton, 'Canon Rawnsley and the English Lake District', *Armitt Library Journal* 1 (1998), 1-17.

40 Marshall and Walton, *Lake Counties*, chapter 9 and 'Conclusion'; C. O'Neill, 'Windermere in the 1920s', *Local Historian* 24 (1994), 217-24; Welberry, 'The Playground of England'.

41 See especially Taylor, *A Claim on the Countryside*, and also W. Orr, *Deer Forests, Landlords and Crofters* (Edinburgh: Donald, 1982); H. Hill, *Freedom to Roam* (Ashbourne: Moorland, 1980); B. Rothman, *The 1932 Kinder Trespass* (Altrincham: Willow Publishing, 1982); T. Stephenson, *Forbidden Land* (Manchester: Manchester University Press, 1989); N. Evans (ed.), *National Identity in the British Isles* (Harlech: Centre for Welsh Studies, 1989), 62.

42 Withey, *Grand Tours and Cook's Tours*, chapter 7; Paul Bernard, *The Rush to the Alps: The Evolution of Vacationing in Switzerland* (New York: Columbia University Press, 1978).

43 M. Blume, *Cote d'Azur: Inventing the French Riviera* (London: Thames and Hudson, 1992), chapter 2.

44 *Majorca Sun*, 7 January 1934, and 29 April 1934.

45 J.M. Zorrilla, *Veraneo en Mar del Plata* (Buenos Aires, 1913), 46, 62 [pamphlet in British Library].

46 H. Ritchie, *Here We Go* (London: Hamish Hamilton, 1993); Charles Wilson, *Benidorm: The Truth* (Valencia: Agencia Valenciana del Turismo, 1999).

47 I. Wallerstein, *The Modern World-System* (New York: Academic Press, 1974).

48 See above, note 6.

49 For an early perception, see L. Turner and J. Ash, *The Golden Hordes: International Tourism and the Pleasure Periphery* (London: Constable, 1975).

50 G. Ritzer and A. Liska, '"McDisneyization" and "Post-Tourism"', in Rojek and Urry (eds), *Touring Cultures*, 96-109.

51 Garland, *The Beach*, 19.

52 See above, note 10.

53 D.H. Robertson, *The Control of Industry* (Cambridge: Cambridge University Press, 1928), 31.

54 J. Barnes, *England, England* (London: Jonathan Cape, 1998). On Barnes's novel, see also Barbara Korte's contribution in this volume.

55 Craik, 'The Culture of Tourism', in Rojek and Urry, *Touring Cultures*, 117; Walton, *British Seaside*, 161f.

56 Walton, *British Seaside*, 116-9.

57 For example in S. Gunn and R. Morris (eds), *Making Identities: Conflict and Urban Space, c. 1800-2000* (London, 2001).

58 Transferable ideas can be found in E.A. Wrigley, 'A Simple Model of London's Importance in Changing English Society and Economy, 1650-1750', *Past and Present* 37 (1967), 44-70.

59 See, for example, J. Belchem (on the Isle of Man) and J.K. Walton (on the Basque Country) in N. Kirk (ed.), *Northern Identities* (Aldershot: Ashgate, 2000).

60 See Sue Wright's essay in this volume.

61 See Urry, *Tourist Gaze* and *Consuming Places*; R. Shields, *Places on the Margin* (London: Routledge, 1991); Said, *Orientalism*; G. Priestley and L. Mundet, 'The Post-Stagnation Phase of the Resort Cycle', *Annals of Tourism Research* 25 (1998), 125-48; R. Evans, *In Defence of History* (London: Granta, 1997).

62 See, for example, C. McEwan, *Gender, Geography and Empire* (Aldershot: Ashgate, 2000); A. Blunt, *Travel, Gender and Imperialism* (London: Guilford, 1994); S. Foster, *Across New Worlds: Nineteenth-Century Women Travellers and Their Writings* (Brighton: Harvester Wheatsheaf, 1990); S. Mills, *Discourses of Difference* (London: Routledge, 1993).

Marketing British Tourism

Government Approaches to the Stimulation of a Service Sector, 1880-1950

John Beckerson

Towns, cities and even nations in the twenty-first century have brand-like identities which are created, manipulated and sold, a process which has reached new heights in recent years. Marketing and place promotion have become important areas of local and regional government policy, and the efforts made in this direction have sparked research in areas as wide as geography, planning, tourism, sociology and heritage studies. Such image generation has spread far outside its origins in tourism to reflect the increasing importance of the service sector within most Western economies. In the UK, the efforts of the British Tourist Authority and the English Tourism Council underpin economic strategy in many needy areas. But ailing tourist towns are not the only beneficiaries. Image-driven regeneration efforts abound in towns as different as Liverpool, Glasgow and the resorts of the 'English Riviera'. The image of place has become a valuable commodity.

The generation of image therefore received a measure of attention. However, little attention has been directed to organisations and structures behind the scenes, or to discover how the use of tax revenues for civic and national boosterism evolved. As Morgan remarks: 'the tendency to describe place marketing as a relatively recent phenomena obscures the long tradition of resort advertising in Britain and seriously undermines the sophistication of the early marketing strategies.'[1] Such strategies were not only sophisticated: they were often controversial. This new historical analysis soon reveals that many obstacles were placed in the way of tourist marketing by local councils and non governmental organisations. The story of how official advertising became acceptable throws light on the progress of the UK from a manufacturing to a service economy, and also on the commercialisation of leisure. It started in the seaside resorts, and came to encompass the attractions of a nation.[2]

1. Victorian Britain: The Heyday of Voluntarism?

Much has been written on the advertising of large leisure firms such as Thomas Cook. This article hopes to open up a somewhat different historical seam. It focuses on the tourist promotion activities of the British state. It was in the late nineteenth century, at seaside resorts, that local government first began to use ratepayers' money to fund town publicity committees. Before the 1890s, advertising by government was almost unknown, and those few excursions which were made were directed at specific, short term ends. A prevailing ideology of laissez-faire liberalism firmly opposed unnecessary state intervention, and nothing seemed more ephemeral or useless than spending ratepayers' money on town publicity. However, in seaside resort towns, a style of civic government began to evolve which questioned the status quo for the most pragmatic of reasons. In large resorts, such as Blackpool, a spirit of 'municipal enterprise' began to emerge. This was quite distinct from municipal socialism. It was a conservative, business-driven ideology, which pragmatically accepted that certain common measures were necessary for a town composed of individual (and even competing) businesses to thrive.[3] One such measure was town publicity.

Competition was the imperative for this action. Durie reminds us that, by the late nineteenth century, 'tourism was becoming a highly competitive business: resort against resort, region against region.'[4] The coming of the mass market meant new opportunities as well as new threats. Most British resorts did not have to worry unduly about international competition, but even those offering standard domestic seaside holidays could ill afford to be complacent. In the late nineteenth century, as the mass market in holidays grew and advertising became more sophisticated, prominent individuals in many resorts began to club together and make advertising efforts, with the aim of boosting their towns. Of course, a good deal of private advertising was also being generated. An average town might be 'sold' by its railway company, its larger leisure providers, and the more substantial hotels. Railways tended to advertise whole areas or groups of towns, and much was done by the companies.[5] But the attention lavished on the railways by historians has somewhat skewed our perceptions. Even the advertising undertaken by larger tourist businesses has been half-forgotten, and the problems of a vast number of small boarding houses – which were almost unable to advertise with any regularity or efficacy until the coming of the municipal guide-book – have barely been considered. It was to these needs that the town advertisers addressed themselves.

The first steps in town advertising were usually taken by setting up voluntary committees to work alongside councils. Advertisements were placed as early as the mid-nineteenth century, and not just in newspapers. Some towns even used the catalogue of the Great Exhibition.[6] Established spas such as Bath and Harrogate were joined by aspiring resorts such as Great Yarmouth and the Isle of Man.[7] In the latter, a 'committee for advertising the Island' was formed, consisting of local merchants, traders, and above all, hotel keepers. Its aim was to 'extend the [advertising] project of the Isle of Man Steam Packet Company.'[8] Advertisements were placed in about 20 English newspapers. The Island was promoted as both a watering place and a permanent residence. Sights were set realistically enough to call 'parties of limited means to the advantages of the Island'.[9] Fourteen thousand 'views' were distributed, and four hundred requests for information were received in the first year of operation.[10] More than half the £ 87 subscriptions raised were spent on newspaper advertising. Enquiries were optimistically reported 'from Lands' End to John O'Groats', and the work was firmly identified as a task of entrepreneurial boosterism.[11] Yet the weakness of the voluntary funding upon which the committee depended soon became clear. A list of subscribers defaulting on their pledges was published in the local press in October in an attempt to secure promised money, but it was not forthcoming, and efforts folded. The story was repeated in many other resorts as seaside tourism grew. However, as the importance of the task was realized more widely, by the late 1880s most resort towns of any size had established more-or-less permanent committees to generate publicity and drum up business.[12] Commercial firms worked alongside them to draft advertising, and some, such as Emmison Brothers of London, worked for several resorts including Blackpool, Douglas and Scarborough. All were eager to follow the railway companies' lead in producing colourful booklets and posters. But in other respects they deviated from railway publicity, which was not always an ideal model. Ward notes that 'the resorts themselves were developing into self-conscious holiday towns [...] they were no longer content to leave the destiny of their towns to the whims of railway companies.'[13]

LIVERPOOL JOHN MOORES UNIVERSITY
LEARNING SERVICES

This discontent further manifested itself in a desire to create reliable and enduring publicity bodies, which could generate municipal advertising, funded ideally through the rates. It was a development which first began in Blackpool, as Walton has pointed out. Discontent with its railway company spurred Blackpool to raise an advertising rate in 1879, and the Advertising Committee soon plastered the railway stations of its hinterland with posters generated by a well funded publicity committee riding high on the town's ever-increasing rateable value.[14] But Blackpool's advertising rate only got through on a parliamentary oversight, and applications by other towns for the same powers were strongly opposed by the Local Government Board (LGB) for decades.[15] This opposition was important. One of the Board's duties was to scrutinize proposed local Bills (such as legislation to permit municipal borrowing, public municipal works or an extension of powers) for legal problems or conflicts with government policy.[16] If the Board vetoed a clause or an entire Bill, this was almost impossible to overcome. Because the Board held the view that town advertising was an unsuitable waste of public money, government ministers were content to agree with its advice. In this situation, the British state chose to limit, not extend, its own local powers, via a central civil service which broadly espoused laissez-faire liberal policies and which reminds us of the relative weakness of statist doctrine in the UK.

On the continent, by contrast, French resorts had benefitted under the *syndicat d'initiative* system, which had brought private and public interests together for publicity and development with no opposition from the state.[17] Moreover, state-owned railways took up the job of national publicity, often with the encouragement of central government. In the UK, only Irish resorts were allowed a Health Resorts and Watering Places Act in 1909. It was presented as 'a simple bill to protect Irish seaside resorts to raise a twopenny rate for advertising; to protect themselves against growing foreign competition' and was originally planned to apply to the whole of the UK.[18] But at the last moment it was adjusted to apply to Ireland alone, and the LGB slashed the rate to a penny, somewhat to the confusion of Irish MPs of all persuasions who had thought it 'entirely non-contentious'.[19]

Why were England, Scotland and Wales excised? Looking back, in the 1920s, the President of the LGB claimed that his predecessors thought that Ireland was an especially needy case, where a tiny struggling industry needed support. In contrast, England, Scotland and Wales boasted a well-established series of resorts. The Board took the view that if every British town advertised, they would only be throwing money away to remain in the same relative positions as before. Resorts outside the self-governing Isle of Man (a Crown Protectorate) were frustrated in their attempts to advertise on the rates. This did not stop demand from building up in resorts across the country. But the pressure cooker lid was firmly on and the towns grew increasingly frustrated in their thwarted desires for official advertising. The *Municipal Review* of May 1908 reveals a growing interest. It stated:

> During the latter half of the last century, advertising among the large businesses was carried out on a gigantic and profitable scale, and with almost the research of a science. But it was only with the dawn of the present one that *towns* in any number have awakened to the fact that there was *no reason* why *their* prosperity should not be materially increased by adopting the methods by which many of the great commercial houses had risen to fortune.[20]

Although resorts as an industrial sector were booming before 1914, it was still essential for them to advertise. It is commonplace to state that a technology cannot be 'un-invented', and this is also true of a business method. For example, by the 1900s Blackpool was using the municipal guide to try to increase its share of the middle class holiday market without alienating its traditional visitors.[21] Once a few enterprising towns had begun to manage their image in such a way, there was little that the rest could do other than to adopt similar tactics. Abundant and aggressive advertising was a simple fact of late Victorian and Edwardian society.[22] The resorts had to keep up with this trend or face decline. There were many businesspeople in resort towns who put the argument forcefully to councils: in turn, the councils put their arguments to Whitehall and Parliament.

As more and more towns rushed to begin advertising their attractions, a multitude of inventive means were found to fund publicity efforts, from mayoral salaries to deckchair profits, and the period 1900-20 was something of a free-for-all, as towns sought to find the most effective means of achieving their objectives.[23] One mayor even admitted that a lot of 'wangling' went on to find the money, and to avoid the threat of LGB surcharging.[24] But the prize of permissive legislation proved elusive.

2. Local Advertising Grows

It took until 1914 for the resorts to secure a reasonable parliamentary chance to promote an advertising Bill. The year before, Asquith himself had stated that the government had no objection to the bill: there was simply no parliamentary time to consider it.[25] His civil servants were less sanguine. The LGB again made known its disapproval, with Sir Herbert Samuel as their spokesman complaining that 'the only advantage would be to the press [...] and poster industry'.[26] However, the bill had a good chance of success, with many MPs supporting the view that the provision of health and pleasure was 'as good an industry as any other', and equally worthy of state support.[27] Political changes which Harris suggests were part of 'a drift towards a more mass-produced, spectator sport style of political life' had softened opposition to the idea of advertising and publicity.[28] The Liberal reforms of 1906-14 extended the principle of state intervention in economic life and local government, and we might also note signs such as the 1909 local development commission, empowered to use public funds to assist depressed towns.[29]

Thus the climate of opposition to an Act weakened, and in 1914 its passing was likely. But war intervened, and it was not until 1921 that it was finally passed. Remarkably, it still did not allow rate-borne advertising, due to objections from the Lords. But it did regularize the position for all resorts, and a compromise in the upper house allowed all the watering places to utilize profits from municipal enterprises up to the equivalent of a penny rate. Opposition from a few Lords notwithstanding, government attitudes were softening, and whilst the administration did not officially adopt the bill, it gave facilities, time and 'an attitude of general sympathy' to it; whilst leaving voting free.[30] The post-war desire for reconstruction gave an added fillip, as a supporter stated:

> We all know how, during the war, our health resorts and watering places have suffered [...] they have had very bad times, and we find our continental friends always advertising in our papers. [...] Why then, should we deprive our own people, in our own country, of the opportunity of making known [...] places in this country worthy of being visited?[31]

The Act was hailed by the advertising industry as 'a long overdue measure', a fact that reveals how closely the world of commercial advertising was watching the resorts.[32] The resorts were also watching the industry, and many of the more enterprising seized on the powers given by the 1921 Act to update their images in line with the advances in publicity and marketing that the private sector had created.

Underlying these developments was a factor which few parliamentary commentators realized, but which was all too obvious on the promenades. This problem was structural to the tourist industry, underpinning the rationale for tax funded publicity. The trade was largely composed of numerous small businesses. Although every larger town had its dominant hotels and entertainment companies, the backbone of any resort was its numerous small boarding house keepers. They needed municipal guidebooks as a means of creating cheap advertising space and to raise awareness of the resort in a way that they simply could not afford single-handed.[33] Only government could underpin the provision of impartial national networks of publicity and tourist information and, later, market research which businesses large and small could use. This was why the circulation, appearance and price of advertising in the town guide were white-hot issues in every resort town, meriting many column inches in local newspapers. Yates postulates that guides simply sold this space to survive. This was of course true, but it is also important to reiterate that the generation of affordable space for small business advertising was, in reality, a *primary purpose* of the medium.[34]

Businesspeople in resorts knew that they had a measure of control over their town guides. They were locally controlled and could be quite democratic. In contrast, railway advertising was often arranged to suit the needs of the railways.[35] It often advertised regions, not towns, or was too broad in scope for many resort businesses. One hotelkeeper's journal analyzed this longstanding advertising problem in the 1930s, and put it as follows:

> The cost to us per square inch in the Great Yarmouth guide and the LMS railway guide are the same, but whereas practically every one of the 75,000 people who receive the Great Yarmouth guide are directly interested in a visit to that resort, this cannot be said for those who purchase the railway publication. [Approximately] five per cent of the 100,000 purchasers of 'holidays by LMS' must be the *very maximum* who are interested in Great Yarmouth. The value of the town guide for advertising, therefore, becomes immediately clear.[36]

The post-1921 period was a good one for local government advertisers. Grounded on a broad base of public support, and enabled by their Act, many publicity committees around the coast of Britain became more adventurous and dynamic in their output. This was a crucial period of image establishment for most British resorts. New ideas, styles and techniques first employed in these years came to have an enduring presence. The influence of the modern movement was felt in poster and booklet design, and some striking work was the result. This explosion of graphic art and colour has remained in popular favour, and continues to be exploited as a heritage commodity. What is has been forgotten is that it was created by the increasingly professional structures of tourist promotion which grew within British local government. Stability had come at last to underpin the resorts' image creation efforts. A period of consolidation and steady growth in marketing resulted, as the seaside holiday product took on a firm pattern of marketing and consumption that endured (for good or ill) until its dramatic decline. This decline was of course not foreseen in the thirties, and some resorts began to dream of attracting visitors from overseas in these years. This was also the goal of the 'better class' hoteliers who already made up the backbone of Britain's small international tourist industry just after World War I. Municipal advertisers and hoteliers were to have a significant influence on the course of coming events.

3. The Inter-War Years: New Growth and a National Movement

The beginnings of international aspirations opened up the possibility of a national tourist organisation. In a typically British way, it was hardly planned at all, but grew as a series of *ad hoc* responses to crises and pressure.

The inter-war years formed a particularly important period of development, growth and transition for state-supported tourist promotion. Britain's nascent international tourist sector was beginning to find a lobbying voice. Encouraged by the example of co-operative resort advertising in the home market, a group of hoteliers, led by Sir Francis Towle, and welcomed by Douglas Hacking at the Department of Overseas Trade, created a new organisation in 1926: the 'Come to Britain' Movement. The Movement used a well-tried model of voluntary coalition of trade interests, led by the great and the good. Shipping lines, railways, London stores and the Association of Health and Pleasure Resorts were all represented.[37] They had no other choice. The Department of Overseas Trade, within whose remit fell the international question, maintained until the early 1930s 'that it was simply not desirable for the government to get involved in an issue that was 'a matter for private enterprise'.[38] But on the international stage, events were leaving Britain behind.[39] Just as the 'Come to Britain' Movement was struggling through its first year, the French government was being criticized for granting its national tourist office 'only' £ 25,000, in comparison to Italy's grant of £ 250,000. Germany was spending £ 60,000 per year on publicity in America alone.[40] The British movement had raised only £ 1,945. It needed £ 20,000.[41] All was not entirely gloomy, for the movement could point to an increase of 10,000 in actual landings of American citizens at British ports. But in New York, the French were busy preparing for a *Maison de France* in Madison avenue as part of that nation's new publicity drive.[42] Such 'odious comparisons' against other countries were particularly worrying to the British, for to be active in the American market was the epitome of all that the Movement (and later the TA) desired.[43] France also had the twin advantages of a cheap currency and an image of fashionability. Senior figures in British tourism worried over this, but dismissed the prospect of opening casinos and night-clubs in England as impossible without generating widespread public outrage. Heritage, ceremony, and tradition were deemed much safer selling points.[44]

The lack of support for the Movement can be compared and contrasted with the approach taken to the promotion of manufacturing industry. The Board of Trade, the Empire Marketing Board and the British Industries fairs were all supported to a reasonable extent.[45] Many industrialists were happy to maintain the status quo, and the Federation of British Industry weighed into the fight in 1928 with a request that the government would *not* support place promotion through taxation.[46] However, life was not entirely rosy in the garden of industrial promotion. Maguire has demonstrated that British manufacturers were not always well projected.[47] The Board of Trade was accused of creating a downright boring British pavilion at the Paris trade fair of 1925, and in addition there were those prepared to claim that Britain was not 'as good at selling as some of our competitors [...] the Americans are very much better, and their methods of advertising are excellent'.[48] Critics of the government with an interest in tourism pointed out the existence of state support for the propaganda of the Empire Marketing Board, and drew direct comparisons with the puzzling lack of it elsewhere. Weighed against these such comparatively well-funded programmes, the movement was puny indeed. In fact, it swiftly collapsed. But its collapse was a catalyst that spurred long-delayed action in Whitehall. At the Department of Overseas Trade, the MP and businessman Douglas Hacking became convinced that voluntarism had failed, and that genuine support was needed if tourist promotion activities were to succeed. Influential figures such as the newspaper magnate Lord Astor pressed Churchill (then Chancellor of the Exchequer) for action, noting dryly that the Board of Trade had 'played with the matter, but in a futile manner'. They did not have enough 'big guns'.[49] In his arguments to the Treasury for a grant, Hacking also understood this:

> [...] if the proposed organisation were organised on really national lines, there is no doubt that it would command the attention of government in a way that sporadic protests and supplications from individual sources are unable to achieve.[50]

This was of course the hope of many tourist interests, including shipping lines, hoteliers, travel agents and resort towns. They saw the potential of a co-operative NGO, which not only created publicity, but would enable them to command greater influence over government policy. The purchase of political leverage would make their subscriptions doubly worthwhile. However, it was hard to obtain. The Treasury disapproved of releasing public funds, complaining that it was 'not the practice of government to subscribe to associations of this nature'.[51] The ideology behind the stance was made plain. 'Private enterprise must have greatly weakened in the country if the powerful [travel] interests [...] cannot do this work for themselves'. This attitude was not restricted to publicity. British hoteliers struggled to improve their premises unaided by the state, whilst in France the *crédit hôtelier* fund was assisted by a grant of almost Ff. 40 million between 1930 and 1936.[52]

Supporters of tourism at the Board of Trade countered reluctance in other areas of the government with the argument that even if it was not possible to make a permanent commitment, the tourist industry needed the psychological boost given by state interest and support. Eventually in 1928 it was agreed to make a grant of £ 5,000 for a couple of years only to a new organisation, in the form of the Travel Association. This was pump-prime funding: official policy was that a permanent grant would be impossible, but a shot of public money would revive the old voluntary model. Therefore the support of the travel trade which had assisted 'Come to Britain' was also vital. The new organization was to be run on conciliar lines. It was to be independent of the state, but involved with it. Its grant was never intended to be permanent. However, the Association began to establish itself and to change attitudes in government. In their funding case put to Whitehall and the travel trade, the founders of the TA argued that 'the visitor is a national asset':

> The tourist as an individual benefits those among whom he travels in a direct financial manner. From the moment he sets out for our shores - in most cases in a British ship - he is contributing towards the maintenance and employment of a long list of our businesses and trades and of individual workers. Immediately after arrival he is a customer of our hotels, railways, motor services and theatres. He is a considerable purchaser of our goods, and becomes an important factor in the country's trade. Multiply the individual visitor by 200,000, or even by 500,000, and it is obvious that travellers from abroad become of extraordinary importance. The actual expenditure of visitors from abroad while in the country will amount to millions a year, apart from subsequent purchases of British goods after their return home, as a result of contacts made or tastes formed in this country. In fact, such visitors become salesmen for British goods. Then there is the political and international aspect of the matter. The visitor who comes over here, reads our newspapers, shares our recreations, talks with our people and makes friends, with many of whom he keeps in touch afterwards, recognises the common interests of the nations and becomes an ambassador of this country as well as a salesman.[53]

National pride was a handy device that helped the Association to gain the Prince of Wales (later Edward VIII) as its patron. But, by placing tourism in the context of the British *economy*, the TA was helping to initiate a deeper change in the approach of government towards the industry. It was not entirely alone. In the wider public sphere, the economic significance of tourism was becoming more apparent, and research such as Sir Frederick Ogilvie's *The Tourist Movement* of 1933 did much to demonstrate that scholars had begun to take the subject seriously.[54] The government's own Chief Industrial Adviser also came to see that the tourist industry had 'obvious potentialities for expansion and [had] a very important bearing on the balance of trade'.[55] Nevertheless, the 1920s were not an auspicious time to start a new NGO. The post-war boom of 1919-20 had been followed by the swiftest economic collapse in Britain's history. The eyes of the nation were on core export industries of coal, iron, steel, engineering, shipbuilding and textiles, which were worst affected. Between them, these industries shed 1.1 million of their 4.5 million employees. Turmoil ensued.[56] The cost of depression led to heavy pressure on government spending. But this made the Travel Association grant all the more remarkable, given the circumstances. The Association was to have an economic breathing space of eight years to establish itself before the Great Depression hit its primary target market of the United States. This was fortunate. Most of the 1920s would be good years for those in the UK with a heavy interest in American custom such as upmarket London hotels and parts of the Scottish highlands.[57] But when depression hit, they took consolation from the suffering of tourist destinations all over Europe. Britain had received 500,000 in 1928, falling to 457,500 in 1929. 1930 saw a further decline to 454,000.[58] However, she experienced a smaller fall in percentage terms than her competitors. Whilst other nations' receipts from tourism fell off during the slump by as much as 75 per cent, the fall in Britain was 50 per cent.[59]

The Travel Association grant was unquestionably inadequate to achieve its objective. But it is important to recall that manufacturing industry was not receiving much largesse from Whitehall either. The governments of the twenties were simply not committed to direct intervention or to the expenditure of large sums of money on industrial regeneration. Even Sir Edward Bridges, Permanent Secretary to the Treasury (looking back at the actions of his predecessors) admitted that although World War I had been catastrophic, in its aftermath there had been 'few far reaching changes [in government economic thinking]'.[60] Nevertheless, the grant to the TA marked the tentative beginnings of a new approach. Bridges noted that:

> The inter-war years [...] were years of ferment in economic theory [...] there was very little agreement between economists on any course of action which would materially diminish the burden of unemployment. [But] far greater importance would be attached in future to the obligation of the State, to do what it could, to ensure that the conditions which made for good trade and high employment were as favourable as possible.[61]

Fig. 1: An early Travel Association graphic, with a somewhat optimistic dual message. (Courtesy of the British Tourist Authority Library.)

Some economists pointed firmly to the processes of change. F.W. Ogilvie wrote in 1933 that the tourist movement was simply the most noteworthy example of the striking tendency in modern times for consumers, after a point, to devote a large proportion of their total resources to economic services as distinct from goods; – a tendency which is in part cause and in part effect of the re-orientation of business which is taking place.[62]

4. The Infancy of an NGO

It was a slowly growing sense these changes within the government that kept the TA tenable. The early years of the Association's existence were vulnerable ones. The means by which it fought for its existence reveal how novel it was within the British system of industrial promotion. Arguments for free trade, national pride, propaganda and tourism were conflated in a concoction that is fascinating in itself, and reveals that much was at stake in an ideological free-for-all as the Association struggled to define and stabilise its position. The Board of Trade began to absorb some of these arguments, and by late 1929 it was arguing for the TA on the basis that it was 'impressed by the definite prospects of substantial and permanent benefits accruing to the trade and industry of this country.'[63] However, times were not auspicious: the late 1920s and 1930s tourist scene was dependent on shaky international economies, vulnerable to exchange controls, and relied on the sale of expensive services which only more prosperous members of the bourgeoisie could afford.[64] An idea of traffic levels may be gained from table 1.[65]

Table 1: Visitors to the United Kingdom 1921-1931

Year	Total visitors	Holiday visitors
1921	318,463	107,31
1922	299,313	127,38
1923	331,822	129,76
1924	380,472	189,855
1925	365,568	185,599
1926	336,224	172,76
1927	418,485	205,348
1928	441,243	244,815
1929	451,659	238,391
1930	444,479	245,865
1931	351, 338	195,142

These flows, though not huge, were nevertheless high enough to encourage established resorts which had grown prosperous through the domestic mass market to become interested in obtaining a section of the international traffic with its attendant benefits.[66] They lobbied alongside the TA for legislation which would enable them to make a contribution to the national tourist promotion effort. Even before World War I, the Association of Health and Pleasure Resorts (mostly seaside municipalities) had tried to attract foreigners to holiday in Britain.[67] Local government was certainly far more dynamic that its national counterpart in the promotion of tourism for much of the inter-war period.[68] The demands of the resorts - supported by the TA which had much to gain - resulted in the Local Authorities Publicity Act of 1931. This permitted vital municipal funds to be added to the promotion of Britain overseas.[69]

The 1931 Act opened up an important new source of income. It was indeed vital for the continued work of the Association, which was able to place its publicity activities on a more stable footing. However, continued underfunding by central government meant that truly large-scale efforts could not be pursued. Despite an awareness by senior figures in the TA of more expansive (and expensive) American boosterism, the British continued to tread cautiously. This vexed the tourist industry. The Association of Health and Pleasure Resorts tried to explain to the Ministry of Health why the traditional approach of government was not working in the face of ever-increasing competition in a growing leisure marketplace.[70]

> It is contrary to all the principles and purposes of advertising that a business should not be permitted to advertise unless it makes a profit, as it is for the very purposes of enabling a profit to be made that advertising is undertaken.[71]

But the ministries of the inter-war period were simply not committed to direct intervention or to the expenditure of large sums of money on industrial regeneration, and were only beginning to consider tourism to be an industry worthy of attention. In Britain, the estimated total expenditure by international tourists had reached £ 20 million per annum by 1933. Yet the grant to the TA of £ 4,000 - reduced due to depression - represented an application of merely 0.02 per cent of this sum to the industry which produced it.[72] The Travel Association pressed on, under the slogan of 'national projection'. These were buzzwords of 1935, and were seen by the advertising industry as evidence of changing government attitudes. Sir Stephen Tallents, public relations manager of the Post Office, agreed. He foresaw a considerable growth in the use of advertising by government. In the past, noted Tallents, most departments feared advertising, maintaining a 'tradition of aphasia [which made] the publicity world, seen through the panes of Whitehall windows, wear at times a hazardous and alarming air'.[73] Now most departments had a public relations office. The Ministry of Health, the Board of Education, and the Post Office were all experimenting with increased publicity, encouraged by the example of the Travel Association. 'All these straws show how the wind is blowing', proclaimed the *Advertising World*: 'State acceptance of advertising'.[74]

This was encouraging news, and indeed the 'thirties were a period of some growth for the TA. In 1934-5 its income reached £ 34,000 (yet only £ 4,000 was from central government) to fund radio and film publicity in addition to traditional posters and booklets. A total of 1,167,000 booklets were issued, but only 15,000 posters. The Association was developing targeted marketing for the modern age and built up a database of 12,000 addresses in the process.[75] Modern methods were certainly necessary. Competition was on the increase all over Europe, and 'with each and every country fighting for a share of the tourist traffic, the amount of advertising [had] never been so great'.[76] In an attempt to cope with this competition, increase income, and ride out the depression, the TA formed an alliance with manufacturers to become the Travel and Industrial Development Association. Local authorities urged the government to grant more money for the work, resolving that:

> The need for the sustaining, as part of the national economy, of an organisation of this kind [is self-evident] since, if the Association were to die, an overwhelming demand would be made upon the government to undertake this work at the sole charge of the state, as is done by many foreign governments.[77]

These efforts resulted in the grant being increased to the pre-depression £ 5,000, but private industry was still bearing most of the burden of running the Association. Slowly, state aid rose. By 1937-8 it was £ 6,658.

5. Nationalization, the Command Economy and the Travel Association

In the last full year of peace, a breakthrough in government funding for the TA had at last been reached. The grant was raised to £ 15,000 on condition that twice this sum was forthcoming from other sources.[78] Prospects for growth were promising. Overseas visitors to Britain had risen from 475,000 in 1932 to a new high of 725,000.[79] The devastation caused to international tourism by total war was equally total. Although most normal work was shut down, the Travel Association continued to work with a skeleton staff and devoted its full attention to post-war planning. An influential memorandum was put to government which set out the steps that Britain would have to take to compete in the international marketplace. It stressed the advantage that a flourishing tourist sector could bring to the nation's balance of payments.[80]

With the coming of the post-war labour government, the level of state support for which the Association had long been pressing was achieved. This was part of a wider set of changes in the British state. With the coming of the 1945 Labour government, its political agenda of economic command, nationalization, state welfare and a hitherto unseen preparedness to regulate the peacetime economy (at least for a few years) surged to the fore. This had several immediate effects on the operation of the tourist industry, to which the new ministry took a two-fold approach.[81] On the domestic front, it sought means to manage such longstanding troubles as low wages, seasonal labour shortages, and a desperately aged infrastructure. The command economy began to impact on a traditionally laissez-faire business, accustomed to being left to its own devices. Much protest ensued. The home holidays programme affected the TA and its members, but the real changes were felt on the international front, where the Travel Association operated. Closing the dollar gap was an urgent priority in the post-war years, and tourism offered a quick and easy way of increasing invisible exports, thus helping to reverse what Keynes called the nation's 'financial Dunkirk'.[82] The aim of attracting tourists from the dollar area was no longer an ideal: it was an urgent demand; a core measure of national economic policy, to which 'substantial funds' were now directed.[83] Tourism was becoming increasingly important to the national economy. In 1946 overseas visitors spent £ 12 million in the country; by 1948 this sum was £ 33 million, and by 1951 this had more than doubled to £ 75 million. On average, traffic levels were to rise at an average annual rate of 13 per cent from the end of the war until 1970.[84] In the late 1940s, this trend was not entirely foreseen; but it was hoped for, and signs of growth were becoming apparent enough for the government to take a greater interest.

Seeking to manage more closely an industry and an organization over which it had little control, the government demanded that the TA relinquish its independent status. From 1948 it was forcibly incorporated as the tourist division of the British Tourist and Holidays Board, which incorporated home holidays, catering and hotel divisions under one umbrella. There was spirited resistance to the enforced merger at the time, a fact which was simply written out of the official history of the TA. In this we find that senior TA figures pressured officials to set up the Board: in reality they gave speeches protesting that tourism was 'not to be nationalised'.[85] The process continued regardless, with civil servants preparing back-up plans for a new organisation should the TA fail to acquiesce. The nationalisation (first called an 'absorption' at the Board of Trade, then toned down into a 'merger') ushered in a new era for Britain's tourist promotion activities. Government had become intimately interested in the fate of the industry for reasons enunciated at the highest levels. The pound was at stake. The promotion of Britain had reached a new level of seriousness and integration into economic policy. The work of the Association greatly increased. The promotion was a success, and the TA's report for 1949 was pleased to boast: 'For the second year running the contribution of tourism to the drive for exports to the USA ranks higher than any other manufacturing industry.'[86]

What had begun as a two year 'start up grant' to 'pump prime' the voluntary publicising of Britain in the USA had turned into a fully fledged non governmental organisation, which would gradually take on responsibilities not just for publicity but for strategic planning, market research, and many other areas of tourism promotion. This was not confined to Britain. Although she had lagged behind her competitors (especially France) in the 1920s and 1930s, by 1948 it was London that took the lead in forming an International Union of Official Travel Organisations. This was part of the plan to reconstruct and manage tourism in post-war Europe. Government involvement in the industry had moved on to a new level.

Fig. 2: Historic landscape juxtaposed against a symbol of modernity and confidence, in a postwar cover for the TA magazine *Coming Events*. (Courtesy of the Cambridge University Library.)

6. Conclusion

We can assemble a framework which will support our analysis of the developments outlined above and which will encompass the historical events which research to date has revealed. This begins at a local level; where town publicity committees and local authorities were the first to become involved in advertising which was supported by tax revenue. Their efforts were aimed at a domestic market. They were often modest; yet their introduction was controversial in the eyes of central government. It took a long time for the resorts to obtain the legislation they desired to advertise using public money with ease.

At the national level – in the late 1920s, and some thirty years after local developments took off – things moved faster. The Board of Trade took an interest in boosting Britain. Other departments in Whitehall were *relatively* quick to accept the idea of a government grant to persuade foreigners to 'Come to Britain'. But this was only possible because the resorts had prepared the way, with thirty years of nagging.

By the late 1950s, the British Travel and Holidays Association had come of age. It was an established NGO with considerable experience in its field. However, its increasingly sophisticated research had only begun to reveal the true complexity of the task in hand. As a report on *American Visitors to Britain* revealed:

> Selling a destination is a complex process. In other fields it may be enough to stimulate a desire for the product [but] persuading people to decide on a trip may be different. After advertising has succeeded in projecting a desirable image of the destination, potential travellers are still left with a mass of questions and detailed agendas. The product is a complex one [...].[87]

This 'mass of questions', appropriately, also resembles the manner in which historians must approach the subject. Some are now being answered. It is clear from the exploratory overview above that between the 1880s and the 1950s considerable changes came about. From small, voluntary origins in Victorian seaside resorts, the technique of selling places grew to encompass the selling of Great Britain itself. For this to happen, an awareness of the importance of the service sector needed to grow within local and national government. Therefore we may conclude that current efforts to sell places, so often thought of as novel, are in fact 'rich with historical precedents'' as Ward points out.[88] The same amnesia applies just as strongly to national tourist promotion. Very little attention has been given to the organisations which promoted nations, and it is to this void that further research will be addressed.

Notes

1 N. Morgan and A. Pritchard, *Power and Politics at the Seaside: The Development of Devon's Resorts in the Twentieth Century* (Exeter: University of Exeter Press, 1999), 101.

2 A note on historical source material for this field may be found in J. Beckerson, 'Making Leisure Pay: The Business of Tourist Marketing in Great Britain 1880-1950', *Business Archives Sources and History* 76 (1998), 1-11.

3 The town boasted of its 'masterly and exemplary spirit of municipal enterprise' in the 1906 municipal guidebook. Cited in D.B. Shaw, *Selling an Urban Image: Blackpool at the Turn of the Century* (Birmingham: University of Birmingham School of Geography, 1990), 9.

4 A. Durie, Draft M.S. courtesy of Dr Durie, 'The Promotion of Scotland; Publicity and Photography' (1999), 1.

5 See a variety of works, from the light-hearted M. Palin, *Happy Holidays: The Golden Age of Railway Posters* (London: Pavilion, 1987), to the more serious R.B. Wilson, *Go Great Western: A History of GWR Publicity* (Newton Abbot: David and Charles, 1970).

6 Itself a great image-selling event, as much as the manufacturing and trade fair that was and is still commonly supposed, as T. Richards finds when trying to make a case for a commodity culture before commodities in *The Commodity Culture of Victorian England: Advertising and Spectacle, 1851-1914* (London: Verso, 1991). The above-mentioned advertisements in the catalogue are pointed out by S.V. Ward, 'Promoting Holiday Resorts: A Review of Early History to 1921', *Planning History* 10.2 (1991), 7.

7 J. Beckerson, *Advertising the Island: The Isle of Man Board of Advertising 1894-1914* (Norwich: MA dissertation, University of East Anglia, 1996).

8 *Manx Sun*, 3 April 1852.

9 *Manx Sun*, 19 July 1852.

10 *Manx Sun*, 16 September 1851.

11 *Manx Sun*, 19 July 1851.

12 Tynwald (1894), *Advertising the Island.* Isle of Man Government commission of enquiry into official advertising with minutes of evidence.

13 Ward, 'Promoting Holiday Resorts', 8.

14 Ibid.

15 *Hansard*, 41 HL Deb. 5 ser. (1920), 556f.

16 C. Bellamy, *Administering Central-local Relations, 1871-1919: The Local Government Board* (Manchester: Manchester University Press, 1988).
17 Ward, *Selling Places,* 35.
18 *Hansard,* 11 HC Deb. 5 ser. (1909), 2164.
19 *Hansard,* 11 HC Deb. 5 ser. (1909), 1980 and 2164.
20 W.H. Reid, 'Town Advertising', *Municipal Journal* 17.5 (1908), 441.
21 Shaw, *Urban Image,* 18.
22 See T.R. Nevett, *Advertising in Britain: A History* (London: Heinemann, 1982) and Richards, *Commodity Culture,* with its particularly pertinent explanation of the use of the seaside girl as an advertising device.
23 At least thirteen large boroughs possessed powers to divert money from their Borough Funds to advertise by 1914. See *Hansard,* 61 HC Deb. 5 ser. (1914), 2051. Also note N. Yates, 'Selling the Seaside', *History Today* 38.8 (1991).
24 'Fortnightly Bulletin', *Come to Britain Movement* 33 (1927), 3.
25 *Hansard,* 65 HC Deb. 5 ser. (1913), 1742.
26 *Hansard,* 61 HC Deb. 5 ser. (1914), 2016.
27 *Hansard,* 61 HC Deb. 5 ser. (1914), 2034.
28 J. Harris, *Private Lives, Public Spirit: A Social History of Britain 1870-1914,* (Oxford: Oxford University Press, 1993), 192.
29 Harris, *Private Lives, Public Spirit,* 207.
30 *Hansard,* 41 HL Deb. 5 ser. (1920), 560.
31 *Hansard,* 41 HL Deb. 5 ser. (1920), 551.
32 Editorial, 'A Long Overdue Measure', *Advertising World* 34.4 (1921), 320.
33 A similar argument applies to international tourism, as proven by numerous BTHA surveys such as *American Visitors to Britain* (1959-60), which found that 73 per cent of those surveyed were staying, or intended to stay, in hotels which had been featured in BTHA guidebooks.
34 Yates, 'Selling the Seaside'. Up to two-thirds of a guide might be composed of advertisements. My hypothesis is supported by extensive oral history interviews into the boarding house trade carried out by the Manx Heritage Foundation in 1999. Many small and medium sized boarding houses relied entirely on the Official Guide for their advertising needs.
35 Although many local Advertising Committees co-operated with the companies both over long periods and for special campaigns.
36 G. Erskine, 'Your Advertising Analysed', *Hotel* (October 1936), 573. This was not a new problem. See the earlier remarks by Fell in the House of Commons, *Hansard,* 61 HC Deb. 5 ser. (1914), 2049: 'railway companies advertise [...] for their own benefit.'
37 *British Travel and Industrial Development Association Annual Report 1934-5,* (London: BT and IDA, 1935), 2.
38 *Hansard,* 217 HC Deb. 5 ser. (1928), 170. Douglas Hacking, Secretary, Department for Overseas Trade.
39 For an overview, see Ward, *Selling Places,* chapter 3.

40 Sir F. Towle, 'Fortnightly Bulletin', *Come to Britain Movement* 24 (April 1927), 2.
41 Anon., 'Come to Britain Movement: Précis', *Monthly Report of the British Hotels and Restaurants Association* 14.11 (1927), 289.
42 Anon., 'Come to Britain Précis'.
43 C. Mackay, Co-operative Advertising and Holiday Resorts', *Advertising World* 65.3 (1934), 138.
44 Astor to Churchill, 9 June 1928. PRO: T161/1229.
45 The publicity grant for the 1928 British Industries Fair was £ 25,000.
46 Federation of British Industry to Neville Chamberlain, Minister of Health, 11th January 1928. PRO: HLG 29/179.
47 P. Maguire, 'Craft Capitalism and the Projection of British Industry in the 1950s and 1960s', *Journal of Design History* 6.2 (1993), 97-111.
48 Sir A. Mond, addressing the Board of Trade Supply Committee. *Hansard,* 186 HC Deb. 5 ser. (1925), 94.
49 Astor to Boothby MP, 9 June 1928 re: meeting with Chancellor of Exchequer. PRO: T161/1229.
50 Memorandum by Douglas Hacking, 17 November 1928. PRO: T161/1229.
51 Stocks, Treasury, to Comptroller-General, 6 February 1929. PRO: T161/1229.
52 Extension of UK tourist traffic. PRO: BT156/19.
53 Pamphlet: 'Why Leading Men Support the Travel Association' (London: Travel Association of Great Britain, 1929).
54 F.W. Ogilvie, *The Tourist Movement: An Economic Study,* (London: P.S. King, 1933).
55 Minutes by Chief Industrial Adviser, H.D. Henderson, 14/3/1931. PRO: BT156/19.
56 D. Baines, 'The Onset of Depression', in P. Johnson (ed.), *Twentieth Century Britain* (London: Longman, 1994), 171f.
57 Visitors to Britain of the type which patronized such facilities in this period were divided by Ogilvie into a 'wealthier group' and a 'less wealthy group'. The number of 'wealthier group' visitors to the UK increased by 77 per cent between 1921 to 1929, before commencing a steep fall of 18 per cent in 1930. Ogilvie, *Tourist Movement,* 76.
58 Rounded figures, source *infra.*
59 R.G. Pinney, *Britain, Destination of Tourists* (London: British Travel Association, 1944), 86. Also PRO: BT156/19: Analysis of international tourism by the Travel Association for Chief Industrial Advisor, 11 March 1931. France and Germany also experienced falls, though their market was larger overall and the two countries received 1,800,000 and 1,000,000 arrivals respectively at the turn of the decade.
60 Sir E. Bridges, *Treasury Control* (London: Athlone Press, 1950), 8.
61 Bridges, *Treasury Control,* 8.
62 Ogilvie, *Tourist Movement,* vii.

63 DOT to Treasury, 16 November 1929. PRO: BT61/54/2.

64 Indeed, even in the 1960s, it was to upper-income professionals that most British tourist advertising in the USA was addressed.

65 Source: Ogilvie, *Tourist Movement,* 74-6, in turn based upon Cmd. 1670 (1922) and subsequent annual returns [issued by the British government].

66 It was ultimately futile, for the resorts were offering a product that the international tourist had little interest in. Although happy to take their money, the image of coastal resort towns in the UK was little heeded by the TA, which from the start preferred to use images of rural landscape and heritage to sell Britain. This will be explored further in a forthcoming article.

67 *Hansard,* 130 HC Deb. 5 ser. (1902), 841. Chairman of AHPR.

68 Or, as one resort publicity officer put it, 'So the resorts are asked to help again!' Mackay, 'Co-operative Advertising'.

69 Local Authorities Publicity Act (1931). Urban District Councils and Boroughs were given powers to contribute to organisations for promoting the amenities of the British Isles *overseas, not* in the UK, using the proceeds of a 1/2d. in £ rate.

70 The Ministry of Health was, confusingly, responsible for many matters of local government administration in the 1930s.

71 AHPR to Minister of Health, 19th February 1935. PRO: HLG 52/117.

72 Lickorish, *British Travel Association,* 9.

73 S. Tallents, 'Advertising's Next Big Job: The Projection of National Policy', *Advertising World* 67.5 (1935), 13.

74 Editorial, 'Looking Ahead', *Advertising World* 67.8-9 (1935), 9. See also article by Parliamentary Secretary to the Department of Overseas Trade; A.M. Samuel, 'Goods Do Not Sell Themselves', *Advertising World* 51.3 (1927), 350f.

75 *Travel Association Annual Report 1934-5.*

76 Editorial, 'Politics Upset Travel', *Advertising World* 68.8 (1936) 11.

77 Resolution of TA Executive Committee, 1935. Lickorish, *British Travel Association,* 9.

78 Lickorish, *British Travel Association,* 10.

79 Lickorish, *British Travel Association,* 11. I have rounded his figures.

80 Pinney Memorandum. BL: 010358.r.17

81 For example, see reports of the Catering Wages Commission.

82 A. Calder, *The People's War: Britain 1939-45* (London: Pimlico Press, 1992 [1969]), 586.

83 Balcon to Sich, Board of Trade, 6/11/1946. PRO: BT64/4052.

84 Lickorish, *British Travel Association.*

85 Various remarks by Sir Harvey Shawcross in the *Times* (1948), collected as press cuttings in PRO: T161/1229..

86 *Travel Association Annual Report 1948-9* (London: BTA, 1949).

87 *American Visitors to Britain* (London: BTHA, 1959-60), 1.

88 S.V. Ward, *Selling Places: The Marketing and Promotion of Towns and Cities 1850-2000* (London: Spon, 1998), 2.

From Privilege to Commodity?

Modern Tourism and the Rise of the Consumer Society[1]

Hartmut Berghoff

In 1975, Louis Turner and John Ash painted a dark, if not apocalyptic picture of modern tourism, which they called

> King Midas in reverse; a device for the systematic destruction of everything that is beautiful in the world. [...] the heart of the industry is people-processing. Just as the great meat-packing companies take live cattle into slaughter houses and find a profitable use of every part of the resultant carcass [...] so do the great tourist conglomerates try to control as many stages as possible as their clients are separated from their money in the course of the holiday. [...] This [...] is the quintessence of today's Mass Tourist Industry. Everything is standardised, [...] The search for simplicity ends in technological complexity [...]; the pursuit of the exotic and diverse ends in uniformity.[2]

Hans Magnus Enzensberger's famous 'theory of tourism' had, almost two decades ago, struck an equally gloomy note. It defined tourism as an escapist movement delivering synthetic illusions and producing passive consumers: 'The liberation from the industrial world has become an industry, the supposed journey out of the consumer society a commodity.' Enzensberger described tourism as a child of the 'industrial revolution' dependent on the principles of mass production.[3] He wanted to raise a genuinely political issue by challenging the consumer society as such. In line with the Frankfurt school of sociology Enzensberger attacked the destructive potential of a commercialized mass culture, at whose heart seemed to be subliminal mechanisms of repressive manipulation and the inculcation of 'false needs', which allegedly fostered psychological alienation and political quiescence.[4]

Tourism, thus, was regarded as an epitome of consumerism. Its popularization allegedly rested on the transformation of a social privilege into a commodity for millions. As the masses began to emulate the manners of the social strata above them, upper-class habits percolated down the social scale finally creating a mass market for tourist products. Holidays, according to this view, were transformed from 'privilege to human right'[5] by consecutive phases of 'democratization'. In the first half of the twentieth century, the welfare-capitalist state finally established a regime of universal entitlement.

These rather crude views of tourism history serve as a starting point to analyze the interrelation between tourism and consumerism through the following four questions: First, is mass tourism a child of the industrial revolution and a result of a top-to-bottom diffusion of leisure patterns? Second, to what degree and by what means is tourism linked to the rise of the consumer society? Third, what actually is the 'product' of the tourist industry, and what is consumed by its customers? Fourth, does the economic and social history of modern tourism confirm the charge that de-individualization and uniformity are its inevitable results?

1. The Ancestry of Modern Tourism

Given that the origins of modern tourism are multifarious and reach back to the Renaissance, if not to antiquity, the idea of tourism as a 'child of the industrial revolution' is misleading. Moreover, economic historians increasingly doubt the concept of an 'industrial revolution' as a sudden, cataclysmic change starting around 1760 and instead stress the evolutionary nature of the transformation. Replacing eruptive images like 'take-off' or 'great spurt' with such gradualism is now becoming a new paradigm in economic history in general and consumer studies in particular, laying less stress on 'revolutionary events' like the invention of the steam engine but rather on long-drawn-out processes involving the reconfiguration of the institutional and cultural framework. The rise of industrial society, according to this revisionist view, was not only driven by supply factors, especially technology, but also stimulated by new patterns of demand based on new mentalities.[6] Jan de Vries coined the catchy phrase of an 'industrious revolution' and demonstrated how social aspirations changed patterns of time allocation.[7] From the seventeenth century onwards, the desire to emulate one's superiors induced people to work more and more intensively in order to buy status symbols.

Neil McKendrick claims that in eighteenth-century Britain such status enhancement caused an unprecedented dissemination of former luxury goods and acted as the prime mover of economic development because additional demand and income was generated and spread down the social scale.[8] Thus many features of the industrial consumer society were found well before the machine age, especially fashion, systematic marketing, buying for pleasure, and conspicuous consumption. Claire Walsh has recently demonstrated that elements generally considered typical of department stores – like window-shopping, browsing, seductive interior design, 'carefully constructed dream worlds' and fixed prices – were already in operation in eighteenth-century luxury shops.[9]

Tourism fits neatly into this discussion. At first glance, its emergence seems to coincide with the rise of industrial discipline in the nineteenth century, but on closer inspection we find many traces of precursors and continuity. In terms of social emulation, some impulses came from above and others from below. Rather than complying with linear concepts of trickle-down or trickle-up, we face a complicated mélange best described as 'two-way traffic'. The concept of emulation has been grossly overrated in consumer studies, masking the fact that people decided on their own terms for certain options because they liked them rather than yielding to outside influence.

Among the precursors of modern tourism was for example the pilgrimage, which had been the most important from of travelling for non-utilitarian purposes since Medieval times. The pilgrim hoped to redeem his or her soul by leaving home for a sacred site. Pilgrimage involved highly organised mass travel already displaying many traces of the package tour. Moreover, it included all social strata, in particular many paupers.[10] Modern tourism may partly be characterized as a secularized form of pilgrimage because the underlying assumption is that 'recreation' – the term itself has strong religious connotations – requires absence from home.[11] Religious travel still is an important segment of the world's tourist market, as a look at Rome, Jerusalem, Mecca, and Lourdes proves.

In contrast, other precursors of modern tourism more or less conform to the trickle-down theory. In the Grand Tour young aristocrats, and increasingly sons of the upper middle classes, rounded off their education by visiting Europe. Their voyages to places of cultural significance created a canon of attractions and a certain infrastructure, which later generations of tourists could develop and expand. Moreover, touring Europe was already a badge of status, which increasingly became attractive to people further down the social scale, as soon as they could afford it.[12]

The use of mineral water springs for health and pleasure dates back to Greek and Roman times. In modern England, spas became leisure towns for the landed aristocracy and gentry from the late seventeenth century onwards. They provided recreation, and arenas for conspicuous consumption, as well as opportunities for social mixing because it was impossible to exclude the upper middle classes. Spas flourished on status enhancement, display, recreation and hedonism.[13] These principles could easily be adopted by the seaside resorts, the new type of leisure town springing up from the end of the eighteenth century to become Britain's most popular holiday destination until the 1970s. Originally, it welcomed the same clientele as the spas, but it widened its market much faster, and as early as 1800 visitors included shopkeepers and farmers.

Large numbers of industrial workers entered the seaside resorts only after 1850. What might appear an entirely new phenomenon does, however, entail strong elements of continuity. The pre-industrial leisure system was not replaced over night by the industrial time regime. In northern England, especially in Lancashire's textile towns, old folk customs like 'St. Monday' survived and paved the way for modern tourism. As John Walton has demonstrated in his by now classic social history, traditions of wakes and fairs as well as Whitsuntide festivities played a crucial role in creating seaside resorts. Besides there was a lower-class tradition of sea-bathing, long before the middle classes discovered the 'lure of the sea'.[14]

The rise of factory discipline and proletarian tourism were parallel developments responding to the stubbornness of pre-industrial customs. Walton observed that 'employers in the cotton industry were unwilling to tolerate frequent and unpredictable absenteeism' but by the 1840s they were

> coming to terms with the established customary holidays [...] The total closure of a mill at [...] the Wakes was preferable to constant disruption throughout the summer, and there were advantages in channelling holiday observances into agreed periods. [...] Lanca-

> shire cotton workers consistently had longer consecutive summer holidays than anywhere else in industrial England [...] Moreover, the observance of a regular working week for the rest of the year made it easier for them to save and prepare for a seaside holiday.[15]

Tourism was becoming a social practice which safeguarded disciplined labour and mediated the delicate transition from the pre-industrial to the industrial work schedule. Proletarian holidays can be seen as a result of negotiation in which the traditional laxity and fluidity of the work process was traded off against rigorous discipline and rising incomes. Pressures from below, folk traditions and modern management methods interacted to create temporary breakaways from the rules of the factory, which were then reaffirmed even more strongly. Examples from 'above' like spa visiting only played a minor role in shaping mass seaside tourism in Britain. The romantic traveller's search for solitude and identity hardly contributed to the emergence of the larger resorts, which offered collective pleasures and often carnivalesque, distinctly unquiet escapades which had their roots in traditional folk festivities. At the same time, however, severe constraints were in operation. Landladies imposed their own discipline on their customers, helped by the high probability of encountering one's neighbour, foreman, or Sunday School teacher.

This collective heritage from 'below' does not mean that pre-industrial travel and recreation by social elites did not contribute to the formation of modern tourism, which in itself is an enormously diverse phenomenon. Educational tourism and cultural sightseeing had an elite pedigree reaching back to the Renaissance-inspired concept of the Grand Tour. Romanticism promised a return to a more authentic, unadulterated world and linked travelling to notions of personal freedom and sensitivity. Encounters with idealized landscapes and culturally significant sights which apparently purged the corrupting forces of 'civilization', released true identity, and secured harmony between nature and the self,[16] were images far from irrelevant for building up demand for mass tourism. Advertisements for holidays have from the very beginning heavily drawn on romantic stereotypes, and keep doing do so today.

In promising authentic experiences and an escape from modern life, the tourist industry still uses the anti-industrial images of the romantic movement. To this extent, Enzensberger is right to argue that modern tourism has been an attempt of industrial society to flee from itself, from pollution, noise and overcrowding, and from the tedium, rigours and alienation of factory and office work. The problems created by industrialism played a major role in whipping up demand for mass tourism, although there was a rather long time-lag before it could be satisfied, since real wages only rose substantially and continuously after 1870. Nonetheless, industrialization provided technological innovations which dramatically altered the supply conditions of tourist businesses. Steamers and then railways reduced everybody's transport costs and journey times. Without being restricted to upper-class models, pre-industrial travel experiences and patterns of leisure served as important preconditions of modern tourism, which, however, needed the full impact of industrialization to reach the mass market. Even then, in the 1890s, holiday-making was far beyond the means of most working class families.

2. Tourism as a Pacemaker of Consumerism

Tourism does not belong to the biologically rooted set of basic needs but to the realm of Adam Smith's 'decencies and desires' which require excess purchasing power. Rather than consuming 'necessities' the holiday-maker tries 'to gratify the five senses and the seven sins, to define a lifestyle if not a persona itself'.[17] In the twentieth century, holidays have become a staple commodity of mass culture, although their popularization was resisted by those losing privileged access. Ironically, the quest for exclusivity became a driving force of mass tourism. Those searching for the tranquillity of untouched landscapes involuntarily acted as the industry's trend scouts. Thomas Cook, the inventor of the package tour, attacked travel privileges enjoyed by social elites. As an advocate of free-trade, he claimed that widening the market was in the best interest of civilisation: 'it is too late in this day of progress to talk of this exclusive nonsense [...] railways and steamboats are the results of the common light of science, and are for the people [...] The best of men, and the noblest of minds, rejoice to see the people follow in their foretrod routes of pleasure.'[18]

In the twentieth century, paid holidays became almost universal in all western societies. Today, they are guaranteed by the state or by collective wage agreements, and even the unemployed are entitled to them. Whereas the first tourists had to legitimize their absence from home by referring to medical and educational reasons, their present-day successors take holidays for granted. Many frankly admit that all they want is to 'have a good time'. Vacations have also become a kind of social obligation. Not to go on holiday is nowadays perceived as deviant behaviour, as it contradicts the dominant pattern of consumption. It requires an explanation, almost an excuse. Not treating oneself to holidays has become a 'sign of social maladjustment almost as strong as the refusal to work'.[19] However, the number of people staying at home is still quite high. In 1989 a remarkable 41 per cent of the British population took no holidays at all.[20]

Holidays are not only a commodity of advanced consumer societies but also closely interwoven with other main practices and agents of consumerism. Mass tourism in a way ushered in new, more hedonistic patterns of spending and living, first 'only on holiday', but later also at home. However, the relationship between consumerism and tourism is full of ambivalence. On the one hand, tourism initially reconfirmed values like frugality and discipline, because most middle- and working-class holiday makers had to save through the year for their vacation. Making sure not to waste a minute and miss an important sight on Cook's tours or self-presentation as a respectable citizen on the promenade entailed strong elements of restraint and even prolonged the work ethos. On the other hand, holidays became a time of less careful spending and more relaxed behaviour. In a way, holiday resorts increasingly developed into training grounds for more affluent lifestyles and tourists became 'consumers par excellence'.[21]

Tourism prompted a whole range of supporting industries, from souvenir manufacturing to mass entertainment. Many new consumer items like cosmetics and cameras found their way to the mass market via the tourist track. Most of them have a low utility, but a high symbolic value. Souvenirs and pictures are basically trophies to demonstrate that one has been there, fetishes of distinction. Department stores, the admired as well as despised cathedrals of consumption, soon became tourist attractions and part of the standard itinerary designed by guidebooks for large cities. Some stores like Bon Marché in Paris organised guided tours of their premises.[22] Tourism's central role in the formation of the consumer society is illustrated by the fact that protests against the widening of the tourist market were often embedded in much broader discourses on consumption and social status. In 1865 the *Pall Mall Gazette* compared Thomas Cook to a 'cheap haberdasher and tailor' serving a customer 'who wants to make himself look like a gentleman at the lowest possible figure'.[23] Yet even the Russian radical Alexander Herzen had complained in 1862: 'Everything – the theatre, holiday-making, books, pictures, cloths – everything has gone down in quality and gone up terribly in numbers [...] Everywhere the hundred-thousand-headed hydra lies in wait [...] to look at everything indiscriminately, to be dressed in anything, to gorge itself on anything [...]'.[24]

Twentieth-century academics partly adopted this pessimistic stance when they bemoaned the 'lost art of travel' or complained about the lack of educational ambition among tourists and their preference for 'mere relaxation'.[25] It has to be remembered that in the nineteenth century the idea of self-improvement through edification rather than self-gratification through consumption played a prominent role in legitimizing tourism. The Baptist preacher Thomas Cook saw tourism as his 'mission to humanity' rescuing workers from alcoholism and enlarging their minds.[26] In the inter-war years, even the Trades Union Congress (TUC) campaigned for paid holidays claiming that workers needed them in order to engage in the 'freely chosen development of the human personality'.[27]

Despite all noble claims to the contrary, mass-tourism tied itself to rampant commercialization. Its emergence, however, was not simply the result of rising real incomes but also of new social dispositions. Tourism itself shaped the mentality of the consumer society, especially during its final breakthrough after World War II.

> The values encoded within modern mass vacations – of individual choice, pleasure, self-gratification, [...] abundance and comfort, beauty and youth [...] helped create the values of post-war consumer culture. This synergy of escapist, pleasure-oriented values and an individualist consumerist culture [...] relied upon a logic of individual needs to be met by commercialised leisure pursuits targeted toward various mass markets.[28]

After 1945, tourism's demonstration effect operated with great vigour. It taught people how to leave behind traditional attitudes of thrift, which had been powerfully reinforced by the wartime plight. In the 1950s and 1960s, tourism helped to popularize a new, more carefree way of living and spending. Significantly, this watershed between austerity and prosperity coincided with the heyday of the British holiday camp. It offered low-budget, highly structured holidays en masse. At first, accommodation and food were plain and discipline rather strict. Comradeship, competitions and freedom from boarding house landladies added up to an attractive proposition. After all, the idea of spending a week in a camp originated in the anti-commercial ethos of youth movements like the scouts.

At the same time, holiday camps allowed their customers a glimpse of future comfort and increasingly brought in elements of luxury and glamour. The camps widened horizons and amplified desires. Their message was: 'Enter the gate of a world of fun and perhaps, one day, it might become the same outside too.' There was plenty of food and drink, swimming pools and dance halls, stage entertainment and amusement parks, show and sporting celebrities, as well as a whole range of services from catering to child minding. 'Images were compressed and interwoven to create' a land of dreams. 'Hawaiian bars and Viennese coffee lounges, Hollywood terraces and South Sea pools, de luxe Grand Hotel ballrooms and sundecks named after Atlantic Liners [...].'[29] By the end of the 1950s, the camps virtually embodied the affluent society that was beginning to take shape. In 1961 a visitor to Butlin's newest camp at Bognor had the impression of entering the 'apotheosis' of consumerism.

> You leave behind the worries of the factory, [...] and go into the pipe-dream that lurks at the back of [the] modern industrial world. [...] It is like living inside commercial television [...] There are advertisements on the outside walls for every brand of cigarette; [...] Newspapers sponsor the innumerable competitions [...] There is half an hour a day of commercials over Radio Butlin's.[30]

When the tourists moved on to sunnier destinations, the demonstration effect remained close to their heels. Holidays seemed to have profoundly altered British dietary habits and, for example, popularized Italian food. In the 1970s and 1980s many familiarized themselves with credit cards while on holidays abroad but kept on using them at home. The fashion and cosmetics industries linked their products to tourist images by making the shots for their advertisements on exotic beaches. Cars in television commercials tend to drive on empty roads in picturesque landscapes, if not on beaches. The subliminal message is: buy this article and your holiday feeling becomes part of your everyday life.

Urry speaks of a progressive 'de-differentiation of leisure, tourism, shopping, culture, education, eating, and so on'.[31] Trade fairs, exhibitions, advertisements, malls, hotels, restaurants, pubs, leisure centres increasingly draw on tourist images by attaching themselves to certain themes. Supermarkets proclaim Italian weeks or rebuilt German wine villages. Hotels offer Arabian suites. Guinness has recently opened hundreds of Irish Pubs all over the continent providing originally looking interior design and Irish personnel. The average high street anywhere in the western world now unites an impressive array of holiday themes. It is one of the main trends of advanced consumer society to incorporate a growing number of tourist images into everyday life.

Tourism is a symbol as well as a motor of consumerism. To less developed countries tourists introduce their model of consumption, which dangles before the eyes of the host country. It is taken up first by social elites and people working in tourism. They attempt to imitate western life-styles and create a demand for imports from the industrial world. 'The community strives to adopt the obvious marks of affluence: transistors, sunglasses, pop, imported food and drink.'[32] In this way tourism acts as a global agent of consumerism and westernization.

3. What is Consumed by Tourists?

Historical consumer studies have long been preoccupied with material consumption or in the words of Brewer and Porter with 'the world of goods'. A rich literature on 'objects' has proliferated over the last 15 years or so.[33] We are well informed about eighteenth-century increases in the consumption of tea and tobacco, spices and wine, books and paintings, jewellery and dresses, buttons and buckles, pots and pans. An intangible product like tourism, however, does not leave any traces in trade statistics or inventories. The tourist buys a combination of related services like transport, accommodation and catering as well as such elusive phenomena like images, experiences and prestige. Obviously there is some material consumption involved, when hotels are constructed, planes fuelled, meals eaten, or souvenirs bought. Yet, these phenomena only depict the surface of tourist consumption. Essentially it is 'a form of imaginative hedonism', centred around dreams and desires of alternatives to everyday life.[34] Eric Leed classifies tourism as the 'experience industry' par excellence.[35] John Urry claims that the 'tourist gaze' is at the centre of tourism. In fact, Cook's first parties visiting Italy were charged for coming 'to stare and laugh at us'.[36] Tourists take pictures of key images to prove what they have looked at. They essentially document conspicuous consumption in the form of scenic views and exotic encounters, but also feature the material side of their consumption, i.e. hotels, food, swimming pools, and fashionable clothes. The pleasures of tourism rely on the availability of ever-new objects to gaze at, many of them specially staged for this purpose. For Urry, the tourist largely consumes novelty itself. Poon, from an ecological perspective, claims that the tourist consumes and finally destroys the environment. In any case, tourism turns out to be paradigmatic of consumerism, which rests on a 'dialectic of novelty and insatiability'.[37]

New tourist objects to gaze at are created with an astonishing speed. The number of recognized British tourist sites soared from 800 in 1960 to 2,300 in 1983.[38] There is a proliferation of museums, heritage trails, and theme parks. Everything can become a tourist destination, a country mansion as well as a derelict steel works, a shopping mall just as well as graveyards and sewage systems. Outside Britain a constant 'widening of the Pleasure Periphery' has occurred.[39] Today only very few parts of the world have not been opened up by the tourist industry. Cheap air fares have deprived geographical distance of its meaning and deterrent effect, as the staggering success of the Dominican Republic demonstrates. The whole world is becoming one giant tourist destination.

Apart from the constant widening of the supply, there is a considerable growth of demand as well. More and more people all over the globe go on holidays, and the number of holidays per person is also increasing, as second and third holidays are becoming commonplace. Tourism might turn out to be the ultimate consumer commodity because it is almost infinitely expandable as a product. Like consumerism tourism has an inherent growth dynamics and seems – despite glaring ecological problems – as yet far away from the point of saturation.

As today tourist attractions are constructed anywhere and around anything, critics complain about the inauthenticity of the experience. However, tourism from its earliest days strongly relied on the perception of destinations through a prism of culturally defined notions of meaning and significance. Besides, carefully arranged landscapes and man-made spectacles, often specially built for tourists, were core elements of the itinerary, from the late eighteenth-century artificial ruins in the Lake District[40] to the Eiffel tower or the Millennium Dome. A pier was a must for British seaside resorts which also built promenades, parks, aquaria, winter gardens and assembly rooms, towers as well as shops, hotels, pavilions and concert halls. Fairgrounds and amusement parks, skating rinks and illuminations were established parts of the tourist experience by 1900.

In the late twentieth century larger and enclosed ensembles of artificial attractions like holiday clubs and theme parks emerged. Disneyland, Sea World, Las Vegas, Centre Parks epitomize the tourist 'pseudo-reality' isolated from the environment. Obviously disgusted with 'a replica of an Elizabethan Inn' in Japan, Turner and Ash complain about a world in which there is 'no need for the real thing' anymore.[41] Yet, real and unreal, authentic and inauthentic are vague and normative terms which obscure the characteristics of these phenomena. It is useless to insist on clear distinctions in a world in which the borderlines between 'real' and virtual realities increasingly become blurred. Umberto Eco argued that in postmodernity the imitation seems more real than the real. Therefore, visiting such tourist artefacts are in his words 'Travels in Hyperreality'. 'Disneyland can permit itself to present its reconstructions as masterpieces of falsification' and teaches visitors 'to admire the perfection of the fake. [...] In this sense Disneyland not only produces illusion, but - in confessing it - stimulates the desire for it [...] Disneyland tells us that the faked nature corresponds much more to our daydream demands' and 'that technology can give us more reality than nature can.'[42] In simple words, the tourist industry has created new, synthetic products which are accepted by millions of visitors, who seem to be particularly delighted about the artificiality they encounter. Postmodernism even celebrates the ironic enjoyment of attractions which are known to be fabricated.

Tourism's diversity is the main reason for its untiring vitality at the beginning of the twenty-first century. Many other commodities have fallen victim to the product life cycle taking them from launch to maturity and mortal decline. In contrast to particular holiday destinations, tourism as a whole has escaped this fate mainly due to its adaptability. Because the tourist gaze is central and essentially a constructed experience, there is considerable scope for innovation. The history of tourism is a history of invention and constant reinvention, which keeps the frontiers of the 'pleasure periphery' in motion. Tourism has been flexible enough to survive major changes of key economic, social, cultural and political parameters. It successfully incorporated new life styles and fashions, shifting expectations and predilections, customers' whims and fancies. Tourism managed to legitimize itself by very different discourses varying from the medical to the ideological, from philanthropy to hedonism, from laissez-faire to welfare state rhetoric.

This high degree of flexibility is reflected in the interrelation between tourism and the media. Poets and painters were the first – in Urry's words – to 'construct and develop our gaze as tourists'.[43] Later on other professional experts joined these designers of images and metaphors. With the rise of the mass press in the nineteenth century, journals, newspapers and advertisements began to play a prominent role in constructing, sustaining and reinforcing tourists' expectations. In the twentieth century the cinema, radio, and television participated powerfully in organising the tourist gaze. Films sometimes redirect tourists' movement. The enormous success of Roger Vadim's movie *And God Created Woman,* which was set in Saint Tropez and 'heavily drew on the theme of living in paradise', played a major role in turning the serene village into the preferred meeting place of the jet set and those who wanted to be part of it.[44] Settings of novels, TV series and movies have become tourist attractions mainly because visitors hope to immerse themselves in the 'unique atmosphere' of the place.

As with other consumer items, media accentuated not the utility, the intrinsic quality of the product, but increasingly appealed to psychological and social needs. Consumerism rests on the process of encoding commodities with social meanings, on the imagination and values attached to them.[45] Tourism has been tied to many images from physical to moral health, from social reform to self-indulgence, from eternal youth to education. One of the greatest myths may be the romantic view of nature as a humanizing force. Similarly powerful was the belief that travelling as an act of conspicuous consumption guaranteed social distinction or that it reflected the possibility of upward social mobility. In reality, the distinctiveness of certain destinations proved to be a highly perishable commodity. Exclusive territory sooner or later was invaded by people striving for exclusivity and destroying it in the process. The quest for superior status triggered off a 'leapfrogging process' to new enclaves of exclusivity. Sociologists have categorized tourists experiences as 'positional goods' subject to 'relational consumption'. This means that satisfaction of each individual 'depends upon the position of one's own consumption to that of others.' Hence, there is a strong element of 'coerced competition' among tourist striving for social distinction.[46]

4. Tourism: A De-Individualizing Form of Consumption?

Enzensberger claims that the tourist industry produces uniformity as it works along assembly-line principles. Beyond doubt it has always heavily relied on economies of scale and scope, i.e. on the advantages of processing large quantities of related services and on generating synergies between them. Cook's revolutionary innovation hinged on combining transport, accommodation, catering, guidance and entertainment into one care-free product, buying these components in large contingents and selling them to groups of travellers. He lowered both unit costs and profit margins. High turnover and massive throughput became essentials. Therefore, group travellers had to be fitted into prearranged structures, to observe a strict timetable and to obey their guides. Naturally, they became easy targets for satire. They 'reminded me of a string of pet dogs going to be fed',[47] wrote a journalist who had been on one of Cook's Swiss trips in the 1860s. Another critic thought of 'convicts who could no longer be sent to Australia'.[48] *Punch* likened tourists to mental patients and mocked their predilection to consume ready-made experiences provided by tour operators like Cook or publishers of guidebooks like John Murray, whose books were famous for their red covers. 'Learns to like and to look / By his Guide or his Book / [...] With his own eyes once looked: / Now he likes his routes Cooked / His Opinion Red-booked, [...]'.[49]

Why was there so much of this derision despite a still relatively small number of tourists? Admittedly, the behaviour of group travellers was bizarre in many ways and needed some time to get accustomed to. More importantly, new patterns of consumption automatically raised questions of social hierarchy and evoked fears of losing one's status symbols and with them eventually one's social position. Cook's system met with so much disparagement because it encouraged people, in the words of Piers Brendon, 'to travel above their station'.[50] Attacks on social privileges provoked counterattacks on those aspiring to intrude into formerly exclusive territory and forcing upon their superiors 'coerced competition'. Emulation by one's inferiors puts pressure on the former holder of status symbols, as they have to find new ways of distinction. Criticizing tourism meant in fact fending off those who were perceived as parvenus or pretenders. After all, Victorian class society was obsessed with status barriers and was extremely sensitive to all questions of social demarcation. Consumption patterns served as core markers of class, and travelling for pleasure represented a very conspicuous form of consumption. For an upper-middle-class family the prospect of meeting their tailor outside his shop, let alone on holidays, amounted to a cataclysmic idea.

Enzensberger and others who rely on the judgements of nineteenth-century critics of tourism are rather naive to take propaganda from a war for contested social territory at its face value and fail to notice that such sources are full of condescension and snobbery. Despite frequent allegations Cook's travel schemes did not generally encourage collectivism and passivity. There is some evidence that being in a group lowered the threshold of security, and once people had gained some experience and confidence, they dared return on their own. According to Brendon, as early as 1865 over 95 per cent of those visiting Switzerland with a ticket issued by Cook travelled independently, though initially about two thirds had joined one of his parties. Cook's voucher system and the guidebooks were specially geared to individual travellers. It enabled them to benefit from economies of scale and scope and yet to draw up their own itinerary. Moreover, group travel did not automatically imply passivity. Members of Cook's parties prepared their journeys by reading about their destinations and learning foreign languages. They were notorious for inundating their guides with questions. Some of them kept diaries, which were occasionally enriched by quotes from romantic poets.[51]

Outside the package tour industry rambling, mountaineering, and cycling opened up chances for highly individualistic forms of tourism, although many people preferred to pursue them collectively in clubs and associations. The British seaside resorts were far from uniform. Instead they catered for very diverse needs and increasingly sought to specialize in various segments of the expanding market. Resorts offered a wide range of individual experiences. The boarding house was renowned and sometimes dreaded for its family atmosphere, in which the guests developed personal relationships to the owners and among themselves.

The main thrust towards mass travel and standardization occurred in the inter-war years of the twentieth century. The taylorization of the factory floor prompted the taylorization of leisure. The TUC had put the right of workers to paid holidays on the agenda in 1911 and kept on fighting for it after 1918. The International Labour Office, formed in 1919 as part of the League of Nations, was an influential promoter of holidays as universal entitlements. In fascist Italy the 'Opera Nazionale Dopolavoro' was formed in 1925 to modernize and rationalize people's leisure and grant holidays to the masses. In the 1930s, the French Popular Front government and the German KdF (Strength through Joy) adopted many elements of the Italian model and provided opportunities for low-cost tourism. In Britain, the 1938 Holiday-with-pay Act finally turned holidays into a politically guaranteed right of citizenship at a time when most major European nations introduced or substantially extended paid holidays. The 'state encouraged the development of mass tourism' and replaced 'a regime of privilege' by one of 'access'.[52] The full result of this political landmark decision became visible only after the war, but the late 1930s saw the rise of organized, highly standardized tourism for the lower middle and the working classes. The KdF resort Rügen with a giant five kilometre long hotel for 20,000 people symbolizes the ugly face of Fordist mass tourism.[53]

In Britain there was no giant public organisation for 'social tourism'. Voluntary, non-profit bodies like the Polytechnic Touring Association, the Co-operative Holidays Association, the Worker's Travel Organisation and a variety of regional and local societies were tiny by KdF standards, but added up to an extensive network. The large commercial holiday camps set up by Billy Butlin and others from 1937 onwards organised a collective, low-budget holiday which would have pleased KdF-functionaries in many ways. There were strict regulations and timetables, loudspeakers to wake up the 'campers' and send them to bed, uniformed supervisors, communal recital of slogans and songs as well as a strong emphasis on group activities and sports.[54]

The holiday camp permitted millions of low-income earners to spend their first holidays away from home. Nonetheless, the rise of collective mass tourism coincided with an increase in new and old forms of individual travel. Motorization, the diffusion of buses and motorcycles and – for the more affluent – cars and caravans, turned out to be a powerful force of destandardization. More dispersed accommodation became available. Hotels did not have to be near railway stations any more. Camping opened up cheap travel opportunities to low-budget individual travellers.

In the 1950s and 1960s, high rates of economic growth, rising real wages and shrinking work times, combined to fuel an unprecedented tourist boom. The opening up of cheap tourist destinations outside Britain and falling costs of air travel increased the numbers of Britons travelling abroad from 1.6 million in 1955 to 16 million in 1986.[55] In this process the standardized package played a key role.

No doubt, the artificial atmosphere of a cordoned-off hotel somewhere on the Mediterranean coastline fostered uniformity to some extent. Some people found it hard to remember whether they have been to Spain or Greece, as long as the beach was fine.

Tourism just like consumerism partly eradicates distinctiveness and creates standardized look-alike places. The difference between the McDonald's in Madrid and Budapest may be just as hard to tell as the one between hotels and beaches around the world. But this does not really signify total de-individualization and the disappearance of choice. The advanced consumer society does not only turn out uniform products but also creates ever growing opportunities for selection. Although commodities are standardized to exploit economies of scale, there is a huge and still swelling variety of goods on offer. Not the difference between Spain and Greece matters but the type of holiday that is spent there. Today tourists can choose among hundreds of different packages according to their preferences. The tourist industry has developed special products for different age and interest groups as it vigorously pursues product differentiation policies.

According to marketing historian Richard Tedlow we live in the age of market segmentation, in which companies divide their customers into subgroups defined by lifestyles as well as by demographic and social factors.[56] As the diversification of lifestyles progresses, the industry increasingly caters for more specialized and volatile tastes. Just as manufacturing industry switches from mass to flexible production, the tourist industry strives for more specialization, flexibilization, and customization. Thanks to more adaptable technology especially in information processing a symbiosis between mass production and individual requirements is emerging. Tourists, who are generally more experienced and better educated than ever, already demand more flexibility. Far from being 'one-dimensional', totally manipulated fools, they actively react to what is put forward to them and participate in product development. The industry meets this challenge by offering a widening range of different but in themselves highly standardized options.[57]

Equally important is the regularly forgotten fact that a considerable number of tourists have always avoided package tours altogether and made their own, highly idiosyncratic arrangements. Visiting friends and relatives may be archetypal for a personal, non-commercial type of holiday. The growth of car ownership in Great Britain from 2.2 to 13.6 million between 1950 and 1974 was accompanied by a rise in self-catering, independent holidays, which often are rather individualistic affairs. In 1979 nearly half of all holidays spent in Britain were self-catering.[58] Foreign tourist coming to Britain are enchanted by the survival of a very personal type of accommodation in the form of Bed and Breakfast. Cheap air and train fares have opened up a huge market for low-budget travel outside the package sector.

Thus, cultural pessimism about tourism as a levelling force producing homogeneous, inactive masses is ill-founded. Tourism has never been Fordist in the sense of delivering identical products to an 'undifferentiated clientele'.[59] Even the strongly regimented holiday camp or the simple, rigidly packaged tour allowed a certain degree of individuality and a dialectic process full of feed-backs and creative responses. Moreover, these highly standardised provisions have long passed the climax of their life-cycle. In retrospect they may turn out to have been a transitory stage in the development of tourism, which was needed to familiarize inexperienced people with tourism. In its long history, tourism has proved very adaptable and full of innovative power. Increasingly segmented markets, more demanding and volatile customers do not overtax the tourist industry's potential. On the contrary, it will react with more flexibility and a mind-boggling range of options. Tourism has always closely reflected the state of the consumer society. At the beginning of the twenty-first century it testifies not only to unprecedented affluence but also to a high level of diversity.

Notes

1 I would like to thank John Walton for valuable comments on an earlier draft. The usual disclaimer applies.

2 L. Turner and J. Ash, *The Golden Hordes: International Tourism and the Pleasure Periphery* (London: Constable, 1975), 15, 107, 111 and 292. See also A. Poon, *Tourism, Technology and Competitive Strategies* (Wallingford: C.A.B. International, 1993), 29-61.

3 H.M. Enzensberger, 'Eine Theorie des Tourismus', in id., *Einzelheiten* (Frankfurt/M.: Suhrkamp, 1962), 147-68; originally published as 'Vergebliche Brandung der Ferne: Eine Theorie des Tourismus', *Merkur* 12 (1958), 701-20 [my translation]. More examples are quoted in C. Rojek, *Ways of Escape: Modern Transformations in Leisure and Travel* (Basingstoke: Macmillan, 1993), 173-5.

4 M. Horkheimer and T.W. Adorno, *Dialektik der Aufklärung* (Frankfurt/M.: Fischer, 1971), 108-50.

5 J. Reulecke, 'Vom Privileg zum Menschenrecht: Die Anfänge des Urlaubs in Deutschland vor dem Ersten Weltkrieg', *Journal für Geschichte* 1 (1979), 28-32.

6 E.A. Wrigley, *Continuity, Chance and Change: The Character of the Industrial Revolution in England* (Cambridge: Cambridge University Press, 1988) and N.R.F. Crafts, *British Economic Growth during the Industrial Revolution* (Oxford: Clarendon Press, 1985). For a short summary, see D. Cannadine, 'The Present and the Past in the English Industrial Revolution 1880-1980', *Past & Present* 104 (1984), 131-72. P. Hudson, *The Industrial Revolution* (London: Edward Arnold, 1992), and others contradict the evolutionary concept and emphasize revolutionary changes at regional level, masked by the aggregate national statistics.

7 J. De Vries, 'The Industrial Revolution and the Industrious Revolution', *Journal of Economic History* 54 (1994), 249-70.

8 See the highly critical article by B. Fine and E. Leopold, 'Consumerism and the Industrial Revolution', *Social History* 15.2 (1990), 151-79.

9 C. Walsh, 'The Newness of the Department Store: A View from the Eighteenth Century', in G. Crossick and S. Jaumain (eds), *Cathedrals of Consumption: The European Department Store 1850-1939* (Aldershot: Ashgate, 1999), 47-71.

10 K. Herbers, 'Unterwegs zu heiligen Stätten – Pilgerfahrten', in H. Bausinger et. al. (eds), *Reisekultur: Von der Pilgerfahrt zum modernen Tourismus* (Munich: Beck, 1991), 23-31; J. Sumption, *Pilgrimage: An Image of Mediaeval Religion* (London: Faber, 1975), especially 168-210.

11 In Victorian England 're-creation' meant the improvement of body, mind and soul by socially approved leisure practices at home or on holidays. See P. Bailey, *Leisure Class in Victorian England: Rational Recreation and the Contest for Control, 1830-1885* (London: Routledge, 1978).

12 J. Black, *The British Abroad: The Grand Tour in the Eighteenth Century* (New York: St. Martin's Press, 1992); J. Towner, *An Historical Geography of Recreation and Tourism in the Western World 1540-1940* (Chichester: John Wiley, 1996), 96-138.

13 R.S. Neale, *Bath: A Social History 1680-1815; or, A Valley of Pleasure, yet a Sink of Iniquity* (London: Routledge, 1981); Towner, *Geography*, 53-95.

14 J.K. Walton, *The English Seaside Resort: A Social History*, 1750-1914 (Leicester: Leicester University Press, 1983); A. Corbin, *The Lure of the Sea: The Discovery of the Seaside in the Western World, 1750-1840* (Berkeley: University of California Press, 1994). Even in typical industrial towns, the factories never employed more than a minority of the adult male labour force, which explains the strength of the non-industrial heritage.

15 Walton, *English Seaside Resort*, 32f.

16 For Hasso Spode tourism resembles a gigantic time machine conveying the illusion of travelling into the past. H. Spode, '"Reif für die Insel": Prolegomena zu einer historischen Anthropologie des Tourismus', in C. Cantauw (ed.), *Arbeit, Freizeit, Reisen: Die feinen Unterschiede im Alltag*

(Munich: Waxmann, 1995), 112. Tourism, however, also celebrates novelty and looks to the future.

17 B. Fine and E. Leopold, *The World of Consumption* (London: Routledge, 1993), 3.

18 Quoted in M. Feifer, *Going Places* (London: Macmillan, 1985), 168-9.

19 J. Viard, quoted in E. Furlough, 'Making Mass Vacations: Tourism and Consumer Culture in France, 1930s to 1970s', *Comparative Studies in Society and History* 40 (1998), 247-86, here 262.

20 Defined as four or more days away from home; see J. Demetriadi, 'The Golden Years: English Seaside Resorts 1950-1974', in G. Shaw and A. Williams (eds), *The Rise and Fall of British Coastal Resorts: Cultural and Economic Perspectives* (London: Pinter, 1996), 49-75, here 58. J. Benson, *The Rise of Consumer Society in Britain, 1880-1980* (Harlow: Longman, 1994), 86, states that in 1979, 37 per cent of the UK's inhabitants did not go on holidays at all. Statistics relating to tourism are still notoriously soft.

21 J. Reulecke, 'Kommunikation durch Tourismus? Zur Geschichte des organisierten Reisens im 19. und 20. Jahrhundert', in H. Pohl (ed.), *Die Bedeutung der Kommunikation für Wirtschaft und Gesellschaft* (Stuttgart: Steiner, 1989), 358-78, here 377.

22 G. Crossick and S. Jaumain, 'The World of the Department Store: Distribution, Culture and Social Change', in eid. (eds), *Cathedrals of Consumption*, 1-45, here 29.

23 Quoted in Brendon, *Thomas Cook: 150 Years of Popular Tourism* (London: Secker and Warburg, 1991), 90.

24 Quoted in D. Engerman, 'Research Agenda for the History of Tourism: Towards an International Social History', *American Studies International* 32 (1994), 3-31, here 12.

25 D. Boorstin, 'From Traveller to Tourist: The Lost Art of Travel', in id., *The Image: A Guide to Pseudo-Events in America* (New York: Atheneum, 1971), 77-117 and J.A.R. Pimlott, *The Englishman's Holiday: A Social History* (Brighton: Harvester, 1976 [1947]), 239.

26 Brendon, *Cook*, 2 and 27.

27 Quoted in Pimlott, *Englishman's Holiday*, 239. To what extent the TUC's position was rhetorical is difficult to decide.

28 Furlough, 'Vacations', 284-5.

29 C. Ward and D. Hardy, *Good Night Campers! The History of the British Holiday Camp* (London: Mansell, 1990), 147.

30 N. Mosley, quoted in Ward and Hardy, *Campers*, 158.

31 J. Urry, *The Tourist Gaze: Leisure and Travel in Contemporary Societies* (London: Sage, 1990), 152. See also Rojek, *Ways of Escape*, 188 and 203.

32 P. Rivers, quoted in Turner and Ash, *Golden Hordes*, 197.

33 J. Brewer and R. Porter (eds), *Consumption and the World of Goods* (London: Routledge, 1993).

34 C. Campbell, 'The Sociology of Consumption', in D. Miller (ed.), *Acknowledging Consumption* (London: Routledge, 1995), 96-126, here 119.

35 E.J. Leed, *The Mind of the Traveller: From Gilgamesh to Global Tourism* (New York: Basic Books, 1991), 5-7.
36 Quoted by B. Cormack, *A History of Holidays 1812-1990* (London: Routledge, 1998), 34.
37 Urry, *Tourist Gaze*, 13.
38 Ibid., 5.
39 Turner and Ash, *Golden Hordes*, 124 and 12.
40 In an island near Derwentwater. See also N. Nicolson, *The Lakers: The Adventures of the First Tourists* (London: Robert Hale, 1955), 104-7.
41 Turner and Ash, *Golden Hordes*, 140-8.
42 U. Eco, *Travels in Hyperreality* (London: Picador, 1986), 43f.; Rojek, *Ways of Escape*, 179.
43 Urry, *Tourist Gaze*, 1.
44 Turner and Ash, *Golden Hordes*, 86. The film featured Brigitte Bardot as leading actress.
45 R. Marchand, *Advertising the American Dream: Making Way for Modernity, 1920-1940* (Berkeley: University of California Press, 1985) and C. Cambell, *The Romantic Ethic and the Spirit of Modern Consumerism* (Oxford: Blackwell, 1987), 77-95.
46 J. Urry, 'The "Consumption" of Tourism', *Sociology* 24 (1990), 23-35, here 29. See also Walton, *Seaside Resort*, 74-102 and 225.
47 Quoted in Brendon, *Cook*, 82-3.
48 Brendon, *Cook*, 89.
49 *Punch*, 9 September 1876, 100.
50 Quoted in Brendon, *Cook*, 90.
51 Brendon, *Cook*, 81-100.
52 Furlough, 'Vacations', 260 and 252. See also K. Maase, *Grenzenloses Vergnügen: Der Aufstieg der Massenkultur 1850-1970* (Frankfurt/M.: Fischer, 1997), 188-95; D.G. Liebscher, 'Organisierte Freizeit als Sozialpolitik: Die faschistische Opera Nazionale Dopolavoro und die NS-Gemeinschaft Kraft durch Freude 1925-1939', in J. Petersen and W. Schieder (eds), *Faschismus und Gesellschaft in Italien* (Cologne: SH-Verlag, 1998), 67-90.
53 H. Spode, 'Ein Seebad für zwanzigtausend Volksgenossen: Zur Grammatik und Geschichte des Fordistischen Urlaubs', in P.J. Brenner (ed.), *Reisekultur in Deutschland: Von der Weimarer Republik zum 'Dritten Reich'* (Tübingen: Niemeyer, 1997), 7-47.
54 Ward and Hardy, *Campers*.
55 Cormack, *History*, 109 and 112.
56 R.S. Tedlow, *New and Improved: The Story of Mass-Marketing in America* (New York: Basic Books, 1990).
57 Poon, *Tourism*, 9-23 and 73-83.
58 Demetriadi, 'Golden Years', 61-3 and Benson, *Rise*, 89.
59 Poon, *Tourism*, 32, exaggerates gravely the uniformity of what she calls 'old tourism'.

Sun, Sea, Sand and Self-Expression
Mass Tourism as an Individual Experience

Sue Wright

The contemporary history of tourism tends to be presented as an economic phenomenon, with an emphasis on the environmental and cultural damage which it has caused being set against the economic miracles that it has brought about. In particular, the concept of 'mass tourism' tends to connote a negative image of a standardized holiday experience, with visitors herded by tour operators to resorts (particularly on the Mediterranean coast) where the emphasis is on sun and beach rather than 'foreign culture':

> Innocents abroad, they go armed with the simple faith that they will enjoy themselves and feel better for it [...] Each summer they all pay a two-week homage to sun, sea, sand and sex. There are other motivations too - curiosity, adventurousness, the need for a rest, escape from squalor, keeping up with the Joneses - but it's the unholy quartet that attracts millions to the magic fringe.[1]

Here we have the 'four Ss' of mass tourism. The masses who choose the packaged holiday experience are, it is implied, the victims of a capitalist plot - to exploit both them and the people and places they visit.[2] That is, the need to take this kind of a foreign holiday has been falsely created by the tour operators, who, encouraged by foreign governments anxious to import foreign money, impose an alien culture upon the foreign hosts, who have to comply because of their individual dependence on the work that tourism creates. Thus the implications for the resorts are also viewed as negative, with the main criticisms being that they are spoilt by the commercialization, and that the host culture is undermined because of meeting the demands of the visitors.[3] An extreme summary of this is taken from the same text:

> Local dances, music, costumes, dishes die, to be replaced by those of the tourist, while local customs soon degenerate into tourist entertainment [...] it is not worth losing a cultural heritage for a transistor radio.[4]

Little attention is given to the ways in which the host culture might have changed without tourism (especially in the light of globalization), or to the hardships and poverty that went alongside the 'host culture'. This paper will challenge critiques of this kind, by uncovering the individual experiences of these so-called mass tourists and by showing some of the ways in which the relationships between hosts and visitors were both positive and negotiated. More recent work by sociologists and anthropologists of tourism is showing that tourism needs to be studied as a social process if we are to understand the complexities of both its nature and impact.[5] Through work such as this, attention is being drawn to the ways in which tourism has affected the lives of its participants: both the holiday makers and the holiday providers. Beginning with a brief history of post-war package tourism, this paper will then deconstruct the mass tourism critique, as it has been applied to package tourism. It will also challenge the 'trickle down' model of consumption, which assumes that changing consumption patterns are as a result of social emulation. The paper will then go on to reassess package tourism, looking at the experiences of package tourists, and, by concentrating on the meaning that these experiences represented, will argue that package tourism does have a cultural value.

1. Post-War Package Tourism

The air-inclusive package holiday tends to be presented as having begun in 1950, when Horizon Holidays first chartered a flight to offer an inclusive 'package' to Corsica.[6] However, if we define a package holiday as one whereby the whole holiday is bought, as a package from one source, regardless of the means of transport, then the package holiday began well before this. Thomas Cook offered package holidays from the 1860s: 'by ensuring that "even delicate persons may, with tolerable ease, reach Geneva", he turned what had once been an adventure into an institution.'[7] However, because Horizon chartered the flight, rather than using scheduled services, they provide the starting point for this study - because it is the package holiday in this form that is usually dismissed as mass tourism.

Foreign package holidays came within the reach of ever increasing numbers after the war. Increased real wages and paid holidays, alongside rationing, meant that more people had more money for holidays (and leisure generally) than ever before - initially without too much in the way of alternative consumer goods to distract them.[8] Add to this surplus aircraft, trained pilots and access to the airfields that were also a product of World War II, and you have the makings of a new industry. An important consequence of the Horizon innovation was that the cost of foreign travel was reduced and therefore made available to a much larger market than before, although there was a range of other factors involved. Prices fell because once companies chartered flights they could undercut the fixed prices of the scheduled airlines.[9] The companies could then link this in with pre-booked accommodation at the destination, and so use the power of block bookings to reduce prices even further. As the popularity of foreign holidays grew, the tour operators encouraged further development by direct investment in resort facilities (for example, hotels), which guaranteed their share of the rapidly expanding market.[10] However, this did not happen overnight, and the above summary has moved the development of the package holiday well into the 1960s. The economies of scale that the tour operators achieved were initially made all the more significant because of the currency controls that were in existence. From the end of the war, until the later 1970s, there was a limit on the amount of sterling that individuals were allowed to take out of the country.[11] It is perhaps ironic that in its attempts to keep sterling in the country the government gave impetus to something that would enable even greater numbers of people to spend their holidays (and pounds) abroad. Serious problems with the economy from the late 1960s to the mid-1970s threatened the industry and revealed major flaws in its organization and structure. Very briefly, the problems were connected to inflation, which was partly due to wages rising faster than productivity, pushing up retail prices; and partly due to balance of payment deficits, which resulted in the devaluation of sterling and therefore higher import prices - both of which led to increased wage demands and industrial action as governments tried to control the spiral through a series of income policies in the form of wage restraints. This was compounded by the Arab-Israeli conflict, and the subsequent oil embargo - which saw imports cut by 15 per cent and the price quadruple towards the end of 1973. The oil shortage combined with industrial action by the miners pushed the uncompromising Heath government towards drastic measures – which included a three-day working week, which lasted just over two months, from January to March 1974. The value of the pound continued to fall throughout this period.[12] All of these issues affected package tourism, and 1974 is usually seen as the crisis year for the industry. This culminated in the collapse of Court Line (the group who owned Clarksons and Horizon, two of the UK's largest operators) on August 15th:

> The collapse of Court Line has meant the whole travel industry taking a long hard look at itself. The problems that brought Court Line to bankruptcy were many – over-ambitious expansion plans [...] inadequate financial control [...] rising fuel costs and, particularly important, the generally depressed economic situation which led to falling markets, all account for it. But the main factor [...] was the cost of a package holiday.[13]

This final factor was also related to the economic climate, in that the price war which had been taking place since the mid-1960s between several of the top operators had been waged on assumptions of increased growth. Profit margins were tiny, and greatly dependent on occupancy levels of at least 90 per cent.[14] Bookings had fallen in 1973, but in 1974 they were down by 20 per cent – despite some operators having commitments which were based on increased sales.[15] Prior to the Court Line crash, a whole series of smaller operators had already collapsed. The outcome for those who survived the crisis was greater attention being paid to consumer confidence and protection, an acceptance of more realistic pricing policies, and relative reductions in capacity. For example, Thomson Travel (who had been Clarksons main rival in the price war) announced a price increase of 15 per cent in their 1975 brochures and no increase in capacity, despite the obvious gap left by the bankrupt operators.[16]

The way in which the industry survived these crises shows the way in which expectations had changed, because – although numbers did fall off during these years – the drop was less than anticipated, and bookings began to increase again in 1975.[17] Once tried and approved, the package holiday tended to become the norm (especially for young people and married couples without children – at both ends of the age range). Deregulation in the 1980s (particularly the abolition of the stabilizer) led to further expansion (by which time jet aircraft had dramatically increased capacity). Key areas of growth during this decade were in sales of winter holidays (although this trend had started in the 1970s); there was also a substantial shift towards the self-catering package and the more specifically designed family package (free child places and dedicated children's representatives in the resorts being two of the key innovations, along with the 'freedom' of self-catering). Arguably, the growth of the family package saw the package holiday 'come of age', as participants were less likely to revert to domestic holidays after having children. This was also the decade that saw the package holiday formula applied to far-flung destinations, although the focus of this paper will be on the European package. It is apparent from even this brief summary that the growth of the industry reflects a process of interaction between consumers and suppliers and this argument is further supported by considering the very diverse range of packages on offer at a given time, and the way that these have changed over time. This enormous range of choice also convincingly challenges the way in which package and mass tourism are usually dismissed as the same thing.

2. The Diverse Nature of Package Tourism: Mallorca in the 1960s and 1970s

The diversity of packages can be illustrated by looking at the way three tour operators, Thomas Cook, Cosmos and Pontinental, presented their packages to Mallorca in the 1960s and 1970s. Of the three, Cook's gave much more detailed descriptions of the individual resorts, and made more of features other than the beach. This suggests that Cook's clients expected more from their holiday. This is supported by the way in which the island's capital was described: by 1968, Cook's still offered seven hotels in Palma (this number had gradually dropped through the 1950s and 60s as resorts had developed around the coast). Palma was described as a cosmopolitan and lively place:

> All kinds of people gather in Palma, locals for business and holiday makers for entertainment. It's a gay town where there's so much you can do and see. There are historic buildings as well as many little shops and gay cafes for music and dancing. But these are comparatively simple pleasures. After a lazy day on nearby beaches or sightseeing in the island's interior, Palma's nightlife is as lively as anyone could wish. It has nightclubs, cinemas and dancing displays in the traditional Majorcan manner [...].[18]

Consider now, the Cosmos description of Palma:

> Palma de Mallorca, the modern and attractive capital, offers every kind of entertainment to the visitor, but has no bathing beach. Cosmos holidays are therefore arranged at resorts near to the capital for those who like visiting the city during their holidays, and in smaller resorts on beautiful beaches for those whose principal requirement is to lie in the sun and who wish for no reminders of the bustle of life at home.[19]

Cosmos were making some sort of distinction among their own clients, showing (especially when compared with the differences between them and Cook's) that there were layers of gradations. Nevertheless, Cosmos presented the beach as the primary criterion for choice. The differences between types of package can be extended even further if we consider another company which started to package continental holidays from 1963: Pontins. In his autobiographical account, Fred Pontin described how his attempts to promote Pontinental as 'Blackpool with the sun' did 'not really catch on'.[20] This implies that, despite 'most of [his] overseas visitors [being] Pontin's clients of very long standing', they wanted more than just the sun to tempt them abroad.[21] Cala Mesquida, the first Pontinental development on Mallorca, opened in 1964:

> This was formerly a camping site, operated and mainly frequented by Germans. Before I transformed it by adding 142 brick-built double chalets, shower block, dining room, kitchen and bar it was totally lacking any modern facilities and services. The approach road was nothing but a rough track, but it was the lovely bay, clear blue water and wide beach which always captivated the new arrivals.[22]

The holiday camp experience was much closer to the ideal 'Fordist' mode of consumption than the packages of the other companies discussed here.[23] Consider the description from the 1975 *Honest Guide*:

> Cala Mesquida is set on a beautiful remote bay with dunes stretching back towards barren hills. It is mainly occupied by a holiday village, which supplies ample facilities and amusements. It needs to, for it is isolated and difficult to get away once there.[24]

The 1976 Pontinental brochure does not seem to challenge this description: Cala Mesquida was presented as 'the most British' of the camps on the island, where visitors (or 'friends' as they are addressed) could be sure of 'hot sun, sea breeze, golden sands, comfortable chalets, homely food [...] an atmosphere of good fellowship, humour and romance'.[25] The camp was presented as a self-contained holiday village, and there was little mention of the island's culture. There is no mention of car hire, or even of organized excursions: the holiday presented does not suggest that visitors would want to leave the campsite. Cook's clients had been offered the option of car-hire since 1960: 'Think of the freedom [...] you can go where you like, when you like.'[26] Thus there was the opportunity for independent travel as part of the package. There was no mention of car-hire in the 1968 Cosmos brochure, where little was made of optional visits or nearby places of interest. Cala Mesquida differed massively from the holidays offered by the Cook's and Cosmos and therefore challenges the linking of mass tourism and package holidays. This brief survey shows that there were just too many different packages for them to be lumped together.

The argument is strengthened further because of the way that the Pontinental packages changed over time. By 1976, the Pontinental programme included three camps on Mallorca. The two other clubs were described as having 'a more cosmopolitan atmosphere than, say, Cala Mesquida':

> Guests can enjoy life with foreign people in a foreign land. It's adventurous, exciting, different and meant for the young at heart and families who are not too conventional in outlook [...]. If you only like English habits, bingo, and chips with everything, Holiday Club may not be for you.[27]

A key difference was that the food was more 'exotic'. However, the newer clubs were placed in the context of the island. Potential clients were given information about bus services, and the 'ample opportunities to join interesting excursions to other parts of Majorca'.[28] The clubs represent yet another package holiday experience: bearing some resemblance to the Cosmos and Cook's experiences; but with some of the features of the older-style Pontinental camps. The Pontinental experience gradually became more exotic: the 1979 brochure made much more of opportunities to sample the culture of the places visited; car hire is offered by 1983. This supports Urry's description of the way that holiday camps tried to change their image in response to the post-Fordist mode of consumption; it also makes the stereotypical package holidaymaker even more difficult to find.[29]

3. 'Romantic' versus 'Collective' Tourist Gaze

John Urry has identified different forms of the tourist gaze.[30] The 'romantic' form emphasizes 'solitude privacy and a personal semi-spiritual relationship with the object of the gaze'.[31] This gaze is focussed on the scenic: mountains, gorges, torrents; any unspoilt and awesome natural grandeur can become the object of this gaze. Romantic because of its associations with poets and artists, it will become apparent that the gaze in this form is the one which dominates the critique of mass tourism, although its origins can be traced back much further. However, as Urry points out, some places are defined by their visitors: 'It is in part other people who make such places. The collective gaze thus necessitates the presence of large numbers of other people [...]. They indicate that this is *the* place to be and that one should not be elsewhere.'[32]

Urry suggests that other characteristics of the collective gaze include 'gazing at the familiar' and 'a series of shared encounters'.[33] Thus, the 'ideal' form of the collective gaze would seem to fit closely with the package tourism critique, which assumes that participants take comfort from the familiar and demand the safety of group activities. This is a useful starting point in making sense of the conventional distinction between travellers and tourists – and especially if we accept Urry's comment that 'those who value solitude and a romantic tourist gaze do not see this as merely *one* way of regarding nature. They consider it as "authentic", as real. And they attempt to make everyone else sacralise nature in the same way'.[34]

Acceptance of the collective gaze as an equally valid form of gaze is a crucial aspect of this study, because of the way that it supports the counter-hegemonic argument being presented. It is also a reminder of the way that popular leisure (outside the home) has usually tended to require the presence of other people – often in large numbers. When set against the way that 'whole towns went on holiday' to English seaside resorts, the package holiday actually shows a move to independence.[35] That is, that although the presence of other people still mattered, they were relative strangers compared to the 'other people' of the late nineteenth and earlier twentieth century holidays. It is here as well that the 'trickle down' model of consumption can best be challenged. It is perhaps inevitable that people will travel down paths first taken by social superiors, because if their expectations include a sociable experience, which is shared with other holiday makers, then this will influence where they choose to visit. Historically, the rich and leisured class, who had the time and money to travel abroad, initiated a process of change (provision of services and transport networks) that gradually opened up ever more sites to the tourist gaze. As the numbers of people who could afford to travel increased, so did the provision of services. That the 'masses' *chose* to follow these paths when they had the time and money does not necessarily mean that they were motivated by social emulation. That they then spent their time in different ways suggests that the later ('mass') tourists were motivated by a very different set of expectations, and that these played a big part in the development of package tourism. Thus time and money plays the larger part in changing trends, not social emulation.[36]

4. Benidorm

Drawing on the work of Walter, Urry points out that it is those who seek the romantic gaze who are 'part of the mechanism by which tourism is spreading on a global scale and drawing almost every country into its ambit, thereby providing uniformity, minimising diversity, and encouraging the 'romantic' to seek ever new objects of the romantic gaze'.[37] The development of Benidorm (one example of a place which has been used to epitomize the negative aspects of 'mass tourism') would appear to support this model. A 1956 travel guide, which described itself as 'the ideal book for the traveller in France and Spain who wants to see the real life of those countries as opposed to the synthetic, highly commercialized existence of the popular tourist centres', is a good example.[38] The book signposted resorts such as Benidorm seemingly without recognition that it must contribute to increased visitor numbers - when this is apparently what its readers wanted to avoid. The section on Benidorm, 'that lovely blue and white fishing village clustered around its little rock', advised readers that

> servants and nursemaids are quite easy to obtain, but in the high season are more difficult. They can, however, be found in the neighbouring towns. And *if* you are fond of Spanish music a circle of young men may be persuaded to come some evenings to

> your veranda, *as friends,* and sing delightful Spanish songs to their guitars.[39]

This extract illustrates two important points. Firstly, Benidorm is presented as an authentic village, unspoilt by tourism - yet clearly the availability of servants and singers shows that visitors were already changing the local economy by demanding such services and that the providers of these services were being drawn from outside. Secondly, the author also described the availability of accommodation, and gives details of three hotels being built as he wrote. Thus Benidorm was already on the tourist map - and this guide, despite its introduction, was a further signpost. The increased popularity can in part be explained by books such as this, which is clearly appealing to the pretensions of 'travellers', yet the description shows that the place already exhibited many of the features of 'mass tourism'. This example can be used to challenge Williams who wrote: 'places such as Benidorm [...] are virtually the creation of the ITCs.'[40] What Williams ignored when he made this statement was the role of the Spaniards themselves. Charles Wilson's very detailed history of Benidorm suggests that the most dramatic changes took place between 1956 and 1966, and comments on the role of the Mayor, Pedro Zaragoza Orts, who 'instigated many of the changes'.[41] He describes Orts as 'a man with enormous foresight and imagination', and draws on a range of newspaper articles and interviews to show the extent of local support that he had over the period of change and beyond.[42] This suggests that the changes were negotiated, and that they were generally seen as positive by the 'local' population. By 1966, 'the damage' had been done:

> *Benidorm* (pop. 6,500) is the phenomenon of the Costa Blanca. In the last few years it has developed from a small, *unknown,* fishing town into one of the major holiday resorts of the western Mediterranean. Its fortune is its three-mile long sandy beach [...]. Along it are hotels, apartments villas, cafes, nightclubs. All the development is spacious and orderly. Expansion is planned to continue at the rate of fifteen per cent per year [...]. The original village stands on a slight hill overlooking the new town. It is today a shopping centre [... it] has been occupied for many centuries [...].[43]

This later description of Benidorm is from a cheap (five shillings) guide. This implies the guide was being sold to the popular market, especially since it contains information about sites of 'mass tourism'. Whilst the book gives some advice to independent travellers, it seems more directed at package holiday makers - since it gives limited details of any accommodation, route or transport. It therefore seems fair to use it to challenge several assumptions about the nature (and evolution) of mass tourism: firstly, that the development is random. Whilst it might not be to everybody's taste, the planned nature of Benidorm's expansion is still mentioned in books written much later than this one. Secondly, that it destroys the nature of places, whereas here we have the old alongside the new (albeit as a shopping centre): even the 1994 *Rough Guide to Spain* says 'the old part's still there, but so overshadowed by the miles of towering concrete that you'd be hard-pressed to find it'.[44] Thirdly, that the above description was followed by a detailed account of places of local interest and local fiestas shows that local cultural heritage remained - and presumably acted as a tourist attraction, implying interaction with the host culture. Wilson supports this, and shows how Benidorm used its fiestas as part of its publicity campaigns of the late 1950s and 60s.[45] Fourthly, the history of Benidorm indicates that readers might want to know the background to the en-masse beach experience. Finally, the listing of places of interest and information on how to reach them indicates that the readers wanted to do more with their holiday than eat, drink and sunbathe. The cheap guide also contained a detailed section on the types of food which visitors might expect: again, the implication being that people were not expecting 'chips with everything'.[46] If people were buying a standardized brochure package, why would guides such as this have been written for the popular market? It is time now to examine the experiences of some package holiday makers, in an attempt to show how these challenge the stereotypes of mass tourism.

5. Individual Experiences and Meanings of Package Tourism

This section will draw on letters from, and interviews with, package tourists. These were generated through letters sent to a range of local newspapers, which briefly outlined the project and asked people to write about package holidays. The replies were followed up with questionnaires asking for more information about the nature of the holidays, and also for more abstract details such as the impression that the holiday had made on the participants and also the reactions of family and friends. The questions were tailored according to how much information was in the original letter, but aimed to build up a standardized 'data base'. This information was then used to establish an interview 'short-list'. Even where there was no follow-up interview, the letters and questionnaires have still been drawn upon. The material generated challenges the stereotypes of mass tourism.[47]

5.1 Local Culture

A common criticism is that the package tourist demands home comforts, and ignores or destroys 'local culture' in this quest. This has already been challenged, because of the way in which guidebooks are produced for the popular market – the existence of this market implies that holiday makers want to move beyond the boundaries of their package. One man wrote that he liked to use some of the local language when on holiday, which he described as 'good fun'. He 'always used guide books [...], mainly pocket Berlitz [which] give you the do's and don'ts.'[48] The evidence overwhelmingly supports the idea that package tourists are motivated by the search for otherness, at some level. A 1954 visitor to Spain wrote of the resort as follows:

> Tossa-de-Mar was *in those days* a delightful unspoilt village and tourists were not commonplace [...], *no high-rise, of course*. The people were far from affluent but everyone was friendly and pleasant. The church in Tossa relayed music in the evenings which filled the village and was very atmospheric [... in the evenings] we visited local bars and there was a lot of flamenco dancing and singing and playing of guitars [...], we *loved* the nightlife, the music and the dancing [...]. The food was [...] certainly very different [...]. One of our earliest meals in Tossa was paella, which arrived with a chicken's foot on top! [...] We enjoyed the food.[49]

This extract shows how the writer's memory of the holiday was based on difference: on one level the cultural 'other' that the holiday represented at the time it was taken; but also the 'other' that she imagined it represented to a present day Tossa-de-Mar. The suggestion is that her memories have been constructed through the mass tourism discourse, which is supported by her further comment that: 'We have never been back [...] but believe now it has been ruined, with lots of high-rise hotels and too many package holiday visitors, and so has lost its true Spanish atmosphere which we found so delightful in 1954.'[50]

This suggestion is further reinforced if we compare these comments with those of a 1958 visitor, who gave a rather different description of Tossa:

> The resort [...] was quite small, very lively and cosmopolitan to us. There were young people of many nationalities. There was a buzz and fression [*sic*] of excitement about the place, especially at night [...], we could come and go at all times and do what we liked. English resorts seemed very staid by comparison.[51]

By comparing the two descriptions it is possible to identify the romantic and collective forms of tourist gaze mentioned in section three. A comparison of the two accounts indicates that little had changed in the four years between the visits and that the differences were in how the two holidays were experienced and remembered. What particularly supports the suggestion that memories are constructed through the mass tourism discourse is that the second woman had returned to Tossa (for the first time) in 1998, and said that she was

> *glad* to see that it has retained its original character [...], the general structure and layout of the town was very similar to how I remembered it. There were no outstanding changes like *high-rise* developments. The original streets were the same [although] the town was more commercialised and cleaner [and] the streets and buildings have been upgraded.[52]

Her use of the word 'glad' implies that she had expected to see it changed, and indicates that her expectations were influenced by the mass tourism critique, in much the same way as the woman who had not returned. The 1954 visitor spoke in some depth about the food offered, and how much they enjoyed it. This again challenges the stereotypes, because most of the people that have spoken to me also confirm this. For example, a visitor to Ibiza in 1963 told me: 'I was a really faddy eater, but on holiday I tried everything. Fish that was not battered and had a head and tail on was a real shock.'[53] A visitor to Palma Nova, Mallorca, in 1971, complained about the food saying that there were 'lots of 'English and German establishments selling "food just like at home", and that the alternatives were 'mainly international food - little proper Spanish food'.[54] Again, this challenges the stereotype - because although the changes made in the resort must have been influenced by demand, it also shows that these changes did not suit everybody. Most people agreed that foreign holidays have influenced our own culture, partly because of the ways that they have encouraged people to experiment with a wider range of food and drinks. Package holiday makers suggest that their experiences have also influenced attitudes to licensing hours and to children, a general relaxation around meals and mealtimes and home décor and furnishings. The following extract illustrates the way in which tastes changed:

> we seemed to get a lot of spaghetti, which we thought was wonderful because, you see, in those days there weren't pizzerias here like there are now [...]. One thing I remembered, when we came home, coffee wasn't drunk here like it is now, and we used to buy this cappuccino coffee, you know, the frothy coffee, and [...] we found this place in Manchester that did cappuccino coffee, and I mean you wouldn't have any problem now, but we couldn't find it anywhere, and eventually we found this cafe in Manchester that did this cappuccino coffee like they did in Rimini.[55]

The way in which the interviewee distinguished between 'England then' and 'England now' is very telling. She did this to emphasize the otherness of the holiday, aware that the things she described are now relatively commonplace. Their pleasure at finding the cappuccino in Manchester was two-fold: firstly because they liked it; secondly because it reminded them of the holiday. Whilst the socio-cultural changes mentioned here need to be seen in a wider context of globalization, it seems fair to suggest that post-war travel opportunities have played a significant part in this spread of ideas and culture - and also in the construction of local identities, which it has been argued elsewhere is an intrinsic part of the globalization process.[56]

5.2 Differentiation and Meaning

As well as the assumption of undifferentiated experience, the stereotype also assumes that from its inception in the 1950s the package holiday has not changed at all, that it remained in the 1990s as it was in the 1950s. The study of brochures in section two showed the diversity of packages available at a given time and how these changed over time. It is fairly obvious that as time and money made a foreign holiday an option for an increasingly large market, some aspects of the holiday would inevitably have had to be standardized to enable the physical movement of so many people. However, it is interesting to note that even these elements of the holiday had different meanings to different participants, as the following extract shows:

> The purpose built hotels in the holiday resorts always had private bathrooms, and swimming pools. This, compared with English seaside hotels was real luxury. And the hot sunshine was also something England couldn't compete with [...]. For young people holidays abroad were suddenly affordable and good fun, and as the resorts developed there were more bars, clubs, etc. and it was a good way to spend a fortnight.[57]

The point being made is that even the most criticized aspects of package tourism represented 'otherness' to the consumers. Harry Ritchie, writing of the package holidays of his 1960s childhood, supports this:

> [planes] whisked you to places that greeted you with an unbelievable heat, places where you could swim all day and learn all about new foodstuffs like peaches, places where you could stare up at the night sky and realise that the Milky Way meant something more than a bar you could eat between meals, then fall asleep under a single sheet that felt like eight blankets, to wake up and step onto your balcony (a balcony!) and start another day in paradise.[58]

Ritchie raises some important points here, and the extract especially draws attention to the emphasis on individual meaning, which this paper argues for. Package holidays may, to an outsider, seem standardized, but to their participants they held a variety of meanings. For example, a married couple who had first gone on a package to Spain in the mid-1960s, with two very young children, gave the following reason for their decision:

> Well, the weather to be honest, we'd been to North Wales the year before, and it rained and it blew a gale and we'd literally to hold the child down and we'd paid a lot of money at a nice hotel and it was a beautiful beach and it really was [...], we spent a lot of time

> in the car travelling round and Carolyn didn't like that, it's not a child's sort of thing but you had to do something because it wasn't beach weather.[59]

Here we can see how their existing expectations of a holiday influenced their decision to take the package holiday. They had a clearly constructed notion of what a family holiday should be like, and this included the beach. But, this was not a uniquely British activity, nor was it unique to the lower classes - as demonstrated by the fact that this family is best described as middle class. Yet, it is the supposed emphasis on the beach (sun, sea and sand), which is most frequently cited in the mass tourism critique.

5.3 Perceptions of Danger

The stereotype also tends to present package tourists as being in need of reassurance, and that the tour operators provide this by creating a 'tourist bubble', which ensures the safety of their clients.[60] The 1976 Pontinental brochure introduced Cala Mesquida to potential holiday makers with the following reassurance: 'You will feel secure here because we control and manage the hotels or holiday villages at which you stay [and ...] the chefs are trained to allow for British tastes.'[61]

That such reassurance was thought to be needed in 1976, when the Pontinental package was thirteen years of age, indicates that there were still people who were daunted by the idea of a foreign holiday. This market was explicitly targeted by the brochure, when it stated that the holidays were 'made to measure for first-timers abroad'.[62] It should be noted that given the isolated nature of the camp site, and its recent history as a camp for foreign holiday makers, it would be very difficult to make a case that such an 'English' holiday experience was in any way damaging the host culture - it seems likely that the site had never had any culture except as a 'resort'. The way in which the Pontinental packages changed suggests that there was a developing 'sophistication' among more seasoned package holiday makers. It seems fair to suggest that there was a gradual confidence building process, as regards foreign travel, over the period studied. A recent newspaper report supports this:

> A new survey shows that, for the first time since mass tourism began in the Sixties, more Brits are now organising their own

> breaks than taking the packages offered by tour companies [...]. Independent travel is no longer associated only with back-packing and far off destinations [...]. Top of the free-thinking traveller's list of destinations is France, followed by Spain.[63]

However, given that Fred Pontin acknowledged the failure of his attempts to promote Pontinental as 'Blackpool with the sun', it could perhaps be argued that they changed because there was not enough demand for such a 'safe' experience.[64] One woman, speaking of a school trip to Switzerland in 1952 said, 'looking back I'm surprised that my parents let me go [...] abroad because my parents weren't travelling people'.[65] In 1957, aged 21, she went to Italy with a friend, and remembers that her parents' reaction was: 'Cagey, very cagey, two girls on their own going to Italy. But it seemed to be quite an organized thing that we went with, and my cousin had been and said it was all right, so they said I could go.'[66]

Here then it was not the package holiday makers themselves who needed the reassurance, but those left behind. This is borne out from other comments, where it was the attitudes of others that tended to reflect a fear of foreign travel. One woman remembered how her grandfather 'looked at me sorrowfully before we embarked on our adventure and [said] why don't you go to Skegness instead'; she also remembered an elderly neighbour who said in awe, 'you've been all that way and are safely home again'.[67] Word of mouth also helped to encourage others to take holidays, as well as to reassure those left behind. The next extract illustrates this:

> We were the first out of the people we knew [...] that had done anything like that. It was quite a brave thing to do. *What were the responses of friends and neighbours?* [...] They were quite interested and quite surprised and when we came back they asked us how we'd managed, and how the children were, and the people over the road, in fact, went. I don't think it was quite the next year but we'd obviously set the seed for them and they did go. We were like pioneers, pathfinders![68]

This was referring to a 1965 package holiday to Lloret-de-Mar. The couple can best be described as middle class when they took their holiday (he was a brewery manager, she was a housewife; they had two children). It was their first holiday abroad. This example suggests that package tourism was a far from universal experience, if the middle class still contained pockets such as this. The various reactions described all suggest that this form of tourism was not considered the safe experience that the critics assume, again showing how individual meanings differ from the stereotypes. Two women who went on a package to a holiday camp in the South of France in 1958 (as part of a group of five young women in their early twenties) said how they

> didn't think of it like a package holiday [...]. It was an adventure really [...]. I don't remember them doing what they do now, where you have a meeting on the first morning and they tell you what excursions there are. There was nothing like that. I don't think there was a rep half the time. I can remember going off, we went off and did different things, a lot of them we did on our own.[69]

Here again, there is recognition of the stereotypes of mass tourism, and the memories being constructed in opposition to them. Again this is done by comparing 'then' to now': with 'then' being an adventure compared to the better organized 'now'. However, this extract also brings us to the strongest theme to emerge from the research, which is that people used package holidays for their own purposes. Whilst it has been argued that the meaning which individuals placed on packaged experiences challenges their being dismissed as mass tourism, the ways in which people moved beyond the boundaries of the package supports the argument that this form of tourism tended to represent the cheapest means to an end (that is, to be abroad) but once that was achieved the actors took control of their holiday, and created their own individual experience. Let us now examine some of the examples of this.

5.4 The Package as Springboard

Staying with the same interview, the women described the camp as follows:

> It was a kind of a very open-air Butlins [...], the chalets were extremely basic, where we had the meals at night there was a sunroof on top, and they had dancing [...] and they were playing Victor Sylvester and we thought "no way"! So we went off exploring and there was a little beach cafe called Miami La Plage. It

> was right on the seashore and you could hear the water lapping around us and all these little fairy lights it was really romantic. It was just records, but the local people went there not just the British [...], we thought it was fantastic, brilliant.[70]

Clearly the model for the holiday camp was based on something which is often seen as the purest form of mass tourism. However, the way in which the women reacted to the entertainment shows that this was not what they were expecting of a holiday, nor did they feel restricted by it. This set the pattern for future holidays. Although they have since married and no longer holiday together, one of the women said that she and her husband tend to use public transport to get around: 'it is far cheaper than the coach tours offered by [the] travel companies. We also prefer the freedom to do our own thing.'[71] They use guidebooks to help plan this, usually before starting their holiday. Speaking of her stay at Palma Nova, Mallorca in 1971, she said: 'You needed to get out of the resort to see something of the country.'[72] This example supports the suggestion that people used the package as a springboard to independent activity, and that although there was recognition of resorts developing to match perceived demands of tourists, such initiatives were not always welcomed. This method of selecting to take parts of the package, whilst rejecting others in favour of a more independent experience was common to all of the people that I interviewed or received letters from. Whilst the tour operators may still, to an extent, provide the agenda, by signposting the sites of tourism, many prefer to visit the sites independently. This is supplemented by the use of guidebooks and probably other media representations such as travel programmes, newspaper supplements, magazines and films. Word of mouth also played a part, as another interviewee commented: 'people say before you go "you must do this, you must do that"'.[73]

6. Conclusion

This paper has shown that to dismiss package tourism as mass tourism is to ignore the multiplicity of experiences and meanings that package tourism represents to its participants. The huge extension of leisure time since the Second World War, and the corresponding increase in real wages were essential preconditions for the rapid development of package tourism, although it has been argued here that a desire for some level of otherness was also an important factor in people's motivation. Given the expansion, it could be argued that there is not the space for vast numbers of people to have a totally independent travel experience. However, to many people, a holiday involves other people. It is a social experience, far removed from the romantic solitude which critics of the package holiday seem to crave. Trickle-down theories have also been challenged because they do not take into account the interactive nature of the relationship between 'elite', 'host' and 'mass' cultures. Thus, as the elite 'discovered' an exclusive destination, so the hosts were made aware of its potential as a tourist attraction and so it was developed to cater for larger numbers of visitors – to the exasperation of the seekers of the 'authentic', who seem unaware that what the resort becomes is, to at least some of the hosts and visitors, still authentic.

Notes

1 P. Rivers, *The Restless Generation* (London: Davis Poynter, 1972), 151.
2 Ibid., especially chapter 9, 'The Crowded Sky'.
3 From many examples see A.M. Williams, 'Mass Tourism and the International Tour Companies', or R.J. Buswell, 'Tourism in the Balearic Islands', in M. Barke, J. Towner and M.T. Newton (eds), *Tourism in Spain: Critical Issues* (Wallingford: C.A.B. International, 1996).
4 Rivers, *Restless Generation*, 162-72.
5 Examples include C. Rojek and J. Urry (eds), *Touring Cultures* (London: Routledge, 1997); V. Smith (ed.), *Hosts and Guests* (Oxford: Blackwell, 1986); J. Waldren, *Insiders and Outsiders: Paradise and Reality on Mallorca* (Oxford: Berghahn Books, 1996); J. Boissevain (ed.), *Coping with Tourists: European Reactions to Mass Tourism* (Oxford: Berghahn Books, 1996).
6 M. Feifer, *Going Places* (Basingstoke: Macmillan, 1985), 223.
7 P. Brendon, *Thomas Cook: 150 Years of Popular Tourism* (London: Martin, Secker and Warburg, 1991), 82. Brendon is quoting *The Excursionist* (28 August 1863), Cook's in-house journal.
8 P. Addison, *Now the War is Over* (London: BBC/Cape, 1985), esp. chapter 5, 'Living it up'.
9 To an extent this was regulated by 'the stabilizer', a pricing control that meant tour operators were not allowed to charge less for the whole package than the cost of the cheapest scheduled flight. This began to be relaxed for winter holidays in 1972-3 but was not completely abolished until the late 1970s.
10 For a fuller discussion of the way that the International Tour Companies (ITCs) reduced Spanish holiday prices see Williams, 'Mass Tourism'.
11 This fluctuated over the period, depending on the economic situation. Initially set at £ 25, it had been increased to £ 100 by 1956, to £ 250 by the mid-1960s and was drastically cut to £ 50 in 1967.

12 For more detailed accounts of the economy over this period see A. Sked and C. Cook, *Post-War Britain* (Harmondsworth: Penguin, 1984), 256-81, or N. Tiratsoo (ed.), *From Blitz to Blair* (London: Phoenix, 1998), 163-90.
13 *International Tourism Quarterly* (*ITQ*) (Sept. 1974), 2.
14 Ibid., 3.
15 Ibid.
16 Ibid., 4.
17 Ibid., 3.
18 P. Yale, *The Business Of Tour Operations* (Harlow: Longman, 1995), 5.
19 Cosmos brochure (1968), 4.
20 F. Pontin, *My Life Always ... Thumbs Up* (London: Solo Books, 1991), 88.
21 Ibid., 94.
22 Ibid., 89.
23 J. Urry, *The Tourist Gaze* (London: Sage, 1990), 14.
24 R. Dewhurst, *Pickford's Honest Guide to Holiday Resorts* (Cambridge: Woodhead Faulkner, 1975), 119.
25 Pontinental brochure (1976), 59.
26 Thomas Cook brochure (1960), 45.
27 Pontinental brochure (1976), 69.
28 Ibid., 72f.
29 J. Urry, *The Tourist Gaze*, 14.
30 Urry, *Consuming Places* (London: Routledge, 1995), 22.
31 Urry, *Tourist Gaze*, 45.
32 Urry, *Consuming Places*, 138.
33 Ibid.
34 Ibid.
35 J.K. Walton, 'The Demand for Working-Class Seaside Holidays in Victorian England', *Economic History Review* 34 (1981), 249-65.
36 G. Cross, *Time and Money: The Making of Consumer Culture* (London: Routledge, 1993).
37 Urry, *Consuming Places*, 139.
38 D. Gratrix, *Little Roads to Spain* (London: Herbert Jenkins, 1956), back cover.
39 Gratrix, *Little Roads*, 97f. [my italics]. A. M.Williams uses Benidorm as an example of a site of mass tourism.
40 Williams, 'Mass Tourism', 121.
41 C. Wilson, *Benidorm: The Truth* (Valencia: Comunitat Valenciana, 1999), 251. In fairness, one has to say that Wilson's account does support other points made by Williams, particularly the way in which the local hotel owners were exploited by tour operators, to which he makes several references in chapter 9. However, in terms of the nature of the development, the chapter clearly supports negotiation.
42 Ibid., 251f.
43 R. Dixon, *The Costa Blanca* (London: Collins, 1966), 57.

44 M. Ellingham and J. Fisher, *Spain: The Rough Guide* (London: Rough Guides, 1984), 698. The Rough Guides are written for 'independent travellers' – the Benidorm entry (which contains advice, for example, on where to stay), seems to assume that the audience will not really want to go there.
45 Wilson, *Benidorm,* chapter 9.
46 Ibid., 36-42.
47 It should be mentioned here that the sample was small and relatively random; therefore no attempt has been made to quantify the material. Whilst it is also impossible to say how representative the experiences are, there are enough common themes for some generalizations to be made. The evidence certainly supports the larger argument that the individual meanings of these experiences defy the stereotypes of mass tourism.
48 Letter 7.
49 Letter 10.
50 Ibid.
51 Letter 17.
52 Ibid.
53 Letter 22.
54 Letter 15.
55 Interview transcript 5.
56 M. Featherstone, *Consumer Culture and Post-Modernism* (London: Sage, 1991); M. Waters, *Globalization* (London: Routledge, 1995).
57 Letter 21.
58 H. Ritchie, *Here We Go: A Summer on the Costa del Sol* (London: Hamish Hamilton, 1993), 4.
59 Interview transcript 5.
60 P. Fussell, *Abroad* (Oxford: Oxford University Press, 1980), 43.
61 Pontinental brochure (1976), 4.
62 Ibid.
63 *The Observer* (12 March 2000), 7, reporting on a survey by market researchers, Mintel.
64 Pontin, *My Life,* 88.
65 Interview transcript 5.
66 Ibid., 5.
67 Letter 10.
68 Interview transcript 5.
69 Interview transcript 20.
70 Ibid.
71 Letter 15.
72 Interview transcript 15.
73 Interview transcript 5.

Engineer's Holiday
L.T.C. Rolt, Industrial Heritage and Tourism

Christopher Harvie

1. Tourism – Holiday – Busman's Holiday

The paradoxes of tourism and culture do not diminish on closer inspection. Their elaboration shows not so much a Janus-face as a character multifacetted as a fly's eye. Tourism can be a pattern of development, and a record of exploitation; it can inflict acculturation or stage cultural rescue; stress the national or the international, the local or the global. It can be xenophobic or cosmopolitan or both at the same time. Think further on the word itself: it can mean recreation, excursion, holidaymaking, escapism, educationalism, application, hedonism. Think, too, of its relationship to work. It is an escape from routine work, but also an industry (sometimes the only one around). But it can also be an escape *into* work: the culture of the 'busman's holiday'.[1]

Given these complexities, further problems set in as the service sector expands and the line between tourism and manufacturing industry becomes more and more blurred. For tourism can reflect both the 'mature' and the 'immature' economy. In some areas where 'modern' manufacturing has been displaced or overwhelmed, tourism-generated demand can sustain or revive 'archaic' modes: 'modern' clockmaking has fled the Black Forest, cuckoo clocks remain; textile mills close in Scotland but hand-weaving and knitting flourishes; English local breweries shut but micro breweries open. The transactions of all of these are classed with 'tourism' but they have as little of the mass-service-industry about them as they have of leading-edge technology. We could buy cuckoo clocks, Shetland sweaters and real ale in Marks and Spencer (probably much cheaper), but 'it's not the same thing'.

Is this because a certain type of tourism both requires and enables something more than hedonistic self-satisfaction: that fundamental but neglected aspect of Smithian economics, 'sympathy', a learned drive with which is combined trust and decorum.[2] Anent tourism, the dividing line between leisure and sloth is as difficult to determine, as is that between the carefree and the irresponsible. A substantial qualitative motive in post-1960s tourism and its migration from the English seaside to the Mediterranean *was* post-Smithian, indeed post-Freudian, hedonism: sun, beaches and cheap drink were equated with sex – a migration of desire from the furtive darkened world of cinemas, car parks and dance halls to a semi-tropic where clothes and inhibitions were in short supply. There the young could mate, married women look around, and middle-aged fathers compensate for sexual boredom by the Page 3 frieze around them. This was a smutty postcard world but less that of Donald McGill than that of Bamford's of Holmfirth. George Orwell wrote that McGill's postcards 'imply a stable society in which marriage is indissoluble and family loyalty taken for granted'.[3] Bamford's world was and is one of less grotesquerie, more sex and little expectation of social or marital continuity.

Enough tourist centres – Lebanon, Sri Lanka, Yugoslavia – have recently, all too rapidly, lurched from pleasure to something as atavistic, but far more brutal, for us to postulate the existence of a fundamental dysfunction within the 'hedonism-facilitating' society they generate. Football in its international aspect is maybe the most obvious, the decline from the innocence of the recruits to Kitchener's army in Philip Larkin's 'MCMXIV' ('Those long uneven lines / Standing as patiently / As if they were stretched outside / The Oval or Villa Park, / The crowns of hats, the sun / On moustached archaic faces / Grinning as if it were all / An August Bank Holiday lark [...]')[4] to the oafishness, if not thuggery, of today's new laddism.[5] But even in a less confrontational form some awkward questions about 'the long slide to happiness' persist. In the moral sense holiday Britain presents one definition of the Enlightenment: a secular, sensual assent to the postulates of Mandeville, Hume and Bentham: the pleasure principle made incarnate. The 1960s and 1970s saw the decline of the McGill film, with the last of the British *Carry Ons*, in step with that of the traditional coastal resorts, and the acceleration of the 'sexualization' of British society, holidays in particular.[6] Heritage could be seen as a subsection of this democratization of Thorstein Veblen's 'leisure class'.[7] But 'heritage' and the involvement of voluntary workers in organizing it connects with a parallel notion that work – or at least 'useful work versus useless toil' – was in itself valuable, derived from the counter-utilitarian social criticism of Thomas Carlyle, John Ruskin and William Morris, and made much of both by the Leavises and by such contemporary 'Anglo-Marxist' writers as Francis Klingender and Raymond Williams.[8]

'Work' and 'leisure' are both blended and made problematic through the economic space opened by tourism and holidaymaking. (I think there is a distinction between the two, perhaps summed up by 'second home', which applies as much to the Liverpudlian caravan at Rhyl as the Islington cottage in Llanbadarn). This could release impulses which contradict the hedonistic, revive the ethical/ sympathetic and in fact transcend both, in a sort of Utopianism. In the history of the link between tourism and industrial heritage three themes - work, hedonism and culture - intersected in one career, which turned out significant for one outmoded infrastructure, and for at least one traditional holiday area in difficulties. L.T.C. Rolt was a highly literate figure but his career is almost wholly unknown to the guardians of the canon of English literature, or to their post-modernist successors. This may suggest, by implication, something about the fragility of both.

2. British Railway Enthusiasm

In *Theatres of Memory*, Raphael Samuel, the great Anglo-Jewish social - and socialist - historian, remarked on the blindness of his Marxian friends, the students of class politics, to the existence of a huge strata of 'amateur' activity in English society. Besides the usually-observed institutions of sport, do-it-yourself, pets and preserving old buildings (the National Trust has over two million members), involvement in quasi-industrial activities attracts tens of thousands, in an economy habitually castigated for its indifference to technology. Samuel guessed at 250,000 railway enthusiasts in Britain, many of whom are engaged in actually running railway lines and maintaining (even building) rolling stock. Adding other forms of industrial heritage, industrial archaeology, ship and vehicle preservation, and those involved in inland waterways, the total may reach around a half-million.[9]

Moreover, a great proportion of the investment in what has become a substantial tourist resource, with for example about 400 km of preserved railways offering summer services, and carrying upwards of 50,000 passengers annually per line, is effectively part-time, donated and voluntary. Companies are co-operatively organized, an example of the 'mutualism' commended by some economic reformers such as Will Hutton in *The State We're In*[10] and - momentarily - by Tony Blair, before his surrender to 'Anglo-American' turbo-capitalism. This 'green' economy apparently stands at an angle to the multinational world of commercialized leisure, being largely rurally-based, concerned with distinctiveness and social and ecological conservationism.

It is not immune to changes in society. In Britain, where every second marriage ends in divorce, 'somewhere to take the kids for the weekend' by one or another single parent, fills steam trains and industrial heritage centres. The kids themselves, the Internet-Nintendo-'dumb is cool' generation, may not be as keen on trains (except on spraying them with hip-hop graffiti) or in doing anything as energetic as their parents. Yet writers trying to reach the qualities most valued in the British, and the English in particular, will eventually find themselves - like Paul Theroux in *The Kingdom by the Sea* and Bill Bryson in *Notes from a Small Country* - coming back to the branch lines as well as the small platoons. That they do so is due to one career which, fairly remarkably, bridges the 'two cultures' whose divorce concerned the scientist-novelist C.P. Snow back in the ambiguous decade of the 1960s.[11]

3. L.T.C. Rolt: 'Premium Apprentice'

Lionel Thomas Caswall Rolt (1910-74) had literary ambitions, and his impact on English culture has been as significant as another 'unwelcome guerilla' from a 'lower-upper-middle-class', non-university background, George Orwell, in the sense that both altered the ways of seeing the industrial landscape. Rolt, however, helped make it into a part of the national cultural heritage. That Wigan Pier itself is now a heritage site - a grasped-at chance of economic diversification in a depressed region - is perhaps more his legacy than Orwell's.[12]

The two were near-contemporaries. Rolt was born an only child on the Welsh border, in Chester, into a family like that of the Blairs, on the social frontier between gentry, military and business. His father was an unambitious rentier - an enthusiastic traveller and expert fisherman and shot - who brought the boy up in a new but fairly affordable villa at Hay-on-Wye, just on the Welsh side of the border, in Brecon. This was the countryside connected with the Victorian diarist and naturalist Francis Kilvert (1840-1879), and much earlier with the metaphysical poets Thomas Traherne (1636-1674), Henry

Vaughan (1622-1695) and George Herbert (1593-1633), with all of whom - as well as with the remarkable landscape - the young Tom Rolt identified. His family lost money in the crash of 1920 and moved to a smaller medieval house at Stanley Pontlarge, near Cheltenham. In 1924 he was sent to Cheltenham College, the nearest public school, which he hated, and then through the agency of an engineer-inventor uncle, Kyrle Willans, to an agricultural engineering firm.

Rolt's training, typical of a section of the English bourgeoisie and gentry, has now completely died out: he was a premium apprentice. This was a youth, usually out of a public school, who was apprenticed to a prominent engineer or, later on, to a railway works, on payment of a fairly substantial annual fee: an education whose contents were somewhat arbitrary, but was equivalent to the sessions his German contemporary would spend at a *Technische Hochschule*, and his French contemporary at the *École Polytechnique*. It had theoretical deficiencies, much remarked on in critiques of Britain's industrial backwardness, but the elements of craftsmanship and adaptability it imparted were almost unique. Notable products of this system included the Hon. Charles Rolls (apprenticed at Crewe Railway Works) and Lord Reith of the BBC (apprenticed at the North British Locomotive Company in Glasgow).[13]

Rolt served his time (1927-29) at Kerr Stuarts, a Stoke-on-Trent manufacturer of steam locomotives and tramcars, which was also trying to diversify into motor lorries until forced into bankruptcy by a fraud, which could not be recovered because of the 1929 slump. His experience of Arnold Bennett's 'Five Towns', a stark contrast to Hay-on-Wye, he later made the subject of a novel, *Winterstoke* (1953), effectively the biography of an industrial town, its rise and fall. But he came away with a respect for the works' engineering craftsmen which he never lost. Thomas Hardy characterized the engineer, in a famous passage in *Tess of the D'Urbervilles*, as a literally hellish apparition, 'a creature from Tophet'. To Rolt his skill, pride and good-humour had a continuity with the same qualities that marked the rural craftsmen celebrated in George Sturt's *The Wheelwright's Shop*, and broadcast by the Leavises.[14]

However, to avoid unemployment, Rolt used his mechanical training to go back to the agricultural engineering which was undermining Sturt's world, at a works not far from Stanley Pontlarge, which became his permanent base for the rest of his life. He maintained the last steam traction engines as well as the first generation of diesel tractors. Then what had started as a sideline became running a garage, founding the Vintage Car Club and becoming a racing driver. In the latter guise, he might almost have fitted into a quite different part of the twenties cultural scene, that rackety fringe of the Bright Young Things which Evelyn Waugh describes in *Vile Bodies* (1928). Rolt's was, actually, a high craft-input, low-cost business, based on buying wrecks of cars and reconditioning them. It could have led to a role in the growing motor industry, or among those inter-war heroes, 'speed-kings' such as Sir Henry Segrave and Sir Malcolm Campbell, but did not.

4. Rediscovering the Canals

At the end of the 1930s, Rolt underwent a career shift and reorientation of values. His Kerr Stuart experience had left him deeply disillusioned with capitalism, and his politics had briefly moved to the far left. Then he seems to have discovered the metaphysical poets and, through an affair with an Anglo-Irishwoman, unidentified but bisexual and some years his senior, he was introduced to the bohemia of Fitzrovia and the works of W.B. Yeats. Yeats's anti-materialism - expressed in his mid-period poetry and in *Autobiographies* (1913) - and the influence of English critics of industrialization, such as Ruskin and H.J. Massingham, seem to have led Rolt to take a sideways move, a few years after J.B. Priestley's *English Journey* (1933-34) and Orwell's *The Road to Wigan Pier* (1936). He rediscovered, with his first wife Angela, and on a narrow boat converted into a passenger craft by Kyrle Willans, the almost secret world of the English canals.

The canals built to carry the raw material and products of the first industrial revolution, between 1760 and 1830, occur in the culture of the Auden/Orwell years as an accompaniment to pictures of industrial depression. But in the course of a two-year voyage round the Midlands on the 'Cressy' - the first, literally, of thousands - Rolt uncovered a hidden world, of 'Number Ones' (independent canal traders), 'scholars' (the few literate canal boat people), boat and lock-gate builders, and families brought up in the tiny cabins of the surviving narrow-boats and their 'butties', with long traditions of crafts in painting, singing, drinking and poaching. All of this took place in an environment which, through disuse, had scarcely changed since the early nineteenth century.[15] *Narrow Boat* was written by 1941 but not published until 1944 after a round of fruitless visits to publishers. It had atmospheric woodcuts by Denys Watkins-Pitchford (Rolt had wanted to use his wife's 'documentary' photographs) and was praised by V.S. Pritchett and Compton Mackenzie. Publicized by the documentary film *Painted Boats* (script by Louis MacNeice, research by Rolt), and widely marketed through the Readers' Union book club, it had sold 35,000 copies by 1946. It was this report from a vanishing world that became, post-war, the keynote of the revival of the canals as a tourist-oriented system.

When war broke out Rolt volunteered as an engineer. He had deeply respected the skilled workers with whom he worked at Stoke-on-Trent, but was appalled by conditions on the assembly line at Rolls Royce's Crewe plant. From Cressy, moored at Tardebigge, between Birmingham and Worcester, he worked as a munitions controller. After the war he met Robert Aickman, a writer involved in the Social Credit movement (like Ezra Pound and Hugh MacDiarmid) and Charles Hadfield, canal historian, but also a former Labour councillor and publisher. Together they founded the Inland Waterways Association in 1946, to revive the canals both as carriers and for pleasure cruising. After initial success they split. Aickman supported those who wanted to reopen as much of the old system as possible, believing (accurately, as it turned out) that it could only survive through recreational use. Hadfield saw the canals as part of a 'green' transport reform, with much large-scale modern construction. Rolt was involved in a severe personality clash with Aickman - they never spoke for two decades after 1949 - and his hopeless campaign to preserve the fast-vanishing world of the freight boatmen, coupled with the break-up of his marriage, might have destroyed him.[16]

5. The Talyllyn Railway: Industrial Heritage and Tourism

Although no advocate of unrestrained capitalism Rolt, like John Betjeman, whom he met in the late 1940s, rebelled against the bureaucracy and featurelessness of Labour's new order. They indicted an unimaginative British Transport Commission which took over the canals in 1947 and then did nothing about them. The railways, now nationalized, found themselves in a situation of near-collapse.[17] Rolt was at the same time working on a series of essays called *High Horse Riderless* 'on the need for a re-establishment of a Christian philosophy of life' (1947); through this he moved towards Welsh nationalism, attracted by the 'small is beautiful' ideas of Plaid Cymru, and its adviser the Austrian 'proto-green' Leopold Kohr, and his friendship with the actor Hugh Griffith, 'Captain Cat' in Dylan Thomas's *Under Milk Wood* (1953).[18] This involvement led, along with his expulsion from the IWA, and wartime memories of the line – 'No Train Today' – to the rescue of the Talyllyn Railway in central Wales, recorded in *Railway Adventure* (1953).[19]

The Talyllyn is the star of a remarkable book. It was an industrial fossil, whose equipment had never altered since it was first built in 1865 to connect the remote Bryn Eglwys slate quarry and the upland village of Abergynolwyn, at the foot of Cader Idris, with the small seaport and resort of Towyn on Cardigan Bay, six miles away down the valley of the Afan Dysinni. Living as the Talyllyn 'Toy Railway' from year to year as the quarry's traffic ran down (it closed in 1946) its two engines and five wooden, unheated, carriages carried summer tourists through the efforts of its owner, an elderly ex-Liberal MP, Sir Henry Haydn Jones. When he died in 1950 the line seemed doomed. But Rolt and a group of enthusiasts, mainly from the Birmingham area (which traditionally went to Cardigan Bay for holidays) took the operation of the line over and, with the ancient and temperamental 'Dolgoch', managed to run it through the 1951 season.

Railway Adventure is at one level a drama of cylinders, connecting rods and steam injectors, of the sort that only impinged on Eng Lit in Kipling's lesser-known fiction.[20] At another, its tone is closer to Ruskin's *The Stones of Venice* (1851-53) than to anything else from the 1950s. Think of its opening:

> The setting of this adventure is a part of the ancient Welsh kingdom of Gwynedd, a land of mountains bounded on the north and south by the estuaries of the Mawddach and the Dovey and on the west by the shores of Cardigan bay. The central keep of this region is Cader Idris whose storm-bitten peak of naked rock commands the coast of Wales from Bardsey Island to St David's Head and wave beyond wave of mountains from Snowdon to Aran Mawddwy and Plynlimmon Fawr. Like three extended fingers of a hand, its outliers point westwards to the sea, enclosing between their narrow, knuckled ridges two deep and secluded valleys.[21]

Compare this with the prelude to Ruskin's second volume, the gondola journey from Mestre to St Mark's Square.[22] And we are not subsequently disappointed; not only is Ruskin cited, but a similar blend of technology and morality follows. When Rolt considers the country folk who use the line and cluster in the guard's van, the result is a short but fierce essay on tourism, the market and identity – going beyond even Wordsworth to the *Mabinogion* and the Arthurian 'matter of Britain':

> To allow the money in the visitors pocket to outweigh local needs would be as fatal for us as it would be for a farmer with a houseful of summer guests to leave his sheep to rot upon his mountain. For at once railway and farm alike would fall out of the regional and historical context of which they have so long been a part and in which alone they have their true being. This is the great danger of the growth of 'tourism' in Wales, and the more dependent the Welsh become on the summer visitor the greater grows the risk that an ancient birthright will be squandered for the proverbial mess of potage. For Wales is not merely a landscape of mountain and waterfall and beach, a convenient empty space on the map where the population of our swollen cities can find a breathing space. Nor is it a no-man's-land to be covered by a regimented forest of conifers, flooded by new reservoirs or blasted by high explosive weapons. Wales is the ages old association of people with landscape in an ecological partnership intimately interlinked. To the landscape the people have given the sheep, the black cattle and the small hill farms; the dry-stone boundary walls and mountain quarries; the little market towns and sea-ports. To the people the mountains have given a way of life and, until the twentieth century invasion, they have nursed and protected the language and the traditions of a people which are the expression of that way of life. But these mountain dykes are down now. Every summer a tide of tourists, each stronger than the last, spills over them to flood Wales just as surely and inevitably as successive tides battered down those sea walls that the drunken Seithenyn so slothfully failed to guard and so drowned the lost kingdom under Cardigan Bay.[23]

And yet, and yet .... The Talyllyn's example gained it publicity of the most modern sort – featuring, for example, in live TV broadcasts and inspiring Charles Crichton's 1952 Ealing comedy 'The Titfield Thunderbolt'[24] and the Emett Festival Railway at the Festival of Britain's Battersea Fun Fair. These, as well as Rolt's book, soon encouraged imitators. The Festiniog railway, once a mighty slate-carrier, was revived in 1955 and the Welshpool and Llanfair in 1963. By then the Talyllyn was carrying over 70,000 passengers per season. The movement spread to England with the reopening of the Bluebell Railway in Sussex in 1958, and was mightily accelerated after the Beeching Report of 1961, with its threat to close over a third of the railway system down. Rather than taper off, it has in fact accelerated with the return of business to the railways. There are now about 120 such lines around the country, and a cognate number of industrial heritage centres, such as the National Museum of Wales's Dinorwic Slate Museum in North Wales, the Beamish open-air museum in Durham, and the Ironbridge museum at Telford. In the survival of Britain's beleagured seaside resorts, the role of 'heritage rail' – from the Dart Valley at Torquay to Blackpool's trams – has been a significant factor.

Preserving the Talyllyn was not totally revolutionary. Railways had been 'restored' earlier, notably the 3′0″ gauge Cumberland mineral line, the Ravenglass and Eskdale, which closed down during World War I and was rebuilt in 1922 by the model railway pioneer W.J. Bassett-Lowke (1877-1953) as a miniature line on the 1′3″ gauge.[25] This demonstrated a paradoxical link between small railways and giant enterprises, as ultra-narrow gauge lines pioneered by Sir Arthur Heywood, a Derbyshire landowner-engineer, were built after the 1900s to carry fuel and supplies to large mansion-houses (notably the Duke of Westminster's vast Eaton Hall near Chester) and were later, with Bassett-Lowke-style engines, used to shift literally millions of visitors at great exhibitions. Wembley in 1924 was the first. Germany subsequently and enthusiastically adopted this technology from England. In the Soviet sphere of influence 'pioneer railways' with scaled-down equipment were used both to give access to suburban pleasure-grounds and to train children as future railway staff. By contrast proto-preservation was undertaken in America when wealthy men, including Henry Ford and Walt Disney, equipped such estate railways with rolling stock from minor lines which were succumbing to road competition, fortified by the writings of Lucius Beebe (1902-66), socialite, journalist and millionaire who collected the discarded private saloons of other millionaires.[26] Disneyland (1955) was a vast elaboration of these projects.

Rolt's initial idea had been to rebuild the Talyllyn to 10.25″ gauge, with a short length on which the 'old ladies' – the original 'Talyllyn' and 'Dolgoch' – could run. The decision to keep going with the original material was thus crucial. Ultimately it shifted the balance of the project from engineering-plus-tourism to a type of engineering with quite ambitious social implications. Rolt concluded *Railway Adventure* thus:

> for railways are no longer run by railwaymen and engineers but by civil servants and economists, whose ruling principle is that before any improvement can be sanctioned a financial economy must first be proved on paper. So your railwayman struggles on, throttled in red tape and fighting a losing battle with obsolete or worn-out equipment [...].
>
> In the ancient kingdom of Gwynedd, under the shadow of Cader Idris [tr. Arthur's Seat], we have striven against odds not merely to preserve a railway but to keep alive a spark of that fine tradition which flourished so richly when the Talyllyn line was born. Is it not worth cherishing.[27]

Note, again, the symbolism - and the book's date! Could this be a last echo of that invocation of Arthur, King of Britain, which the Tudors had so resonantly employed, at the start of what was billed as the New Elizabethan age?[28]

Rolt lost money through managing the Talyllyn. He had also married again, and soon had two boys to support. So he turned to history writing, which sustained him for the rest of his life. His works of philosophy and criticism from the 1940s and 1950s seem to have made scarcely any direct impact. *High Horse Riderless* (1947) took its title from the *Kulturpessimismus* of W.B. Yeats's 'Coole and Ballylee, 1931':

> We were the last romantics - chose for theme
> Traditional sanctity and loveliness;
> Whatever's written in what poets name
> The book of the people; whatever most can bless
> The mind of man or elevate a rhyme;
> But all is changed, that high horse riderless,
> Though mounted in that saddle Homer rode
> Where the swan drifts upon a darkening flood.[29]

The Clouded Mirror (1955) has a passionate attack on the 'peaceful' as well as military use of nuclear power, two years before the birth of the Campaign for Nuclear Disarmament. These writings were, however, perceptive as a guide to an eclectic social thought which had much in common with 'modernism', and perhaps a more lasting impact. Rolt's point of departure was not the industrial revolution but an 'undivided sensibility' sought in common with T.S. Eliot, in the poetry of the metaphysicals from his home countryside, Herbert, Traherne and Vaughan. Against their religious concern with the small community – something akin to Ferdinand Tönnies's concept of *Gemeinschaft*[30] but involving a continuing link with the industrial craftsman – he saw opposed the 'great society' enabled by mechanical communications.[31]

Rolt's opposition to coercive power – whether of the state or of the atom – aligned him with figures like Kohr and the Welsh poet R.S. Thomas, born in 1913, as a conservative green. The tone of *Railway Adventure* echoes Thomas's famous 'Cynddylan on a Tractor' composed about the same time:

> Yes, you should see Cynddylan on his tractor.
> Gone the old look which held him to the soil.
> He's a new man now, part of the machine,
> His nerves of iron and his blood of oil.[32]

Yet at the same time Rolt was fascinated by the craftsmanship and calculation which went into the artefacts of the new society: the roads, bridges, canals, railways and their vehicles. This was a paradox which, he later admitted, he had never managed to square, except at the existential level of action: something which may reflect, as in the case of Thomas, the influence of Soren Kierkegaard.[33]

Rolt's major occupation – indeed near-obsession – for the last two decades of his life was the writing of industrial histories and biographies.[34] *Red for Danger* (1955), a history of railway accidents and safety precautions, proved in a somewhat more ghoulish way as popular as *Narrow Boat*, and has rarely been out of print. If his friend Betjeman celebrated Victorian architecture and poetry, Rolt documented its engineers, with his standard biographies of – among others – Isambard Kingdom Brunel (1957), Thomas Telford (1958), Richard Trevithick (1960), and George and Robert Stephenson (1960). He also became a leading figure in the Newcomen Society, the main organization for the history of technology, which had existed since 1920, and in 1973 was founder-member and first President of the Association for Industrial Archaeology. For the generation which formed the movement to preserve industrial heritage Rolt's books were essential reading and he was also quick to see the mutual interaction of preservation, scholarship and tourism.

Latterly Rolt's position was quasi-academic - he calculated his annual income from commissions and royalties in 1969 as £ 3600, which would put him at a professorial salary level - and he acted as godfather to the first generation of industrial archaeologists and outdoor museum organizers, such as Kenneth Hudson, Angus Buchanan and (Sir) Neil Cossons.[35] Writing up to the last, overweight, chain-smoking, he died of cancer in 1974, aged only 64. But by then the industrial heritage movement was in full swing, with multi-million projects such as the Beamish Museum in Durham, with its reconstructed north-east mining community, and the Ironbridge museum in Shropshire, which became the tourist centre of a new city which bore the name of a master-engineer, Thomas Telford. It is, to say the least, unlikely that this project, or indeed the city itself, would have proceeded, had Rolt not resurrected this golden age of engineering.

6. Conclusions: 'What Poet-Race ...?'

This has been a difficult essay to write. It ought to be simple by being biographical, yet Rolt's career subverts so many of our accustomed paradigms. He came from a *rentier* class which lived off industrialization in a 'touristic' way. His life resembled 'ours' in its combination of economic and social insecurity, hedonism and *Spieltrieb*, but he also came to mirror the obsessive activity of the men he wrote about. By, literally and culturally, reactivating an earlier, more human-scaled and accessible form of technology, he made it attractive to voluntary providers and marketable in a society grown anonymous. Yet his mission would not have succeeded without the space and income that 'tourism' provided: to charter canal-boats and restore canals, to holiday on the Welsh coast, to make day trips to places like Ironbridge. But he put the division of work and leisure under question, and in doing so returned to one of the fundamental issues of the Enlightenment.[36]

Rolt's research was thorough and his engineering knowledge (rare among economic historians) contributed to biographies which were well-informed and undogmatic. In these and his histories he continually emphasized the technical problems which have to be overcome before an invention could become an economic proposition - alloy steel for high temperatures, flawless castings, accurately-machined shafts and cylinders - and how ingenious and theoretically feasible schemes such as the atmospheric railway or the monorail could be frustrated by such details.[37] Yet he continued a practice of studying technology through men and inventions which had been pioneered by the Scots doctor, Carlyle-disciple and individualist Samuel Smiles, over a century earlier. He was only marginally interested in the relation between technological innovation and economic organization, the corporate structures of research and development which enabled, say, the Walkman or the mobile phone.

As an epigraph to his Stephenson biography, Rolt cited G.K. Chesterton's 'Kings Cross Station':

> Or must Fate act the same grey farce again,
> And wait, till one, amid Time's wrecks and scars,
> Speaks to a ruin here, 'What poet-race
> Shot such cyclopean arches at the stars?'[38]

The influence of this poetic-humanist *gestalt* cannot be underestimated. As an historian Rolt was attracted by the fusion of individual craftsmanship with steam and steel, not by the mass-production of the motor age. He maintained his motoring interests, but these took the form of a 1928 Alvis touring car. In fact, his ruralism accorded with Smiles's observation - probably with Telford in mind - that many of the great engineers of whom he wrote had themselves come from pre-industrial backgrounds, 'brought up mostly in remote counting places, far from the active life of great towns and cities'.[39]

As a result of the power of this *gestalt*, the 'community element' propelling public transport policy in Britain remains strong and innovative - and has even made something out of the chaotic privatization of the railway system. At the same time the objective history of transport is peculiarly patchy. While every siding on every branch line has been logged, the history of road haulage is almost unwritten, despite its 80 per cent dominance of freight transport since the 1960s, and the environmental and ethical problems that this has brought. Some critics of British industrial culture, such as Martin Wiener and Corelli Barnett, would see this as evidence of the retrospective, rural-oriented values which have over the years slowed down Britain's rate of technological development. Perhaps the railway restoration movement has a certain culpability here: many of the Talyllyn's early activists were quite senior managers opting out of the profit-through-innovation main line. Alan Pegler, boss of a leading engineering firm, saved the Festiniog Railway, and then Nigel Gresley's famous Flying Scotsman, but at the cost of his own business.[40]

On the other hand, industrial heritage is not only perhaps the most thriving part of Britain's visitor-oriented tourist industry (the high £ has hit the stately-home business sharply), it has also done much to conserve both skills and the sense of identity that Rolt stressed in *Railway Adventure*. In Wales the major sites, such as the Dinorwic slate museum, the Big Pit at Blaenavon, lead mines near Aberystwyth, several restored canals and regional museums are, as the historian Dai Smith has argued, necessary to the self-understanding and self-confidence of the communities around them, although their incomes are now drawn from quite different sources.[41]

There will soon be more miles of narrow-gauge line than there were in 1900, with the rebuilding through Snowdonia, from Carnarfon to the Festiniog Railway at Porthmadog, of the spectacular but hopelessly uneconomic Welsh Highland Railway, abandoned in 1939. This has been funded by the National Lottery and EU structural funds and will cost about £ 30 million. It has been very controversial, but has won government backing as it offers an environmentally-tolerable way of securing access to the mountain region and cutting car traffic. Preserved railways have never been subject to any searching analysis of their regional economic role, and indeed the only text linking them to 'the condition of England' is a novel, Graham Coster's fine but undervalued *Train, Train* (1989).[42] But does not this success stand in sharp contrast to New Labour's unvisited mausoleum, the £ 800 million Greenwich Dome, reached by £ 3.2 billions of Jubilee underground line?[43]

Anent mausoleums, with the closure in 1993 of the Trawsfynndd nuclear power station after thirty years service (the core will remain radioactive for a further 30,000 years) the 'Great Little Trains' have emerged as among the biggest employment and visit generators in North-West Wales. Moreover, in turn they have promoted manufacturing industry, with the engineering and maintenance skills that they require, and this has contributed to a growing green economy, spreading out from the Centre for Alternative Technology in the Corris Valley, not far from the Talyllyn, and itself a major tourist attraction. Neither enterprise has been slow to use new communications technology. An outcome which would have pleased, as well as surprised, Tom Rolt.[44]

Notes

1 The *OED* gives the earliest use of this term as 1893.

2 A. Smith, *A Theory of Moral Sentiments* (1759) (Oxford: Oxford University Press, 1976), 9f.; with this can be coupled Adam Ferguson's 'idea of play' as a socially-unifying activity, which Fania Oz-Salzberger argues lies behind Friedrich Schiller's notion of *Spieltrieb*, and which returns to British civic discourse via Thomas Carlyle. See Oz-Salzberger, *Translating the Enlightenment: Scottish Civil Discourse in Eighteenth-Century Germany* (Oxford: Clarendon Press, 1995), 114-6.

3 Orwell, 'The Art of Donald McGill' (1941), in *Critical Essays* (London: Secker and Warburg, 1954), 105.

4 Larkin, *Collected Poems* (London: Faber, 1988), 127.

5 It may be prudent, however, not to rush to judgement. Max Dennis, arch-lad editor of *Viz*, and creator of Johnny Fartpants, Sid the Sexist and the Fat Slags, is using his gains to reopen the Alnwick to Alnmouth railway.

6 J. Richards, *Films and British National Identity* (Manchester: Manchester University Press, 1997), 165. Orwell's puritan point seems echoed by the most hedonist of movies, Dusan Makavejev's satire on the hang-ups of the Cold War, *WR: Mysteries of the Organism* (1971). This invocation of William Reich's assault on inhibitions accompanied the post-religious, easy-going sexuality of beach life in Tito's Yugoslavia.

7 Veblen, *The Theory of the Leisure Class* (New York: Macmillan, 1899), 1-18.

8 See F.R. Leavis and D. Thomson, *Culture and Environment* (London: Chatto and Windus, 1933); F.D. Klingender, *Art and the Industrial Revolution* (London: Noel Carrington, 1947) and R. Williams, *Culture and Society* (London: Chatto and Windus, 1958).

9 R. Samuel, *Theatres of Memory* (London: Verso, 1994), 6.

10 W. Hutton, *The State We're In* (London: Cape, 1995).

11 See Theroux, *The Kingdom by the Sea* (Harmondsworth: Penguin, 1984) and Bryson, *Notes from a Small Country* (London: Transworld, 1996). It is an intriguing reflection on the peculiarities of the British that of Rolt's seventy-odd books fourteen remain in print, of Snow's only *The Two Cultures* (London: Macmillan, 1961, last edition 1979).

12 The books by Rolt relevant to this study are, in order of publication: *Narrow Boat* (London: Eyre and Spottiswoode, 1944); *High Horse Riderless* (London: Allen and Unwin, 1947); *Railway Adventure* (London: Constable, 1953); *Winterstoke* (London: Constable, 1954); *The Clouded Mirror* and *Red for Danger* (London: Bodley Head, 1955); *Victorian Engineering* (London: Allen Lane, 1970). The three volumes of autobiography are *Landscape with Machines* (London: Longman, 1971); *Landscape with Canals* (London: Allen Lane, 1977) and 'The Gifts of Grateful Time', written in 1971-74 but not published until 1994 as *Landscape with Figures* (Stroud: Sutton).

13 See Rolt, *Landscape with Machines*, 25-32; W.H.G. Armytage, *A Social History of Engineering* (London: Faber, 1960).

14 Hardy, *Tess of the D'Urbervilles* (London: Macmillan, 1891), chapter 47. See Leavis and Thomson, *Culture and Environment*; G. Sturt, *The Wheelwright's Shop* (Cambridge: Cambridge University Press, 1923) and Williams, *Culture and Society*.

15 Rolt, *Landscape with Canals*, 140-55. A comparable, and only slightly later 'rediscovery' was that of the folk-songs preserved in the oral culture of tinkers and travellers, by such researchers and political activists as A.L. Lloyd and Hamish Henderson.

16 See I. Mackersey, *Tom Rolt and the Cressy Years* (London: Baldwin, 1985), 67; and see J. Boughey, *Charles Hadfield: Canal Man and More* (Stroud: Sutton, 1998). In fact the marriages of all three ended at about the same time, a degree of instability which was then unusual. All the wives concerned were distinctive characters and were set on their own careers (Rolt's joined a circus, Aickman's became an Anglican nun); the same also applied to their successors. So this episode is perhaps of some account in the socio-sexual history of the time.

17 See Betjeman's introduction to Rolt's *Railway Adventure* (London: Constable, 1953), xixf.

18 *Landscape with Canals*, 165; see also *Welsh Nation*, July 1949, 6.

19 Rolt, *Railway Adventure*, xiii-xv.

20 See C. Harvie, 'The Sons of Martha: Technology, Transport and Rudyard Kipling', *Victorian Studies*, 29.3 (1977), 269-82.

21 Rolt, *Railway Adventure*, 1.

22 See Ruskin, *The Stones of Venice* (London: George Allen, 1906), II, 1-3.

23 Rolt, *Railway Adventure*, 85f.

24 See Richards, *Films and British National Identity*, 134, 137.

25 Bassett-Lowke was partly of German descent, and set up his model shop network through marketing German-built models, by Bing of Nuremberg and Märklin of Göppingen, of British trains. A Fabian socialist, he was influenced by the Werkbund and commissioned designs from C. Rennie Mackintosh and P. Behrens.

26 See L. Beebe, *Mixed Train Daily* (New York: Dutton, 1947).

27 Rolt, *Railway Adventure*, 151.

28 See G.A. Williams, *When was Wales?* (Harmondsworth: Penguin, 1985), 123-5.

29 Yeats, *Poems of W.B. Yeats: A New Selection* (second ed. Basingstoke: Macmillan, 1988), 12f.

30 See F. Tönnies, *Gemeinschaft und Gesellschaft* (1887); translated by Charles P. Loomis: *Community and Society* (New York: Harper and Row, 1957).

31 Rolt, *Victorian Engineering*, 281.

32 In R.S. Thomas, *Collected Poems* (London: Phoenix, 1995), 30.

33 Rolt, *Landscape with Machines*, 18. Kierkegaard was only translated into English in the decade after 1939. There was a considerable vogue for things Danish among Welsh nationalists in the 1940s, and Rolt's *High Horse Riderless* was actually translated into Danish as *Stolten Ganger oden Rytter* (1948).

34 I. Rogerson, *L.T.C. Rolt: A Bibliography* (London: Baldwin, 1994) notes at least seventy books, most of them dating from the post-1953 period.

35 Salary from article in *The Author* (1969). In 1970, making a television programme on Brunel for the first humanities foundation course of the Open University, I initially found Rolt reserved and laconic, but once past this surface impression, enthusiastic and original in his contribution. I subsequently joined the Inland Waterways Association, and possibly because of his influence with Charles Hadfield, had several years collaborative work, both on inland shipping and transport history, with the latter – of much more value to me than to the cause of inland shipping.

36 Oz-Salzberger, *Translating the Enlightenment*, 306f.

37 Rolt, *Victorian Engineering*, 178-88.

38 Chesterton, 'King's Cross Station', *Collected Poems* (London: Methuen, 1933), 338.

39 S. Smiles, *Lives of the Engineers* (London: John Murray, 1862), II, 292; and see Asa Briggs, 'Samuel Smiles and the Gospel of Work', in id., *Victorian People* (Harmondsworth: Penguin, 1967 [1955]), 124-48.

40 See C. Harvie, 'The English Railway Enthusiast', *Anglistik und Englischunterricht*, 46/47 (1992), 107-22.

41 D. Smith, 'Work and Heritage', in E. Bort and N. Evans (eds), *Networking Europe* (Liverpool: Liverpool University Press, 2000), 311-20.

42 Coster, *Train, Train* (London: Bloomsbury, 1989). See R. Scarlett, *The Finance and Economics of Preserved Railways* (Huddersfield: Transport Research and Information Network, 1998), as well as G. Coster, *Train, Train* (London: Bloomsbury, 1989). D. Marks, 'Great Little Trains? The Role of Heritage Railways in North Wales in the Denial of Welsh Identity, Culture, and Working Class Identity', in R. Febre and A. Thompson (eds), *National Identity and Social Theory* (Cardiff: University of Wales Press, 1999), a title which seems to say it all.

43 The preservation business has, however, to be set beside its most remarkable spin-off, 'Thomas the Tank Engine'. The Rev. Wilbert Awdry's 'The Three Railway Engines' series, started in 1947, was a fixture of middle-class boyhood, with twenty-six books selling eight million copies between then and 1983. An early Talyllyn member, he featured the line in *Very Old Engines* (London: Edmund Ward, 1965). But an animated TV series, narrated by Ringo Starr, and spin-off marketing by the Britt Allcroft organization, raised sales to 50 million by 1996. With turnover in that year $ 170 million *from Japan alone*, Thomas's drawing power has been such that most preserved lines have to operate 'Thomas' specials,

from which Ms. Allcroft draws a hefty royalty (BBC2: *Bookmark*, 9 March 1997).

44 See Centre for Alternative Technology, *Crazy Idealists* (Machynlleth: CAT, 1995); B. Nowak, 'Virtual Trainspotting', unpublished paper, University of Tübingen, 2000. So much had the narrow-gauge lines come to symbolize Wales that the French film director François Truffaut featured the Talyllyn in *Anne and Muriel* (1971). As he filmed only in France, 'Dolgoch' was played by a Mallet locomotive of the Reseau de Vivarais.

True Copies
Time and Space Travels at British Imperial Exhibitions, 1880-1930

Alexander C.T. Geppert

1. Imperial Exhibitions and Modern Tourism

'As a cultural phenomenon', Werner Sombart observed in 1908, 'the exhibition is exceptionally interesting, for it appears in entirely different meanings, can be judged by very different criteria and classified in quite different contexts'.[1] Such versatility, together with the necessity of a complete *mise-en-scène*, largely explains the fascination of the universal exhibition as a mass medium, yet at the same time it augments its analytical complexity. Exhibitions represent complex historical phenomena. Their character is transient, without a narrative of their own or a prescribed single and central perspective, a given chronology or an easily decipherable hierarchy of meanings.

As the *sujet de délire* of the nineteenth century, in the words of Gustave Flaubert, exhibitions were conceived as fleeting microcosms of national self-representation which had however also to be placed both physically and mentally within the metropolis.[2] By first reflecting the meanings with which they were charged, then condensing and catalyzing them, exhibitions also interacted with their urban and intellectual environment, through this often achieving symbolic character themselves. They were soon considered welcome tourist attractions and figured in widely-read guidebooks such as *Baedeker* or the *Guide Bleu* - even having special editions issued featuring them. However, imperial exhibitions were not only the object of tourism, they also claimed that they sent their visitors on imaginary tours through time and space. Time and again, British imperial exhibitions claimed this 'imaginary travelling' function, which could aptly be labelled 'internal tourism', even if it certainly constitutes a formidable analytic and methodological challenge *not* to take the exposition's advertising rhetoric at sheer face value, but to examine their internal functioning and popular appeal. At the same time, the exhibition areas soon turned into tourist attractions in their own right, contributing to the surrounding city's attractiveness and giving potential visitors an additional incentive to tour the metropolis as well – which could well be described as 'external tourism'. The common denominator of 'internal' and 'external' tourism is that they both refer to space, although to very different versions of it. As exhibitions are dense, materialized textures, an in-depth spatial analysis is called for.

This essay puts forward three hypotheses: first, many of the features of the British Empire Exhibition, rather than being new, were clearly structured by the accepted medium 'exhibition' and a specific language which seems to have evolved quite slowly. As an example, an analysis of the Wembley exhibition can, however, demonstrate some of the more general principles and practices of representation at work in this 'mass medium of modern civilization', as a prospectus described the genre in 1922.[3] Second, exhibitions play an important but largely overlooked role in the wider history of tourism and vice versa. Here I seek to draw attention to the institutional affinities and interdependencies between the two, arguing that this relationship was two-dimensional and mutually supportive. Third, this argument is not specific to Britain but genuinely European in context and character. From the 1880s onwards imperial exhibitions were held in almost all European capital cities, Berlin being the only notable exception, and in each case the city as much as the exposition was on display. The exhibitions constituted focal points of local and regional, national and international travel and tourism, providing domestic, if not always metropolitan 'contact zones' for encounters with the wider, colonial world.[4] What was specific, though, was the existence of a densely-knit network containing single instances that imitated and quoted from each other.

Imperial exhibitions were subject to enormous inter-municipal and inter-national controversy and competition. Already in 1887, their analytical potential was recognized by Patrick Geddes, the Scottish biologist, sociologist, and pioneer city planner: 'The spectacle of not only grown men but intelligent chiefs of industry, naively working up their contributions to a museum of production into the exact likeness of the ornaments made in every kindergarten, is as instructive from an educational and anthropological point of view as it is grotesque from the artistic and utilitarian',[5] was how he, rather tartly, described their intellectual appeal.

2. Internal Tourism: The British Empire Exhibition at Wembley (1924/25)

British imperial exhibitions of the late nineteenth and early twentieth century have a family resemblance to London's 1851 Great Exhibition of the Works of Industry of All Nations. International exhibitions and world fairs are now widely regarded as a most central feature of European cultural history whose popular impact was anything but ephemeral. After the immense and entirely unexpected success of London's 1851 Great Exhibition of the Works and Industry of All Nations, international exhibitions were quickly established both in public life and the collective imagination. Despite a strong family resemblance, later exhibitions were marked by thematic specialization as well as emphasis on entertainment, amusement and spectacle and went beyond the claim 'to forward the progress of industrial civilization' made for the Crystal Palace. The scientist and computer inventor Sir Charles Babbage predicted well before the actual event of 1851, that it would 'bring to London from every quarter a multitude of people greater than has yet assembled in any western city'.[6] Subsequent imperial exhibitions, like world fairs, attracted a mass audience of millions. But despite a number of material, symbolic and functional similarities to the latter, the impact of the British imperial exhibitions dwindled with the Empire itself. According to the first Labour government's Secretary of State for the Colonies J.H. Thomas at least, there was complete correspondence between the two: 'Anyone who has seen the Exhibition,' he proclaimed, 'has seen the Empire'.[7]

World and imperial exhibitions, as technologies which allowed a society's representation of itself, are often considered both one of the most characteristic inventions of the nineteenth century and one of its few genuinely international cultural institutions. By the beginning of the twentieth century, however, the medium had reached a certain maturity, and complaints about 'exhibition fatigue' were being heard. Given that the general strategies of representation had steadily been refined through a process of ongoing inter-urban, particularly British-French competition, each such could draw upon a specific use of architectural forms, a grammar and semantics well-established in public life, and fall back on a long-accepted array of images.

While there were no exhibitions as great as 1851 in London until 1924, the medium had established itself with the Colonial and Indian Exhibition of 1886 as the first British exhibition exclusively devoted to imperial themes, and the first instance of complete 'spectacularization' came with Imre Kiralfy's large-scale Franco-British Exhibition held in Shepherd's Bush in West London in 1908. Although Wembley was by no means the last imperial exhibition (Glasgow in 1938 was also spectacular) it still constituted a preliminary endpoint in terms of size, grandeur, and impact.

Opened by King George V on April 23, 1924, it remained so for 150 days, and reopened in 1925, attracting a total of 27 million visitors over the two seasons. Its main objectives, the *Official Guide* declared, were 'serious':

> It is to stimulate trade, to strengthen the bonds that bind the Mother Country to her Sister States and Daughter Nations, to bring all into closer touch the one with the other, to enable all who owe allegiance to the British flag to meet on common ground, and to learn to know each other.

In short it was to be 'a Family Party, to which every part of the Empire is invited, and at which every part of the Empire is represented'.[8]

The vast, 216-acre site was dominated by the Empire Stadium (Fig. 1), built on the exact site of the so-called 'Watkin's Folly', London's notoriously uncompleted imitation of the Eiffel Tower from Paris's 1889 Exposition Universelle.[9] Divided by a double road axis and situated around gardens and lakes were Palaces of Industry, Engineering and Art, exhibition pavilions dedicated to the 56 participating colonies and dominions, and a special building for the British Government (Fig. 2). To the east, this 'serious' part of the Exhibition was supplemented by an amusement park with an abundance of 'fun-makers' and 'thrill-producers'. According to the numerous advertisements, this 'City of Pleasure' together with the 'City of Concrete' (or 'Poem of Empire' as the main section was called, Rudyard Kipling having named its streets) made Wembley 'The Empire's Metropolis', and London the 'host of the world'.[10] Actually, the site, clearly a city within a city and through good public transport within a quarter of an hour of Piccadilly Circus, was 'some way out of London', as *The Times* already noted in autumn 1921.[11] The advertisements did not mention this. As a matter of fact, after the Colonial and Indian Exhibition of 1886 had been held in South Kensington, exhibi-

Fig. 1: The Empire Stadium.

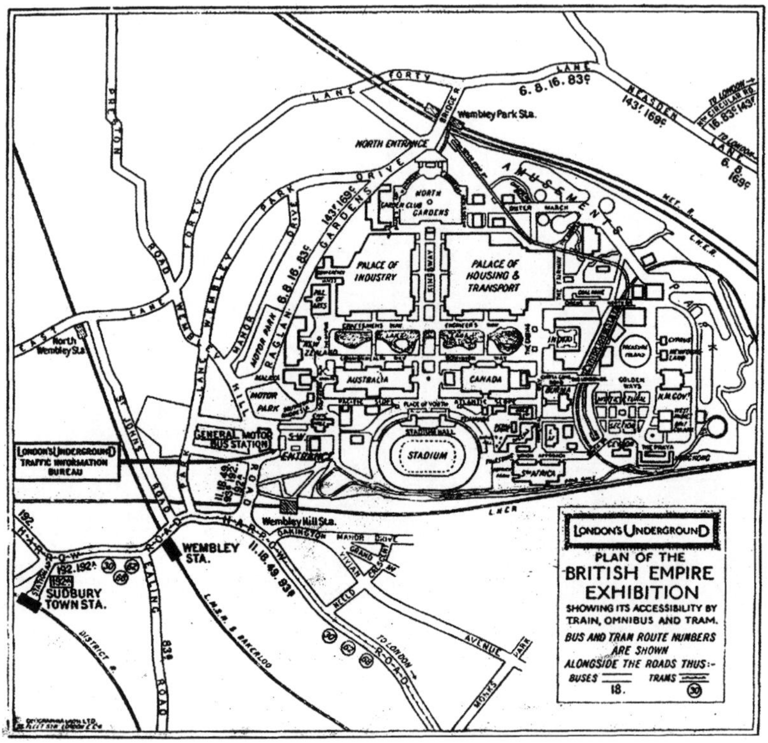

Fig. 2: London's Underground Plan of the British Empire Exhibition, showing its Accessibility by Train, Omnibus and Tram.

tions were increasingly driven to the outskirts, and by and large 'suburbanized'; it was only with the Festival of Britain in 1951 that town planners and urban designers realized the enormous possibilities for post-Blitz redevelopment connected with it, and decided to bring the spectacle back into the city centre. Wembley could easily be interpreted as a further, if transitory attempt in a long line of urban development projects aimed at permanently 'imperializing' London's character, and thus lessening its inferiority complex - representational in general, and architectural in particular - when comparing itself to cities such as Paris. This time, however, it did so from the edges, via suburbia.

But what kind of images both of home and of the far-flung reaches of empire did 'the Empire City' actually disseminate?[12] In order to construe the kinds of knowledge the exhibition provided, specifically designed for popular rather than specialist consumption, my analysis concentrates on the representation of the Indian and West-African colonies on the one hand, and the 'domestic section' such as the British Government Pavilion on the other.

The pavilions for the first two regions were situated close to each other, at the south-eastern end of the site. As India was the most important British possession overseas, arousing deep emotions in the London audience, its pavilion played a significant part in the overall concept of a British Empire Exhibition. At the same time, India's earlier dominance in the representations of empire showed a decline from its core role in the Indian and Colonial Exhibition in 1886. With the emergence of the Indian National Congress in 1885, steady concessions to repeated calls for autonomy and the transfer of much decision-making to the provincial governments were needed to sustain economic and military cooperation. India was no longer suitable for the projection of European fantasies of colonial exoticism.

This political-cultural change found its direct expression in the conception of the Indian pavilion of 1924/25. While the *Daily News Souvenir Guide* carefully stated, 'India is changing rapidly and the change can be seen here' and then continued to list exhibited indigenous industrial products, the Commissioner for India for the British Empire Exhibition proved much brisker when he described his (at least partly) demystifying objective for the Indian section: 'From a dependency, India has grown to the status of a partner in the empire.'[13]

However, in realizing this concept, certain concessions to the audience's taste were imperative. On the one hand, pains were taken to ensure that the traditional 'arts and crafts' exhibits did not dominate the huge, five-acre exhibition pavilion; the emphasis was instead placed on the domestic and industrial products of the 27 Indian provinces represented. On the other hand, it was still considered necessary to offer the audience more direct experiences by providing pseudo-authentic recreations of Indian lifestyle. In an Indian restaurant, for instance, guests were served by Indian waitresses and chose from a menu composed entirely of Indian dishes. There was also a traditional Indian theatre whose performers included jugglers, a troupe of 'Tibetan devil's dancers' and numerous wild animals such as 'a real live cobra, slowly swaying its deadly hook'.[14]

As India, for the reasons outlined, was no longer suitable as a foil for European fantasies of 'savagery', West Africa became the place where conflicting ideas and representations of foreignness collided and exploded into controversy. In the exhibit, the British colonies in Africa were divided according to geographical location. Their sections, one each for South, West and East Africa, were situated east of the Empire Stadium. Nigeria, the Gold Coast and Sierra Leone together formed the so-called West African 'Walled City', which the author of the *Daily News* guide rated particularly high in terms of attractiveness for the seekers of the exotic: 'Both inside and out, the Walled City of West Africa is subtly different from all other parts of the Exhibition'. The attentive visitor could further read:

> Within the red mud walls, with the tang of wood smoke in the air, amid the thatched huts, with natives of many tribes passing to and fro, such far-off places as Sierra Leone and the fabled Gold Coast become fantastically real. Within the halls the same illusion is maintained. The dark dim lanterns in the mud vaulted pavilion of the Gold Coast itself, the blue sunshine roof of the Nigerian hall, the mud and thatch of the Sierra Leone hut, all have a quality of reality.

In other words: 'This *is* West Africa.' Striving to surpass even reality itself, such a 'quality of reproduction' was also kept up in the 'African compound behind the bamboo gates', which, according to the same source, offered a faithful copy of 'native life': 'A real princess lives here, and the natives carry on with their ordinary tasks much as if they were at home, weaving, making pots, weaving baskets and mats.'[15]

This exhibiting of non-European peoples led for the first time to open controversy. In May 1924, a London-based group of mainly West African students, the Union of Students of African Descent, used the appearance of an article full of unsubtle sexual allusions in the *Sunday Express* as an opportunity to lodge an official complaint with the Colonial Office about the 'Holding up to public ridicule of Africans at Wembley'.[16] In the article, entitled 'When West Africa Woos', the reporter had set out to write the 'story of love as it is made in Akropong'. For his investigation, he had interviewed the putative 'princess' and questioned her bluntly about sexual practices and native marriage rituals. Though the students' protest was rejected by the Colonial Office, which (although under a Labour government) brusquely argued that the group had no 'earthly right to aggrandize itself this way' and that the Office had something better to do 'than to rush round in sympathy wherever a black "student" thinks his dignity is hurt,' the 'African village' was consequently closed, first to the press, then to the public. After consultations with the West African governments, and under a new Tory government, it was reopened in the following year, this time without exciting any further public outrage.[17]

Further east, towards the amusement park, and flanked by 'Newfoundland' and 'the West Indies', the official 'British Government Pavilion' afforded a contrast to the other pavilions. Devoted neither to a specific territory nor some specific industry but aiming at illustrating the British Government's activities and functions as a whole both abroad and at home, this section was 'more general in scope'. One of its approximately five million visitors described the building's ferro-concrete, two-storey architecture as 'of massive dignity [...] almost classical with its imposing colonnaded doorway and the six majestic lions guarding the entrance'.[18] If the Empire Stadium dominated the entire area architecturally, its organizational equivalent and the exhibition's domestic centre lay here.

That Wembley had such a pavilion was a direct consequence of a policy formulated by the Board of Trade's Exhibitions Branch, set up on the recommendations of a 1907 committee under Sir Alfred Bateman.[19] Without any government participation in an 'exhibition of this magnitude' and with no effort made 'to visualise to the public at home and in the Empire what H.M. Government is doing [...] for the public benefit', the Branch feared, 'there would be somewhat of a gap', rendering the enterprise 'incomplete' and 'open to criticism'. So the necessary funds were granted.[20] Nonetheless, the debate about building the pavilion is evidence of the government's ambivalent position towards a semi-public, semi-private project. The government was, unlike at most earlier exhibitions, represented by its own building. But the fact that this was the subject of debate clearly indicates the state's general distancing. It even had to pay, for example, for the space used for the Pavilion.

Employing a wide variety of sub-media, the Pavilion was a small exhibition in itself. Displays presented the achievements of modern civilization in the fields of military defence, communication, settlement and economic development. Military, aerial and naval displays were especially prominent, like a re-staging of the famous 1918 raid on the German U-boat base at Zeebrugge.[21] Its central exhibit in the Court of Honour, immediately visible on entrance, was a 'living', large-scale relief map of the world. Set in water, small model ships incessantly ran along the main ocean routes from port to port, connecting the various parts of the empire, painted red as usual, with both the mother country and each other. According to the *Official Guide*, they thus served as a 'medium for the exchange of commodities between the manufacturing centres of overcrowded countries and the vast agricultural centres of the younger [sic] lands'. 'It is impossible', the *Guide* continued, seemingly awed by this mobile spectacle,

> to spend even a few moments watching the vessels in pursuit of their lawful occasions and the ever-changing lights which indicate the growth of this mighty empire without a sobering sense, not only of civilisation's vast achievement, but of its still vaster requirements.[22]

Displaying a wide range of British governmental activities and the superior state of the technologies employed for its purposes, the Pavilion presented a contrast with the non-European colonial displays. At the same time, it was intended to provide the Empire with a symbolic centre, otherwise yawningly absent. London was supposed to be to the empire what the British Government Pavilion was to the exhibition, but, in fact, this meant that Wembley's symbolic order became almost incomprehensible. The 'living map' installation was yet another attempt to domesticate the empire (and by implication the entire world) by replicating, reducing and representing it on a small scale as the conflated centrepiece of the centre (the British Government Pavilion in the British Empire Exhibition) of the empire's centre and 'the world's greatest metropolis', London. The empire's heart turned out to be a map of it.

3. Time and Space Travellers: Critics, Visitors, Tourists

Apart from the troubles over the West African 'Walled City', there were few controversies over the British Empire Exhibition in the press, at least about its political status in the wider context of empire. Although agreeing to a large extent with the exhibition's official objectives in general, the majority of commentators presented a set of different, mostly functional arguments that tried to prove the desirable character of such initiatives in general and the indubitable success of this project in particular. The following four arguments can be isolated from the press coverage.

The first argument stated that the exhibition would act as a 'stocktaking of our Imperial position in production, manufacture and merchanting'. It would directly contribute to the advancement of the British economy and result in an upturn in trade with the colonies (Fostering-Trade argument).[23] Second, the holding of such a 'family party' as a 'great agency of empire development' would strengthen the cohesion of the colonies and the unity of empire. Already at the beginning of February 1924, the former industrial trouble-shooter Lord Askwith, for example, was arguing in the *Daily Telegraph* that this would mark a significant step forward in comparison with the Great Exhibition of 1851, where the colonies had been greatly underrepresented (Bonds-of-Empire argument):

> It was not till the Indian and Colonial Exhibition and the Jubilee Pageants of 1887 and 1897 that the nation began to awake to a better knowledge of the import of the British Empire. It is but fitting that some stock should now be taken and education spread more widely than ever, to make us realize that the British Empire is a living and growing entity, bound together in a manner different from any other known to history.[24]

Third, the exhibition would not only contribute to the improvement of the general living standard in Great Britain, but also have positive consequences for the welfare of mankind. According to this argument, the unstoppable progress of science, whose promotion was an integral part of this exhibition, made such results inevitable. In the end, this was a 'step towards ultimate understanding and co-operation between the nations of the world' (Unity-of-Mankind argument).[25] Last, an argument was often put forward which, unlike the former ones, could serve to motivate an individual visit rather than to justify the exhibition as such: for an 18-pence admission fee, a visit to the exhibition could take the place of an entire world tour. George Clarke Lawrence, for instance, stated succinctly: 'To visit the Exhibition is to visit every Continent of the earth', and a prospectus promised both a problem- and care-free panoramic insight into nothing less than the entire world (Around-the-World-in-a-Day argument).[26]

Together with constant attempts at evoking what Roland Barthes calls 'reality effects' this argument was probably as intrinsic to the entire 'exhibitionary complex' and its rhetorical universe as the critique of tourism is to tourism. Both were roughly of the same age.[27] The imaginary world tour, despite being confined to one place, was nonetheless celebrated as a truly historic achievement. The exhibition seemed to promote a further democratization in travelling in a way which was politically both correct and desirable, that is imperial. 'In the old days', began the *Official Guide*'s introduction,

> the Grand Tour was the prize of the fortunate few. Young men of wealth and position devoted two or three years to travel, often in circumstances of acute discomfort, and came back having caught no more than a glimpse of Europe. The Empire as we know it did not exist. Even the beginnings were small and far away. To-day the Grand Tour is within the reach of all, and the actual cost of it is just eighteenpence![28]

A development that had begun with the decline of the 'Romantic Grand Tour' as well as the first indications of a more organized tourist industry around 1820 and the subsequent rise of international exhibitions peaking just before 1900, seemed to have arrived at a climax. Tourism was possible without travelling. To adopt the tourist's gaze at the outer world did not even require leaving one's own city. However, a certain undertone of paternalistic pity vis-à-vis the social newcomers was not too well hidden when Lord Stevenson, Chairman of the Board of the Exhibition, intimated in a lecture given to the Royal Society of Arts after the first year that 'to the great majority of 17 million people who visited "Wembley" it is the only Empire they know'.[29]

How was the relationship between fair-like amusement, entertainment and spectacle on one hand, and the display of imperial themes and propaganda on the other, received by the individual visitor? The consumption of the imperial project by a mass audience is obviously difficult to ascertain. However, some conclusions can be drawn. First of all, most visitors seem to have been impressed by what they experienced. For Arthur Mason, the son of an English butcher growing up in Wembley, the British Empire Exhibition was 'a big thing in our life'. Having never seen a non-European before, Mason was, like many others, deeply moved by the completeness and remoteness of a world still in his hands and under his control:

> Every time you went you were entering into another world, a fascinating world. [...] The most vivid thing is the anticipation when you actually went in and paid your ninepence and you went through and you were, now this whole world was spread in front of you. All these pavilions and people, and, well, it was just like a fairy land really to a small boy.[30]

Ibrahim Ismaa'il, on the other hand, wrote about a visit to Wembley from the perspective of a young Somali, who had been living for some time in a Socialist community near Cardiff. After a trip to the site he found himself impressed and confused, but above all distanced from his European colonizers:

> [At Wembley] we saw big machines moving by themselves and all sorts of other strange and wonderful things. I felt overwhelmed by it all. It appeared to me as if the world had been made for Europeans, who had only to stretch out their hands to bring before them, as by magic, all the products of the Universe.[31]

Finally, Eric Pasold, an immigrant from Eastern Europe, was likewise 'overwhelmed' by the 'colourful, bustling spectacle' whose lasting impact on him could not be 'conveyed in words': 'The nostalgic picture of this mightiest of all empires as displayed at Wembley is so deeply engraved in my subconscious that its influence still lingers after all the years that have since passed', he wrote a few years later in his autobiography. However, the visit to Wembley also left an ambivalent mixture of envy and admiration. Describing the reasons for such an uneasiness in more detail than Ismaa'il, Pasold revealed why such feelings did not alter his wish to be naturalized; quite the contrary:

> The more exotic the pavilions the more they thrilled me. [...] India held an irresistible fascination [...] Nigerians in their colourful robes, cowboys from Calgary, dusky East African beauties, Indians, Malays, Chinamen, Australians, New Zealanders and Fiji islanders in an endless variety of human types, colour of skin and national costume, and in a profusion of tongues with which the Tower of Babel itself could not have competed - yet all were members of one great empire, united under one king and flag, linked by the English language, financed by sterling, ruled by British justice and protected by the Royal Navy. How proud they must all feel, I thought, and how I envied them.[32]

Thus, the majority of both domestic and foreign visitors found themselves impressed by the wide range and exotic diversity of easily digested objects on display rather than by the accompanying industrial or educational exhibits. The immediate reaction to the multiplicity of meanings these images conveyed was a diffuse imperial 'feeling' or 'sentiment', as the Earl of Meath had it, that was supposed to 'hasten materially the unification of the British Empire' and have London finally officially recognized as its centre and capital.[33]

Exhibitions became an integral part of the urban environment, both material and cognitive, but also helped to form it. Sometimes, in fact, the relation between the exposition ground and the urban context seemed in danger of being inverted. Especially for the numerous foreign or colonial visitors, so-called 'colonials', the metropolis itself *was* the actual exhibit, rather than their 'exported homes' at the exhibition site. For them, the relation between the 'real world' beyond the gates on the one hand, and the exhibition site on the other could be blurred, if not entirely reversed. London itself became the actual exhibit. From such a perspective, their experience could even be considered as complementary to the general trend of importing and concentrating the entire world in the imperial centre. It thus reflected the colonial situation - but *in* the metropolis.

The results and consequences of the imperial exhibitions were ambivalent: on the one hand, by demonstrating cultural exoticism to a mass audience, ethnic displays and debates about the representation of foreign cultures helped create a certain idea of Britishness. The overall effect lay not so much in the knowledge acquired but in an emotional mapping, the subjective creation of an imaginative topography. On the other hand, however, the partially successful protests of the Union of Students of African Descent must be read as the first signs of dissolution of the centre's monopoly in ascribing meaning. The vision of 'Empire' as embodied in the British Empire Exhibition had lost most of its former ideological and conceptual connotations. Spectacle had replaced them as the prevailing form of representation, the empire itself became a salesman's package. Deprived of its meaning, the flotation of empire on the stock exchange of images would precede its political demise, its 'kingdoms of the mind'[34] revealing themselves as mere fantasies intended for consumption rather than for education. Viewed in this light, the British Empire Exhibition of 1924/25 represents both another attempt at reinventing the empire and, simultaneously, the beginning of its end. If this did not in fact prescribe the empire's political disintegration, at least it was announced *in nuce*. Taken together, the representations analysed here represented neither the empire nor themselves. Rather, they overlapped each other in meaning to such an extent that an unambiguous interpretation is impossible to make. Although a major component of the 'complete colonization of social life',[35] the British Empire Exhibition proved to be tautological. Simultaneously, it was a real spectacle and a true copy.

4. Imperial Exhibitions as Travel Destinations and Tourist Attractions

Given that national and international industrial exhibitions were generally understood as 'Flash Photographs of Civilisation on the Run', the media visualization of progress achieved, as well as the ritualized communication of national identities for a mass audience, are commonly considered the primary functions of each international exposition.[36] The reduction of the whole world to a strictly limited space in the exhibition form served as the supreme principle of the representation and orchestration of cultural encounters in the age of empire. Fin-de-siècle imperial exhibitions resembled their surrounding metropolitan areas in many ways and were in fact often considered 'cities within the city'. To use Louis Wirth's classical attributes of urbanism yet again,[37] both kinds of cities, the 'real' and the 'fake' one, were relatively large, spatially dense, and socially heterogeneous. Unlike their environs, however, there was very little that was coincidental about the expositions, and one of their essential, often-discussed features consisted precisely in their transitory character, not in their permanence.

Taken together, all these expositions exposed 'frozen times' and distant places in an urban setting, and thus seemed to open up undreamed-of opportunities of travelling in time and space for their visitors. Pseudo-medieval ensembles labelled 'Alt-Berlin', 'Old London' or 'Vieux Paris' were integral, often very popular, parts of each exhibition's standard repertory, and were aptly described by the French writer Adolphe Démy as 'ce mélange des âges, cette juxtaposition des temps'.[38] Wembley took part in this web of representations and references which referred back and forth to each other; here, for instance, an 'Old London Bridge' was to be found between a Burmese pagoda and the Indian pavilion. It led directly to the amusement section of the exhibition (Fig. 3).[39]

It could therefore be argued that imperial exhibitions included and provided, in Bakhtin's suggestive term, so-called 'chronotopes': fictional sites where different times and spaces were brought together, thickened and compressed, where activities, stories and events were simultaneously staged and enacted, and sold to contemporary spectators and visitors. These times and spaces varied enormously in their qualities, and, implied in the contrasting displays, were very different political stances on historical achievements, the state of civilization, and the future progress and prospects of mother country and its colonies. While the scope and usefulness of this argument are still open to debate, it nonetheless allows exhibitions to be studied according to the character and ration of their temporal and spatial categories – even if represented in a quite bizarre mixture – without privileging either category. The chronotope, as Bakhtin's editor Michael Holquist puts it, 'is an optic for reading texts as x-rays of the forces at work in the culture system from which they spring'. The three concepts put forward here – the exhibitions' transitional nature, their spatial layout and urban context, and their chronotopic character – mark by necessity important points of departure for a theory of European exhibition practices which has still to be written.[40]

Yet, the relationship between turn-of-the-century British imperial exhibitions and the history of early mass tourism was not limited to such forms of internal tourism. Like most guidebooks written before the event, *The Marlborough Pocket Guide to the Empire Exhibition at Wembley* predicted that the exposition would make London develop into a 'microcosm of the world, where men of every race and clime will meet'.[41] Its author could only make such a forecast because the medium's history seemed to guarantee that both aspects – the reduction of worldwide space and its reproduction in a single spot, and its

Fig. 3: The Old London Bridge between the Indian Pavilion and the Burmese Pagoda.

direct counterpart, the occasion provided by the exhibition for world-wide travelling and meeting – would prevail yet again.

In fact, ever since Thomas Cook (in cooperation with several railway companies) had organized special low-cost excursions to London and the 1851 exhibition for the British working classes from all parts of the country (and thus helped to make Sir Charles Babbage's forecast come true), a pattern had been set. A newspaper specially launched on that purpose, *The Excursionist and Exhibition Advertiser*, combined articles with technical information about the journey with hints about how to visit both exhibition and metropolis. Simultaneously, it served to market Cook's package tours. Once developed and refined, for later expositions in Paris and elsewhere, these methods of attracting tourists would simply be revived, though obviously on a much larger scale. An already well promoted, popular product like the Great Exhibition suited the developing tourism industry perfectly, and it is precisely with the excursion trains that the democratization of English leisure is often said to have begun. At the same time, employers sometimes provided special travel grants to reward a few selected groups of workers and to foster their industrial education; these, in turn, were given the opportunity to embark on a journey about which they had to write lengthy and often quite detailed reports upon their return. It does not come as a surprise then that exhibitions were mediated, communicated and popularized through the same sort of advertisements, newspapers, travel literature, guidebooks, picture postcards and other ephemera as was 'normal' tourism, and therefore formed part of one and the same universe of travel.[42]

The precise numbers which illustrate such a close, interdependent relationship between large-scale universal, industrial or imperial exhibitions and mass tourism are rather difficult to come by. Fig. 4 shows the number of passengers embarking or disembarking at eight different French, Belgian and Dutch ports connecting with Great Britain between 1850 and 1914. Three general trends immediately catch the eye: first, the almost exponentially, or at least extremely rapidly-growing number of passengers over the course of roughly sixty years; second, until 1900 the holding of exhibitions always caused clearly distinguishable peak points in the growth curve; third, after 1900, with the overall number of passengers several times greater than in 1850, the peaks became less distinct but were nonetheless still recognizable.[43]

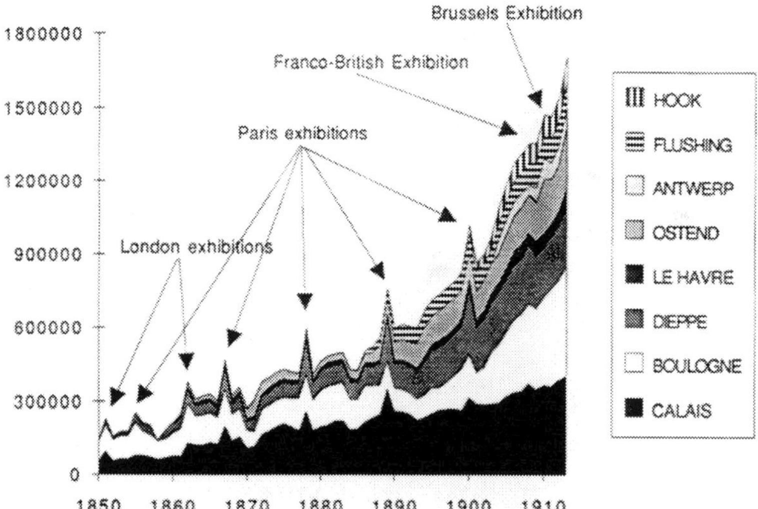

Fig. 4: PRO, RAIL 633/425, 411/655.

While clearly indicating a significant correlation, these figures say very little about individual visitors' travel routes, their places of origin and points of departure. However, as the examples discussed above – Mason, Ismaa'il and Pasold – demonstrate, exhibitions were certainly attractive travel destinations for international, national, regional and even local tourists and visitors. Mason was a Londoner from Willesden, Ismaa'il a widely travelled Somali temporarily living in Cardiff (who was likewise impressed by two further British institutions, the Tube and the British Museum) and Pasold the eighteen-year old son of Bohemian industrialists whose parents had sent him to England for a whole year to finish his education. Wembley, however, he visited together with his father and an uncle on a small conducted tour of a dozen businessmen, starting from Leipzig; the objectives of this tour were to see 'modern and traditional London, the great exhibition, and the City'.[44]

Forty years earlier, in 1886, the Colonial and Indian Exhibition had already provided a similarly welcome occasion for numerous visitors of either British or indigenous origin, to pay London a visit. In addition to the participating 'natives' a number of public figures were invited and looked after by a specifically founded Reception Committee of the Royal Commission under the supervision of the Duke of Abercorn. A complex system of 14 different categories was used to decide whom to invite and how the guests would be treated. According to several estimates approximately 5,000 to 6,000 official 'colonial and Indian visitors' accepted this invitation. Yet, the number of 'unofficial', that is private visitors was clearly much higher. On similar criteria it was estimated that over 5,000 visitors from India alone came to see Wembley.[45] Thus, imperial exhibitions like the Colonial and Indian Exhibition or the British Empire Exhibition were not only attractive to former emigrants seeking a reason to visit their old home, but also brought a multitude of British visitors to London, many of them for the first time ever.

5. Travels in Hyperreality?

In advertising the British Empire Exhibition and other such hallmark events, the Around-the-World-in-a-Day-argument was popular because it elegantly conflated elements of internal and external tourism, thus parallelling the exposition's alleged structure. If bourgeois travelling opened up new temporal and spatial dimensions, simultaneously translating spatial travelling into time travelling, then exhibitions clearly were part of a long-term development which they also helped to catalyze.[46] Here, however, the general reduction of the time formerly spent on the Grand Tour was taken to an extreme: by no means completely annihilated yet but rather exceedingly compressed, chronotopic elements still dominated the time-space ratio. While theoretically numerous places were still visited, the Tour now concentrated on one major destination only. At Wembley, as elsewhere, every effort was made to ensure the site's representational credibility. It is no accident, then, that its 'native villages' first came under public fire. Their contribution *in situ* was of essential importance to the entire arrangement, for only they seemed capable both of guaranteeing authenticity and turning virtual worlds into reality: living 'natives' could not be faked. Yet, if such an attempt at 'staged authenticity' failed, the exposition was itself exposed. True or not, a vast majority of critical commentators seems willingly to have accepted at least this argument.[47] Having devoted a six-day-long in-depth visit to the exhibition to disentangle 'appearances and reality' of the staged empire, the German publicist Fritz von Hake concluded 'that one had, in just a few days, most comfortably gained the same impression as if one had travelled through the entire world-embracing British empire'.[48]

Last but not least, the sheer existence of the exhibitionary complex 'world wide web' renders all standard arguments about national specificities or even identities unsatisfactory and calls for a new, transnational form of network analysis.[49] By responding and reacting to each other, these representational spaces developed a specific use of forms, thus giving further shape to the medium, codifying a certain standard repertoire but still further differentiating its specific language. While exhibitions could *prima facie* be easily added to the many similar sites in which, according to Michel Foucault, 'history unfolds', namely the church, cemetery, theatre, garden, museum, library, fairground, brothel, barracks and, of course, the prison,[50] they differ from all these institutions by a single factor of utmost importance: their transitional character. That all organizers tried to overcome the medium's fleeting nature by issuing thick general catalogues consisting of innumerable single volumes, erecting carefully designed architectural residuals or incorporating all exhibits in a museum before the actual exhibition had even been inaugurated is by no means contradictory. It does not come as a surprise, then, that ever since 1851 the question of the 'day after' has constituted a highly

LIVERPOOL JOHN MOORES UNIVERSITY
LEARNING SERVICES

contested issue. In this, as in many other ways, Hanover clearly did not constitute an exception from the rule: 'Tour the world's future in a single day' was one of Expo 2000's major slogans.

Notes

1 W. Sombart, 'Die Ausstellung', *Morgen: Wochenzeitschrift für deutsche Kultur* 9, 28 February 1908, 249.

2 Flaubert, *Le Dictionnaire des idées reçues et le catalogue des idées chic* (Paris: Librairie Générale Française, 1997), 78.

3 *A City for Sale* (London, 1922), 4; H606.1/WHI/HQM537, Hammersmith and Fulham Archives and Local History Centre, London.

4 See M.L. Pratt, *Imperial Eyes: Travel Writing and Transculturation* (London: Routledge, 1992), 6f. for this concept.

5 P. Geddes, *Industrial Exhibitions and Modern Progress* (Edinburgh: David Douglas, 1887), 26.

6 C. Babbage, *The Exposition of 1851; or, Views of the Industry, the Science, and the Government of England* (London: John Murray, 1851), v.

7 Thomas, 'Preface', in M. Hardie (ed.), *The Pageant of Empire Souvenir Volume* (London: Fleetway, 1924), 3.

8 G.C. Lawrence (ed.), *The British Empire Exhibition 1924: Official Guide*, fourth ed. (London: Fleetway Press, 1924), 13. A few years ago, most of the publications occasioned by the Wembley exhibition were moved from the Grange Museum of Community History in northwest London to the Cricklewood Community History Library and Archives, London Borough of Brent. There is no satisfactory historiographical analysis of the British Empire Exhibition, but see D.R. Knight and A.D. Sabey, *The Lion Roars at Wembley: British Empire Exhibition 60th Anniversary 1924-1925* (London: Barnard and Westwood, 1984); T. August, 'Art and Empire – Wembley, 1924', *History Today* 43 (October 1993), 38-44; J. MacKenzie, *Propaganda and Empire: The Manipulation of British Public Opinion, 1880-1960* (Manchester: Manchester University Press, 1984), chapter 4; J. Woodham, 'Images of Africa and Design at the British Empire Exhibitions between the Wars', *Journal of Design History* 2 (1989), 15-33, and J. Hill and F. Varrasi, 'Creating Wembley: The Construction of a National Monument', *The Sports Historian* 17 (1997), 28-43.

9 The promoter of this project, Sir Edward Watkin, was Managing Director of the Metropolitan Railway Company and planned a spectacular pleasure park in Wembley with the tower as its centrepiece. This project was to increase inner-city tourism and provide his company with more passengers. When it had reached 155 feet (out of 1200) in 1894, the project was halted for want of funds and structural defects but nonetheless soon turned into a popular weekend destination. See Anon., 'The Great Tower in London', *Engineering* 49 (1890), 542-4, F.C. Lynde, *Descriptive Illustrated Catalogue of the Sixty-Eight Competitive Designs for the Great*

Tower of London (London: Industries, 1890), C. Marsillon, 'La Tour Eiffel de Londres', *La Nature* 22 (1894), 387-90, J.M. Richards, 'A Tower for London', *The Architectural Review* 88 (1940), 141-4, F.I. Jenkins, 'Harbingers of Eiffel's Tower', *Journal of the Society of Architectural Historians* 16.4 (1957), 22-9, R. Jay, 'Taller than Eiffel's Tower: The London and Chicago Tower Projects, 1889-1894', *Journal of the Society of Architectural Historians* 46 (1987), 145-56.

10 *The Times*, 16 April 1924, 19 and 23 April 1924, 33.

11 *The Times*, 10 October 1921. Quoted by Hill and Varrasi, 'Creating Wembley', 34. See also Lord Stevenson, *British Empire Exhibition: A Lecture Delivered to the Royal Society of Arts* (London, 16 April 1925), 16: 'The building of Wembley was the building of a huge new city. That it was a beautiful city, no one denies.'

12 L. Richmond, 'The Lure of Wembley', *Studio* 87 (1924), 312.

13 *Daily News Souvenir Guide to the British Empire Exhibition* (London: Daily News, 1924), 56. D.B.T. Vijayaraghavacharya, 'India and the British Empire Exhibition', *Asiatic Review* 19 (1923), 140-5.

14 *Daily News Souvenir Guide*, 56f.

15 Ibid., 72, 74 (emphasis in original). The *Official Guide* also stressed complete correspondence between copy and original: 'The village within the walls at Wembley is *complete to the last detail*. In every way it *reproduces* the *characteristic* village of the West African Hinterland. In it *representatives* of West African tribes live and move and have their being for the period of the Exhibition.' Lawrence (ed.), *Official Guide*, 77 (my emphasis).

16 C. Graves, 'When West Africa Woos', *The Sunday Express*, 4 May 1924, 7. See also C.F. Hayfron-Benjamin: 'The Union of Students of African Descent: Its Work in London', *West Africa*, 25 October 1924, 1179; *Minutes*, 17 May 1924, CO 554/64, 169-325, Public Record Office (PRO).

17 Ibid., 169.

18 See *British Empire Exhibition 1924 Wembley, London April-October: Handbook of General Information* (London, 1924), 8f.; *The Pavilion of H.M. Government: A Brief Record of Official Participation in the British Empire Exhibition, Wembley, 1924* (London: HMSO, 1924), 10; H.B. Grimsditch, 'The British Government Pavilion and the Basilica at Wembley', *Studio* 88 (July 1924), 27-32. F. von Hake, *Wembley: Schein und Wahrheit* (Weimar: Fink, 1926), 20. Embodying 'the might, dignity, power and prestige of the British Empire' and typically British characteristics such as 'strength, honesty, simplicity' at the same time, the lion emblem served as the exhibition's general trademark and official logo. See 'Triumph of Advertising: Making Wembley Popular', *Daily Telegraph*, 28 October 1924 ; 'How Wembley was Advertised: Work of the Publicity Department', *The Times*, 28 October 1924, 10; Lawrence (ed.), *Official Guide*, 103.

19 S. Smith, 'Should Britain Take Part in International Exhibitions?', *The Nineteenth Century* 67 (June 1910), 983-94, here 986f.

20 *The Pavilion of H.M. Government*, 2; and Original Version of a Draft to the Secretary, Treasury, January 1923, no. 7657, BT 60/5/1, PRO.

21 *The Raid on Zeebrugge: An Illustrated Souvenir of the Model Display in the Admiralty Theatre of H.M. Government Pavilion. British Empire Exhibition* (London: HMSO, 1924/25).

22 Lawrence (ed.), *Official Guide*, 44f.; *Daily News Souvenir Guide*, 47.

23 For instance T. Clarke, 'The British Empire Exhibition - Second Phase', *The Nineteenth Century* 97 (February 1925), 175-82, here 180; E. Shanks, 'Reflections on Wembley', *The Saturday Review* 140, 11 July 1925, 36f.; J. Stevenson, 'The British Empire Exhibition', *Landmark/English Speaking World* 6 (1924), 153-8.

24 Lord Askwith, 'Empire Exhibition: Seventy Years' Progress', *Daily Telegraph*, 4 February 1924; F. Young, 'At Wembley: A Pilgrim's Progress XXXVIII', *The Saturday Review* 137 (29 March 1924), 317f.; A. Harrison, 'The British Empire Exhibition, 1924', *The English Review* 35 (July-December 1922), 446-51; G. Barry, 'A Day at Wembley', *The Saturday Review* 137 (17 May 1924), 502f.

25 'The Meaning of Wembley', *The Saturday Review* 137 (26 April 1924), 428. G.C. Lawrence, 'The British Empire in Miniature: A Preliminary Survey of Next Year's Great Exhibition at Wembley', *The World's Work* 42 (October 1923), 429-32.

26 Lawrence (ed.), *Official Guide*, 15. See also the prospectus *British Empire Exhibition 1924. Wembley, London. April-October* (London, 1924), 35.8 (BRI), Greater London Record Office.

27 J. Buzard, *The Beaten Track: European Tourism, Literature, and the Ways to Culture, 1800-1918* (Oxford: Clarendon Press, 1993), chapter 2. See also C. Hennig, 'Touristenbeschimpfung: Zur Geschichte des Anti-Tourismus', *Zeitschrift für Volkskunde* 93 (1997), 31-41. To give but one example, see 'Round the World at the Paris Exposition', *Atlantic Monthly* 43 (1879), 41-8; T. Bennett, *The Birth of the Museum: History, Theory, Politics* (London: Routledge, 1995), chapter 2.

28 Lawrence (ed.), *Official Guide*, 13. The same argument, but with a view to the individual tourist, was made on the official visitors' map: 'You have often wanted to travel around the world. At Wembley you will be able to do so at a minimum of cost, in a minimum of time, with a minimum of trouble, studying as you go the shop windows of the British Empire. You will be able to go behind these windows and see how the goods are produced and meet the men and women who produce them. Every aspect of life, civilised and uncivilised, will be shown in an Exhibition which is the last word in comfort and convenience.' *British Empire Exhibition 1924*, n.p.

29 J. Towner, 'The Grand Tour: A Key Phase in the History of Tourism', *Annals of Tourism Research* 12 (1985), 297-333, here 314, 325. Stevenson, *British Empire Exhibition*, 5.

30 Interview with Arthur Mason, 22 February 1996, Grange Museum of Community History.

31 I. Ismaa'il, 'The Life and Adventures of a Somali: Presented and Annotated by Richard Pankhurst', *Africa: Rivista trimestrale di studi e documentazione dell' Istituto Italo-Africano* 32.2-3 (giugno-settembre 1977), 159-76, 355-84, here 378f. Although a part of Somalia (British Somaliland) had come under British rule in 1884, it was not represented by a pavilion of its own but together with other East African states. This 'East Africa' section is not mentioned by Ismaa'il.

32 E.W. Pasold, *Ladybird, Ladybird: A Story of Private Enterprise* (Manchester: Manchester University Press, 1977), 77-9.

33 Earl of Meath, 'London as the Heart of the Empire', in A. Webb (ed.), *London of the Future* (London: T. Fisher Unwin, 1921), 251-8, here 252f.

34 J.H. Thomas, 'Preface', 3.

35 G. Debord, *The Society of the Spectacle* (New York: Zone Books, 1995), 29.

36 G.F. Barwick, 'International Exhibitions and Their Civilising Influence', in J. Samuelson (ed.), *The Civilisation of Our Day: A Series of Original Essays on Some of Its More Important Phases at the Close of the Nineteenth Century. By Expert Writers* (London: Sampson Low, Marston and Company, 1896), 301-13, here 313.

37 L. Wirth, 'Urbanism as a Way of Life', *The American Journal of Sociology* 44 (1938), 1-24, here 8.

38 A. Démy, *Essai historique sur les expositions universelles de Paris* (Paris: Librairie Alphonse Picard, 1907), 594.

39 See *A Short Description of Burma, Its Inhabitants and Products, Together with an Account of the Burma Pavilion at the British Empire Exhibition of 1924* (London, 1924).

40 As Mikhail Bakhtin puts it: 'We will give the name chronotope (literally, 'time space') to the intrinsic connectedness of temporal and spatial relationships that are artistically expressed in literature. [...] In the literary artistic chronotope, spatial and temporal indicators are fused into one carefully thought-out, concrete whole. Time, as it were, thickens, takes on flesh, becomes artistically visible; likewise space becomes charged and responsive to the movements of time, plot and history.' See Bakhtin, 'Forms of Time and the Chronotope in the Novel: Notes toward a Historical Poetics' (1937), in M. Holquist (ed.), *The Dialogic Imagination* (Austin: University of Texas Press, 1981), 84-258, here 84. See G.S. Morson and C. Emerson, *Mikhail Bakhtin: Creation of a Prosaics* (Stanford: Stanford University Press, 1990), esp. 366-432.

41 H. Moore, *The Marlborough Pocket Guide to the Empire Exhibition at Wembley, 1924* (London: Marlborough, 1924), 2.

42 See J. Reulecke, 'Kommunikation durch Tourismus? Zur Geschichte des organisierten Reisens im 19. und 20. Jahrhundert', in H. Pohl (ed.), *Die Bedeutung der Kommunikation für Wirtschaft und Gesellschaft* (Stuttgart: Steiner, 1989), 365f.; J. Walvin, *Leisure and Society, 1700-1850* (London:

Longman, 1978), 20f., 124; L. Withey, *Grand Tours and Cook's Tours: A History of Leisure Travel, 1750 to 1915* (London: Aurum, 1997), 135-66.

43 See L. Tissot, 'How did the British Conquer Switzerland? Guidebooks, Railways, Travel Agencies, 1850-1914', *Journal of Transport History* 16 (1995), 29f.

44 Pasold, *Ladybird, Ladybird*, 75f.

45 See Royal Commission for the Colonial and Indian Exhibition (ed.), *Report of the Reception Committee* (London, 1886), 18, for a full program. *The Empire* even estimated the total number of foreign visitors that had made the journey specifically for the exhibition at 30,000 to 60,000. See 'The Close of the Exhibition', *The Empire* 656, 12 November 1886, 4. For a fascinating analysis of travelogues written by Indian men about London in the 1880s on this occasion see A. Burton, 'Making a Spectacle of Empire: Indian Travellers in Fin-de-Siècle London', *History Workshop Journal* 42 (Autumn 1996), 127-46. See also the report on *H.M. Government's Participation at the British Empire Exhibition, Wembley 1924 and 1925*, BT 60/14/2, PRO, M.

46 See W. Kaschuba, 'Erkundung der Moderne: Bürgerliches Reisen nach 1900', *Zeitschrift für Volkskunde* 87 (1991), 29-52, here 35 and 40.

47 The complex relationship between authenticity, virtualization and the chronotope cannot be discussed in full detail here, but see D. MacCannell, *The Tourist: A New Theory of the Leisure Class* (New York: Schocken, 1976), 91-107; D. Harvey, *The Condition of Postmodernity: An Enquiry into the Origins of Cultural Change* (Oxford: Blackwell, 1989), 299; U. Eco, 'A Theory of Expositions', in id., *Travels in Hyperreality* (New York: Harcourt Brace Jovanovich, 1986), 296.

48 Von Hake, *Schein und Wahrheit*, 9f.

49 W. Pehnt, *Frankfurter Allgemeine Zeitung*, 5 May 1999, 55.

50 M. Foucault, 'Of Other Spaces', *Diacritics* 16 (1986), 22-7.

Travelling in Transience
The Semiotics of Necro-Tourism

Tobias Döring

1. Graveyards and the Making of Tourism

Let me begin with a common complaint: 'These Tourists, heaven preserve us!' The outcry is familiar and has often been repeated; tourists have never had a good press. For all their social prominence, economic power and cultural relevance since the early nineteenth century, tourists are regularly decried and rarely described in other than negative terms. As soon almost as the word is introduced into the English language, *tourist* is used to suggest disapproving or derogatory attitudes:

> These Tourists, heaven preserve us! needs must live
> A profitable life: some glance along,
> Rapid and gay, as if the earth were air,
> And they were butterflies to wheel about
> Long as the summer lasted: some, as wise,
> Perched on the forehead of a jutting crag,
> Pencil in hand and book upon the knee,
> Will look and scribble, scribble on and look,
> Until a man might travel twelve stout miles,
> Or reap an acre of his neighbour's corn.[1]

This is the opening of William Wordsworth's Lakeland poem 'The Brothers', published in 1800, some twenty years after the first citation of the term *tourist* in the *OED*.[2] The stereotype constructed here is still recognizable: the tourist is regarded as an idle pleasure seeker and sightseer, with no true understanding of the places visited, outside their social nexus, and entirely reliant on second-hand representations. The observation that tourists keep 'pencil in hand and book upon the knee' while they 'look and scribble, scribble and look' is particularly interesting because it emphasizes the closed circuit character of touristic sign systems. The 'book' signifies both the guidebook and the sketch book, from which the tourist gains and to which he imparts all information – whereas the real world of work ('reap an acre of his neighbour's corn') and proper travel ('travel twelve stout miles') escapes his notice. Wordsworth's poem here presents the voice of a country priest who is proffered as a general cultural spokesman. We may take his critical remarks as evidence of how the idea of modern tourism is, literally, made through its critique.

In his recent study on *European Tourism, Literature and the Ways to Culture*, James Buzard has discussed this poem as a prime example of what he terms the 'differential relationship' of true/false-categories between travel and tourism.[3] He points out that the term *tourist* did not gradually acquire the derogatory connotations through negative experience. The very origins of tourism, he argues, are fundamentally determined by an opposition to what is perceived as 'genuine' travelling. Tourism has long been understood as an organized mass activity along beaten tracks and in regulated modes, precluding the possibility of singular experience and of true encounters with a place. In this way, tourism shows a salient effect of modernization: the new mobility it offers is payed for with a presumed loss of individualized and authentic ways to culture.

In England, the Lake District was among the first places thus reorganized for the emerging tourist market in response to popular demand – not least as a consequence of Wordsworth's poetic publicity for this region. Ironically though, his own work rather attempted to salvage it for the solitary traveller and, as in 'The Brothers', fend off all unwelcome intrusions. But this particular poem, placed at the threshold to modernity and set against a background of failing family traditions, is especially interesting for its thoughtful setting: the encounter between tourist/visitor and local priest takes place on the village churchyard. The critique of tourism it offers is staged among the graves.

As I propose in this essay to look at graves in British travelling, this seems to be a highly relevant locale. What does it suggest about the significance of graveyards in the making of tourism? How may their *genius loci* bear on the meaning and topography of modern touring? And in what ways do graveyards function as topoi and targets in British travel practices?

Graves and graveyards are in fact rather conspicuous in the experience and literature of tourism. When Roland Barthes observed that 'Christianity is the chief purveyor of tourism',[4] he was referring to church buildings. But, to a large extent, the same holds true for the burial places associated with them. Graves, tombs, cemeteries and funeral monuments have long been well-established places for the cultural traveller and for the commercial tourist. They structure the itineraries of many journeys and are standard features of the classic guidebooks. The prominence of graves for travel goes back a long way into the past. Arguably, the most important modes of medieval journeying, the pilgrimage and the crusade, were also structured around a tomb as target. And some of the most popular forms of late twentieth-century touring give evidence of rather similar structuring - such as catastrophe tours to the sites of great calamities or the so-called Grave Line Tour in Hollywood to graves, suicide spots and assassination points involving film celebrities. In a chapter about fatal attractions of this sort, Chris Rojek has termed such death points 'Black Spots' and has noted that they clearly serve a strong demand and hold great touristic power.[5]

In the present discussion, I would certainly not want to suggest any trans-historical continuity of 'the grave' or 'death point' as a signifier throughout the literature and across the various versions of travel from the medieval via the romantic into the postmodern period. But I would like to address the question *why* such targets are so prevalent and prominent. What specific interests can they serve for travellers and tourists? And in what ways are they seen and represented in travelogues and guidebooks?

2. Labelling: Sights and Signs of Death

To begin with, one reason to consider here may be the point that graves are always placed at an intersection of nature with culture. Death, after all, seems to be something we all share: an anthropological constant. Funeral practices, on the other hand, are highly different and culturally specific. With his monumental study on the history of death, Philippe Ariès even suggested that death should altogether be regarded as a cultural invention, defined through images and social rituals which try to come to terms with this bewildering experience.[6] Perhaps we might account then for the fact that fatal attractions are so wide-spread in the history of travel by thinking of the ways in which they can be used to negotiate between otherness and sameness. My claims, however, would go further. Drawing on a range of sample texts and discussing the contextual and strategic relevance of the graves presented there, I would like to argue three points: that graveyards and cemeteries, as places of memory and canonization, have a story to tell which attracts outside visitors hoping to encounter 'the authentic'; that sepulchral representations therefore reveal the various understandings of the 'ways to culture' which travellers and tourists seek; and that there is a clear affinity between the semiotics of death and the semiotics of tourism.

This last point can be made with a closer look at the Wordsworth poem and its version of the rural churchyard. The visitor has come to this place especially to look at the graves (he tries to trace his family connections), and his insistent questions to the priest, on behalf of the reader, elicit much information about local burials. What is most remarkable about the graves found here is their lack of all distinctive features: they are not marked by any cultural signs and can hardly be distinguished from the neighbouring fields. As the visitor observes:

> Here's neither head not foot-stone, plate of brass,
> Cross-bones nor skull, – type of our earthly state
> Nor emblem of our hopes: the dead man's home
> Is but a fellow to that pasture-field.[7]

This is indeed a noticeable absence. According to an English funeral historian, common outdoor graves were permanently marked by headstones since the eighteenth century.[8] But the visitor's observation, I would add, is even more remarkable in that it also makes a crucial point about the semiotics of tourism. The local priest explains the lack of all explanatory signs with the closely-knit social structure of the village community where oral tradition keeps history alive and provides such information as the outsider is looking for:

> We have no need of names and epitaphs;
> We talk about the dead by our fire-sides.

At first reading, this answer simply echoes the familiar scepticism against writing as an alienating technique that substitutes dead script for living memory and signs for real presence. In the context of the poem's debate about tourists, however, the problem has a wider meaning: it also highlights the signifying practices by which a place is marked and marketed for tourism.

In a well-known article on 'The Semiotics of Tourism', Jonathan Culler has argued that the world is not only coded *for* tourists in such a way that certain places become saleable as 'authentic' sites, but that the world is also coded *by* them in this manner. Tourists themselves 'are the agents of semiotics: all over the world they are engaged in reading cities, landscapes and cultures as signs'.[9] For the tourist, each encounter with the other must be experienced as an instance of something 'typical', and to assure such an experience a special designation is required. Guidebooks, signposts, postcards, brochures, travelogues, photographs, souvenirs and the various other paraphernalia of the trade are all assistants in this task. They provide ciphers for the code by which tourists recognize the 'real' Orient, the 'typical' Italian piazza or the 'quintessential' English country church. The touristic search for the authentic is thus semiotically motivated: it is directed towards 'a usage perceived as a sign of that usage', as Culler puts it somewhat technically.[10] This is to say that, for example, gondolas or British canals are no longer seen as useful means of transportation but instead as signs of 'Venice' or of 'The Industrial Revolution'. We only *know* about the *genuine* features of a new and unique experience if it forms part of an explanatory and authenticating code and thus conforms to expectation. Whether at home or abroad, the enterprise of tourism, to a large extent, is a quest for signs that serve this purpose.

In the Wordsworth poem, then, the visitor's search for epitaphs points towards this practice of touristic coding. The irony of the poem, to be sure, lies in our awareness that the visitor only *poses* as a stranger and assumes the guise of tourist in order to find out about his brother's fate (whom he once left behind and now suspects dead and buried in his native soil). But this irony just sharpens the semiotic issue. '*We* want / No symbols, Sir', the priest tells the supposed stranger. The 'symbol' is the shibboleth to distinguish between insiders and outsiders, the dividing line between true and false, between local and touristic. And it seems to me entirely appropriate and deeply meaningful that this debate is played out on the graveyard. For, generally speaking, graveyards are always prime sites of symbolization. Graves present what is missing: they display a person lost. Burial practices are employed to mark this absence and therefore often involve great semiotic efforts. The whole repertoire of epitaphs, effigies, tombstones, emblems and sepulchral monuments can be seen as offering cultural signs in place of natural losses. Moreover, the signpost or symbol on the grave is a necessary marker to establish the genuine character of this particular spot and, as such, operates as a decisive defender against indifference and oblivion alike. Only the *naming* of a burial place marks it as authentic because – short of exhumation – this is what identifies the unique but absent dead. Thus, it may indeed be argued that the semiotics of graveyards and cemeteries seem to have intriguing affinities to the semiotics of tourism.

This is my hypothesis which I shall discuss with reference to some sample texts from the nineteenth and the early twentieth centuries. But before I consider this material from the tourist period proper, I would like to ground my discussion historically with one example from the early modern period of cultural touring.[11]

3. Wandering: Early Modern Tombstone Travel

In the history of European travel Thomas Coryate (ca 1577-1617), English gentleman and eccentric wit, may be regarded as a pioneer of the leisure tour. Son of a rector, friend of Ben Jonson and member of the fashionable Mermaid Tavern circle in London, Coryate engaged in an idiosyncratic version of what much later would become a wider social practice: journeying for journeying's sake. He was surely motivated by exotic and humanistic interests but, according to a modern commentator, his extensive pedestrian tours through Europe, the Middle East and into India were largely driven by 'self-conscious wanderlust'.[12] In this perspective, it is significant to note that this tourist *avant la lettre* held such a great esteem for graves that he described himself as a 'tombstone traveller'. What may he have meant by this?

Some of the implications of this term are established in a humourous but nonetheless affectionate poem about Coryate which concludes the 1616 publication of his letters from India. Here we learn that 'Toombs', 'Stones', 'Marble Pillars' and 'dead mens bones' were among Coryate's chief interests in both his touring and his writing.[13] In one of his last letters, addressed 'To his louing Mother' and published in the same collection, the traveller himself suggests some reasons for this sepulchral preference:

> I humbly beseech you euen vpon the knees of my heart, with all submissiue, supplications to pardon me for my long absence; for verily, I haue resolued by the fauour of the supernall powers, to spend 4 entire yeares more before my returne, and so to make it a

> Pilgrimage of 7 yeares, to the end I may very effectually and profitably contemplate a great part this worldy fabricke, determining by Gods special help, to go from *India* into the countrey of *Scythia*, now called *Tartaria*, to the Cittie *Samarcanda*, to see the Sepulcher of the greatest Conqueror that euer was in the worlde, *Tamberlaine* the Great.[14]

Coryate's announcement of this tour seems so interesting to me because it registers both old and new practices of travel. On the one hand, he speaks of his whole journey as a 'pilgrimage' and so frames it in the culturally most validated form of medieval mobility. He has indeed visited Jerusalem and often refers to the Bible when reasoning about his route. But his own desire for travel is neither teleologically nor theologically contained: it does not end at any Christian shrine. Instead, it leads him to the tomb of a notorious pagan emperor. What is it that he hopes to find there?

Johannes Fabian once argued that the point of reference in the history of European travel changed.[15] In the old pre-modern paradigm, travel was directed *to* the centres of religion; with pilgrimages, in particular, all authority and reasoning of travel is teleologically derived from the holy point of destination. In the modern paradigm, by contrast, secular travel leads *from* the centres of learning into the periphery; the motivation derives from the point of departure and so the significance of the enterprise must be mediated home in writing. With his letters to friends and family in England, Coryate does just that, and in the letter quoted he reveals that his projected trip to Samarcand is, in fact, a literary tour: motivated by *Tamburlaine the Great*, Christopher Marlowe's spectacular tragedy, which hit the London stage in the late 1580s and which remained popular into the seventeenth century. As much as Marlowe's mighty tyrant intends to 'confute those blind geographers' who in their maps exclude so many regions of the world,[16] Coryate maps the geography of his projected journey no longer on the authority of the Bible, but on a version of the world according to this stage play. Visiting the late conqueror's tomb, he plans to pay tribute to his worldly power.

Two further points should be noted here. Firstly, Coryate never reached this place. For all we know, he died himself while on his way to Tamburlaine's grave. This irony may well suggest another general reason why tombstone travelling has special fascination. It offers a reminder of the real risks and dangers to which travellers expose themselves and might, potentially, fall victim. The tour to visit others' graves may thus lead to one's own: it enacts the 'life-as-journey'-metaphor, through which travel and the trajectory of death can form a meaningful alliance. In the romantic search for solitude no less than on the beaten tracks of modern tourists, many a hopeful journey therefore may be mapped on such a *memento mori*. Secondly, Coryate's secular (and fatal) pilgrimage to the remains of Tamburlaine seems to be motivated by the same combination of the factual and the fictional that is characteristic of modern cultural touring – whether of the heritage type which takes us to the literary shrines and sites of Wordsworth's Lake District, Hardy's Wessex or Jane Austen's Bath,[17] or of the more recent popular type which takes us to the glamours of Hollywood, to film locations or to the home of Elvis Presley.[18] Even in a contemporary postmodern geography where the experience of space has generally become secularized such spots are marked as remnants of a spatial hierarchy: they remain places inscribed with special meaning. It seems as if, in a world of the profane, the celebrity shrine might offer a last substitute for the sacred.

This may be a contentious claim. To suggest parallels between the touristic functioning of figures such as 'Tamburlaine' and 'Elvis' seems to ignore our crucial move into the media age where stardom is constructed through simulacra in a constant reproduction of images. However, it is precisely for this reason that the burial places of contemporary celebrities gain even more importance and attention. The corpse is the one thing about them that cannot be replicated. The grave remains unique and can therefore be used and marketed as a sign of the 'authentic'. When we accept this as a further factor potentially contributing to the touristic popularity of graves, the question of historical experience, again, arises. Is this a recent development, propelled by the demands of the postmodern tourist trade and caused by the powerful media techniques of our age?

Chris Rojek, in his discussion of celebrity graves and other 'Black Spots', argues in this way. He points out, for instance, that Jim Morrison's grave at the Père Lachaise today is the fourth biggest tourist attraction in Paris.[19] And he goes on to remark that, generally speaking, this famous cemetery is not visited by mourners any longer but exclusively by tourists, who bring their cameras instead of flowers. This, he implies, is a profanation of what was once held sacred. 'Who, in bourgeois culture', Rojek asks rhetorically, 'would have dreamt of allowing the cemetery to become a tourist attraction?' In our times, the gravity and solemnity of graves have been 'reduced by moves to make them more colourful and more spectacular than other sights on the tourist trail'. He analyzes this as a 'relabelling of signs': complete with ice-cream vans and souvenir shops, traditional cemeteries have now been redefined as leisure parks.

The process of 'relabelling' here identified is evident and crucial because it reflects the same touristic transformation to which Culler draws attention when he claims that tourists perceive all usage as a sign. Arguably, the making of modern tourism can generally be accounted for in semiotic terms as providing places relabelled in this way and redefined outside pragmatic use. But while Rojek's diagnosis of the current situation is entirely plausible, his historical account is not. His implication that the contemporary tourist trade in Paris is trespassing on holy ground is highly questionable. It does not take into consideration that the Père Lachaise and, by and large, most of the other famous bourgeois cemeteries of the nineteenth century were constructed not only for the mourner, but also for the urban sightseer and leisure seeker.

4. Leisure Seeking: Victorian Garden Cemeteries

In England, this development took place in the 1830s and gained even more momentum in the Victorian period. Here, both the cemetery movement and the rise of organized touring must be regarded as cultural evidence and as integral part of the project of modernity. In the high industrial age, the Wordsworthian cult of country churchyards and solitary wanderers was soon becoming obsolete, or rather: the romantic cult gained new nostalgic popularity while the social practice changed. Travel as much as burial had to be reorganized for the masses.

In retrospect, this process is reflected in an interesting *Lecture on Epitaphs*, which Robert Wilkinson delivered to a mid-Victorian London audience in 1862. The speaker opens with the observation that 'the village churchyard is an object which will always claim an exception' and merit a thoughtful visit in the style of Thomas Gray's famous elegy.[20] He goes on to talk at length about rural epitaphs and their moral import, before he comes, characteristically, to the following conclusion:

> But the time is gone for making the greatest use of this moral agency. By our former mode of locomotion, when the stage-coach paused for a relay of horses, or other purposes, the Christian traveller, ever ready to acquire lessons on the subject of his mor-

tality, would 'Go search them there, where, to be born and die, / Of rich and poor, makes all the history'.[21]

The speaker here draws a functional connection between the general appreciation of rural graveyards and the traditional mode of transportation. In the 1860s, both were becoming outdated. As long as travel used to be by stagecoach, it could conveniently be practised as a pious peregrination, with the stops along the way used for Christian contemplation of the local graves. In the age of railway journeys this is no longer possible. Travelling by train, the modern tourist reaches his destination on a direct route and so becomes deprived of the particular 'moral agency' of epitaphs.

On the other hand, the establishing of new transport lines across the country coincides with the construction of new interment places in the city to meet the demands of drastically rising numbers. This was especially acute in London, where the growth of population made the disposal of the urban dead an urgent problem. Since the 1820s, the cemetery movement therefore campaigned for the provision of large-scale burial grounds in the outskirts of the metropolis. The first of these was Kensal Green, founded in 1832 and followed shortly after by several others: Norwood, Highgate, Nunhead, Abney Park, Brompton and Tower Hamlet. Significantly though, all these were not only places of burial and mourning; they were also places of leisure and recreation for the urban masses – and what is more, they were consciously designed, planted and constructed for this purpose.

The history of the famous London cemeteries, well documented and much visited, clearly bears this out.[22] Many Victorian visitors and guidebooks could be quoted to illustrate the enthusiastic attitudes of city dwellers when walking through the pleasant gardens at their doorstep. That they were here in fact walking over buried bones does not seem to have troubled them unduly. Highgate cemetery may serve as an example. Founded in 1838, it soon attracted celebrity burials and so became a Victorian version of the traditional poet's corner in Westminster Abbey. At the same time, it was advertised and accepted as a landscape garden next to the metropolis:

> No cemetery near London can boast so many natural beauties. The irregularity of the ground, rising in terraces, the winding paths leading through long avenues of cool shrubbery and marble monuments, and the groups of majestic trees casting broad

> shadows below, contribute many natural charms to this solemn region. In the genial summer time, when the birds are singing blithely in their leafy recesses, and the well-cared-for graves are dazzling with the varied hues of beautiful flowers, there is a holy loveliness upon this place of death, as the kind angels hovered about it, and quickened fair Nature with their presence, in love for the good souls whose bodies repose there.[23]

This is the opening of William Justyne's *Guide to Highgate Cemetery*, published in 1865. Focussing on natural beauties, the description is pervaded by a rhetoric of the picturesque. It does refer in passing to the solemn presence of the dead, but the register of the sublime remains subdued. Rather than glimpses of eternity, the cemetery is said to offer very wordly views. At a later point, it is celebrated for its panoramic - and indeed cartographic - sight of the great imperial city:

> There, spread out like a broad map, is the great metropolis of the world, with its countless spires of every shape and almost every age - some of the design of zealous monks in the far away past, and some light workmanship of modern piety, all more or less dimly depicted in the grey film of smoke which curtains the mighty city by day.[24]

The 'grey film of smoke' mentioned here is the only point at which this description registers that all the natural pleasures are planted and constructed in an urban and non-pastoral setting. Otherwise the cemetery can be seen to offer an entirely sufficient substitute for the traditional landscape garden. Instead of going on a tour into the countryside, the modern metropolitan finds both the natural space and opportunity for recreation on a Sunday afternoon while strolling among tombs. Again, this emphasizes the touristic relevance of burial grounds: conveniently they offer what the leisure seekers need.

5. Reclaiming: English Graves Abroad

But the ultimate significance of graves for tourism and travel only emerges when we look at English graves abroad and consider how their representation functions in travelogues and touristic discourse. I would like to argue that the semiotics of death are particularly productive here for the making of wider cultural meanings. To encounter the grave of a countryman or countrywoman abroad has, for many travellers and tourists, been a hallmark of their journey and a symbolic nodal point in their negotiations of identity and otherness. Placed among strangers, English graves operate as powerful points of recognition and reconnection. They invite identification and so offer reassurance that there is some corner of a foreign field that is forever England. Their visitations and representations therefore often reflect and rehearse gestures of territorial and cultural appropriation - though not all of them are in the last analysis successful.

Many cases might be studied here. Before I concentrate on two rather marginal but highly interesting examples, I would like to mention a central and well-known place: the Cimitero Acattolico del Testaccio in Rome. Situated right at the old city walls and next to a sepulchral monument of classical antiquity (the pyramid of Caius Cestius), this site at the very margins of the *urbs eterna* was used as a modern burial ground since the mid-eighteenth century. As indicated by its name, the 'Protestant Cemetery' offered a last resting place for foreigners, protestants and other 'heretics' who died in Italian exile, the most prominent figures interred here being the English Romantics Keats, Severn (his painter friend) and Shelley. With the great influx of cultural tourists after the Napoleonic wars, this cemetery became so popular with English and German visitors that formal regulations and administrative efforts were necessary to cope with rising numbers. This history of cultural invention through a geography of diasporic interment is extremely fascinating and has been studied elsewhere.[25] I merely cite it here because this is one prominent example where the cultural significance of graves became an issue of international politics. In 1911, a contract was signed between the German Reich and the Municipio di Roma to preserve the cemetery as a historical monument. This ended forty years of bitter dispute which began when, after Italian unification in the 1870s, the city of Rome planned to level the cemetery and use the grounds for road construction. The ensuing diplomatic conflicts, documented by Krogel,[26] are revealing. They suggest how the city authorities viewed foreign interests in this matter with suspicion and saw the cemetery as some fifth column: a protestant and potentially treacherous element. Since the Rome visit of Wilhelm II in 1888, the German government assumed authority to act on behalf of the British and other protestant nations to negotiate a respectful solution with the municipality, in close consultation with high officials of Her Majesty's government. In this way it came about, three years before the Great War, that the Kaiser was instrumental in rescuing Keats's grave for posterity and cultural tourism.

Rather than on such prominent sites, my two final examples focus on graves in peripheral places, off the beaten track: a colonial graveyard in the West Indies as seen by J.A. Froude in the 1880s, and a war cemetery near a notorious battlefield of the Great War, as described in a Thomas Cook guidebook from the early 1920s. Both cases merit attention because they concern English burials in emphatically un-English settings and, in very different ways, attempt to relate the homely graves to their unhomely surroundings. The cultural meanings so constructed are contradictory and complex and, especially in the colonial context, fraught with characteristic problems.

The conservative historian James Anthony Froude sailed to the New World English colonies late in 1886, and he sailed with a clear political agenda. As he explains at length in his travelogue *The English in the West Indies, or The Bow of Ulysses*, this tour was to strengthen the imperial spirit and to reawaken interest, at the domestic front in Westminster, for the English exclaves in the tropics which had been seriously neglected since the decline of the sugar trade and the Gladstonian rise of liberal laissez-faire. The grave political incentive of his voyage notwithstanding, Froude visits many of the natural beauty spots of the Caribbean islands and clearly relishes the sights they offer. But his main and most serious attention is directed at the fate of Englishness abroad. There is one question to which his reflections constantly return: how do English culture and traditions fare on the far-away colonial coasts? As it turns out, they fare best in Barbados. All islands visited are ranked by Froude according to their likeness to, or deviation from, the English cultural norm, and Barbados, colonized in the seventeenth century and never ceded to another European power, occupies the top position: it appears to be thoroughly anglicized.

Froude's visit to a Barbadian parish church provides a strong example of the kind of cultural reassurance he is looking for. Its traditional protestant architecture attracts the English visitor already from afar; and when he enters the building, it feels like a homecoming:

> The door was wide open. We went in, and I seemed to be in a parish church in England as parish churches used to be when I

> was a child. There were the old-fashioned seats, the old unadorned communion table, the old pulpit and reading desk and the clerk's desk below, with the lion and the unicorn conspicuous above the chancel arch. [...] No mass had ever been said at that altar. It was a milestone on the high road of time, and was venerable to me at once for its antiquity and for the era at which it had begun to exist.[27]

The old-fashioned appearance of colonial culture is welcomed for its sense of social preservation. No matter what might happen to faith and Church at home, it suggests, in this West Indian corner old England still exists: the road from such a past leads to a stable future. But all sense of stability and homeliness is lost when the immediate surroundings of the Barbadian church are inspected:

> The churchyard was scarcely so home-like. The graves were planted with tropical shrubs and flowers. Palms waved over the square stone monuments – stephanotis and jessamine crept about the iron railings. The primroses and hyacinths and violets, with which we dress the mounds under which our friends are sleeping, will not grow in the tropics. In the place of them are the exotics of our hot-houses. We too are, perhaps, exotics of another kind in these islands, and may not, after all, have a long abiding place in them.[28]

The description of this familiar-foreign graveyard dramatizes problems of displacement in colonial discourse. The scene is pastoral and the place sepulchral, but they cannot be rendered in the traditionally appropriate terms. The imperial traveller must record uncanny differences that lead him into gloomy speculation. The natural iconography of English graveyards, canonized in Gray's undying elegy, can here no longer be sustained: instead of yews and elm trees, these English graves lie under palms, covered by tropical shrubs and overgrown with foreign plants. As a result, all sense of cultural reconnection wanes. For all the familiar cultural markers of the church, the exotic vegetation in the churchyard serves as an insistent sign that the efforts to plant the mother country's culture in this foreign field are under threat. Through the incongruity between English graves and alien growth, the passage points to the problematic status of colonial projects, determined to reproduce likeness and yet haunted by irremediable otherness. In the final sentence Froude makes an explicit transfer to imperial politics by substituting plants for people: 'we too are, perhaps exotics [...] in these islands'. With this turn from *natural* to *national* history, he anticipates the dreaded turn in the destiny of the English in the West Indies. If the Barbadian parish church appears to the traveller as a milestone on the road of progress, the churchyard disturbingly displays the transience of imperial roads.

Graveyards, I suggested at the outset, are placed at the intersection between nature and culture. The foregoing example shows that this is a precarious balance and not a stable opposition. The natural signs may overpower cultural markers and thus effect quite different, unaccommodating meanings which are especially problematic in the colonial setting. As the Trinidadian-English writer V.S. Naipaul, who travelled in Froude's footsteps through the postcolonial Caribbean, observed with great acuity, the 'associations of an English churchyard' in the tropics are always radically different 'from the associations of a churchyard in England'.[29] The contesting cultural and natural codes cannot come together; colonial death remains engraved in difference.

6. Canonizing: War Cemeteries near Troy

If in Froude's Barbadian encounter the English are interred in hostile grounds, the opposite can be observed with my final example, a 1922 Thomas Cook guidebook for English travellers to Turkey and the Near East. The booklet is explicitly geared towards a new tourist market established after the Great War when, as a forerunner of the death tours analyzed by Rojek, the battlefields of great campaigns were redefined and labelled as attractions. The coast of Asia Minor proved particularly useful for this project because it allows for a combination of classic monuments with recent military sites. In Froude's travelogue the title reference to Ulysses and his bow served merely as a textual figure of the heroic grandeur that the Caribbean traveller must search in vain. In tours through Asia Minor, by contrast, Homeric antiquity *in situ* can meet with British national interests and be employed to offer epic glory. The guidebook by Roy Elston, accordingly, offers detailed tour descriptions to the field of the Gallipoli Campaign of 1915, one of the most spectacular failures of British and Australian troops in the war, soon canonized as heroic martyrdom. However, the author does not just point us to the visible remains of war (mainly the military cemeteries) with the necessary practical information (about boat hire etc); he supplements his account with a vivid retelling of the historic battle scenes that took place there a few years before.

Through this double textual strategy – description of place versus travel through time – the performance of the guide makes up for the lack of observable detail. For this text is not least revealing because it tacitly suggests that, in actual fact, there is not much to see. The uninformed traveller will simply find a plain agrarian landscape, in which 'the gaily-turbaned Turk' sings songs to his oxen and works from dawn to twilight in the fields.[30] The visitor's true interest, however, does not lie in the picturesque but in the heroic and this must constantly be reconstructed through the combination of topographical observation with historical narration. All the imperial cemeteries are here listed and described at length, with details about the brigades and regiments to which they belong, but with special regard to their proximity to Trojan battlefields and the graves of Homeric heroes. This line of argument is already established in the opening passage, dramatizing the recommended approach by sea:

> This section of the journey is of unique interest. On entering the Dardanelles, one sees on the right the ancient realm of Priam stretching down to the sea from the slopes of Mt. Ida; in the midst of this is the Mound of Troy commanding the plain where Achilles and Agamemnon marshalled their warriors; and down by the coast, near the promontories of Sigeum and Rotheum, are the traditional tombs of the heroes. On the opposite shore are the ruined forts of Sedd-ed-Bahr; and behind these, hidden in the folds of the Thracian hills, are the graves of those whose grand exploits in 1915 added further glories to the annals of British heroism.[31]

The keyword here is 'further' in the final sentence: it insinuates historical continuity derived from spatial contiguity. The graves of the Homeric warriors are said to be *next* and hence *akin* to the graves of British soldiers. Historically, the battle of Gallipoli was lost to the Turks. Touristically though, the place is now retaken for the British as the graves become contemporary tokens of the great Homeric types.

7. Symbolizing: Showing the Invisible

In conclusion, all these sample texts and my preliminary discussion may offer some account for the long-standing and continuing touristic popularity of graves and of related fatal sights. Graveyards and cemeteries, clearly, are not constructed for the dead but for the living and, even more clearly, for the living visitor. They are places set aside for collective memory, where the present tries to come to terms with the past - but with a past that must, by cultural convention, remain entirely unseen. Unlike archaeological sites, ruins, temples or other historical monuments, graveyards and cemeteries conceal their one defining property and shield it from the present gaze. The past is literally buried here and must remain interred, if we are not to violate taboos. Thus, with the most important feature categorically invisible, graves attract semiotic effort to construct specific cultural signs that must mark its place. In this way, graveyards and cemeteries should be seen as sites where cultures turn not only retrospective but also self-reflexive. And for this reason, necro-tourism can be seen as a paradigm of cultural tourism in general: essentially concerned with the engagement in signs rather than usage, and with symbolic rather than use value.

To sum up, we may therefore return to Wordsworth's imaginary scriptless country churchyard and assume that, for all his dislike of intruding strangers, the village priest here operates as the archetypal tourist guide.

Notes

1 Wordsworth, 'The Brothers', in *The Poems of William Wordsworth* (London: Edward Moxon, 1858), 68.

2 The *OED* gives 1780 as the earliest reference for the term; in 1800 it records the following definition: 'A Traveller is now-a-days called a Tour-*ist*'.

3 J. Buzard, *The Beaten Track: European Tourism, Literature and the Ways to Culture, 1800-1918* (Oxford: Clarendon Press, 1993), 18.

4 R. Barthes, *Mythologies* (London: Cape, 1972), 75.

5 C. Rojek, *Ways of Escape: Modern Transformations in Leisure and Travel* (Basingstoke: Macmillan, 1993), 136.

6 See P. Ariès, *L'homme devant la mort*, 2 vols (Paris: Editions du Seuil, 1977).

7 Wordsworth, 'The Brothers', 69.

8 D. Cressy, *Birth, Marriage, and Death: Ritual, Religion, and the Life-Cycle in Tudor and Stuart England* (Oxford: Oxford University Press, 1997), 470.

9 J. Culler, 'The Semiotics of Tourism', in id., *Framing the Sign: Criticism and Interpretations* (Oxford: Blackwell, 1988), 153-67, here 155.
10 Ibid., 159.
11 I would like to thank Manfred Pfister for drawing this to my attention.
12 M. Pfister (ed.), *The Fatal Gift of Beauty: The Italies of English Travellers. An Annotated Anthology* (Amsterdam and Atlanta/GA: Rodopi, 1996), 479.
13 Coryate, *Travailer: For the English wits, and the good of this Kingdom* (London: Iaggard and Fetherston 1616; repr. Amsterdam: Da Capo Press, 1968), 56.
14 Coryate, *Travailer*, 51.
15 J. Fabian, *Time and the Other: How Anthropology Makes Its Object* (New York: Columbia University Press, 1983), 6.
16 Marlowe, *The Complete Plays* (Harmondsworth: Penguin, 1986), 160.
17 See I. Ousby, *The Englishman's England: Taste, Travel and the Rise of Tourism* (Cambridge: Cambridge University Press, 1990), 21-57.
18 See Rojek, *Ways of Escape*, 138.
19 Ibid., 170.
20 R. Wilkinson, *Lecture on Epitaphs* (London: C.A. Bartlet, 1862), 7.
21 Ibid., 35.
22 See H. Meller, *London Cemeteries: An Illustrated Guide and Gazetteer* (Amersham: Avebury, 1981), and Ariès, *L'homme devant la mort*, II: *La mort ensauvagée*, 240-5.
23 Quoted from Meller, *London Cemeteries*, 148.
24 Ibid.
25 See W. Krogel, 'Der Alte Friedhof der Nicht-Katholiken in Rom und seine Umgebung: Ein Szenarium im Wandel', in A. Menniti Ippolito and P. Vian (eds), *The Protestant Cemetery in Rome: The 'Parte Antica'* (Roma: Unione Internazionale Degli Instituti di Archaeologia, Storia e Storia dell' Arte in Roma, 1989), 91-160.
26 Krogel, 'Der Alte Friedhof', 153-6.
27 Froude, *The English in the West Indies, or The Bow of Ulysses* (London: Longmans, Green, 1909 [1887]), 101.
28 Ibid., 102.
29 Naipaul, *The Enigma of Arrival* (Harmondsworth: Penguin, 1987), 148.
30 R. Elston, *Constantinople to Smyrna: Notes for Travellers* (London: Thos. Cook and Son, 1922), 31.
31 Ibid., 5f.

Exploring London

Walking the City – (Re-)Writing the City

Eveline Kilian

Jonathan Culler defines tourism as a practice that involves the tourist in a complex set of semiotic processes.[1] He argues that the tourist's encounter with the destinations she or he chooses is always semiotically mediated, that even the experience of the authentic is only possible because certain items are marked as such and allow her or him to read them as 'the real thing'. In more general terms it can be said that tourists 'are engaged in reading cities, landscapes and cultures as sign systems'.[2] This view of culture as a sign system functioning like a text can be regarded as one of the basic tenets of Cultural Studies.[3] Within this framework tourists become 'agents of semiotics'[4] who actively participate in the production of meaning, who create an account of the places they visit depending on the cultural concepts and markers available to them and on their personal approach to travelling as tourists. Consequently we can place the semiotic activity of the tourist within the more general field of cultural practices that have been described by contemporary theory and literature, which variously highlight the processes of construction involved in our reading of reality and history, in our personal world-making.[5]

Applying these ideas to an urban context, we can infer that exploring the city – as a tourist, a researcher, a city enthusiast or simply a city-dweller – also means constructing one's specific version of the city. I will look at the implications of this notion on the basis of a number of contemporary London texts, literature being an appropriate medium for the study of the mechanisms of cultural representation and interpretation, since it presents such processes in a highly condensed and concentrated form.[6] I will examine the different mental realities the metropolis can evoke and the way they affect the very structure of these texts, thus creating what Julian Wolfreys called 'narrative architectures'.[7]

As the title of Penelope Lively's novel, *City of the Mind* (1991), already indicates, the city shapes itself and comes to life in and through the human mind. In the transient meeting between the material reality of the city and the individual observer a personal vision of the city is created: 'We are hosts to the physical world [...]. We see the world, invest what we see with meaning.'[8] This vision is tinged by the perceiving subject's previous experience, memories of particular places, cultural background, by his or her 'personal elsewhere' (176), and, of course, by circumstance. It always consists of a specific selection of items. It is not entirely autonomous but dependent on preconceptions derived from cultural representations of a particular city. It is 'coloured by the many visions of other people, by fact and error and received opinion and things remembered and things invented' (9). As Al, the first-person narrator of Maureen Duffy's novel *Londoners*, says about London: 'We make our choice, make her in the image we need to love or hate.'[9]

For Jane, the protagonist Matthew Halland's eight-year-old daughter in Lively's novel, who at her age still lives in an eternal present, London is 'an anarchic landscape'[10] drowning her in a multitude of impressions from which she picks out the ones that she can tie to her own experience, the world she knows. Her attention focusses for example on billboards advertising her favourite brand of chocolate, on cars that are like her father's, or on buses with destinations she recognizes. Matthew's image of the city, on the other hand, tends to be influenced by his professional view as an architect. He notices architectural features, masterworks of engineering, Japanese businessmen. He combines his impressions to form a narrative of historical change, looking back to rows of decaying or restored Georgian houses and forward to the most recent developments in the Docklands, which epitomize the threshold to the twenty-first century. And Eva Burden, a Jewish refugee who came to England as a child in 1939, feels particularly drawn by the river, which connects London to other places and other people. Consequently she sees London primarily as a kind of melting-pot to which everybody brings their own personal background so that the city becomes 'a reflection of the rest of the globe' (176). These examples outline the mechanisms involved in constructing one's personal image of the city, and they can thus serve as a starting-point for the following analysis, which will concentrate on three texts: Iain Sinclair's *Lights Out for the Territory: 9*

Excursions in the Secret History of London (1997), Geoff Nicholson's *Bleeding London* (1997) and Jonathan Raban's *Soft City* (1974).

1. *Lights Out for the Territory*

In his essay collection *Lights Out for the Territory*, Iain Sinclair describes nine excursions in London, which he undertook with photographer Marc Atkins. He quite explicitly connects walking the city with the act of reading the city and of rewriting it. Their search for graffiti during their first walk is only the most obvious expression for their 'thirst for text',[11] which spills over into a number of different spheres. He and Atkins give the areas they visit a 'close reading' (13), and these readings, in turn, can be transformed into a text, as Sinclair's essays demonstrate. Writers across the ages have presented ever changing faces of London. According to Sinclair, London offers illimitable possibilities and challenges writers to create ever new versions of the city: 'London is begging to be rewritten' (138). And these London texts guide their perception of the metropolis, for example when Sinclair reads Peter Wright's *Spycatcher* as background to a walk around Lambeth, featuring the MI6 building (190), or when his view of the Thames refers him back to Wordsworth's poem 'Composed Upon Westminster Bridge', or when his own route intersects with a passage in Patrick Keiller's film *London* and he has the impression of '[w]alking [...] into another man's film' (194). This corroborates William Chapman Sharpe's thesis that 'there is no unmediated artistic response to the city',[12] that each new version of the city rests on pre-existing 'textual conventions'[13] governing the representation of the city. Consequently Sinclair's exploring London has to be seen not only as a textual but as an intertextual affair.

Each of Sinclair's and Atkins's journeys results in a narrative, uncovers and rewrites part of the city's narrative. They unfold over time and they preserve time in that they follow up traces of the city's past. And this means revealing a partially or almost totally 'Invisible City' (121) whose vestiges have been buried or superseded by more recent developments. A good example is their search for the exact location of the original Temple of Mithras in the City of London, erected by the Romans in honour of the Persian god of light. Its remains were accidentally discovered in 1954 during construction works. They were removed to 'a more convenient site' (115) nearby and realigned in the wrong direction, from north to south, instead of from west to east. People hardly ever notice them: 'It looks like an unfilled paddling pool, a parking space.' (116) In their former place there is now a wine-bar called 'the Mithras'. This is an example of how the surface and texture of the city 'is rewritten, scribbled over, revised' (231). In other words, here, as in *City of the Mind* and in other London texts, we encounter the concept of the city as palimpsest, as a multilayered organism bearing evidence of its former shapes and appearances. In London we find a juxtaposition of different architectural styles; historical monuments exist side by side with the latest products of contemporary city planning:

> [t]his is the city, in which everything is simultaneous. [...] The city digests itself, and regurgitates. It melts away, and rears up once more in another form. People [...] sift through the place in their millions, leaving this sediment of brick and stone, the unquenchable testimony of their existence by way of pediments and cornices, statues of men on horseback and women in draperies and admirals on the tops of columns.[14]

Likewise, the names of places and streets in London - Wood Green, Blackheath, Ladbroke Grove - still bear testimony of a formerly different topography of the city; they are sediments of the past, just as the exhibits in museums and art galleries provide us with an access to history and to a cultural heritage. In *City of the Mind* and in Maureen Duffy's *Capital*[15] the idea of the palimpsest is even reflected in the structure of the books in that they consist of different layers of narratives connected by association. Lively's novel juxtaposes the main plot centring on Matthew Halland with scenes depicting the Blitz, the Covent Garden area in Victorian times, the work of the nineteenth-century palaeontologist Richard Owen, and Martin Frobisher's expeditions in the sixteenth century. In *Capital* the two present-day narratives of Meeper and the history lecturer are interspersed with vignettes from London's past, ranging from prehistoric times to the mid-twentieth century.[16]

The personae in these texts - Meepers in *Capital,* Matthew Halland in *City of the Mind,* Iain Sinclair in *Lights Out for the Territory* - are predisposed to unravel these layers due to a structural affinity between the city and the human consciousness: both are endowed with a capacity to absorb and contain presence and absence, the past and the present at the same time. Just like the city, the human mind is a storehouse of events and representations across time and space that can be evoked simultaneously, recalled at will and linked variously by a chain of associations. In this sense memory also functions as a keeper of the past. Human consciousness is endowed with a sense of history, it is usually equipped with a certain degree of historical knowledge and is thus able to read, order and classify the medley of traces preserved in the urban landscape.

In *Lights Out for the Territory,* uncovering the invisible city, exploring the 'unedited book of the city' (226), not only refers to giving an inventory of ruined buildings. For Sinclair it also implies, quite literally, discovering connections and reference points in London that you cannot see but only conjecture. His aim is to reconstruct the subterranean energy flows of the city, which are strongly connected to places of worship devoted to a certain cult, like the Temple of Mithras mentioned before, sites of occult practices, mysticism or alchemy. He terms this 'the psychic landscape' (347) or 'the psychogeography of the City' (115, 118), a notion further illustrated by an 'alchemical route' they follow in one of the chapters, which was devised by an antiquarian bookdealer and acquaintance of Sinclair's in Vancouver and which draws on the works of the seventeenth-century alchemist Elias Ashmole. It links churches and enclosures associated with St Dunstan and its focal point is St Paul's Cathedral (118-29).

During their excursions, Sinclair and Atkins are driven by a search for meaning. They start out in a 'near-arbitrary' (1) fashion, sometimes they rely on coincidence and chance association, but at other times their meandering develops into a 'quest' (7, 113) or even a 'hunt' (116), into an obsessive pursuit of form and significance, which is produced in an interaction between the material reality of the city and the creative energy and the imagination of the walker and observer. Concentrating on 'the secret history of London' (as the title suggests) results in alternative readings of the city, in opening up new vistas, in looking at familiar things in a new and perhaps unexpected way. These walks, Sinclair says, enabled him 'to subvert what I thought I knew' (269). The meanings he establishes are tentative and provisional. They are closely linked to form. Certain places are singled out as focal points of specific walks, because they seem to be charged with a certain significance in this particular context: St Paul's becomes the centre of the alchemical walk; on their graffiti tour it is the vandalized chapel in Abney Park sprayed with graffiti spelling DOG - the reversal of the expected GOD, the appropriate word for a place of worship, a play on words that gives rise to a number of associations developed in the following chapters on pit bulls and the Isle of Dogs.[17] That it is not just a matter of investing individual excursions with significance but also of finding a certain order or even symmetry for the book project as a whole becomes clear when Sinclair snatches at the opportunity to have a few words with the writer and member of the House of Lords, Jeffrey Archer, because it 'rounds my essay off so neatly' (203). Or when a visit to Lord Archer's luxurious two-level apartment in Lambeth, overlooking the river, appears as 'pivotal in the development of *Lights Out for the Territory*' (166), since it functions as a counterbalance to the marginal sites and characters, 'the parade of shaggy scufflers, my stock company of anarchists, disenfranchised artists and petty criminals' (167), which form the basis for the majority of his essays.

Another way to create meaning is tied to Sinclair's notion that his essays and walks can be assigned letters of the alphabet (159), which might reveal an additional level of signification. The letter V recurs several times. Walking from Hackney to Greenwich Hill and back to Chingford Mount in the first chapter is already 'an act of ambulant signmaking' (2), because their journey describes a V on the map. Their circling the city when tracing the Temple of Mithras provides the letter O. Added to this is an X, which, in one instance is linked to the focal point of the graffiti walk,[18] and in another to Aidan Dunn's book '*Vale Royal*, its poet and publisher: an *X* on the map' (159). This sequence of letters reads '*VOX*. The unheard voice that is always present in the darkness' (159), a further allusion to Sinclair's project to reveal the hidden, the secret aspects of London. In a gesture towards creating a kind of frame for his book, this symbolic reading is taken up again with respect to their last walk in the final section to suggest a circular structure. Now the V from the first excursion links up with 'the *O* of the Maryon enclosure' (358) in Woolwich and the X Marc Atkinson photographed on the hillside in Maryon-Wilson Park (358). All these aspects are supposed to support Sinclair's view that the different walks 'gave this book a form: removed it from the taint of the rehashed essay' (269). But it must be said that his attempts to give the excursions and the shape of the book a coherent form is rather sporadic, haphazard, sometimes even forced, and by no means systematic. Julian Wolfreys presents a perhaps too generous but nevertheless interesting interpretation of the loose structure of *Lights Out for the Territory*, which he sees as a reflection of the shifting structure of the city that can never be grasped as a whole, that consists of different layers and texts producing a variety of resonances, haunting each other and demanding a constant shift of focus.[19]

The character able to unravel the hidden meanings of the city is 'the stalker', someone who makes these journeys 'with intent', who walks 'with a thesis', '[w]ith a prey' (75). Sinclair opposes the stalker to the flâneur, whom he associates with 'aimless urban wandering', 'dawdling', 'browsing', with 'the savouring of reflections in shop windows, admiration for Art Nouveau ironwork, attractive matchboxes rescued from the gutter' (75). It would be more accurate to say, however, that he magnifies one specific aspect of the flâneur, namely his more aggressive, purposeful, investigative pursuit of impressions. This quality has been part of the concept since Edgar Allan Poe's story 'The Man of the Crowd' (1845), in which the protagonist, an impartial and leisurely observer of the crowd at first, suddenly feels the urge to follow an old man almost obsessively to learn about this fascinating individual, about his history and his motives for walking the streets of London all night long, 'to form some analysis of the meaning conveyed', to read him.[20] The flâneur's deceptively casual air and demeanour have always concealed the more systematic attitude of the 'botanizer',[21] and like Sinclair and Atkins, his wanderings lead him into an exploration of the city's past.[22] In Sinclair's stalker, the flâneur's affinity to the detective that Walter Benjamin already commented on[23] is foregrounded and links up with his search for meaning, his almost obsessive preoccupation with the construction of underlying patterns. But his quest is not simply an end in itself; on closer inspection, it reveals a stance of social and cultural criticism.

Sinclair's critical position becomes apparent in his predilection for characters, products and activities of the counter-culture, but also in his unearthing of psychic landscapes, in his uncovering of traces of the city's past, which have long been destroyed and superseded by less desirable structures and constellations. Here he particularly focusses on the City bearing the mark of the Thatcher-Major years and parading a host of submissive and highly competitive professionals (89-92), on the old centre of London, which has been turned into a high security fortress guarded by innumerable surveillance checkpoints and where the old gates of the City have been replaced 'by invisible gates, gates that can be shifted at a phonecall' (104). A glance at Patrick Keiller's film *London*,[24] to which *Lights Out for the Territory* bears a certain resemblance, supports this point. The narrator is asked by his friend Robinson to accompany him on a series of journeys through London, which he calls 'exercises in psychic landscaping'. Keiller highlights the clashing of expectations and encountered reality through the montage of contrasting narrative voice, music and images covering London-based impressions throughout the year 1992: reflections on Romanticism coupled with the view of an oversize MacDonald's situated next to a busy road, the stately area of Lincoln's Inn Fields with a gathering of homeless people, a peaceful, almost rural residential area on the periphery of London with planes and noise from Heathrow Airport, a shot of Brentford Basin accompanied by Peruvian folk music, their 'pilgrimage to the sources of English Romanticism' distracted by an IRA bomb attack, their unsuccessful search for bohemia in the cafés at Tesco and IKEA. What emerges is the picture of a city run down after more than a decade of conservative rule and marked by unemployment, workers' demonstrations, poverty, homelessness and dereliction, but it is a picture that is interspersed with glimpses of a different world, of alternative possibilities that can be traced sporadically, in the margins. It is ultimately the representation of 'a city divided against itself'.[25] Keiller's handling of the camera is equally telling. The camera is completely static, only moves between shots, records from one angle the stillness or movement producing itself in front of the lens. The viewer is forced to focus his or her unswerving attention on one spot, give the vision time to settle. This specific technique can be read as a stance of resistance to the accelerated pace of our everyday visual experience, 'a charm against [...] the culture of speed',[26] and it can be compared to the flâneur's protest against the relentless bustle of the city and the single-minded pursuits of its inhabitants,[27] which he expresses through his ostentatiously leisurely gait, his seemingly aimless wandering, his 'walking "out of step" with the late-modern rhythm of the city'.[28]

2. *Bleeding London*

Sinclair's psychogeography of London represents only one version of how to conceptualize the city, one among a multitude of different patterns. This heterogeneity of visions is one of the central issues in Geoff Nicholson's novel *Bleeding London*. It compiles and juxtaposes a great variety of maps, some of which pertain to the ordinary and expected, while others strike us as more eccentric. There are those devised for the tourists who join the tours offered by the 'London Walker', which centre on a particular aspect of London literature, art or architecture, for example 'the Bloomsbury Walk, the Boswell Walk, the Christopher Wren Walk, The London Crime Walk, the Holmes and Watson Walk, the Art Gallery Walk, the Docklands Walk'.[29] There are the less predictable walks Stuart London sometimes conducts like 'Stuart London's London – The City That Nobody Knows', which features the city's 'unknown quarters' and 'obscure corners' (74). Then there is the compressed, miniature version of London with '[a]ll the tourist attractions [...] on one manageable site' (332) that is to be built on a Japanese island, a project over which Stuart's wife Anita negotiates with some Japanese backers with a view to expand their business. And there are very personal maps like the ones Judy Tanaka collects of places where she and her lovers lived and made love. And this is by no means all, as Judy remarks:

> 'There are an infinite number of maps that could be drawn of London; not just sex maps but death maps, crime maps, drug maps, maps of resistance and insurrection, of liberation and oppression, murder maps, suicide maps'. (136)

One character in particular enables us to study the process by which someone who is a complete stranger to London gradually constructs his own version of the city and thus turns the place into more familiar ground. Mick Wilton lives in Sheffield, but when his girlfriend Gabby, a stripper, comes back from a gig in London and tells him that she was gang-raped by six apparently well-to-do men at a stag-party, he goes to London to take revenge on the men whose names are on a list Gabby gives him. On his arrival he is metaphorically and literally without a map, so the first thing he buys is an *A-Z* at a bookshop. He also has no mental map of the social stratification of the various districts of London and needs to enlist the help of the shop assistant, Judy Tanaka, to locate the different addresses he finds in the phone book under each name.

Mick uses his victims, sometimes in a slightly absurd manner, to familiarize himself more and more with the city. Acquiring a better knowledge of London becomes part of the programme from the very beginning and starts with his first victim Philip Masterson. Mick slashes the hood of Masterson's convertible, gets into the car with him when he wants to go out to work, breaks his little finger, and orders him to drive him through central London on a sightseeing tour and to show him the most important tourist spots and answer questions about London, before he forces him to undress and jump off London Bridge into the Thames. Here Mick tests his preconceptions about the capital, because it is a trip

> around Mick's own idiosyncratic version of London, those places he simply happened to have heard of: the Monument, Stamford Bridge, the Old Curiosity Shop, the Post Office Tower, Portobello Road, Soho, the Hammersmith Flyover. (53)

At this point there is a considerable discrepancy between his hazy notions and what he actually encounters. This shows in his reaction when he says, '"I'm still a bit disappointed. Basically London looks like a big slum with a few famous landmarks scattered through it"' (54). Before meeting his final humiliation, the second man on the list, who is an actor, has to reproduce different London accents for Mick so that he can get an impression of the city's 'many facets and characters, all its rich culture and history' (109). And the third victim has to answer questions from a guidebook called *Unreliable London* as part of his ordeal. By the time Mick comes to deal with his fifth victim, he realizes that his initial dislike of London has turned into a certain fondness and that he does not really want to go back to Sheffield. His increasing topographical competence is reflected in the fact that he is now able to help other people find their way (154), and when he assembles the pieces of a jigsaw of London that Judy gave him, he is conscious that he is 'gaining mastery over this once wholly unfamiliar territory' (156). Forming a whole from a number of disparate pieces also reveals Mick's map of London to be the result of an act of construction. Another important factor that contributes to his starting to feel at home in London is the 'human factor'. Mick's attitude begins to change noticeably after he has agreed to sleep with Judy, who in turn confirms his sense of belonging by adding to the jigsaw the one missing piece she had taken from the box.

Unlike Mick Wilton, Stuart London, co-founder of the 'London Walker', is an enthusiastic connoisseur of the capital. He is also in the process of building his own version of London by realizing his project 'to walk down every street in London' (77), in sections of ten miles per day excluding weekends. He draws a thick black line along all the streets he has walked in his *A-Z*, so that day after day, the street atlas is divested of its original function and is reduced to 'an abstract linear design' (84), to mere 'decoration and ornament' (8). And as the official map of London is gradually blotted out, Stuart's personal version emerges in the form of a diary he writes to document his daily excursions. Stuart's diary and the *A-Z* cover the same areas, but there is an essential difference in that his rewriting of the city is highly idiosyncratic. It consists of a mixture of historical background and literary connections that he happens to remember, and, most importantly, of personal associations, chance encounters and incidents. His emphasis on the ephemeral and everyday turns his walks into very specific experiences and makes it impossible for anybody else to repeat them in exactly the same way; they bear the mark of a specific context and of his personal vision.

Stuart's mission to walk and (re-)write London is intimately linked to his search for identity, especially since he feels more and more redundant due to his wife's competent handling of the business. This connection is expressed in three different ways. Firstly, he likens his own self to a city.[30] They both consist of different layers, change their shape in the course of time and are subject to unpredictable developments:

> As I walk I realize I am no longer the person I was. [...] I know too that it is not merely a question of change and growth, not even of decay, but rather of demolitions, regroupings, blottings out. The opinions, the tastes, the most passionately held beliefs have all disappeared in a blitz of slum clearance and redevelopment. Yes, a man is like a city, a site of erasures, of subsidence, in-fill, subdivision and occasional preservation orders. But there is no blueprint, no foolproof map, no essential guide book. (301f.)

Secondly, he reflects that his selection of items for his London text 'will reveal as much about me as about London' (142), that his personality will outline itself in and through his draft of the city. And thirdly, his rewriting of London amounts to an attempt to reconstruct his identity and his place in the world. In Stuart's case this enterprise shapes itself into an obsession to create a literary work, i.e. his diary, for which he, and his version of London, will be remembered by posterity. He models himself on Samuel Pepys, one of the greatest diarists in English literature. Like Pepys he wants to create a lasting 'city of words' (247), and on several occasions he sees his own history to become conflated with Pepys's (247), a notion that culminates in a dream about the breakout of a fire in London, in which Stuart takes on the role of a present-day Samuel Pepys, advising the Queen about what to do to master the crisis the way that the real

Pepys acted as counsellor to Charles II during the Great Fire in 1666. Pepys's ending his diary unwillingly on account of his failing eyesight sparks off in Stuart the idea to find a means by which 'his own text might be given a similarly beguiling resonance' (248), and, knowing that 'the death of the author could be a great help to a work of literature' (248), he opts for the most drastic of all means, his own death. Thus he would leave a great unfinished work behind, requiring scholars to edit it posthumously, to add some learned footnotes and explanations. Furthermore, he starts flirting with another literary self-stylization, a modification of Dr Johnson's famous dictum that 'when a man is tired of London he is tired of life'[31]. Stuart's version reads: 'When a man is tired of London he's ready for a bullet' (304). He pursues and expands this idea by reading his obliteration of the streets in his *A-Z* metaphorically, and also rather pathetically, as an erasure of his own life: 'I realized that the end of my wandering should be, not simply the blotting out of the city, but also the blotting out of the self. When the map was all blacked in I'd be ready to be snuffed out.' (304)

Stuart's literary production of the city and of the self raises some pertinent questions as to the connection between fiction, truth and reality. First of all we are again made aware that there is no universally acknowledged and generally accepted version, 'no authorized text' (194) of London, that it is 'created in the image of each of its inhabitants' (301), who find their respective views the most convincing and acceptable. Whereas for Stuart his diary entries represent the most authentic view of London, his wife Anita calls them 'a fake' (329), 'not quite like life' and 'a shade too literary', because '[t]hey're not part of the London I know' (330). With respect to Stuart's construction of self, the reader is in a privileged position to understand the complex relationship between fiction and reality, because she or he is presented with different perspectives: Stuart's diary, a third-person narrative giving us details about his biography and his encounters with some of the other characters in the novel, and Anita's reaction to his diary, which she discovers and reads while her husband is out on his final walk. Here a similar discrepancy between individual perceptions and an ambiguous link between mental and material reality becomes apparent. When Anita reads about his plan to commit suicide, she does not 'believe a word of it' (306), and she is right in looking upon it as a part of his literary self-fashioning. Nevertheless, Stuart himself is so convinced of the fiction he created that he actually tries to shoot himself after his last excursion and thus to convert his text into lived reality. But since there are no bullets in the gun he uses, this final touch to his project fails and is again reduced to a mere figment of his imagination. Consequently he returns home just as his wife expected him to do (306), so that for the two characters both their visions of reality seem confirmed. Stuart, however, is left with the problem of having to find a new ending for his text, 'the final page [...] that was much more trashy, much less monumental than he'd wanted' (327), and consequently, of redefining his identity.

3. *Soft City*

In *Soft City* Jonathan Raban conceptualizes the relationship between city and identity in yet another way. Like Nicholson he exploits the structural affinities between the city and the self. Both possess 'plastic qualities'.[32] Cities are 'soft' (3), they allow us to shape them according to our own will and perspectives. In a similar way, identities can be created and refashioned, especially in the context of the city, where we are constantly confronted with images of people we might be desirous to become and that induce us to try out new versions of the self. 'City freedom', says Raban, is 'the freedom to be who you want to be' (175). Here 'personal identity has been rendered soft, fluid, endlessly open to the exercise of the will and the imagination' (63).

Another parallel between the city and identity consists in their both functioning like texts. As in Sinclair's *Lights Out for the Territory*, constructing the city in one's mind is seen as a process of 'imposing order' (164), of reading and (re-)writing it. Raban describes London as 'a chaos of details' (61) and an 'indomitable [...] environment' (158). The ever-changing face of the city and its inhabitants, the rapidity and multifariousness of impressions, the multiplicity of fragments glimpsed and lost are signs that have to be deciphered and read. In that sense the city resembles a complex and fluid literary text full of ambiguity. That Raban applies this semiotic view to both the city and the self becomes obvious in his choice of terminology. He refers both to 'the grammar of urban life' (9) and the 'grammar of identity through which you could project yourself' (56). Seen within this framework, the self is modelled by means of styles and codes, which can then be deciphered and interpreted by one's fellow-beings. Raban translates this affinity between city and identity into a relationship of interdependence. Inventing the city and inventing the self combine in a process of mutual moulding that can set in in a situation of estrangement or distance. Raban dramatizes this moment as a sudden feeling of disorientation when one becomes a stranger to oneself and a stranger in one's own city, when the everyday and habitual stops being familiar and forces the subject to grope for 'anchors to tether you down' (3). As Raban explains at the beginning of his book, this experience can arise when you find yourself at some London traffic lights and you suddenly no longer know the direction of the traffic. You hear people speaking in foreign languages and feel like 'a dizzied tourist' (3) yourself. Such a condition can set off a reciprocal process of creation:

> at moments like this, the city goes soft; it awaits the imprint of an identity. For better or worse, it invites you to remake it, to consolidate it into a shape you can live in. You, too. Decide who you are, and the city will again assume a fixed form round you. Decide what it is, and your own identity will be revealed, like a position on a map fixed by triangulation. Cities [...] are plastic by nature. We mould them in our images: they, in their turn, shape us by the resistance they offer when we try to impose our own personal form on them. (3f.)

4. Conclusions

We can draw a number of conclusions from our analysis of these contemporary London texts. First of all, we are made aware that our encounter with London, with a city, indeed, with the world in general, is not a matter of passive and standardized registering of what is already there. It is rather an active meeting in which impressions and perceptions are subjected to an individual ordering which is based on selection, preconceptions, personal background, cultural patterns and specific situations among other things. This process of active creation and signification necessarily results in the production of a number of 'alternative cartographies of the city', each offering 'a partial meaning structure'.[33] They are not static but can change over time, accommodating new angles and additional information. Such mappings are instrumental in establishing the places we experience as real.[34] Their value resides not so much in their topographical qualities but, more importantly, in their function as 'maps of meaning'.[35]

Secondly, active participation suggests involvement of the self on various levels. It can mean taking a critical stance towards political and social changes leaving their imprint on the surface of the city. Individual visions of the city inevitably allow us to glimpse the personality of the observer. Furthermore, creating a personal vision of the city can be functionalized to establish a new sense of self, can be used as a means of self-stylization, as we have seen in Geoff Nicholson's *Bleeding London*. And finally, the self and the city form a relation of interdependence: the self can be changed in its encounter with the city, just as the city is reshaped and reorganized in the mind during each excursion.

Thirdly, the central metaphor that pervades all these texts, namely the city *as* text, leads us back to the notion of culture as text and to Culler's semiotic approach to tourism. Culture, as Clifford Geertz explains, consists of 'webs of significance' that have to be read and decoded.[36] Consequently the subject must be allocated a central role in the creation and mediation of meanings and structures of signification, since deciphering the city does not simply mean passively registering it in the sense of producing a 'referential duplication', but it implies rewriting it as it is read.[37] This reference to a semiotics of culture helps us to establish a broader context in which to place our specific examples of touring the city or, even more specifically, of urban tourism: our explorers of London operate as cultural agents who produce ever new 'partial meanings' of the city, different 'senses of placement and identity',[38] which are in turn circulated among the readers of their narratives.

Notes

1 J. Culler, 'The Semiotics of Tourism', in id., *Framing the Sign: Criticism and Its Institutions* (Oxford: Blackwell, 1988), 153-67.

2 Ibid., 155.

3 C. Geertz, 'Thick Description: Toward an Interpretive Theory of Culture', in id., *The Interpretation of Cultures: Selected Essays* (New York: Basic Books, 1973), 5; D. Bachmann-Medick, 'Einleitung', in ead. (ed.), *Kultur als Text: Die anthropologische Wende in der Literaturwissenschaft* (Frankfurt/M.: Fischer, 1996), 7-10 and 22-6.

4 Culler, 'The Semiotics of Tourism', 155.

5 I am here referring to semiotic approaches to culture, New Historicism and theories of postmodernism in general. A literary genre that is particularly interested in the ways history is constructed, narrativized and fictionalized is that of historiographic metafiction. See Geertz, *The Interpretation of Cultures;* H.A. Veeser (ed.), *The New Historicism* (New York: Routledge, 1989); L. Hutcheon, *A Poetics of Postmodernism: History, Theory, Fiction* (New York: Routledge, 1988); A. Nünning, *Von historischer*

Fiktion zu historiographischer Metafiktion, 2 vols (Trier: Wissenschaftlicher Verlag, 1995); B. Engler and K. Müller (eds), *Historiographic Metafiction in Modern American and Canadian Literature* (Paderborn: Schöningh, 1994).

6 Bachmann-Medick, 'Einleitung', 25

7 J. Wolfreys, *Writing London: The Trace of the Urban Text from Blake to Dickens* (Basingstoke: Macmillan and New York: St Martin's Press, 1998), 9.

8 Lively, *City of the Mind* (London: Penguin, 1992), 49. Matthew Halland, the protagonist of the novel, makes a similar point: '"This city [...] is entirely in the mind. It is a construct of the memory and of the intellect. Without you and me it hasn't got a chance. [...] What I mean is that significance is in the eye of the beholder."' (7)

9 Duffy, *Londoners: An Elegy* (London: Methuen, 1983), 88.

10 Lively, *City of the Mind*, 86f.

11 Sinclair, *Lights Out for the Territory: 9 Excursions in the Secret History of London*, with illustrations by Marc Atkins (London: Granta, 1998), 39.

12 W.C. Sharpe, *Unreal Cities: Urban Figuration in Wordsworth, Baudelaire, Whitman, Eliot, and Williams* (Baltimore: Johns Hopkins University Press, 1990), xi.

13 Ibid., xii.

14 Lively, *City of the Mind*, 24.

15 Duffy, *Capital* (Harmondsworth: Penguin, 1978).

16 For a discussion of the structure of *Capital* see C.W. Sizemore, *A Female Vision of the City: London in the Novels of Five British Women* (Knoxville: University of Tennessee Press, 1989), 219-33.

17 Sinclair is very conscious of the fact that his attribution of meaning is arbitrary and fictional in the sense that it is constructed in and through the eye of the beholder: 'Everything I believe in, everything London can do to you, starts here. [...] The lovely lies that take you out into the light. That bless each and every pilgrimage.' (34f.)

18 The word DOG 'established this site as the X, the given, the point from which the true walk would begin' (34).

19 J. Wolfreys, 'The Hauntological Example: The City as the Haunt of Writing in the Texts of Iain Sinclair', in id., *Deconstruction – Derrida* (Basingstoke: Macmillan, 1998), 139 and 144.

20 Poe, 'The Man of the Crowd' (1840), in *Collected Works: Tales and Sketches 1831-1842*, ed. T.O. Mabbott (Cambridge/MA: The Belknap Press of Harvard University Press, 1978), 511. For an analysis of the flâneur in Poe's story see H. Neumeyer, *Der Flaneur: Konzeptionen der Moderne* (Würzburg: Königshausen und Neumann, 1999), 31-7.

21 See W. Benjamin, *Charles Baudelaire: Ein Lyriker im Zeitalter des Hochkapitalismus*, ed. R. Tiedemann (Frankfurt/M.: Suhrkamp, 1969), 36; and C.L. Bernstein, *The Celebration of Scandal: Toward the Sublime in Victorian Urban Fiction* (University Park: Pennsylvania State University Press, 1991), 6.

22 W. Benjamin, *Gesammelte Schriften*, ed. R. Tiedemann (Frankfurt/M.: Suhrkamp, 1982),I 524; H.-J. Ortheil, 'Der lange Abschied vom Flaneur', *Merkur* 40 (1986), 30-42, here 31.
23 Benjamin, *Charles Baudelaire*, 41f.
24 P. Keiller, *London* (UK, 1993).
25 Sinclair, *Lights Out*, 306.
26 Ibid.
27 Benjamin, *Charles Baudelaire*, 57.
28 C. Jenks, 'Watching Your Step: The History and Practice of the *Flâneur*', in id. (ed.), *Visual Culture* (London: Routledge, 1995), 150.
29 Nicholson, *Bleeding London* (London: Indigo, 1998), 69.
30 This idea is echoed in Judy Tanaka's identification of the city and the body, expressed in an initial statement to her therapist: 'I display signs of both renewal and decay. Strange sensations commute across my skin. There is vice and crime and migration. My veins throb as though with the passage of underground trains. My digestive tract is sometimes clogged. There are security alerts. There's congestion, bottlenecks. Some of me is common, some of me is restricted. I have flats and high-rises. It doesn't need a genius to see what's going on. Greater London, *c'est moi*.' (12) The equation between body and city becomes even more manifest when she has her torso tattooed with a map of London (344f.) – 'the map made flesh' (345).
31 *Boswell's Life of Johnson* (1791), ed. G.B. Hill, rev. and enlarged edition by L.F. Powell (Oxford: Clarendon Press, 1934), III, 178.
32 Raban, *Soft City* (London: Harvill Press, 1998), 9.
33 Jenks, 'Watching Your Step', 144.
34 See G. King, *Mapping Reality: An Exploration of Cultural Cartographies* (Basingstoke: Macmillan, 1996), 16.
35 P. Jackson, *Maps of Meaning: An Introduction to Cultural Geography* (London: Unwin Hyman, 1989), 2 and 185f.
36 Geertz, 'Thick Description', 5.
37 See T.J. Barnes and J.S. Duncan, 'Introduction: Writing Worlds', in eid. (eds), *Writing Worlds: Discourse, Text and Metaphor in the Representation of Landscape* (London: Routledge, 1992), 5.
38 Jenks, 'Watching Your Step', 144.

Julian Barnes, *England, England*
Tourism as a Critique of Postmodernism

Barbara Korte

The great event of this period, the great trauma, is this decline of strong referentials, these death pangs of the real and of the rational that open onto an age of simulation.
(Jean Baudrillard)[1]

I think that one hundred percent truth is unreclaimable and unknowable, but that we must maintain the superiority of a sixty-seven percent over a sixty-four percent of truth. (Julian Barnes)[2]

1. England Quintessentialized: A Dystopia of Tourism?

Read on its most obvious level, Julian Barnes's novel *England, England* (1998) is a satirical dystopia about the tourist industry and its consequences – the work of an author clearly familiar with the ongoing critique of modern and postmodern tourism.[3] In the central part of the novel, which is set a few decades into the third millennium, a reckless and megalomaniac media tycoon named Sir Jack Pitman (modelled on the Rupert Murdoch/Robert Maxwell type) embarks on the project to realize a final great idea, the crowning achievement of his life. He transforms the Isle of Wight, already an important tourist site in its own right, into a mega-tourist experience. The Isle of Wight is an ideal setting for the novel because '[a]s every schoolboy knows, you can fit the whole of England on the Isle of Wight' (blurb of the original edition). But to Barnes the island also epitomizes the negative effects of tourism:

> It was one of the first places in Great Britain to be perverted by becoming a tourist destination. It was a rather undeveloped, old-

> fashioned, quite primitive offshore island until sunbathing became fashionable. [...] People went there for their holidays, and then built bungalows. The traditional industries of smuggling and boat-building lost out to tourism.[4]

In *England, England,* the Isle of Wight is to become a copy of England that will transcend all former ventures in a blossoming industry of touristic replication:

> 'We are not talking theme park,' [Sir Jack] began. 'We are not talking heritage centre. We are not talking Disneyland, World's Fair, Festival of Britain, Legoland or Parc Asterix. [...] we are talking quantum leap. We are not seeking twopenny tourists. It is world-boggling time. [...] We are offering *the thing itself*'. (59)[5]

Sir Jack's version of England and Englishness, with its mixture of super-authentic theme park and living-history experience, is specifically designed for foreign tourists with sufficient capital ('Top dollar. Long yen', 58). England itself, this suggests, no longer has enough inhabitants who can, in an era after Tony Blair, afford the tourism Sir Jack has in mind. Since well-paying customers deserve to get what they expect, Sir Jack's England is planned on the basis of thorough market research. A poll in twenty-five countries reveals which 'Fifty Quintessences' (sights, historical characters and myths, institutions and stereotypes) foreigners associate with England – or read as signs of Englishness, to adopt Jonathan Culler's terminology of a semiotics of tourism[6] – and which they will therefore have to see in order to get a 'real' impression of the place. They include, among others, the Royal Family, Big Ben and the Houses of Parliament, Pubs, a Robin in the Snow, Robin Hood and His Merrie Men, Cricket, the White Cliffs of Dover, the *Times*, Shakespeare, a Cup of Tea, Stonehenge, Marmalade, London Taxis, TV Classic Serials, Oxbridge, Harrods, Red Buses, Hypocrisy, Homosexuality, Alice in Wonderland, Queen Victoria, Breakfast, (Warm) Beer and Emotional Frigidity (83-5). Eventually the whole catalogue of quintessences is realized: England's built heritage is easily copied; a natural feature on the Isle of Wight similar to the Cliffs of Dover is found without problems; actors are hired to impersonate historical and mythical characters associated with England's collective memory (including Queen Victoria, Dr Johnson, Nell Gwynne, Robin Hood and a few more recent cultural heroes such as the SAS); and a thousand robins have been acclimatized to perpetual snow.[7] After only two years Sir Jack's scheme has become the big commercial success it was intended to be, as a pastiche travel feature from the *Wall Street Journal* appreciates: 'this ground-breaking enterprise is likely to be much copied' (179). Thanks to Sir Jack's political cunning, the enterprise is even more than a success in the business world: the Isle of Wight gains political independence, and with the appropriate financial persuasion a rather undignified Royal Family also moves there. The success of the new state, which is a 'pure market state' (183) gladly admitted into the European Union, soon engenders 'a new proud insularity' (202f.) among the former Wighters, who now find themselves in full employment after all.

Ultimately the existence of the replica - now named 'England, England' with fitting reduplication - means the end of the Isle of Wight as an authentic location and community. Apart from a few spots where no tourists ever go, the island is completely remodelled - even including a replica memento of the tourist site it used to be before Sir Jack. In a street called Bungalow Valley, 'Visitors may wander through a perfectly-recreated street of typical pre-Island Housing' (180). But the existence of England, England also means the end of the original England, which had been considerably weakened before Sir Jack's takeover anyhow (due to the devolution of Scotland, Wales and Northern Ireland as well as its own problems with the EU). When overseas visitors no longer come to see the real thing because Sir Jack's island provides them with 'everything you imagined England to be, but more convenient, cleaner, friendlier, and more efficient' (184),[8] and above all in a time-saving[9] and thus more economical manner, the original England loses a key basis of its national income and cannot prevent its final downfall: 'The world began to forget that "England" had ever meant anything except England, England' (253). The copy has indeed become the thing itself.

All that remains of old England in the end is an 'olde' England indeed: a retrogressive political unity named Anglia, which is depicted in the novel's short third and final part. This version of England has regressed into a far-from-splendid isolationism and fosters a naive ideal of rural and traditionalist Englishness. Anglia is a deindustrialized state that has forbidden most modern media and communication technology and does not welcome visitors from abroad (tourism is banned 'except for groups numbering two or less', 253). After the loss of further counties apart from the Isle of Wight,

Anglia has even restored the old Anglo-Saxon kingdoms.[10] The farcical elements in this part of the novel strongly suggest that the authenticity of Anglia is to be questioned just as much as that of the Disneyfied version of England on the former Isle of Wight.

The critique of tourism is as old as tourism itself; it has become particularly outspoken since the explosion of mass tourism after World War II. In its late twentieth-century forms, tourism has been blamed for many things: for perverting the venerable cultural tradition of travel into just another commodity of late capitalism; for tempting countries to sell their cultural heritage; for its destructive effects on the natural environment and on over-visited tourist sites (such as Stonehenge, the Acropolis or Lascaux); as a new form of imperialism in the so-called developing countries; and last but not least for the alleged superficiality of perception it provokes among its practitioners. Much of this is addressed in Barnes's novel, but it is not tourism per se or the professional provision of tourism which *England, England* sets out to criticize. Rather, the novel uses tourism metaphorically to inquire into the condition of a postmodern England.

2. Tourism and the Loss of Authenticity

Tourism is a pervasive cultural practice of the contemporary world. To Dean MacCannell, it 'is not just an aggregate of merely commercial activities; it is also an ideological framing of history, nature, and tradition; a framing that has the power to reshape culture and nature to its own needs'.[11] Tourism thus provides an ideal ground for exploring the condition of postmodern England and the sense of identity or non-identity it engenders.[12] This timely concern of the novel is underlined by the fact that Barnes has himself called the book an 'idea-of-England novel' and expressly 'wanted the paperback to come out in time for the millennium'.[13] Perhaps he had a premonition of how Britain would be presenting itself in its Millennium Dome, with the 'Self Portrait' pavilion offering just the kind of superficial and heterogeneous image collage which Barnes sets out to criticize in *England, England*.

A metaphor in the novel's first part explicitly suggests that something has gone wrong with English identity. In her childhood during the final decade of the twentieth century Martha Cochrane, one of Sir Jack's chief executives, used to play with a Counties-of-England jigsaw puzzle – the puzzle being an obvious image for the postmodern idea that all nations are constructs or imaginations, to take up Benedict Anderson's influential phrase.[14] Martha, however, cannot complete her puzzle since her father, when he deserts his family, takes one of its pieces (the county of Nottinghamshire) with him. Henceforward, Martha's constructions of England and Englishness will always be marked by a sense of loss, and she has no reservations about working on a project that will actually remove a puzzle piece - the county of the Isle of Wight - from England.

Beyond Englishness, Barnes's novel has an even wider significance as a comment on postmodern existence in general. As one reviewer writes: 'Despite its light touch, *England, England* is a philosophical novel about authenticity';[15] it can thus be seen in line with Barnes's other works of fiction where the theme of the possibility of truth, or of establishing truth, is generally prominent. The loss of the real has been marked as one of the great epistemological problems of postmodernity, whose discussion involves now-familiar conceptualizations such as a preoccupation with images, representations and depthless surfaces, signification without referentials in the real world, the simulacrum, hyperreality, cyberworlds and a general shallowing of experience that is easily satisfied with spectacle.[16] In the words of Chris Rojek:

> Postmodernism reverses the tendency in modernist thought to oppose authentic experience with unauthentic experience and to privilege the former. By throwing the symbolic, processed character of social experience into sharp relief, post-modernism problematizes the realm of the authentic.[17]

The study quoted here is one of several in which late twentieth-century tourism and the terms of postmodern existence have been explicitly linked. To John Urry, tourism is not only 'prefiguratively postmodern because of its particular combination of the visual, the aesthetic, and the popular', but during the final decades of the twentieth century, it has even been universalized into an everyday mode of perception and experience: 'This has the effect, as "tourism" *per se* declines in specificity, of universalising the tourist gaze - people are much of the time "tourists" whether they like it or not.'[18] The link between tourism and postmodern existence is made not least through the concept of authenticity, which has also, however, been central in the discussion of the tourist experience before postmodernism. In an influential study, Dean MacCannell, for instance, has referred to the tourist as 'one of the best models available for modern-man-in-general', since tourism serves a modern *longing* for an authenticity no longer to be found in one's own everyday world. 'All tourists desire this deeper involvement with society and culture to some degree; it is a basic component of their motivation to travel'.[19] This is why the tourist industry 'stages' authenticity that the tourist can gaze at.[20] However, in a time that is *post*modern, tourists may no longer even desire to find the authentic; *mock* authenticity, *surface* authenticity seems to be satisfactory: 'leisure and tourism are now equivalent to mere consumption activity. The modernist quest for authenticity and self-realization has come to an end.'[21]

As a consumable form of travel, tourism seems to embody the commodified, image-and-appearance-orientated mode of existence that is said to characterize late capitalist culture - especially in a form that has indeed boomed only in the final decades of the twentieth century: a tourism centred around simulacra of original tourist spots.[22] In an interview relating to *England, England*, Barnes himself mentions two recent real mega-projects of this kind: the Venice simulation around a Las Vegas hotel (The Venetian) that was opened shortly before the novel appeared, and the Roma Vetus project outside Orvieto, opened in 1999, which reconstructs ancient Rome's 'old buildings but in much better shape'.[23]

Barnes's novel places the England, England project very openly within a postmodern frame-of-mind and rhetoric - most flagrantly through a third-millennium clone of its major French theorists. A 'French intellectual' is invited to deliver the gist of his theories to the Project's Co-ordinating Committee:

> 'It is well established [...] that nowadays we prefer the replica to the original. [...] Permit me to cite one of my fellow-countrymen, one of those old *soixante-huitards* of the last century whose errors many of us find so instructive, so fruitful. "All that was once directly lived", he wrote, "has become mere representation." A profound truth, even if conceived in profound error. For he intended it, astonishingly, as criticism not praise. [...] He understood, this old thinker, that we live in the world of the spectacle, but sentimentalism and a certain political recidivism made him fear his own vision. I would prefer to advance his thought in the following way. Once there was only the world directly lived. Now there is the representation - let me fracture that word, the re-presentation - of the world. It is not a substitute for that plain

> and primitive world, but an enhancement and enrichment, an ironisation and summation of that world. This is where we live today.' (53-5)

A philosophical position that does not even bemoan any more that authenticity no longer matters is the perfect underpinning for Sir Jack's project, where hyperreality triumphs over reality and where the boundaries between real space and cyberspace seem to collapse. When the King of England first visits England, England, he feels transported into cyberspace: 'Lady Godiva had come by on her horse, and just to make sure she wasn't in cyberspace he hoisted a pair of binox to his peepers.' (165) To Martha, the theme park simulation becomes indistinguishable from its electronic representation on a monitor screen: 'There were sights on the Island Martha knew so intimately from a hundred camera angles that she could no longer remember whether or not she had ever seen them in reality.' (185) The tourist project in Barnes's novel is notably created by people who have no scruples regarding truth and authenticity as long as surface images are satisfactory. Sir Jack wears braces that signify all sorts of prestigious memberships but have no actual references (30). Martha manipulates her CV and even openly admits this to her future employer: 'It's as true as you want it to be' (45). In a world where appearance is generally more important than the real thing, it is not surprising that Sir Jack's clientele is content with the product he sells them. In fact, they think that the replica is even better, more authentic, than the original, as the pastiche travel feature for the *Wall Street Journal* emphasizes: 'if given the option between an inconvenient "original" or a convenient replica, a high proportion of tourists would opt for the latter.' (181)[24]

3. Heritage Tourism, or Englishness without Depth

The tourists who visit England, England are foreigners. But the consequences which the abandonment of even the desire for the authentic has on identity, are shown for England and the English. Where signification matters more than referentiality, the idea of authentic selfhood also becomes vain. 'Postmodernism outflanks the notion of the integrated self which underpins modernist thought. It presents the self as a fissile entity which presents in different ways in different social settings.'[25] Presentation or re-presentation is the sole purpose of the actors who impersonate the historical and mythical characters in England, England. Like the Wighters recruited to provide a backdrop of picturesque and friendly native folk, these actors soon start to identify with their roles (the replica becoming real again), which indicates that their real identities have at best been weak in the first place. This is supported by the fact that the actor who identifies with Dr Johnson so much that visitors complain about his filthiness and moodiness,[26] turns out to have adopted the name Samuel Johnson even before he was hired for England, England (210).

Sir Jack's planning committee also consists of characters who are good presenters, careful of what their appearances signify. The Project Historian, for instance, is a tele-don (that is, a professional presenter of images) and a meticulous dresser, while Sir Jack characteristically opts for cruder modes of self-fashioning, such as his only-signifier-braces or the slab of Cornish slate which, in the anteroom of his office, is meant to awe visitors with a kind of pre-mortem obituary (29). Beyond this façade, however, Sir Jack's personality – like that of another media tycoon, Citizen Kane – is most slippery: nobody knows anything definite about his origins (33), and he is read differently by different people (56f.). Sir Jack, to whom authenticity does not matter, also has no respect for personal identity, whether other people's or his own. He calls all his personal assistants Susie (34), once says to his planning committee: '"What is real?" [...] I could have you replaced with substitutes, with ... simulacra' (31), and he even trifles with the elusiveness of his own self: 'Is my name ... real?' (32). It seems a just revenge that after his death Sir Jack himself is replicated for the tourists on his island – particularly because his personal idol, whom he wished to emulate with his project, is Beethoven, a truly original genius in the nineteenth-century sense.

Sir Jack is a quintessentially postmodern personality without depth, and the depth dimension he lacks most obviously is that of a past, which, however, he tries to simulate in a monstrous and perverse manner; Sir Jack fakes childhood experience in a luxury brothel where once a month he indulges in grotesque mock babyhood (155-9).[27] All identity is based on memory, on the faculty to remember one's own past (not least one's childhood) and that of one's culture. In the words of David Lowenthal: 'The past is integral to our sense of identity [...]. Ability to recall and identify with our own past gives existence meaning, purpose, and value.'[28] The past thus generally plays a major role in Barnes's novel. Even as a child, Martha has the central insight into the existential importance of the past – and also the fact that the past is always, to a certain extent, an interpretation of the present, since only then can it become meaningful for nations as well as individuals: 'the past was never just the past, it was what made the present able to live with itself' (6).

Significantly, the form of tourism which Barnes's novel depicts is heritage tourism – a tourism expressly intended to bring the past into the present. It is also a form of tourism associated with postmodern times that are allegedly troubled by their disintegrating present and therefore feel strongly attracted to the past:

> the wish to save England in one of its past forms is a powerful, motivating force in the country. In line with tourists' expectations, the imaginative return to the past is the search for reassurance and confirmation. It runs in direct contradiction to the everyday experience that in elusive ways life is dislocated, rootless and unsatisfying.[29]

Indeed, heritage tourism as a branch of a general heritage cult and industry did not emerge in Britain on a grand scale until the 1970s, and it only started to boom under Thatcher, in the 1980s. The past in Britain then became, in the words of David Lowenthal, 'a foreign country with a booming tourist trade'.[30]

Heritage tourism presents the past for the present in a manner that has been perceived as characteristic of an age of re-presentation, simulation and growing indifference towards authenticity. Heritage tourism has been condemned for engendering a superficial approach to history. To Hewison, heritage tourism offers 'no history in depth', but 'a contemporary creation, more costume drama and re-enactment than critical discourse'. He further claims that heritage 'is bogus history. It has enclosed the late twentieth century in a bell jar into which no ideas can enter, and, just as crucially, from which none can escape'.[31] In *England, England*, Martha (who was trained as a historian but then worked temporarily for the Department of Heritage and the Arts, 45) and the Project Historian discuss whether Sir Jack's is a 'bogus Project' (131). David Lowenthal acknowledges that all history, too, is only a re-construction of the present, but one which – in contrast to heritage – is still committed to verifiability and seriousness:

> But heritage is not history, even when it mimics history. It uses historical traces and tells historical tales, but these tales and traces are stitched into fables that are open neither to critical analysis

> nor to contemporary scrutiny. [...] Historians' pasts, too, are always altered by time and hindsight. To be taken seriously by other historians, however, these revisions must conform with accepted tenets of evidence. Heritage is far more flexibly emended.[32]

Chris Rojek points out that heritage tourist sites like the 'The Way We Were' exhibit in Wigan Pier characteristically blend the authentic and unauthentic: 'authentic historical buildings and artefacts are preserved and actors in period costume present themselves as real living people from the past. The authentic and the unauthentic are displayed as equivalent items.'[33]

Heritage tourism can also be seen more positively as a form of tourism that helps people to come to a better understanding of their own culture's past[34] and may thus be seen as a popular continuation of the long tradition of domestic tourism in the British Isles.[35] In Barnes's novel, however, Sir Jack's project is not directed at domestic visitors. In the early third millennium, an England whose 'tits have dropped', as one character casually phrases it (37), has only its 'accumulation of time' (39) left to capitalize on.[36] England thus sells its heritage off to foreigners - explicitly *not* in order to provide them with a deeper historical understanding of England's past but just for the light consummation of a nostalgic retro experience.[37] Sir Jack hires the Project Historian *not* to develop an educational concept, but 'to advise us on how much History people already know' (71) so that the future visitors' pleasure will not be spoilt by real education. The presentation of the past in Sir Jack's mega theme park has lost all historical depth and seriousness, illustrating the conviction expressed, for instance by Fredric Jameson, that postmodernity is 'a new and original historical situation in which we are condemned to seek History by way of our own pop images and simulacra of that history, which itself remains forever out of reach'. The pastiche in much historical fiction of the late twentieth century is, to Jameson, characteristic of this attitude, since here elements of the past are presented as 'perpetual presents'.[38] As in Sir Jack's England, England, the past thus loses its fourth dimension and becomes a mere space (a park) in which everything is present-ed and time levels have been radically compressed; in perpetual simultaneity, elements of the past become a spectacle for the present moment.

In England, England, visitors can meet historical characters, and items from English cultural memory are re-modelled so that they can be easily enjoyed according to third-millennium family values, fashions and standards of political correctness: Nell Gwynne, the lover of Charles II, retains her impressive bust (making a jealous queen of England wonder whether it can be real, 164), but she is made older than sixteen – the age when the historical Nell met her King – to avoid any suspicion of paedophilia (93). The 'primal English myth' (146) of Robin Hood and his Merrie Men undergoes 'repositioning [...] for modern times' (148) by the inclusion of ethnic minorities, the differently-abled as well as gays. When Robin Hood and his men rebel against this refashioning of their myth and want to make it more real again – by having real fights and consuming real meat instead of a fake vegetable ox – different time levels in England, England are even interfaced: 'a one-off cross-epoch extravaganza' (227) is devised to solve the problem but is somewhat aborted: the island's SAS attacks the Merrie Men but is unexpectedly defeated since meanwhile the mock-medieval band has also replaced its replica weapons with real ones.

Such manipulation of the past perverts the fact that the past has to be interpreted in order to become meaningful for the present. In England, England, the past is reinterpreted in a drastic manner – not, however, to make it meaningful, but to make it consumable and thus profitable. This strategy is embodied in the episode in which a logo is chosen for England, England. This logo adapts an anecdote which Sir Jack's Project Historian has come across on the Isle of Wight: a nineteenth-century egg-seller was blown off the edge of a cliff by a gale of wind but parachuted safely to the ground thanks to her big umbrella and crinoline. The image evokes Mary Poppins, but the woman is christened Betsy.[39] Sir Jack loves the idea of a Betsy logo since the anecdote is '"*here* and it's *magic* and we can make it into *now*"' (122). When attempts fail to have stuntmen re-enact Betsy's actual fall, the anecdote is turned into a tourist experience that is consumable in the literal sense: tourists float safely down the cliff on a camouflaged cable, bearing a basket of eggs that will become part of their Island Breakfast Experience at Betsy's All-Day Breakfast Bar (123).

The novel suggests that such transformation of cultural memory into spectacle is the result of a loss of respect for the past and its culture in contemporary England. This loss of respect is epitomized in Sir Jack's corruption of a line from one of the most famous and most patriotic speeches in Shakespeare's *Richard II*: 'a precious whatsit set in a silver doodah' (61). In Shakespeare's play the respective line ('This precious stone set in the silver sea', II.1, l. 46) is spoken by the dying John of Gaunt, who in the context *bemoans* what has become of his England, explicitly complaining that 'This land of such dear souls, this dear dear land, [...] Is now leased out - I die pronouncing it - / Like to a tenement or pelting farm' (II.1, ll. 57-60).[40] Entirely ignoring the context of the original line, Sir Jack uses it to legitimize his project, since the Isle of Wight, with its diamond shape, is a precious stone indeed, especially as far as Sir Jack's profit is concerned. However, the past is generally held in low esteem in the England which Barnes depicts, and only this general mentality permits Sir Jack to be successful. The novel shows clearly, for instance, that at the end of the twentieth century, something went seriously wrong with history as a school subject. Martha's history lessons consisted of drilling games in which dates and names were associated with mnemonic phrases and anecdotes. 'She [the history teacher] led them in and out of two millennia, making history not a dogged progress but a series of vivid and competing moments [...].' (12) This focus on isolated moments is exactly the superficial and time-levelling attitude towards history which is later realized for the tourists. When the Project Historian tests English people about their knowledge of history, even a university-educated 49-year-old man knows so little about English history that '[i]t seemed to Dr Max positively unpatriotic to know so little about the origins and forging of your nation' (82). Sir Jack's project can only have its wide-ranging consequences because it is erected against the background of a nation that has lost the ability to deal meaningfully with its past, to take the past seriously and make sense of it for constructing its present identity: 'Old England had lost its history, and therefore - since memory is identity - had lost all sense of itself.' (251) A people like this will not mind when its history is Disneyfied into a heritage product, and it cannot react when an historical episode is misused by Sir Jack to claim the political independence of the Isle of Wight (126).

4. Tourism and Personal Non-/Identity

Underlying England's problem with its history and *collective* memory is the problem which individuals have with their *personal* memory and thus identity. The very beginning of the novel mentions Martha's insight that individual memory is nothing 'solid' either (3) but that it is always to a certain extent invented and reinvented, processed through and coloured by everything that has happened in between the now and then (6). For Martha, this insight causes disorientation, since a primal, original moment that might account for an essence of her self cannot be remembered and probably never existed: '"What's your first memory?" [...] "I don't remember"' (3), is the opening of the novel. The absence of a primal moment is also emphasized by the Project Historian: 'there *is* no authentic moment of beginning, of purity [...]. We may choose to freeze a moment and say that it all "began" then, but as a historian I have to tell you that such labelling is intellectually indefensible'. (132)

When memories of the self are constructed, however, then the self too is only an unstable construct. While Sir Jack seems to be immune to all identity problems that result from such problems of remembering, especially of remembering origins, Martha is a character who is at least capable of developing an epistemological crisis since – like tourists before postmodernism – she can still long for what she has lost: the missing piece of her England puzzle, but above all authentic memories on which her sense of self and thus her happiness could be built: 'even if you recognized all this, grasped the impurity and corruption of the memory system, you still, part of you, believed in that innocent, authentic thing [...] you called a memory' (6f.). The fact that happiness and a sense of self are connected reveals itself to Martha in a conversation she has with the fake Dr Johnson by whose authentic depression she is touched. Martha finds out that the secret to find happiness would be to be true to her own nature – 'but what if this nature was no more natural than the nature Sir Jack had satirically delineated after a walk in the country? – because if you were unable to locate your nature, your chance of happiness was surely diminished.' (226)

Childhood disappointments have turned Martha into a cynic unable to enter a satisfactory love relationship or to believe in God and other grand or meta-narratives. After her father's desertion, she is deeply disappointed by the judges of an Agricultural Show, which, for her, is 'a place where [...] there was order, and rules, and wise judgment' (18) and where perfect sets of identical exhibits seem to defy the contingency of natural life. Nevertheless, Martha has preserved a desire for a happier and more serious existence: 'Well, I suppose life must be more serious if it has a structure, if there's something larger out there than yourself.' (236)[41] This desire drives Martha into a long-deserted church of the old Isle of Wight that has remained untouched by Sir Jack's project. Here Martha recognizes what the only possibility of leading a meaningful life could be in a world where everything is understood as a construct and where authenticity does not matter any more. Once reality and the grand narratives have decomposed, the only hope left is *faith* in a more serious mode of existence. (237) Significantly, in her existential anguish, Martha identifies with Betsy, the logo figure of the project. She tries to imagine the feeling of salvation which the original nineteenth-century Betsy must have felt, thus restoring the 'seriousness' of the original event by celebrating 'the original image': 'A woman swept and hanging, a woman half out of this world, terrified and awe-struck, yet in the end safely delivered.' (238) For cynical Martha, whose ability to believe has been shattered, this deliverance seems no longer feasible. To her, only children still have a gift to see through appearances and thus to believe in reality: 'even when they disbelieved, they also believed' (264). But Martha at least seems to reach a resigned old age in Anglia, the place where she grew up but which has now been drastically changed.

5. Anglia, or Tourist England Universalized

Outwardly, old Martha adapts to the new state, but inwardly she keeps her critical distance – not least because the new retro state is so dangerously close to the England, England from which she was exiled. Many of its strategies of re-inventing olde England bear a conspicuous resemblance to the strategies of England, England. In the novel's final episode Martha's village has just invented a festival as a tradition (246), for which the new Anglians dress up as the same historical characters that were also simulated in England, England: Queen Victoria, Boadicea and Robin Hood (264). The simulation is less perfect than in Sir Jack's project, but it is attempted, and some of Anglia's inhabitants also very obviously lack authenticity and seriousness: Martha's fellow villager Jez Harris, for instance, is really an American who has adopted an ur-English retro identity and now constantly invents apparently authentic folklore.

At the end of Barnes's novel, then, the version of English culture that was developed as a reaction against the tourist version of England, England seems to have turned into a permanent heritage condition itself – not one en-acted for tourists, however, but for oneself. In both England, England and Anglia, a tourist version of England has universalized into the thing itself. Barnes's novel may initially seem 'just' a dystopian critique of contemporary tourism, but, through its intricate web of allusions and intertextual references, it turns out to be far more complex than that: *England, England* criticizes not tourism but the postmodern attitudes that have allowed a touristification of England to take place.

Notes

1 J. Baudrillard, *Simulacra and Simulation* (Ann Arbor: University of Michigan Press, 1994), 43.

2 R. Freiburg, 'Julian Barnes [Introduction and Interview]', in id. and J. Schnittker (eds), *'Do you consider yourself a postmodern author?' Interviews with Contemporary English Writers* (Münster: LIT, 1999), 41-66, here 58.

3 In his interview with Freiburg, Barnes comments on the amount of research that goes into his highly intertextual novels. He is aware that, apart from specific research, 'you can be influenced at second hand, and you can be influenced by things that are in the air' (53).

4 J. Lanchester, 'A Vision of England' [interview with Barnes], *Electronic Telegraph*, 29 August 1998. http://www.telegraph.co.uk/.

5 All page numbers in parentheses refer to the original edition of *England, England* (London: Cape, 1998).

6 J. Culler, 'The Semiotics of Tourism', in id., *Framing the Sign: Criticism and Its Institutions* (Oxford: Blackwell, 1988), 153-67.

7 The characters in the novel assume that Christmas cards explain the popularity of the robins (85). But considering the general importance of childhood in the novel (see below), it seems significant that a robin in the snow is also found in a classic of children's literature, C.S. Lewis's *The Lion, the Witch and the Wardrobe* (1950).

8 In this context, see also the Disney quote cited in note 24.

9 The name Sir Jack Pitman suggests a pitbull/John Bull reference appropriate to the novel's main theme, but it might also allude to Sir Isaac Pitman (1813-97), the inventor of a shorthand system, since the version of England presented in Barnes's novel is a shorthand one indeed. I am grateful to Stephen Prickett for this suggestion.

10 According to M. Gee, 'Career, Money, Sex – Why Waste Time on them?', *Electronic Telegraph*, http://www.booksonline.co.uk:80/, the Anglian village depicted in the novel's final part is 'curiously reminiscent of John Major's famous speech about warm beer, cricket and old maids on bicycles', famous for being a plagiarism of Orwell's *The Lion and the Unicorn* (1941). But in its Anglia part, the novel also reminds one of G.K. Chesterton's *The Napoleon of Notting Hill* (1904), a fantasy set in the late twentieth century in which London is unexpectedly transformed into a neo-medieval society. This future society is used to criticize the mercantilism, technology and politics which Chesterton deplored in his own present. The fact that Sir Jack in Barnes's novel plans his project at a battle table and wears a uniform with a tricorn might be a reference to Chesterton's novel. Furthermore, like all of Chesterton's fiction, *The Napoleon of*

Notting Hill demonstrates the importance of human faith, which is also, as will be pointed out below, a major issue in *England, England*.

11 D. MacCannell, *Empty Meeting Grounds: The Tourist Papers* (London: Routledge, 1992), 1.

12 The novel is thus clearly placed in a long tradition which considers travel as an important 'resource in the quest for self-realization'; see C. Rojek, *Ways of Escape: Modern Transformations in Leisure and Travel* (Basingstoke: Macmillan, 1993), 177, and E.J. Leed, *The Mind of the Traveler: From Gilgamesh to Global Tourism* (New York: Basic Books, 1991), part III. See also Helga Quadflieg's contribution in the present volume. On the role that the 'tourist map' has played in defining the specifically English sense of identity, see I. Ousby, *The Englishman's England: Taste, Travel and the Rise of Tourism* (Cambridge: Cambridge University Press, 1990), here 4.

13 Lanchester, 'A Vision of England'. Barnes's interest in Englishness throughout the 1990s is also reflected in his *Letters from London, 1990-1995* (London: Picador, 1995), and the short stories in *Cross Channel* (London: Cape, 1996).

14 B. Anderson, *Imagined Communities* (London: Verso and New Left Books, 1983).

15 J. Carey, 'Land of Make-Believe', *Sunday Times*, 23 August 1998, electronic edition, http://www.sunday-times.co.uk.

16 The influential theory of the simulacrum was formulated by Baudrillard, to whom the present is marked by the third order of the simulacrum: simulation. The simulacra of simulation - especially those produced in the electronic media - are purely 'founded on information, the model, the cybernetic game - total operationality, hyperreality, aim of total control' (*Simulacra and Simulation*, 121). This leads to the abolishment of the real: 'the era of simulation is inaugurated by a liquidation of all referentials - worse: with their artificial resurrection in the systems of signs'; simulation 'threatens the difference between the "true" and the "false", the "real" and the "imaginary"' (ibid., 2 and 3 respectively). Following U. Eco's *Travels in Hyper-Reality* (1986), Baudrillard defines the hyperreal as 'the generation by models of a real without origin or reality' (ibid., 1). On depthlessness as a 'constitutive feature of the postmodern' see F. Jameson, *Postmodernism, or The Cultural Logic of Late Capitalism* (London: Verso, 1991), 6. D. Harvey, *The Condition of Postmodernity: An Enquiry into the Origins of Cultural Change* (Oxford: Blackwell 1989), provides a readable survey of the relevant positions in postmodern thinking.

17 C. Rojek, *Decentring Leisure: Rethinking Leisure Theory* (London: Sage, 1995), 171.

18 J. Urry, *The Tourist Gaze: Leisure and Travel in Contemporary Societies* (London: Sage, 1990), 87 and 82 respectively.

19 D. MacCannell, *The Tourist: A New Theory of the Leisure Class* (New York: Schocken Books 1976), 1 and 10 respectively. See also Culler, 'The Semiotics of Tourism', 158.

20 MacCannell, *The Tourist*, 92-102.

21 Rojek, *Ways of Escape*, 133.

22 However, the origins of this form of tourism predate the postmodern condition at least a century. The great exhibitions in the second half of the nineteenth century replicated 'civilized' and 'exotic' cultural sights that were sometimes even peopled with real inhabitants. See P. Greenhalgh, 'Education, Entertainment and Politics: Lessons from the Great International Exhibitions', in P. Vergo (ed.), *The New Museology* (London: Reaktion, 1989), 74-98, and the contribution by Alexander Geppert in the present volume.

23 Lanchester, 'A Vision of England'. The Venetian and Roma Vetus have web pages: http://www.in-vegas.com/venetian, and http://www.romavetus.com. Almost coinciding with *England, England*, this form of tourism is also addressed in another novel about postmodern England, Geoff Nicholson's *Bleeding London* (1997); see Eveline Kilian's contribution in this volume.

24 This is not without precedent in the real world. See D. Lowenthal, *The Past Is a Foreign Country* (Cambridge: Cambridge University Press, 1985), 293 on the fact that '[r]eplicas like replacements may be preferred to their prototypes. The nineteenth-century English view that "a happy imitation is of much more value than a defective original" has its twentieth-century counterpart in Walt Disney's boast that Disneyland's "Vieux Carré" was just like the 1850s original, but "a lot cleaner".'

25 Rojek, *Decentring Leisure*, 172.

26 Lowenthal, *The Past Is a Foreign Country*, again names real-life precedents for these phenomena: 'Re-enactments are patent anachronisms. But [...] some actors become so involved in bygone events that they feel as though they are really living them.' (300f.) 'True-to-eighteenth-century militiamen at Canada's restored Louisbourg Fortress offended tourists with their rumpled uniforms and rude ways; even when told that the "militiamen" were slovenly and demoralized because that was how they *had* been, back then, visitors were ill at ease, as they were with ticket collectors posing as "syphilitic whores". In the end Louisbourg abandoned realistic animation altogether.' (298)

27 In this context of the grotesque, see the parallel drawn between Baudrillard and Rabelais in Z. Bauman, *Intimations of Postmodernity* (London: Routledge, 1992), 152.

28 Lowenthal, *The Past is a Foreign Country*, 41.

29 J. Taylor, *A Dream of England: Landscape, Photography and the Tourist's Imagination* (Manchester: Manchester University Press, 1994), 214. See also R. Hewison, *The Heritage Industry: Britain in a Climate of Decline* (London: Methuen, 1987), 135, and especially K. Walsh, *The Representa-*

tion of the Past: Museums and Heritage in the Post-Modern World (London: Routledge, 1992).

30 Lowenthal, *The Past Is a Foreign Country*, xvii. In 1983, the National Heritage Act established English Heritage as a quango; it was transformed in 1992 into the Department of National Heritage, in which the arts and tourism were linked for the first time in one government department. In the version of this new ministry, which also looks after sport, broadcasting and the new national lottery, 'the past exists in line with the present; it can be said to have delivered the present, and can be honoured as "tradition"' (Taylor, *A Dream of England*, 218).

31 Hewison, *The Heritage Industry*, 135 and 144 respectively. For influential criticism of the heritage cult see also P. Wright, *On Living in an Old Country: The National Past in Contemporary Britain* (London: Verso, 1989).

32 D. Lowenthal, *Possessed by the Past: The Heritage Crusade and the Spoils of History* (New York: Free Press, 1996), 121.

33 Rojek, *Ways of Escape*, 151.

34 See several contributions in G. Wall and W. Nuryanti (eds), 'Heritage and Tourism', special issue of *Annals of Tourism Research*, 23.2 (1996).

35 For a brief survey of this tradition see B. Korte, *English Travel Writing: From Pilgrimages to Postcolonial Explorations* (Basingstoke: Macmillan, 2000), chapter 4. On the association of travel with education before postmodernism see also Rojek, *Ways of Escape*, 114 and 120.

36 The association between a sense of decline in Britain and the rise of the heritage industry is made by Hewison, *The Heritage Industry*, 9f.

37 'Retro' is a word repeatedly mentioned in the novel that did not emerge in English until the late twentieth century, as a new word in lifestyle and leisure; see S. Tulloch (ed.), *The Oxford Dictionary of New Words: A Popular Guide to Words in the News* (Oxford: Oxford University Press, 1991), s.v. 'retro'.

38 Jameson, *Postmodernism*, 25. See also Baudrillard, *Simulacra and Simulation*, 43f. on the retro approach to the past. On 'time-space compression and the postmodern condition' see also Harvey, *The Condition of Postmodernity*, chapter 17.

39 The reason is that a character in the novel remembers the exclamation 'Heavens to Betsy'. Barnes's intertextual reference here is probably to a well-known book about curious sayings: C.E. Funk, *Heavens to Betsy! & Other Curious Sayings* (New York: Harper and Row, 1955). 'Heavens to Betsy' exemplarily fits a prominent theme of Barnes's novel in that its origin is mysterious, as Funk emphasizes: 'The title selected at the very outset for the book itself turned out eventually to be completely unsolvable. [...] The expression is in daily use in all parts of the United States. [...] But not an inkling have I been able to find that would lead to a positive source.' (ixf.)

40 *The Norton Shakespeare*, ed. S. Greenblatt et al. (New York: Norton, 1997).

41 In this context, see also Barnes's statement that 'God for the characters that I'm interested in doesn't exist anymore, as for most British people. [...] I don't believe in God but I miss him is how I would put it because [...] I think that His absence makes life less grand' (Freiburg, 'Julian Barnes', 56). For the wider context see, of course, J.-F. Lyotard's famous definition of the postmodern as 'l'incrédulité à l'égard des métarécits' in *La Condition Postmoderne: Rapport sur le Savoir* (Paris: Les Editions de Minuit, 1979), 7.

Index

air transport 3, 169, 174, 176, 183f.
Alps, the 5, 9, 12, 47, 75, 85-7, 94f., 101, 116, 121, 123
alterity (see also otherness) 27, 48
Ariès, Philippe 251
authenticity 5, 114, 123, 163, 169f., 188, 190, 200, 243, 249-66, 267, 278, 285-303
Bacon, Francis 23f., 26
Baedeker 6, 223
Bakhtin, Mikhail 238, 247
Barnes, Julian 17, 125, 285-303
Barthes, Roland 234, 251
Bath 117, 135, 256
battlefield tourism 8, 261, 263f.
Baudrillard, Jean (see also simulacrum) 16, 285, 300
beautiful, the (see also the picturesque; the sublime) 5, 9, 11, 13, 69, 73-5, 79f., 86, 88, 93, 102
Benjamin, Walter 273
Benidorm 122, 189-91
Bierstadt, Albert 98, 100-2
Bildungsreise (see educational travel)
Blackpool 3, 114, 125, 134-7, 186, 197, 212
Board of Trade 14, 141f., 145, 150, 152, 231
Brighton 89, 112, 125
Britishness (see also Englishness; identity, national) 39f., 236
British Tourist Authority 133-57, 141
Bryant, William Cullen 99
Brydone, Patrick 51
Bryson, Bill 206
Burke, Edmund 73f., 85-8, 91, 95
Butlin, Billy; Butlinism 3, 166f., 174, 198
Buzard, James 250
Byron, Lord 52, 55, 62, 101
Camden, William 4
canals 16, 208f., 214, 217, 253
Catholicism (see identity, religious)
city walk 17, 67-83
class (see tourism, and class)
club holidays 3
colonial travel 12, 85-107
colonialism; colonialization 4, 12, 22, 92, 99, 223-48, 261f.
Come-to-Britain Movement 140f., 143, 152
commercialization; commodification (of culture) 6, 9,14,

122f., 133f., 159-79, 181, 189, 193, 206, 288
conservation; conservationism (see preservation)
consumer society; consumerism; consumption 3, 6, 9, 13f., 110, 112, 117, 126, 159-79, 182f., 188f., 224, 229, 235, 290, 294
Cook, Thomas 3, 9, 16, 110, 113, 115f., 121, 123, 134, 164-6, 168, 172f., 182, 185f., 240, 261, 263
Cooper, James Fenimore 99
Coryate, Thomas 10, 17, 29-36, 38f., 254-6
crusades 251
Culler, Jonathan 10, 32, 253, 257, 267, 281, 286
Daniell, Thomas and William 87-90, 95f.
day-trippers 12, 70, 76, 83, 113-5, 120, 124f.
Defoe, Daniel 4
difference (see otherness)
discoverer, discovery 4, 22, 28, 32, 37, 86f., 94, 98
Disneyland 170, 212, 286, 288, 296, 301
Duffy, Maureen 268, 270
Eco, Umberto 170
educational travel 4, 10f., 21-45, 116, 163f.
elite (see tourism, and class)
Empire 16, 110, 123, 223-48, 264
empiricism 23f., 33f.
Englishness (see also Britishness; identity, national) 10, 21-45, 110, 119, 125, 260-3, 285-303
Enlightenment 5, 86, 113, 204, 215
environment 7, 69-84, 169, 211, 217
Enzensberger, Hans Magnus 159, 163, 172f.
exhibitions (see also Expo; Great Exhibition; Imperial Exhibitions; Millennium Dome) 8, 16f., 167, 212, 223-48, 301
exoticism (see also otherness) 10, 12, 89, 99, 116, 159, 168, 187, 229f., 236, 254, 262f., 301
explorer (see discoverer)
Expo 16, 244
Fordism 174, 188
foreign; foreignness (see other; otherness)
Forsyth, Joseph 62
Foucault, Michel 113, 243
Frobisher, Martin 22, 270
Froude, J.A. 261-3
Galt, John 55, 64
Garland, Alex 114, 124
Geertz, Clifford 281
Gilpin, William 11
globalization 13, 109-31, 175, 182, 189, 194
Goethe, Johann Wolfgang von 2
Grand Tour (see also educational travel) 2, 4f., 10f., 13, 22, 31, 47-68, 70, 87, 100f., 109, 112, 114, 116f., 121, 123, 161-3, 234, 243
graveyard tourism (see also necro-tourism) 29, 249-66
Gray, Thomas 56, 75, 257, 262

Great Exhibition 16, 135, 225, 233, 240
Guérard, Eugene van 96-8
guidebooks 6, 113f., 116, 123, 135, 139, 165, 172f., 189-92, 199, 223, 238, 240, 250f., 253, 258, 261
Hakluyt, Richard 28f.
Hamilton, Emma 52, 54f.
Harriot, Thomas 37f.
Hazlitt, William 56f., 62, 64
health 5, 117, 164, 171
hedonism (see also leisure; pleasure) 9, 162, 168, 171, 203-5, 215
Heine, Heinrich 2
heritage movement; heritage tourism 8, 13, 16f., 85, 110f., 116, 124-6, 140f., 163, 191, 203-21, 256, 286, 288, 291-6
holiday camp (see also Butlin) 186f.
Holidays-with-Pay Act 3, 174
home tour (see tourism, domestic)
host culture 15, 122, 181f., 200
humanism (see also educational travel) 10f., 21-45
identity, national (see also Britishness; Englishness; otherness) 8-10, 18, 21-45, 121f., 126, 211, 217, 223, 237, 243, 260, 288, 291, 296, 298, 300
identity, personal (see also otherness) 5, 10, 17, 26f., 37, 40f., 60, 85, 120, 126f., 163, 211, 276-81, 291f., 296-8
identity, religious 10, 36-40, 76, 260f.
images (see also sights) 6, 8f., 85, 133, 168, 225, 251, 256, 289, 291
imaginary travelling 223
Imperial Exhibitions 16f., 223-48
imperialism (see colonialism)
industrial heritage (see also heritage movement) 8, 203-21
industrialization 5, 7f., 12f., 71, 74, 76, 78, 109-31, 159-62, 164, 208, 253
Ironbridge 212, 215
Isle of Man 133-57
Isle of Wight 125, 285-303
Italy (see also Grand Tour) 2, 47-68, 100, 197
Jameson, Frederic 294
Jerusalem 21, 33f., 161, 255
Keiller, Patrick 269, 273f.
knowledge (see also educational travel) 23f., 28, 60, 271
laissez-faire 79, 134, 136, 171, 261
Lake District 11f., 69f., 74, 76, 78, 80f., 85, 119-21, 123, 125, 169, 249f., 256
Laker, Freddie 3
landscape (see also nature; tourism, scenic) 5, 8, 11f., 69-84, 85-107, 110, 119f., 121, 169, 207, 211, 253, 271, 273
leisure (see also hedonism; pleasure) 3, 10, 25, 134, 147, 160, 162, 164, 166f., 174, 183, 204-6, 240, 254, 257-9, 290

Leland, John 4
Lithgow, William 21, 29, 31-4, 38
Lively, Penelope 268, 270
London 1, 16f., 35, 52, 69, 71, 83, 91, 101, 126, 223-48, 254, 257-9, 276-83, 286
Longfellow, Henry Wadsworth 99
Macaulay, Thomas Babington 76-83
MacCannell, Dean 6, 288f.
Mallorca 121, 185-8, 193, 199
markers (of sights) 10, 199, 253
mass tourism 3, 11, 13, 15f., 116, 122, 126, 134, 159-61, 163f., 166, 174, 181-202, 224, 238, 240, 250, 288
memory 85, 252, 265, 268, 271, 286, 295-7
metropolis (see London)
Millennium Dome 1, 16, 169, 217, 288
modernism 214, 291
monuments (see also sights) 8, 21, 29, 32f., 37, 64, 89, 251, 253, 258, 260, 262, 265, 270
Moore, John 57
Moran, Thomas 98, 100-4
Morgan, Lady Sydney 49f., 61, 65
Moryson, Fynes 10, 29, 31-41
mountain tourism (see tourism, scenic)
national parks (see also conservation; preservation) 102, 104, 120
National Trust 81, 83, 120, 205
nature (see also landscape) 8f., 11, 13, 52, 61, 69-84, 85-107, 119, 123, 163, 188
necro-tourism 17, 249-66
Nicholson, Geoff 17, 269, 274-9, 281
Normanby, Marquis of 50
Orwell, George 204-8, 299
other; otherness (see also exoticism) 9f., 21, 25-8, 34f., 37, 41, 47f., 50, 59, 64, 110, 119, 123, 188, 192, 194f., 199, 230, 235f., 251, 253, 260, 262
package tour 2f., 5f., 9, 15, 122, 161, 164, 173-5, 181-202, 240
Parsons, William 57
patriotism 4, 21, 34f., 82
Pepys, Samuel 277f.
picturesque, the (see also the sublime; the beautiful) 11f., 70, 88, 92, 101, 110, 119, 259, 264
pilgrimage 4, 22, 25, 33f., 87, 102, 114, 161, 251, 255f.
Piozzi, Hester Lynch 47-9, 52
pleasure (see also hedonism; leisure) 2f., 10-2, 22, 25, 29-31, 47-50, 61, 86, 112, 117, 121, 161, 166, 169f., 173, 185, 204, 212, 226, 249, 259
Poe, Edgar Allan 273
Pope, Alexander 94f.
postcards 6, 204, 240, 253
postmodern; postmodernism 7, 17, 31, 41, 111, 124f., 170, 251, 256, 281, 285-303
Potter, Beatrix 12, 76, 81, 125
preservation 8, 76, 81-3, 110, 120, 206, 212

Priestley, J.B. 208
Protestantism (see identity, religious)
Raban, Jonathan 269, 279f.
railways 3, 9, 11f., 16, 69-84, 100, 102, 104, 110, 115, 119, 121, 134-6, 139, 164, 174, 176, 203-21, 258
replication (see also simulation; simulacrum) 170, 238, 286f., 291, 295, 301
Richardson, D.L 91
Rojek, Chris 17, 251, 256f., 263, 289, 294
Rolt, L.T.C. 16, 203-21
romantic gaze 115, 119, 188f., 193
romantic travel 5, 11f., 60, 69-84, 85-107, 163, 188, 234
romanticism 69-84, 119, 163, 173
Rome 32, 38, 47, 52, 55, 57, 61, 71, 100f., 161, 260
ruins 78f., 82, 86f., 169, 265
Ruskin, John 5, 9, 16, 72f., 76, 80f., 96, 101, 205, 208, 210f.
Samuel, Raphael 205
Scotland 4, 21, 34, 40, 70, 78, 80, 83-5, 112, 120, 203, 287
seaside resorts; seaside tourism 2, 13f., 109-12, 115-9, 123, 125-7, 133-57, 162f., 169, 173, 181-202, 204, 210
Shelley, Percy Bysshe 86, 101, 260
Sherlock, Martin 59, 64
Sidney, Sir Philip 23, 25f., 28
sights 1, 8-12, 16, 22, 29-33, 47-51, 55-61, 64, 85f., 89, 93, 104, 123, 135, 168f., 199, 257, 261, 265
sightseeing 10, 47-68, 249
simulacrum; simulation (see also Baudrillard; replication) 16f., 256, 285-303
Sinclair, Iain 268-74, 279
Smiles, Samuel 216
Southey, Robert 76, 79f.
souvenirs 33, 165, 253
spa resorts 13, 109, 112, 115-7, 162f.
spectacle 30, 39f., 96, 169, 224, 226, 234f., 237, 289f., 295
stagecoach 11, 71f., 86, 100, 257f.
Sterne, Laurence 51
sublimation; the sublime (see also the beautiful; the picturesque) 5, 11-3, 47-68, 69-84, 85-107, 116f., 119, 259
theme park 110, 125, 169, 286, 291
Theroux, Paul 206
Tönnies, Ferdinand 214
tourism, and class 11-5, 70f., 76, 109-31, 137, 160-4, 168, 171-4, 189, 196f., 200, 234, 240
tourism, and cultural change 1, 10, 15, 123, 126, 159, 167, 170, 175, 181f., 192-4, 200, 203, 250, 288
tourism, advertising of 3, 8f., 11, 13, 100, 104, 123, 133-57, 163, 167, 224, 226, 240
tourism, as economic factor 1-4, 13, 111, 116f., 126, 159-79
tourism, critique of 5-7, 9, 15, 25, 70, 72, 75, 80f., 120, 159,

165f., 169, 172, 176, 181-202, 234, 249f., 285-303
tourism, domestic 4, 13, 133-57, 294
tourism, foreign 16, 86, 121f., 181-202
tourism, history of (see also travel, history of) 4, 7, 13, 109-31, 160-4, 170, 224, 238
tourism, marketing of 8, 133-57, 175
tourism, promotion of 13, 133-57
tourism, scenic 47-9, 69-84, 85-107, 110, 115, 119-21, 125, 211
tourism, semiotics of 17, 111, 249-66, 267-83, 286
tourism, urban (see also city walk) 16f., 223-48, 258f., 267-83
tourist attraction (see also sights) 8, 111, 165, 169-71, 191, 223f., 237-42
tourist gaze 7f., 115, 123, 168-71, 188, 193, 234, 289
tourist industry 1f., 7, 17, 21, 32, 85, 139, 147, 148, 159, 163, 169f., 175, 234, 240, 285
tourism, infrastructure of 2, 7, 11, 25, 31, 85f., 89, 116, 119-23, 134f., 168, 172, 183, 189-91, 195
tourism, vs. travel 6, 60, 70, 110, 113-5, 124, 188, 250
transport (see also tourism, infrastructure of) 3, 7f., 12, 69-84, 86, 110, 120, 164, 168, 172, 174, 182f., 189, 191, 199, 205, 216, 226, 253, 258
Travel Association of Great Britain (TA) 142-50
travel literature; travel writing 6, 27f., 30, 33, 37, 39, 47-68, 240, 251, 253, 259, 261, 263
travel, dangers of 10, 22, 26, 32, 60f., 64, 86f., 92-4, 114, 173, 196-8
travel, history of (see also tourism, history of) 6, 16, 251
travel, motivation to 3f., 6, 13, 21f., 31, 85, 181, 290
travel, vs. tourism (see tourism, vs. travel)
trickle-down theory 12, 14, 160f., 182, 188, 200
upland tourism (see tourism, scenic)
Urry, John 7, 115f., 126, 167-9, 171, 187-9, 289
utilitarianism; utility 5, 69, 76, 78-80, 205
Veblen, Thorstein 204
virtual travel 16, 170, 234, 242-4
voluntarism 14, 134-7, 142, 152
Wales 2, 121, 195, 203-21, 287
Waugh, Evelyn 64f., 208
Wentworth, William Charles 94
Wigan Pier 206, 208, 294
Wordsworth, Dorothy 70
Wordsworth, William 5, 11f., 69-84, 86, 91, 95, 119f., 211, 249f., 252f., 256f., 265, 269
Yeats, W.B. 208, 213
Young, Arthur 78